THE RACE QUESTION IN MODERN SCIENCE

RACE
AND
SCIENCE

New York: Columbia University Press

The present volume is the result of a resolution voted by the General Conference of Unesco in 1950 and re-adopted by it at each of the following sessions. According to this resolution, the Secretariat was entrusted with the responsibility of collecting scientific material concerning the race question and giving this material the widest possible diffusion. This volume contains all the brochures which have appeared separately in the series 'The Race Question in Modern Science'.

FOREWORD

Since the beginning of the nineteenth century, the racial problem has, unfortunately, been growing in importance. A bare thirty years ago, Europeans could still regard race prejudice as a phenomenon that only affected areas on the margin of civilisation or continents other than their own. They suffered a sudden and rude awakening. The long-standing confusion between race and culture has produced fertile soil for the development of racism, at once a creed and an emotional attitude. The virulence with which this ideology has made its appearance in the present century is one of the strangest and most disturbing phenomena of the great revolution of our time.

Racial doctrine is the outcome of a fundamentally anti-rational system of thought and is in glaring conflict with the whole humanist tradition of our civilisation. It sets at nought everything that Unesco stands for and endeavours to defend. By virtue of its very constitution, Unesco must face the racial problem: the preamble to that document declares that "the great and terrible war which has now ended was a war made possible by the denial of the democratic principles of the dignity, equality and mutual respect of men, and by the propagation, in their place, through ignorance and prejudice, of the doctrine of the inequality of men and races".

Because of its structure and the tasks assigned to it, Unesco is the international institution best equipped to lead the campaign against race prejudice and to extirpate this most dangerous of doctrines. Race hatred and conflict thrive on scientifically false ideas and are nourished by ignorance. In order to show up these errors of fact and reasoning, to make widely known the conclusions reached in various branches of science, to combat racial propaganda, we must turn to the means and methods of education, science and culture, which are precisely the three domains in which Unesco's activities are exerted; it is on this threefold front that the battle against all forms of racism must be engaged.

The plan laid down by the Organization proceeds from a resolution (116(VI)B(iii)) adopted by the United Nations Economic and Social Council at its Sixth Session, asking Unesco "to consider the desirability of initiating and recommending the general adoption of a programme of disseminating scientific facts designed to remove what is generally known as racial prejudice."

Responding to this request, the Fourth Session of Unesco's General Conference adopted the following three resolutions for the 1950 programme: "The Director-General is instructed: to study and collect scientific materials concerning questions of race; to give wide diffusion to the scientific information collected; to prepare an educational campaign based on this information."

Such a programme could not be carried out unless Unesco had at its disposal the "scientific facts" mentioned in the resolution of the Economic and Social Council.

The 1949 meeting on race, supplemented by the 1951 meeting, sought to set forth in clear and simple terms the state of scientific knowledge, at that time, on the controversial problem of racial differences. The final result of these two meetings was the 1951 statement on race. This was not seen by Unesco as an ex cathedra manifesto, nor was it considered the final pronouncement on the race question.

In 1964, Unesco convened a group of experts with a view to discussing the biological aspects of race. Biologists, geneticists and physical anthropologists were invited to discuss the implications for race relations of the latest discoveries in their particular fields. The proposals unanimously adopted at this meeting have been published and are added to the appendix of this book.

Taking these proposals into account, a subsequent meeting was convened in 1967, at Headquarters. It included moralists, philosophers, social scientists and biologists from the 1964 meeting, who examined more specifically the social and ethical aspects of the race question. A new statement on race and racial prejudice was issued on 26 September 1967.

Since the publication of this book in 1951, there have been important changes in the world with regard to the dimension of the "race" problem. These were reflected in the 1967 Statement on Race and Racial Prejudice mentioned above. Neither the conclusions of the meeting nor the present situation in multi-racial societies have been taken into account in this edition.

The several chapters which make up this volume have previously been published in the form of separate brochures—which explains a few repetitions and a number of discrepancies in the interpretation of facts. The authors have endeavoured to present the facts as simply and clearly as possible and have rigorously avoided any propagandizing tendencies. Nothing could have been more harmful to the ideals of Unesco than a campaign against racism which had the appearance of a sentimental appeal to the emotions. No effort has been made to reconcile the different theories or divergent points. In the field of race as elsewhere, science is constantly changing and it would have been contrary to its spirit to aim at uniformity.

CONTENTS

PART ONE

RACIAL MYTHS

by
JUAN COMAS

*Professor of Anthropology
at the Mexican School of Anthropology*

GENERAL OBSERVATIONS ON RACIAL PREJUDICES AND MYTHS[1]

It is a matter of observation that men are not alike in appearance; there are variations in the external physical characteristics transmitted wholly or partially from father to son. It is groups relatively homogeneous in this respect which constitute what are commonly called 'races'. Not only do such races differ in appearance; they are also usually at different levels of development, some of them enjoying all the blessings of an advanced civilization while others are backward to a greater or lesser extent. This last fact is the true *fons et origo* of racism in all its subsequent developments.

In the Old Testament we already find the belief that the physical and mental differences between individuals and groups alike are congenital, hereditary and unchangeable. The Book of Genesis contains passages apparently assuming the inferiority of certain groups to others: 'Cursed be Canaan; a servant of servants shall he be unto his brethren', while

---

1. For examples of race prejudice extensive use has been made of Sir Alan Burns' excellent little book, *Colour Prejudice* (London, 1948, George Allen and Unwin Limited) which also includes many valuable quotations from works or reviews not available to the present writer. As the nature of the present collection precludes frequent footnotes, the author takes this opportunity to acknowledge his debt to Sir Alan Burns and to express his gratitude for permission to draw on Sir Alan's knowledge.

some sort of biological superiority is implied in the assertion that Jehovah made a compact with Abraham and 'his seed'.

In the New Testament on the other hand, the theme of the universal brotherhood of men is quite incompatible with this point of view.

It is a fact that the majority of religions disregard individual physical differences and regard all men as brothers and equal in the sight of God.

Christianity—though not all Christians—has been anti-racist from the very beginning. St. Paul says: 'There is neither Jew nor Greek, there is neither bond nor free for ye are all one in Christ Jesus', and again: 'He hath made of one blood all nations of men for to dwell on the face of the earth'. We may also recall that traditionally one of the three Magi was a Negro. Racism was condemned by Pope Pius XI and in 1938 the Vatican condemned racist movements as 'apostacy from the Christian faith in spirit and in doctrine'. Moreover the Church's role of the Beatified and of the Saints includes white men, yellow men and Negroes. The 12 apostles themselves were Semitic and so was Mary, mother of Jesus Christ.

Similarly, Mohammedans have never displayed racial intransigence or intolerance to other peoples so long as those peoples adopted the Faith.

Against all this, however, it must be pointed out that we have examples of a contrary attitude from the remotest antiquity. The most ancient reference to discrimination against Negroes, though possibly dictated by political reasons rather than by race prejudice, is found in a stele raised by order of the Pharaoh Sesostris III (1887-49 B.C.) above the second cataract on the Nile:

'Southern Boundary. Raised in the eighth year of the reign of Sesostris III, King of Upper and Lower Egypt, to whom be life throughout all ages. No Negro shall cross this boundary by water of by land, by ship or with his flocks save for the purpose of trade or to make purchases in some post. Negroes so crossing shall be treated with hospitality but no Negroes shall hereafter forever proceed by ship below the point of Heh.'

The Greeks of 2,000 years ago regarded all men not of their own race as 'barbarians', and Herodotus tells us that the Persians in their turn thought themselves greatly superior to the rest of humanity.

To justify the Greek ambition for universal hegemony, Aristotle (384-22 B.C.) evolved the hypothesis that certain peoples are by nature free from birth and others slaves (a hypothesis used, as we shall see, in the sixteenth century to justify the enslavement of Negroes and Amerindians). Cicero however thought otherwise: 'Men differ in knowledge but all are equal in ability to learn; there is no race which, guided by reason, cannot obtain virtue.'

Ideas as to the 'superiority' or 'inferiority' of a people or group of people are subject to constant revision. For proof of this it is enough to recall Cicero's opinion of the Celts of Britain, whom he inconsistently describes, in a letter to Atticus, as exceptionally 'stupid and unteachable'.

The savagery and mystery of Africa which was slowly yielding its secrets to Europeans at the end of the nineteenth century are brought out strikingly in Conrad's great tale *Heart of Darkness,* which draws a parallel with the impression made by the untamed Thames of 1,900 years ago on the captain of a Mediterranean trireme or on the young patrician newcomer from Rome; the latter felt the same 'longing to escape, the powerless disgust, the surrender, the hate', as the colonial administrator of our own day. It is almost redundant to recall the contempt of the Norman nobility for the conquered Saxons, and how the ancestors of the proudest nation of Europe were despised. These are not however, strictly speaking, examples of 'racism', nor had even the fierce antagonism of Christians to Musulmans a racial basis. Hatred or aversion springing from differences in cultural level or religious belief is more human than prejudice claiming to be based on implacable laws of heredity.

All this notwithstanding, it may be asserted that generally speaking there was no true racial prejudice before the fifteenth century, since before then the division of mankind was not so much into antagonistic races as into 'Christians and infidels'—a much more humane differentiation, since the chasm between religions can be bridged while the biological racial barrier is impassable.

With the beginning of African colonization and the discovery of America and of the trans-Pacific sea route to India, there was a considerable increase in race and colour prejudice. It can be explained on grounds of economic self-interest, the resurgence of the imperialistic colonizing spirit, etc. Juan Ginés de Sepulveda (1550) in an attempt to justify the institution of slavery on the strength of the Aristotelian hypothesis, spoke of the inferiority and natural perversity of the American Aborigines, asserted that they were 'irrational beings', that

'Indians are as different from Spaniards as cruelty is from kindness and as monkeys are from men'.

Of course there was Fray Bartolemé de Las Casas to maintain the opposite view and battle unwearyingly for the proposition that all the peoples of the world are men and not 'submen' or 'half-men' predestined to do what others tell them. The main basis for social stratification in Latin America was racial discrimination, the order of excellence being Creoles, half-breeds, Indians and Negroes. In theory the law does not recognize such discrimination, but now, as then, the law is not obeyed.

Speaking of the Brazilian Indian, Montaigne (1533-92) said: 'There is nothing savage or barbarous about this nation save for the fact that each of us labels whatever is not among the customs of his own peoples as barbarism'; he was followed in this view by some of the most illustrious thinkers of the eighteenth and nineteenth centuries. Voltaire (1694-1778). J. J. Rousseau (1712-78) and Buffon (1706-88) were among many determined supporters of the fundamental oneness of human nature and hence of the equality of all men. In the other camp Hume (1711-76) wrote: 'I am inclined to believe that Negroes are naturally inferior to whites'. Renan (1823-92) was another who refused to accept the hypothesis of the equality of men and Taine (1828-93) also combated the theory and denied that 'Greeks, barbarians, Hindus, the man of the Renaissance and the man of the eighteenth century are all cast in the same mould'.

Despite the influence of certain thinkers, race prejudice developed into a regular doctrinal system during the eighteenth and nineteenth centuries. There was indeed a relatively brief period when it appeared as though the spread of the principles of the French and American revolutions and the success of the anti-slavery campaign in England might lessen or even abolish such prejudice, but both the reaction which followed the Restoration and the industrial revolution in Europe at the beginning of the last century had direct and damaging repercussions on the racial question. The development of power spinning and weaving opened ever wider markets to cotton manufacturers, and 'Cotton was king', particularly in the Southern part of the United States. The result was an increasing demand for servile labour; slavery, which was breaking down in America and might have vanished of itself, automatically became a sacrosanct institution on which the prosperity of the Cotton Belt depended. It was to defend this so-called 'special institution' that Southern thinkers and sociologists developed a complete pseudo-scientific mythology designed to justify a state of affairs clean contrary to the democratic beliefs they professed. For the quietening of consciences men had to be persuaded that the Black was not merely an inferior being to the White but little different from the brutes.

The Darwinian theory of the survival of the fittest was warmly welcomed by the whites as an argument supporting and confirming their policy of expansion and aggression at the expense of the 'inferior' peoples. As Darwin's theory was made public in the years in which the greater powers were building their colonial empires, it helped to justify them in their own eyes and before the rest of mankind: That slavery or death brought to 'inferior' human groups by European rifles and machine-guns was no more than the implementation of the theory of the replacement of an inferior by a superior human society. In international politics racism excuses aggression, for the aggressor no longer feels himself bound by any consideration for foreigners belonging to 'inferior' races and classifiable little, if at all, above the beasts.

The notion that the stronger is biologically and scientifically justified in destroying the weaker has been applied as much to conflicts within as to those between nations.

It is unfair to level at Darwin—as many have done—the reproach that he promoted this hateful and inhuman theory: the truth is that with coloured societies becoming potential competitors in the labour market and claiming the social advantages regarded as exclusively the heritage of the whites, the latter were obviously in need of some disguise for the utter economic materialism which led them to deny the 'inferior' peoples any share in the privileges they themselves enjoyed. For that reason they welcomed with satisfaction Darwin's biological thesis and then by simplification, distortion and adaptation of it in conformity with their own particular interests, transformed it into the so-called 'social Darwinism' on which they based their right to their social and economic privileges; it is a thing which bears no relationship to Darwin's purely biological principles. Herbert Spencer (1820-1903) applied to sociology the concept of 'survival of the fittest' and the same idea was used to defend Nietzsche's (1844-1900) doctrine of the 'superman' with whom 'fittest' was equated.

In this way progress in biology was misused to provide

superficially scientific and simple solutions to allay scruples on points of human conduct. However, the distance between science and myth is both brief and easily traversed and that is what happened in this case.

It is obvious that the psycho-somatic inheritance does influence the external appearance and the conduct of human beings, but that does not warrant the argument of the racists that (a) biological heredity is the sole important factor or (b) that group heredity is as much a fact as individual heredity.

Racist doctrine becomes more dangerous still when it is applied, not to separate ethnic groups, but to different social classes within the *same group*. For instance, Erich Suchsland (*Archiv für Rassen und Gesellschafts-Biologie*), argues the thesis that the individuals unsuccessful in life (for instance, those who lack the means to live in the more expensive suburbs) are necessarily the racially inferior elements in the population, whereas the rich are 'racially superior'; hence the bombardment of poor quarters would be a form of selection and would bring racial improvement. Here there is no question of white against black or nordic against non-Aryan; it is a question of finding pseudo-biological support for discrimination against the proletarian classes by the bourgeoisie. Even without any explicit admission, it is quite obvious that racial or class discrimination in this and other instances hides a social-economic antagonism. Alexis Carrel (*Man the Unknown*) does not go as far as Suchsland, but nevertheless maintains that the proletariat and the unemployed are people who are inferior by heredity and descent—men inherently lacking the strength to fight, who have sunk to the level at which fighting is no longer necessary: as though the proletariat did not have a far sterner fight every hour of the day than the well-to-do.

Prenant suggests as a possibility that the main concern of many racists may be, not to provide an apparently objective basis for nationalism and patriotism, but to inculcate the notion that social phenomena are governed by racial factors determined once and for all. Such a biological determinism, unalterable by social action, would absolve Society of all responsibility for each man's heredity, would determine at birth whether he was going to be a great man, a capitalist, a technician, a member of the proletariat or even one of the unemployed, without anyone being able to do anything effective to prevent it.

In any case there is no room for doubt that 'racial' discrimination is only one facet of the broader problem of social discrimination.

The notion of 'race' is so charged with emotional force that objective discussion of its significance in relation to social problems is uncommonly difficult. *There is no scientific basis whatsoever* for a general classification of races according to a scale of relative superiority, and racial prejudices and myths are no more than a means of finding a scapegoat when the position of individuals and the cohesion of a group are threatened.

Persons differing in physical appearance are easily identifiable targets for aggression, while in psychological terms the feeling of 'guilt' is removed or mitigated, given a more or less plausible 'scientific' theory whereby it can be shown that the group attacked is 'inferior' or 'harmful'. Generally speaking, such 'aggression' is directed either against minority groups or against cowed and powerless majority groups.

This brief outline of the origin, development and alleged justification for racial prejudices and myths in general will serve as an introduction for the more detailed analysis of certain of the more widespread and fundamental myths of the racist theory. We hope to demonstrate the falsity and error of these pseudo-biological arguments which are no more than a smoke-screen for their proponents' oppressive aims and policies.

THE MYTH OF BLOOD AND OF THE INFERIORITY OF CROSS-BREEDS

Human miscegenation has been and is the subject of infinite debate. Opinions on the subject are conditioned by the views of the disputants on race and racial differences, the opponents of miscegenation starting from the assumption of racial inequality, whereas its defenders take the view that the differences between human groups are not such as to constitute an objection to cross-breeding between them. Hence the first thing needed in the study of the problems raised by human inter-breeding is a clear definition of what is meant by race and the selection of criteria for deciding whether or not any pure races exist.

Even under the loosest definition, race implies the existence of groups presenting certain similarities in somatic characteristics which are perpetuated according to the laws of biological inheritance, allowing for a margin of individual variation.

The peoples of Europe are of such mongrel origin that any attempt at classification according to only two characteristics (colour of eyes and hair) would exclude two-thirds of the population in any region studied; the addition of a third characteristic (cranial formation) would leave us with a still smaller fraction of the population presenting the required combination of all three characteristics; and with the inclusion of stature and nasal index, the proportion of 'pure' types would become infinitesimal.

We may take it then that there are no pure human races; at the very most it would be possible to define a pure race in terms of the incidence of one selected somatic characteristic, but never in terms of all or even of the majority of hereditary traits. Nevertheless there is a widespread belief that there was a time in antiquity when racial types were pure, that miscegenation is of relatively recent date, and that it threatens humanity with a general degeneration and retrogression. This belief lacks the slightest support from science. The mixing of races has been going on since the very beginning of human life on earth, though obviously the improvement of communications and the general increase in population has stimulated it in the last two centuries. Migration is as old as the human race, and automatically implies cross-breeding between groups. It is quite possible that the Cro-Magnon type of the upper Paleolithic interbred with Neanderthal man, as seems to be indicated by the discovery of remains displaying intermediate characteristics. Moreover the existence of Negroid and Mongoloid races in prehistoric Europe is a further proof that cross-breeding is not a recent phenomenon, and that the oldest populations of Europe are no more than the product of such miscegenation over thousands of years. Yet they show neither the disharmony nor the degeneration which many writers believe to result from racial interbreeding.

History shows us that all the areas in which a high culture has developed have been the scene of the conquest of an indigenous race by foreign nomadic groups, followed by the breaking down of caste divisions and the creation of new amalgams; these, though regarded as racially homogeneous nations, were in fact no more than new nationalities comprising different races.

Those who, like Jon A. Mjoen consider miscegenation

dangerous for the future of mankind, assert that it is a source of physical degeneracy and that immunity against certain diseases diminishes. They allege that prostitutes and vagrants are commoner among half-bred than among pure-bred races, while an increased incidence of tuberculosis and other diseases is observable among the former group, with a diminution of mental balance or vigour and, an increase in criminal tendencies (*Harmonic and Disharmonic Race Crossing and Harmonic and Unharmonic Crossings,* 1922). These data are not valid because the writer does not specify the types of individuals studied nor the general characteristics of the races which have interbred; he ought also to prove that the specific families whose interbreeding produced the half-breeds examined were physically and mentally healthy and free of any sign of degeneracy or disability. Mjoen also entirely overlooks the influence of the social background on the subjects' behaviour.

C. B. Davenport also demonstrates (in *The Effects of Racial Miscegenation,* 1917) the existence of disharmonic phenomena in half-breeds—relatively small digestive organs in a bulky body, well developed teeth in weak jaws, large thighs out of proportion to the body, etc. It is not disputed that there are individuals displaying such characteristics, but it has not been shown that the phenomena are due to miscegenation; similar cases are found among old families while generally speaking crossbreeding between black and white produces well proportioned individuals.

S. K. Humphrey, M. Grant, L. Stoddard and many others argue that, as a result of crossbreeding with foreign elements, there is a likelihood of the North American population losing its present stable and harmonic character. Some writers have gone so far as to assert that such a disharmony would be productive of a whole series of social evils and immoral tendencies.

A line of reasoning rebutting the validity of such arguments as those under discussion is that advanced by H. Lundeborg (*Hybrid-types of the Human Race,* 1931), demonstrating that miscegenation is more frequent among the lower social classes than among the middle and upper classes: hence the phenomena observed by Mjoen and Davenport are due not to the assumed correlation between hybridism and degeneracy or debility, but to the fact that it takes place between individuals belonging to the most impoverished sections of the human groups concerned. The same phenomena would result from endogamy as from exogamy and the interbreeding of races

21

has nothing to do with it. In point of fact the human families in which endogamy has been consistently practiced are frequently marked by a degree of degeneracy equal to or even greater than that which Mjoen and Davenport purport to find in half-breeds.

Both endogamy and exogamy are utilized according to the requirements of the case for the improvement of animal strains; if a strain is good from the point of view of the characteristics interesting the stock-breeder, inbreeding can be continued for many generations without outside crosses and without exhibiting signs of degeneracy. Endogamy further serves to reveal all the hereditary potentialities of a group as it brings out all the recessive hereditary characteristics which would remain latent if they existed in one of the parents only; in such cases, if the characteristic in question is undesirable, the logical and necessary step is exogamic crossing (miscegenation) so as to introduce a dominant hereditary factor to counter the undesirable recessive characteristic.

Thus the immediate result of crossbreeding is to check the outward manifestation of any recessive defects peculiar to either of the races interbreeding. In other words, endogamy makes recessive anomalies and defects visible or tangible, whereas exogamy tends to extirpate or, at the least, to minimize them.

The same line of reasoning can be applied in the case of useful hereditary talents, characteristics and aptitudes. Hence, it is impossible to assert in general terms that the effects of endogamy or exogamy on the descendants of such unions are good or bad; the nature of the result depends in each case on the genetic characteristics of the individual's interbreeding.

The champions of miscegenation argue that endogamy or marriage between members of the same group conduces to the deterioration of the race, and that hybrid races are more vigorous because the infusion of 'new blood' increases the vitality of the group, etc. This dangerous generalization can be refuted by the same arguments as the first.

Neither the partisans nor the enemies of miscegenation have determined certain aspects of the question, which the writer feels should be examined: (a) results of miscegenation between groups definitely above the average and more particularly between groups definitely below the average; (b) the form taken by the environmental obstacles against which half-breeds usually have to fight.

If half-breeds in any country are treated by law or custom

as second-class citizens (from the social, economic and political point of view), it is highly probable that their cultural contributions will not be commensurate with their innate abilities. Under a rigid caste system in which there is no possibility of a half-breed's raising himself above the social status of the lower-caste parent, clearly any assessment of the effects of racial miscegenation should not be based on the level attained by individuals of mixed blood. On the other hand, under a system where individual merit alone is the basis for social classification, the achievements of half-breeds would be a very definite indication of their intrinsic qualities.

It is, in fact, difficult to distinguish between the effects of racial miscegenation as such and those of crossbreeding between lower-grade population groups independently of their race. Instances of interbreeding between groups higher in the social scale have produced a large proportion of high-grade human beings, but in none of these cases should the results be attributed exclusively to the cross. In the present state of our knowledge there is nothing to prove that crossbreeding produces either degeneracy in the descendants of the cross or groups of improved quality.

The notion of humanity as being divided into completely separate racial compartments is inaccurate. It is based on false premises, and more particularly on the 'blood' theory of heredity which is as false as the old racist theory. 'Of one blood' is a phrase without meaning, since the genes or factors of heredity have no connexion whatever with the blood, and are independent elements which not only do not amalgamate but tend to become most sharply differentiated. Heredity is not a fluid transmitted through the blood, nor is it true that the different 'bloods' of the progenitors are mixed and combined in their offspring.

The myth of 'blood' as the decisive criterion regarding the value of a cross persists even in our own day and men still speak of 'blood' as the vehicle of inherited qualities, 'of my own blood', 'the voice of blood', 'mixed blood', 'new blood', 'half blood', etc. The terms, 'blue blood' and 'plebeian blood' have become a permanent part of everyday speech as descriptions of the descendants of aristocratic and plebeian families respectively, the last being used in a depreciative sense. 'Blood' is also the mean nationality: 'German blood', 'Spanish blood', 'Jewish blood', etc. The criterion reaches the nadir of absurdity in such cases as the classification in the United States of those individuals as 'Negroes' or 'Indians' who have one-sixteenth part of 'Indian blood' or 'black blood'—that is, when one of their sixteen direct ancestors (great-great-grand-parents) was a Negro or an Indian.

People who still think in this way are quite incapable of understanding the inwardness of hereditary phenomena or of the social phenomena in which heredity plays a part. If there is inheritance by blood how are we to explain why children of the same parents differ in character when the *same blood* runs in their veins? Again, how are we to explain why certain individuals exhibit characteristics found in their grandparents but absent in their parents?

The truth is that many people are ignorant of the fact not only that the blood has nothing whatever to do with the genetic process, but that it has also been proved that the mother does not supply blood to the foetus which develops its own blood from the beginning (F. M. Ashley-Montagu, *The Myth of Blood,* 1943)—this indeed explains why a child may be of a different blood group from its mother.

Lastly, the fact that successful blood transfusion between individuals of different races is possible, given congruity of serological types, is a new and striking proof that the 'myth of blood' lacks the slightest biological foundation.

It is beyond dispute that all the major races are of hybrid origin, and during the millenia which have elapsed since the original fission of the basic human stock, crossings have gone on continuously. Dixon points out that the brachycephalic Alpines despised by Grant and others were an important element in the building of the Babylonian culture; that the immigration of the Alpine Dorians into Greece immediately preceded the flowering of Hellenic culture; that Rome did not attain its full glory until after the conquest by an Alpine stock of the Mediterranean-Caspian population of Latium; that the development of Chinese culture followed the absorption of Caspian by Alpine elements; and that the amazing development of modern European civilization has occurred in the zone where the mixture of Alpines, Mediterraneans and Caspians has gone farther than anywhere else in the world. There are many other examples of great civilizations such as Egypt, Mesopotamia and India arising at the points where different peoples mingled.

Of course racists such as Gobineau, who regard miscegenation as necessarily disastrous, are capable of such absurdities as to claim that of the 10 most brilliant known civilizations, six are the work of 'Aryans', the 'higher' branch of the white race (Hindu, Egyptian, Assyrian, Greek, Roman and German); while the other four major civilizations (Chinese, Mexican, Peruvian and Maya) are the work of the white race slightly interbred with inferior races. Gobineau concludes that the signs of degeneracy occurring in cross-bred stock are egalitarian ideas, democratic movements, etc., and that miscegenation, produces mediocrities, as it were 'men with the herd mind', 'nations dulled by a fatal somnolence' . . . 'people like buffaloes chewing the cud in the stagnant wallows of the Pontine marshes'. It is unnecessary to refute yet again ideas so absurd, based solely on racist criteria of a political and philosophical nature and on pseudo-scientific biological arguments which have already been discussed and rebutted.

By way of examples of crossbreeding in what are accepted as civilized nations, from the earliest ages England (Britain) was occupied by human groups of the Cro-Magnon type and by Nordics, Mediterraneans and Alpines, and in later ages was invaded by Saxons, Norwegians, Danes and Normans. Thus far from it being possible in our day to speak of a pure English race, we have an excellent example there of a racial mosaic.

In the Palaeolithic Age France was settled by a number of different races, Neanderthal, Cro-Magnon, Chancelade and Grimaldi; in the Neolithic Age a number of branches of the Mediterranean race and certain primitive Alpines came in from the east and in the seventh century B.C. Celtic invaders conquered the first colonists. About the first century of our own era France had a foretaste of the barbarian invasion which was, however, contained for the time being by the power of Rome; two centuries later the Vandals conquered Gaul and the Visigoths founded a kingdom in southern France which continued in existence until the eighth century. Even these few points give an idea of the degree of racial heterogeneity in France and show the extent of the interbreeding which has taken place. 'Western France is perhaps more Teutonic than south-western Germany and much of eastern Germany is more Slavonic than Russia.'

The course of events has been very similar in other continents, and if we get the impression that the mixture of races has been carried to its farthest point in post-Columbian America this is merely because the phenomenon of interbreeding is occurring before our eyes and is not merely a record in the history books. It should further be recalled that the pre-Columbian population of America was also heterogeneous in nature from the beginning.

In all the regions in which an advanced culture is found there has been conquest of one people or peoples by others. The claim that crossbreeds are degenerate is refuted by the actual fact that the whole population of the world is hybrid and becoming increasingly so. Isolated human groups have had little or no influence on the cultural progress of humanity, whereas the conditions which allow of any group playing an important role in civilization are promoted by crossing with other races.

The influence of Caspian-Mediterranean immigrants into Northern Italy may well have been a factor in the brilliance of the Renaissance in that area. Again, is it mere coincidence that a European culture, after the Dark Ages, began to emerge at the point in time when the racial mixtures had crystallized into new peoples? Finally the supreme instance of a racial melting pot is the United States; that country is also one of the principal centres of contemporary civilization.

Accordingly we can sum up the position more or less as follows: (a) miscegenation has existed since the dawn of human life; (b) miscegenation results in a greater somatic and psychic variability and allows of the emergence of a great variety of new gene combinations, thus increasing the range of hereditary characteristics in the new population group; (c) speaking biologically, miscegenation is neither good nor bad, its effects being dependent in every case on the individual characteristics of the persons between whom such crossbreeding takes place. As, in general, miscegenation occurs more frequently between individuals on the lower social levels and in unsatisfactory economic and social circumstances, the causes of certain anomalies observable must be sought in this fact rather than in the fact of miscegenation as such; (d) examples of 'pure races' or of isolated human groups having developed a high culture independently are the exception; (e) on the contrary the great majority of areas of high civilization are inhabited by obviously cross-bred groups.

COLOUR PREJUDICE: THE NEGRO MYTH

So far as can be seen, few of the physical traits used for the classification of human races have functional value for the individuals displaying them. Our own civilization attaches special importance to the colour of the skin and relatively dark pigmentation is a mark of difference condemning numerous human groups to contempt, ostracism and a debased social status. In certain persons colour prejudice is so strong as to give rise to almost pathological phobias; these are not innate but reflect, in an exaggerated form, the prejudices of the social environment. To maintain that a man is an inferior human being because he is black is as ridiculous as contending that a white horse will necessarily be faster than a black horse. Nevertheless, however little basis there may be for colour prejudice, the importance of the resultant attitudes and behaviour in many countries is indisputable.

The exploitation by the whites of agriculture and mining in the newly-discovered countries from the fifteenth century onwards created slavery, particularly the enslavement of Negroes and American Indians. Simultaneously the pride of the white man and his superiority complex towards men of colour was increased and strengthened still further by the fact that he was a Christian whereas Negroes and Amerindians were pagans. In point of fact, however, the causes of white aggression were fundamentally economic; the whites seized the richer lands inhabited by coloured populations and reduced the latter to slavery to secure a ready source of labour which would increase the value of their recent acquisitions.

While it is true that we have in Las Casas a fierce champion of the abolition not only of Indian but of Negro slavery, 'because the same reasons apply in their case as in the Indians', there were more people who sought to maintain the *status quo* on the grounds that the Negro was 'inferior' to the white man. For instance, in 1772 the Reverend Thomas Thompson published a monograph, *The Trade in Negro Slaves on the African Coast in Accordance with Humane Principles and with the Laws of Revealed Religion,* in 1852 the Rev. Josiah Priest published *A Bible Defence of Slavery,* while C. Carroll (1900) in his work *The Negro as a Beast or In the Image of God* includes a chapter ('Biblical and Scientific Proofs that the Negro is not a Member of the Human Race') in which he asserts that 'all scientific research confirms his typically simian nature'.

The final division among themselves by the white men of colonial territories for exploitation and government in the last third of the nineteenth century (more particularly at the Conference of Berlin in 1884 for the division of the African continent among the European powers) afforded glaring proof of their complete indifference to the legal and ethical point that none of them had the slightest right to dispose of any part of Africa and still less of the lives, goods and labour of its inhabitants.

Despite the proclamation in the Declaration of Independence of the United States of the equal rights of all men and the explicit provision of the Fifteenth Amendment 'that it shall be illegal to deny or restrict (those rights) in any state of the Union on the grounds of race, colour or former condition of slavery', despite the inclusion of equivalent provisions in the Constitutions of most countries and despite the solemn agreement to the same effect in Article 2 of the Universal Declaration of Human Rights signed by the United Nations on 10 December 1948, it is all too obvious in practice how widespread throughout the world is social, economic and political discrimination against Negroes in particular and coloured races in general, based mainly on false racial concepts.

One of the major absurdities of colour prejudice in the United States is the classification of anyone admitting to an African ancestor as a 'Negro' regardless of his physical appearance. The result is that in this case a 'Negro' is not a biological term but denotes membership of a particular cultural, economic and social group. Some 'Negroes' are indistinguishable from white men and pass themselves off as such to escape anti-Negro discrimination. The lack of logic in this attitude becomes still clearer if we reflect that if a person with the smallest proportion of 'Negro blood' can be classified as a Negro, it is just as logical and fair to classify everyone with one drop of 'white blood' as white.

It has been reckoned that the coloured races represent approximately three-fifths of the world's total population. Obviously so large a proportion of the human race can neither be regarded as a negligible quantity nor relegated to a secondary and subordinate status. There must be mutual respect; men must learn to live with one another, without fear, hatred or contempt, without the urge to exaggerate differences at the expense of similarities, but seeking to understand their true extent and importance. If this is not done Dubois' prophecy of 1920 may well be fulfilled that the 1914-18 war 'would be nothing to compare with the fight for freedom which black and brown and yellow men must and will make unless their oppression and humiliation and insult at the hands of the White World cease. The Dark World is going to submit to its present treatment just as long as it must and not one moment longer'. Another Negro leader, Marcus Garvey, has said much the same: 'The bloodiest war of all is yet to come when Europe will match its strength against Asia and that will be the Negro's opportunity to draw the sword for Africa's redemption.'

The greatest humiliations suffered by Negroes are social restrictions and personal insults: the exclusion of Negro travellers from certain trains and motor-coaches, the provision of restricted vehicles and waiting rooms, special schools, prohibited restaurants and hotels, etc., are to the Negro insulting and ridiculous. In South Africa, where colour prejudice is very strong, there was an instance in 1944 of certain officials being dismissed from their posts for refusal to obey Government instructions that the same courtesy terms should be used in official documents addressed to coloured persons as in those to whites.

It would appear that those most insistent on discrimination against Negroes are the lower class whites; they are the first to fear Negro competition in the economic field, and as they have no other argument to warrant their attitude of superiority towards Negroes, they rely on skin pigmentation to which they give an altogether exaggerated importance.

Colour prejudice has not only served as the basis for introducing a caste system in our society; it has also been used as a weapon by labour unions to combat competition by a black or yellow proletariat. The colour barriers raised by American, South African or Australian labour federations and unions, themselves subscribing to socialist ideals and setting themselves up as the defenders of the working class, throw a lurid light on the economic rivalries which are the real motives behind racial antagonisms and the myths evolved to justify them.

Assumptions about psychological and social characteristics based on the colour of the skin are not merely absurd but disingenuous, they vary with circumstances. As an example we may take the changes in the views held about the Japanese: in 1935 the majority of North Americans thought of them as 'progressive', 'intelligent', and 'industrious'; in 1942 they had become 'cunning', and 'treacherous'; in 1950 things have changed again. When there was a shortage of Chinese labourers in California they were described as 'frugal', 'sober' and 'law-abiding'; the moment competition became severe and it was necessary to exclude them, they were described as 'dirty', 'repulsive', 'unassimilable' and even 'dangerous'. The same lack of objective criteria might later be found in India: while North American troops described the natives as 'dirty', and 'uncivilized', the Hindu intellectuals described the Americans as 'boorish', 'materialistic', 'unintellectual' and 'uncivilized'.

Regarding the supposed inferiority of the Negro's psychosomatic attributes to those of the white man. Hankins claims that the bulk of the brain is less in the Negro and deducts that the Negro is mentally inferior. H. L. Gordon (1933) asserts that congenital cerebral deficiency is a characteristic of the Negroes of Kenya, resulting, in his view too, from the lesser cranial volume and the difference in conformation of the Negro brain.

In many instances the peculiar body odour of the Negro and his marked prognathism have been regarded as proof of his biological inferiority. However, it is above all in the psychological field that the most sustained effort has been made to prove the superiority of the white man over the Negro. Admittedly Negro and white are in no respect identical either physically, intellectually or emotionally; nevertheless this does not warrant the assertion that the differences imply any superiority of the one over the other.

The investigations of Leaky in Africa and Steggerda among the Negroes of Jamaica have shown that their cranial capacity is not inferior, and even superior in some cases, to that of the white man. This is confirmed by the work of J. Huxley and A. Keith. For further confirmation of this view we may turn to the work of J. H. F. Kohlbrugge (1935) on the formation of the brain, based on earlier research by such eminent anthropologists and doctors as Reezius, Weinberg, Sergi and Kappers. He draws the following important conclusions:

1. The weight of the frontal lobe, regarded as the seat of the intellect, is 44 per cent of the total weight of the brain in men and women, *black and white alike.*
2. No racial differences are observable as regards the weight of the brain; there are however, marked variations between individuals within each human group or 'race'.
3. Men of marked intellectual powers have not necessarily possessed brains greater in weight or volume.
4. Comparison of the incisures and convolutions of the brain afford equally little support for the view that there are discernible differences between the races; *all* variations are found in *all* 'races'. The writer concludes: 'If the specimens available were mixed up there is no one who could dis-

tinguish the brains of Australians from those of Europeans nor those of people of high intelligence from average brains.'

The work of Sergi on Negroes and Kappers on Chinese confirms these important conclusions, which explode the unwarranted assertion *that the presumed* intellectual inferiority of the Negro is due to the (*presumed and arbitrary*) fact of the brains of coloured races being smaller in volume and less complex structurally.

Admitted the prognathism frequently found in Negroes is a primitive somatic trait. However, the lack of body hair, the thickness of the lips, and the texture of the hair of the head, etc., are all consistent with a more advanced stage of evolution in the Negro than in the white man. We can say with Ruth Benedict that 'No race has an exclusive claim to represent the final stage in human evolution; there is no valid argument to confirm that certain selected traits may indicate the superiority of the white race'.

In this connexion the terms 'good', 'bad', 'superior' and 'inferior' are meaningless as they are all subjective terms; in every case they should be used in a specific connexion, e.g.: 'the majority of Negroes are superior to white people in their resistance to malaria'; or 'the majority of white people are superior to the majority of Negroes in resistance to tuberculosis', etc. The result would be to show that every human group is superior in some respects and inferior in others.

In comparisons of the position of the white and Negro races today there is a tendency to assume the inferiority of the latter from the fact that their economic, political and cultural evolution is far behind that of the whites. This, however, is not due to an 'innate racial inferiority', but is purely the result of circumstances and due to the régime of exploitation under which almost all Negroes live today as a result of white colonization and of the existence, if not of slavery in law, of conditions equivalent to it in practice.

Too often the Negro is still in a position of economic semi-slavery, he is enmeshed in a network of restrictions, partly legal and partly not. Poverty, contempt and disease have made him what he is today.

Regarding the supposed laziness of the Negro (as also of the American Indian) the cause may well be lack of incentive. As Burns rightly points out, the vast yield of the West African colonies, where some land is still in Negro hands, shows that the Negro is not lazy by nature. When he is interested in and understands his work he will expend energy without stint, but he wants to select his own hours of work without feeling himself the prisoner of the time-recorder. Similarly the Amerindian, in a position to till his own land and secure the full fruit of his endeavours, undoubtedly works with a degree of energy, enthusiasm and efficiency unknown in cases where he is aware that it is the 'boss' who will draw the profit. Booker Washington holds that the greatest harm inflicted on the Negro by slavery was to deprive him of the sense of personal independence, method and the spirit of initiative.

There is no reason why whites and Negroes should not dwell together amicably as fellow citizens of a country and of the world, why they should not show mutual consideration and respect without either group having to sacrifice anything of its individuality, in just the same way as Catholics and Protestants in many countries can remain on excellent terms without slackening their religious standards.

What offends Negroes is their systematic exclusion on grounds of colour from certain social facilities open to white men of very doubtful culture and education. It is the general attitude of white people towards them, the lack of consideration and the deliberate slights which make them desire increasingly every day to be delivered from this everlasting ostracism and from the degradation which brands them as almost members of another species, as sub-human (Mathews, quoted by Burns).

There are Negroes whose quite understandable inferiority complex leads them to read hostility to their race, and the wish to keep them down, into any painful or even disagreeable action or decision, even when it relates to an individual only and colour prejudice does not enter into it in the slightest degree. The seething rancour and hatred born of past offences, the mistrust of advances by white people, the bitter and sometimes overt loathing of everything white, must all be conquered, subdued and forgotten if a real spirit of understanding is to grow up between the two races.

At various points in history religious wars put an end to all tolerance in religion. The writer believes that war between the races can be prevented if white people throughout the world stop inflicting on the Negro slights, oppression and injustice, and adopt a civilized and decent attitude towards coloured peoples distinguished by tolerance and good neighbourliness. We must make it impossible for any coloured man to say, as a Hawaian did to a missionary: 'When the white man came you had the Bible and we owned the land; now we have the Bible and you have the land.'

The contributions of Negroes as a race or as individuals to world civilization are not an adequate basis for prognostication of what the race may be able to achieve in the future in terms of its own aptitudes and under more satisfactory environmental, social and economic conditions. Moreover, we must not forget that the twelfth century Negro university of Timbuctoo could stand comparison with European schools and the same is true as regards the respective levels of civilization in Europe and in the three great Negro kingdoms of the age. Moreover, it is quite possible that the working of iron, which is fundamental to all modern technology, was a Negro discovery. Lord Olivier (1905) has said truly, 'the Negro is progressing and that disposes of all the arguments in the world that he is incapable of progress'.

To sum up, all the evidence of biology, anthropology, evolution and genetics demonstrates that racial discrimination on grounds of colour is a myth without the slightest scientific warrant, and hence that the supposed 'racial inferiority of coloured peoples' is untrue. It is unfavourable environmental, political and social-economic factors which alone keep these groups at their present level.

THE JEWISH MYTH

Jews are a human group which have aroused deep hatred in almost all countries and almost all ages.

Anti-Semitism, as a social and political attitude, infecting whole States in some instances and extensive sectors of the population in others, and defended to a greater or lesser extent on religious and economic grounds, is a long-standing antagonism of which examples are found far back in history. To indicate its persistence, we may quote such instances as the mass expulsion of the Jews from Spain in the fifteenth century, the segregation of Jews in Christian Europe during the Middle Ages, the Dreyfus case in France, the notorious pogroms of Jews at various times and in various parts of Eastern and Central Europe, and the use for world-wide propaganda of the spurious 'Protocols of the Learned Elders of Zion', with which it was sought to exacerbate anti-Semitic feeling among the masses.

Today, however, anti-Semitism has resorted to the *myth of a Jewish race* in an attempt to justify itself and to provide a pseudo-scientific cloak for its political and economic motives. The type regarded as typically 'Jewish' is actually very common among the peoples of the Levant and the Near East, though most of these peoples are not Jews and never have been, either in religion or in other aspects of their culture.

The fact that some Jews can be identified as such on sight is due less to inherited physical traits than to the conditioning of emotional and other reactions productive of distinctive facial expressions and corporal attitudes, mannerisms, intonation and tendencies of temperament and character, by Jewish custom and the treatment inflicted on Jews by non-Jews.

If the Nazis had had genuine distinctive 'Jewish' characteristics to go on, why were Jews obliged to display the Star of David on their clothing to allow of their identification by Aryans?

As far as Italy is concerned, Mussolini said in 1932: 'There are no pure races and there is no anti-Semitism in Italy. Italian Jews have always behaved well as citizens and have fought valiantly as soldiers.'

In 1936 the German-Italian alliance forced him to begin an anti-Jewish campaign, although the more obvious heterogeneity of the Italian people resulted in Italian racism differing from German. The Fascist manifesto of 14 July 1938 proclaims: 'There is a pure Italian race. The question of race in Italy should be dealt with from a purely biological angle independently of philosophical or religious considerations. The concept of race in Italy must be essentially Italian and Aryan-Nordic. . . . Jews do not belong to the Italian race. Of the Semites who have settled throughout the centuries on the sacred soil of our fatherland, it is generally true to say that none has remained there. Even the Arab occupation of Sicily has left no traces save the memorial of a few names.' This Fascist claim that there exists in Italy a pure Italian race of Aryan-Nordic type would be laughable if it were not tragic. The principal point the writer wishes to stress is that the anti-Semitic attitude of Italian Fascism is a clumsy imitation of Nazism, thus, like it, based on false biological premises.

What are the alleged anthropological characteristics distinguishing the Jewish race?

The Jews were a nation until the taking of Jerusalem by Titus in A.D. 70. At the beginning of the Christian era and perhaps earlier, there was emigration of Jews from Palestine to various countries from which, in many instances, they were later expelled, thus giving rise to what might be called secondary migrations and population movements. It would be interesting to know the racial characteristics of the Hebrews of antiquity who are probably the main ancestors of the Jews of today; so far, however, it has not been possible to ascertain them and thus it becomes necessary to conduct the investigation along other lines.

At a very early date, the Semites interbred with such neighbouring peoples of western Asia as Canaanites, Philistines, Arabs, Hittites, etc., and thus, even if the Hebrews were originally a pure race, there had been extensive crossing with several other races even in antiquity.

In addition to the new State of Israel, there are extensive Jewish colonies in Asia such as those in Transcaucasia, Syria, Mesopotamia, the Yemen (Arabia), Samarcand, Bokhara (Turkistan), Iran, Herat (Afghanistan), etc.

Jewish settlement in North Africa (Morocco and Algiers) began in 1000 B.C. and there were further settlements later. Three distinct types are found in this part of the world, reflecting distinctive ancestral origins: (a) Jews of the old stock, now few in number, who frequently present the classical Hebrew traits of light complexion, dark hair and eyes and large hooked nose; (b) Jews in whom Spanish characteristics predominate; (c) Jews of the Arab-Berber type: these are the most numerous and are barely distinguishable from the native peoples among whom they live. Thus while some Jewish communities in Africa resemble each other in somatic characteristics, others bear a much closer resemblance to Asiatic peoples.

In Spain there was an important Jewish colony from the beginning of the Christian era. On their expulsion in 1492, the Spanish Jews scattered to North Africa, the Balkans and Russia. Jews of Spanish origin are dolichocephalic whereas Russian Jews are brachycephalic, a difference explainable by the fact that the skull conformation of each group resembles that of the Spanish and Russian populations among which they live. A similar general observation may be made regarding the Jews of Poland, Germany and Austria. Of English Jews, 28.3 per cent are dolichocephalic, 24.3 per cent mesocephalic and 47.4 per cent brachycephalic, whereas of the Jewish population of Daghestan (Caucasus), 5 per cent are dolichocephalic, 10 per cent mesaticephalic and 85 per cent brachycephalic.

With respect to cranial conformation, it may be said, generally speaking, that in Asia the predominant type is brachycephalic, though there are some dolichocephalic groups; in Africa the predominance of the dolichocephalic group is absolute; while Europe contains both dolichocephalics (more particularly stocks of Spanish origin), mesaticephalics and brachycephalics. It is not possible in the present paper to quote the detailed statistics proving the variability of all the other somatic characteristics in the misnamed 'Jewish Race'; however, it may be mentioned that 49 per cent of Polish Jews are light haired and 51 per cent dark haired, while there are only 32 per cent of blonds among German Jews. Thirty per cent of the Jews of Vienna have light coloured eyes. The hooked nose, which seems so typically Jewish, occurs in 44 per cent only of the individuals of certain groups while straight noses are found in 40 per cent, the so-called 'roman' nose in 9 per cent and tip-tilted in 7 per cent.

All the above is clear proof of the variability and lack of morphological unity of the Jewish peoples. In confirmation of this view R. N. Salaman says: 'The purity of the Jewish race is imaginary; the widest variety of ethnic types is found among Jews ranging, as regard cranial conformation only, from brachycephalics to hyperdolichocephalics. More particularly in Germany and Russia, there are Jews who do not display the smallest Semitic characteristic.'

Fishberg adds: 'The percentage of light-eyed blonds and their irregular distribution in the various centres of Jewish population, the extreme variability of the cranial index—at least as great as that observable between any of the peoples of Europe the existence among Jews of negroid, mongoloid and teutonic types, the variations in stature, etc., are other proofs of the non-existence of one Semitic race unmodified since biblical times. Hence the claims of Jews to purity of descent are as vain and baseless as the allegations of a radical difference between Jews and the so-called Aryan race on which anti-Semitism is based.'

The Jews who emigrated from their country of origin at various times in history were crossbreeds to a degree varying directly with the date of emigration. On arriving in the new country, some of the settlers married among themselves and thus perpetuated the original cross, but far more frequently they interbred with the aborigines. This is not mere supposition for there are facts to prove it, despite the widespread belief that the Jews keep themselves apart:

1. From very early in the Christian era numerous laws were promulgated prohibiting marriage between orthodox Christians and Jews, e.g., the codex of Theodosius II in the sixth century; the Council of Orleans in 538; the laws issued by the ecclesiastical authorities in Toledo in 589, in Rome in 743, and by King Ladislas II of Hungary in 1092. The fact that such prohibitions were necessary suggests that unions between Jews and Christians were frequent. Spielmann quotes numerous instances of marriages between Germans and Jews which resulted in the partners being deported by the Merovingian king to different cities of the Rhineland.

2. It is calculated that in Germany, between 1921 and 1925, for every 100 Jewish marriages, there were 58 all-Jewish and 42 mixed. In Berlin, in 1926, there were 861 all-Jewish marriages and 554 mixed. The figures speak for themselves, especially if we take into account the large number of partners who became Jews by religion although there was nothing 'Semitic' about them.

3. It is obvious that all Jewish communities are of mixed stock whatever the country in which they reside, since, even if they were segregated at certain epochs, these measures could never be strictly, nor for long, maintained or complied with. This is so far true that the general analysis and classification of Jews according to origin gives us the following separate groups: (a) descendants of Jewish emigrants from Palestine (very few); (b) descendants of unions between Jews of mixed Asiatic descent or between Jews and other groups, who might be called cross-cross-breeds; (c) Jews by religion but having anthropologically no connexion whatever with the Jews of Palestine and consisting simply of individuals of other human strains converted to the Hebrew religion. A typical example of this class is Boulan, King of the Khazars, converted to Judaism in 740 with many of his nobles and peoples; there are still numerous Jews in Poland and South Russia tracing their descent from this group.

Thus despite the view usually held, the Jewish people is racially heterogeneous; its constant migrations and its relations—voluntary or otherwise—with the widest variety of nations and peoples have brought about such a degree of crossbreeding that *the so-called people of Israel can produce examples of traits typical of every people*. For proof it will suffice to compare the rubicund, sturdy, heavily-built Rotterdam Jew with his co-religionist, say, in Salonika with gleaming eyes in a sickly face and skinny, high-strung physique. Hence, so far as our knowledge now goes, we can assert that Jews as a whole display as great a degree of morphological disparity among themselves as could be found between members of two or more different races.

This raises a problem: if, scientifically speaking, it can readily be demonstrated that the Jewish people is heterogeneous and that there is no such thing as a Jewish race, how is it that in fact some Jews can almost infallibly be identified as such at first glance? The probable explanation is that the Jews in question are those who retain certain ancestral Jewish characteristics: aquiline nose, pale skin in combination with dark eyes and hair. Nevertheless, we fail to notice and identify a much larger number of Jews who have taken on the traits of the people among whom they live and thus pass unnoticed.

Another point is that individuals professing the same religion attain a degree of similarity in gestures, habits, dress, etc., which facilitates their identification. Among the Jews, whose rites and customs are extremely rigid, this outward similarity arising from their ethnographic, linguistic and religious affinities is strongly marked though quite unconnected with the variety of morphological types making up that people.

There is therefore no foundation for the claim that there is a Jewish race; it is a biological *myth* affording no valid basis for an anti-Semitic attitude.

THE MYTH OF 'ARYAN' OR 'NORDIC' SUPERIORITY

Racists were not content with proclaiming the 'superiority' of white over coloured races nor with discriminating against Jews nor even with combating miscegenation and asserting *a priori* that it was dangerous as leading to racial degeneration. They also felt it necessary to erect biological and psychological hierarchies within the white race itself in an attempt to justify new rights of conquest, domination and overlordship vested in a still more exclusive caste.

That is the origin of 'Aryanism' or 'Nordicism' as a basic doctrine of racial superiority. The Aryan myth is the common source of other secondary myths—Germanism, Anglo-

Saxonism, and Celticism, evolved concurrently in Germany, England, the United States and France.

Let us consider the origin, distribution and essential characteristics of the superior 'Aryan' type.

ORIGIN OF THE ARYANS

The philological similarities between Sanskrit, Greek, Latin, German and the Celtic tongues observed by W. Jones (1788) led Thomas Young (1813) to adopt the term 'Indo-European' to designate the common root of these and other languages. The view quickly gained currency that there had been an Indo-European people and J. G. Rhode (1820) located their original home in Central Asia. Later J. von Kalproth suggested that the term 'Indo-European' be replaced by 'Indo-Germanic', a term whose use was made fairly general by the works of Prichard (1831) and F. Bopp (1833). In 1840 F. A. Pott suggested the valleys of the Oxus and Iaxarte and the slopes of the Hindu Kush as the home of the primitive Aryan people; though without any solid basis, this hypothesis was accepted until the end of the nineteenth century.

With Max Müller (1861), belief in the Asiatic origin of the Aryans became very widespread; Müller repeatedly stressed the desirability of replacing the terms 'Indo-Germanic' and 'Indo-European' by 'Aryan' on the grounds that the people which invaded India and whose language was Sanskrit called itself *Arya*. According to Müller the primitive Aryan language implied the existence of an 'Aryan race' which was the common ancestor of Hindus, Persians, Greeks, Romans, Slavs, Celts and Germans. Later, however, he reacted against the notion of 'racial' Aryanism and, as we shall see later, reverted to the view that it was a purely linguistic term.

J. J. d'Omalius d'Halloy (1848-64), R. T. Latham (1862), Bulwer Lytton (1842), Adolphe Pictet (1859-64) and others denied the alleged Asiatic origin of the Indo-Europeans. Benfey (1868) held that the Aryans came from the northern shores of the Black Sea between the Danube and the Caspian. Louis Leiger (1870) located them on the south shore of the Baltic and J. G. Cunok (1871) in the area between the North Sea and the Urals. D. G. Brinton (1890) believed the original home of the Aryans to have been West Africa while K. F. Johanson (around 1900) took the view that the waves of Aryan emigration had spread outwards from the Baltic. Peter

Giles (1922) thought they came from the plains of Hungary. V. Gordon Childe (1892) argued for south Russia as their place of origin, while G. Kossina (1921) believed them to have come from northern Europe. At the same time there were others such as R. Hartmann (1876), G. de Mortillet (1866) and Houzé (1906) who maintained that the Aryans were no more than a figment of certain writers' imagination, 'begotten in the study'.

The examples quoted demonstrate the variety of opinions held on the subject—opinions which in many cases flatly contradict each other. This must bring us to the conviction that the existence of the so-called Aryan 'people' or 'race' is a mere myth since we find purely subjective criteria employed in the attempt to determine its home, without the slightest factual and scientific foundation.

DOCTRINE OF ARYANISM AND TEUTONISM

The first to propound the theory of an aristocracy of 'German blood' was Count Henri de Boullainvillers (1658-1722), but it was Arthur de Gobineau who laid down the doctrine of 'Aryanism' in all its fullness (*Essai sur l'inégalité des races humaines,* 1853) and proclaimed the superiority of the 'Aryan race' over the other white strains. His ideas had a considerable influence on philosophical and political thought in Europe and from the first he was well known in Germany, where he made contact with Richard Wagner who helped to spread his ideas. However, it was only later that his theory exercised any influence or achieved any degree of acceptance in France, his native country.

Gobineau was the descendant of a burgher family of the seventeenth century who wished to prove the nobility of his family's origin, and his work is primarily the result of research designed to demonstrate the 'superiority' of his own caste. Hence Gobineau's racism is not a *nationalist* but a *class* concept of aristocracy, to defend the latter's position against a bastard proletariat. His 'Aryan' race was a 'superior' caste, the pure-bred, select and privileged minority born to govern and direct the destinies of the 'inferior' crossbred masses in any nation. Gobineau was neither pro-French nor pro-German; he merely asserted the 'superior pure Aryan descent of the aristocracy' in whatever country.

It was after the Franco-Prussian war of 1870 that 'Aryanism' as a doctrine proclaiming the innate superiority of a social class became transformed into a dogma of 'the superiority of certain nations'. While it was erroneous—as we shall see—to postulate the biological purity of a social class, it was a still greater absurdity to assert the racial purity of a nation. Nevertheless among the French, the Germans and the Anglo-Saxons alike, men of letters, politicians and pseudo-scientists were found to devote their energies to demonstrating that the triumphs of civilization were due exclusively to their own respective 'races'. The champions of Aryanism lauded the Nordic element as the source of all higher civilizations and major achievements of humanity in whatever age and place. In Gobineau's view, for instance, the Chinese civilization arose as a result of the infiltration of 'Aryan blood'.

Gobineau is not very definite as to the characteristics or traits of 'Aryans'. They may be brachycephalic or dolichocephalic; the eyes are usually light in colour, but may be dark or even black (it should be remembered that he himself was a dark-eyed Frenchman). It is his followers who ascribe to the exclusively 'Aryan' type, tallness, blue eyes, fair hair and long heads with the following psychic qualities as well: virility; innate nobility; natural aggressiveness; imperturbable objectivity; dislike of useless words and vain rhetoric; distaste for the amorphous mass; precise intelligence; the spirit of independence; sternness to themselves and others; well-developed sense of responsibility; great foresight; tenacity of will; the qualities of a race of leaders, men of great undertakings and large and well-thought-out ideas, etc.

Houston Stewart Chamberlain (1899), a pro-German Englishman and son-in-law of Richard Wagner, was the keenest supporter of the racist theory of the 'blond, dolichocephalic Nordic'; he adopted the terms 'Teutonic race' and 'Teuton blood', thus giving a frankly nationalist twist to Gobineau's class thesis. Assuming that the 'blond German' has a God-given mission to fulfil and that 'the Teutons are the aristocracy of humanity', whereas 'Latins are a degenerate population group', the conclusion drawn is that European civilization, even in countries classed as Slavonic and Latin, is the work of 'the Teuton race': e.g., Greece, Rome, the Papacy, the Renaissance, the French Revolution and the Napoleonic Empire. He goes on to assert: 'where the Germanic element has not penetrated, there is no civilization in our sense'.

Let us examine a few examples of this fantastic theory. The

'Aryan Greeks' were successful in the arts, but lacked the spirit of political organization as a result of miscegenation between their race and the Semitic, the latter containing a proportion of black blood. By the same process of imagination run mad, Julius Caesar, Alexander the Great, Leonardo da Vinci, Galileo, Voltaire, Marco Polo, Roger Bacon, Giotto, Galvani, Lavoisier, Watt and many others are all claimed as Teutons and Napoleon himself is regarded as probably descended from the Vandals.

Other great figures in history are described as products of the mixture of 'Teuton blood' with the 'dark southern race'; this class includes such men as Dante, Raphael, Michelangelo and Shakespeare, who are described as 'men of genius, not on account of, but in spite of their mixed blood'; 'their natural gifts represent the heritage received from the Teutonic race'. Referring to the apostle Paul, whom they seek to include in the 'Aryan group', writers of this school conclude that so great a man could not be a 'pure blooded' Jew and accordingly they purport to discover that he was the son of a Jewish father and a Greek mother. Of Jesus, Waltmann says: 'There is not the slightest proof that his parents were of Jewish descent; there is no doubt that the Galileans had a proportion of Aryan blood: moreover, Christ's Aryanism is obvious in his Message', furthermore, 'Joseph was not his father, because Jesus had no father'. Nevertheless, when Hitlerian Nazism clashed with the Church, no racial theorist any longer dared to refer to the 'Aryan' origin of St. Paul and of Jesus Christ.

Exaltation of the Teutonic race reaches its final pitch of absurdity in Waltmann's assertion on the strength of imaginary philological homologies of the Germanic origin of other great figures of the Renaissance: e.g., Giotto, formerly Jothe; Alighieri, formerly Aigler; Vinci, formerly Wincke; Tasso, formerly Dasse; Buonarotti Michelangelo, formerly Bohurodt; Velazquez, formerly Velahise; Murillo, formerly Moerl; Diderot, formerly Tietroh, etc.

ANTHROPOSOCIOLOGY AND SOCIAL SELECTION

This school of thought, introduced by G. Vacher de Lapouge (1896) in France and Otto Ammon (1898) in Germany, is a special variant of 'racial determinism' based on statistical researches of considerable interest in themselves, but whose results were interpreted in conformity with the preconceived idea of 'the superiority of the blond dolichocephalic type'. As a result of his examination of seventeenth and eighteenth century skulls in Montpellier, de Lapouge thought he could prove that members of higher social classes had a lower cephalic index than the common people, i.e., the latter's skulls were rounder or brachycephalic.

Certain of his conclusions may be summed up as follows:

1. In countries of mixed blood, wealth increases in inverse ratio to the cephalic index; i.e. individuals with a lower cephalic index (dolichocephalics) are the richer.
2. City-dwellers are predominantly dolichocephalic whereas brachycephalics are dominant in rural areas.
3. Urban life exercises a selective influence unfavourable to brachycephalic elements.
4. There is a greater tendency to dolichocephalism in the higher than in the lower classes; competition for the higher social positions tends to eliminate brachycephalics, who are more frequently found among workmen.
5. Since prehistoric times there has been a steady increase in the cephalic index in Europe. De Lapouge accordingly forecast the extinction of the 'blond dolichocephalic' and hence a subsequent Dark Age in the world.

All the above hypotheses are based simply and solely on the so-called Ammon's Law which asserts the concentration of dolichocephalics in the city and their social 'superiority' to brachycephalics.

The work of Levi in Italy (1896), Oloriz in Spain (1894), Beddoe in England (1905) and Houzé in Belgium (1906) demonstrated the falsity not only of Ammon's Law but also of the over-hasty deductions made by its supporters. There is no doubt that according to statistics for Germany and northern Italy students (representing the higher social classes) were predominantly dolichocephalic; however, the opposite is the case in southern Italy. Furthermore, anthroposociologists themselves reckoned that the Mediterranean dolichocephalic type was 'inferior' to the brachycephalic Alpine, whereas their own theory should have led them to accept the Negro, the most dolichocephalic type in the world, as one of the 'superior' peoples. Furthermore, Ammon draws attention to instances of brachycephaly and dark complexion among intellectuals, and to explain it away writes: 'a slight admixture of brachycephalic blood is advantageous as it tends to modify the excessive ardour of the Aryan and gives them the spirit of perseverance and reflexion which makes them better fitted for scientific studies'; 'instances are found of people of true Germanic type as regards colour of skin, eyes and hair but brachycephalic and hence psychologically of the brachycephalic type'; 'skull formation is however the important point as it determines the shape of the brain and hence the psychological type'. Vacher de Lapouge went so far as to assert that 'a brachycephalic skull is evidence of total incapacity in the individuals concerned to raise themselves above barbarism'.

However, statistical research, including that of de Lapouge and Ammon themselves, showed that (contrary to their assertions) there was a tendency to brachycephaly in intellectuals and even a preponderance of dark complexioned types among the so-called superior classes. Accordingly de Lapouge took refuge in another sophistry and labelled intellectuals 'false brachycephalics', an expression devoid of the slightest anthropological meaning.

In fact somatic study of people classed as intellectuals in the different countries would show the utmost variety of combinations of the anthropological traits attributed to the different so-called primitive races.

We accordingly see that the theories and data put forward by anthroposociologists are obviously contradictory and prove nothing as to the alleged 'intellectual superiority of the dolichocephalics'. Nor have they been able to confirm that the alleged selective influence of the great cities on newcomers operates according to the shape of the skull, and even less that the proportion of dolichocephalics is higher in the 'superior classes'.

Anthroposociology believed in and preached the superiority of dolichocephalic blonds, but all it really achieved was to reinforce powerfully the racial arrogance of self-styled 'Aryans' and to increase the aggressive tendencies of Teuton and Pan-German chauvinism by giving it the false illusion of having ethical warrant.

THE 'ARYAN' THESIS OF CONTEMPORARY NAZISM AND FASCISM

The nationalist application of 'Aryan racism' in H. S. Chamberlain, Waltmann, Theodor Pesche, Karl Penca, and Richard Wagner found convinced adherents, who played a powerful part as propagandists and caused the hypothesis of the supremacy of the 'Aryan' or 'Teuton' race to take root in Germany. In 1894, belief in the God-ordained superiority of Germany became a quasi-religious cult with the foundation in Freiburg, under the chairmanship of L. Schemann, of the 'Gobineau Vereinigung'. Hence, the doctrines of 'race purity' and 'race superiority' attained much greater importance in Germany than elsewhere, and finally became articles of faith, dangerous by the time of the first world war. While the German leaders stirred up the popular frenzy for the defence of Teutonic culture and its propagation among the other 'less civilized' races of Europe, these in their turn alleged that the German 'blonds' were not Europeans but of Asiatic origin and descendants of the Huns, lacking all the elements of true culture, without the smallest notion of the concept of liberty and democracy, and deserving extermination to the last man.

In connexion with the non-existence of the 'Aryan' or 'Nordic' type, there is an historical anecdote worthy of recollection. Before 1914, William II wished a racial map of Germany to be produced displaying the incidence of the 'Aryan' element; however, the data assembled could not be published since heterogeneity was so marked, and in whole regions such as Baden there were no Nordics.

The post-war period (1919-39) did nothing to improve relations between the peoples and the Aryan racist myth again served political ends, those of the Nazis and Fascists. J. L. Reimer (*Ein Pangermanisches Deutschland*) even proposed the establishment of a system of castes based on the varying proportion of 'German blood': (a) an upper caste of 'pure-blooded' Germans, 'ideal Teutons', to enjoy full political and social privileges; (b) an intermediate caste of 'partly German' blood to have restricted privileges only; (c) a caste of non-Germans deprived of all political rights who should be sterilized so as to safeguard the State and the future of civilization.

One of the theorists of Hitlerite racism, F. K. Günther (1920-37) has described the Alpine type as psychologically 'specially fitted to end up as the muddle-headed owner of a cottage and a patch of garden', while the Alpine woman will turn into a 'faded little creature growing old in a debased and narrow world'; Alpines according to him are 'petty criminals, small-time swindlers, sneak-thieves and sexual perverts'. Nordics on the other hand are 'capable of the nobler crimes'. However, there are racist fanatics even wilder than Günther; according to Gauch (*Neue Grundlagen der Rassenforschung,* 1933), the difference in anatomical and histological structure (hair, bones, teeth and tegument) between man and animals is *less* than that between Nordics and other human races; only Nordics possess perfect articulate speech; only in Nordics do we find the correct biped position, etc. He ends by suggesting that a strict line should be drawn between 'Nordic' man and the animal world, the latter comprising all non-Nordic humanity.

Hitler himself (*Mein Kampf*, 1925), on the question of German superiority writes: 'It is outstandingly evident from history that when the Aryan has mixed his blood with that of the inferior peoples, the result of the miscegenation has invariably been the ruin of the civilizing races. In the United States where a vast majority of the population consists of German elements among whom there has only been a small degree of interbreeding with inferior peoples belonging to the coloured races, both the human population and the civilization are different from their counterparts in Central and South America where the bulk of the immigrants have interbred with the aborigines . . .'; 'The German who has maintained his racial purity without interbreeding has become the *master* of the American continent and will continue to be its master as long as he does not commit suicide in his turn by an incestuous contamination.' In other words the Latin-American—according to German racists—is predestined to irremediable biological degeneration and hence to live under the rule of the pure 'Aryan' or 'German' race. Comment is needless.

In the previous chapter we pointed out that Italian Fascism not only proclaimed its anti-Semitism but also its 'Nordic' racism as the basis of national unity and of political and economic alliance with Nazism.

America itself is not free of this aberration and can show genuinely racist authors such as Madison Grant (*Passing of the Great Race,* 1916), Clinton B. Stoddard (*America's Race Heritage,* 1922) and Lothrop Stoddard (*The Revolt against Civilization; The Menace of the Underman,* 1922) who maintain and propagate their standard of 'Nordic superiority' with such statements as these: 'The proportion of Nordic blood in each nation is an exact measure of its power in war and its place in civilization'; 'The Nordic element in France decayed and with it the country's strength'; 'The superstition and lack of intelligence of the Spaniard of today is due to the replacement of the Nordic element by Alpine and Mediterranean strains, etc.'

THE ALLEGED 'ANGLO-SAXON' TYPE

The alleged somatic uniformity of the *Anglo-Saxon* race can be exploded as readily. If North Americans were direct descendants of the Pilgrim Fathers, and if England at that period could be deemed an exclusively Anglo-Saxon country, there might be some basis for the thesis of this type's 'purity'. It has been said that 'the Teutonic invaders exterminated all the native inhabitants of England in a glorious universal slaughter'. The truth is, however, that the Teuton conquerors were no more than a new element in the racial complex of the British Isles, and they themselves were very far from being morphologically homogeneous.

As far as the United States are concerned, there is no doubt whatsoever that the original settlers in New England were drawn from many different strata of English society and accordingly presented great physical differences among themselves. Stature and the cephalic index alike show a considerable degree of variability in the English people and Parson (1920) proved statistically that while just under 25 per cent presented the combination of dark eyes and brown or black hair, those combining light eyes and blond hair were no more than 20 per cent; and that the most frequent combination was light eyes and dark hair, though there were individuals with dark eyes and blond hair. No evidence is to be found in the British Isles, and *a fortiori* even less in the United States, to justify the alleged identification of the 'Anglo-Saxon' race with either nation.

'CELTICISM'

Celticism, another variant of 'Aryanism', is one of the fruits of the strong nationalist tendency which developed in France after the war of 1870. It is asserted that it is the Celtic type which inhabits France and distinctive somato-psychic characteristics are ascribed to it which make it 'superior' to the rest of the white races. Whereas Gobineau, de Lapouge, Ammon, Chamberlain, Waltmann, etc., attribute the creative genius of France to the 'Aryan' and 'Teutonic' element, Celticism presents equally valid arguments for the 'racial superiority of the Celt'.

A. de Quatrefages (*La race prussienne,* 1872) holds that the racial descent of the Prussians is entirely different from that of the French and concludes: 'There is nothing Aryan about the Prussians'. In 1871 Broca affirmed that France was a nation of brachycephalic (Alpine) Gauls and maintained the superiority of that strain over the dolichocephalic German 'Nordic'. Isaac Tylor (*The Origin of the Aryans,* 1890), was another scientist who held that the Celts were a tall, brachycephalic race and the only Aryans.

The ambiguous use of terms and the confusion as to somatic characterization grow still greater when an attempt is made to define the Celt and the Gaul. Joseph Widney (1907) speaks of two Celtic types, the first tall, blond and dolichocephalic (like the Highland Scot and the people of Northern Ireland), the second short, dark and brachycephalic (like the Southern Irish). He regards the first as the true Celt, while the second is descended from a more ancient conquered race and has merely adopted the 'Celtic tongue'. However, he continues: 'The Celt has never maintained his blood unmixed'; 'the fatal propensity of the Celt to miscegenation has brought about the ruin of his race'. Widney claims that the blond dolichocephalic Celt is the dominant element in France; in France itself, however, the tendency is more to identify the Celt with the brachycephalic Alpine of intermediate stature and complexion.

Some schools of thought in France regard it as peopled by Celts, others by Gauls, though there is no agreement between French scholars as to which was which, nor whether they were or were not in fact the same race. Hence certain investigators hold that 'Celt' is a historical term of little scientific precision used to designate peoples speaking related languages and presenting every morphological variety from short, dark dolichocephalics through moderately fair brachycephalics of medium height to tall, blond, dolichocephalics. However, these entirely correct observations have little influence on a mentality imbued with 'racism'.

Whatever the 'Celtic' type may be, the fact is that between 2000 B.C. (end of the Neolithic Age in France) and the Teutonic migrations in the fifth century of our own era, very little is know about racial mixtures in western Europe. It seems fairly certain that there were successive waves of brachycephalic Alpine types or peoples in which that type preponderated. Like Germany and northern Italy, France was the meeting point of the three main races of Europe, as well as of any surviving palaeolithic groups: (a) the Mediterranean race was the indigenous stock in southern France, where it is still predominant; (b) Alpines penetrated towards the north-west and today constitute the bulk of the population of Savoy, Auvergne and Brittany; (c) the Nordic or Baltic races (Normans, Teutons, Saxons, Franks and Burgundians), all of whom were of extremely mixed stock, spread over France from north to south and one of them gave its name to the country. Even today the Germanic element predominates in extensive areas of northern France. To sum up, if we take into account the shape of the skull, colour of eyes, hair and skin and stature, it becomes evident that morphologically the French people was and is amazingly heterogeneous.

CRITICISM AND REFUTATION OF THESE THEORIES

The fundamental error of 'Aryanism' or 'Nordicism' in all its forms lies in a confusion of ideas which is very wide-spread but by any reckoning unscientific: the term *race* is used indifferently as a synonym for *language* and *nation*.

It has already been pointed out that the term 'race' has an exclusively biological significance. Nevertheless, the terms 'Latin race', 'Slav race', 'German race' and of course 'Aryan race' are in common use, and thus men fall into the error or regarding human groups which are only linguistically homogeneous as anthropologically uniform. In 1900 Havet wrote: 'Language and race are two entirely different concepts. In a discussion of linguistics not a single anthropological term should ever be used and similarly in anthropological studies the vocabulary of linguistics must be avoided.' Max Müller himself, who was one of the first to use the term 'Aryan race' (1861), abjured its biological interpretation and re-emphasized its purely linguistic significance. He wrote: 'To me an ethnologist who speaks of Aryan race, Aryan blood, Aryan eyes and hair, is as great a sinner as a linguist who speaks of a dolichocephalic dictionary or a brachycephalic grammar.' However, the concept of the 'Aryan race' had become so wide-spread that Müller's retraction and the views of Havet were without practical effect.

There is indeed a group or family of related languages labelled 'Indo-European' or 'Aryan'. Language, however, spreads and is transmitted from one people to another by migration, conquest and commercial exchanges, without, on that account, implying membership of the same biological human group by those speaking similar tongues.

The best illustration of this is to be found in the United States, whose 150 million citizens are a new type to which a multitude of races from all points of the world have contributed. Though the main strains of the population range from tall, long skulled blonds (Nordic type) through short, sub-brachycephalic blonds (Eastern European type) to tall, dark-skinned dolichocephalics (Atlantic-Mediterranean type), all of them speak English. In other words there are a number of groups somatically distinct with a common language, not to mention the numbers of English-speaking North American citizens of Negro, Amerindian, and Chinese stock.

In other words, a nation can consist of more than one race, while—conversely—biologically similar groups may be subdivided into separate nations. The inhabitants of North America bear more resemblance to the people of Denmark and Sweden than to the people of south Germany, while the latter are physically akin to parts of the population of France, Czechoslovakia and Yugoslavia. How then is it possible to speak of German, Aryan or Anglo-Saxon 'races'?

Generalizations about the 'Aryan' race and its superiority are based on arguments which lack all objective validity and are erroneous, contradictory and unscientific.

It is in the strictly morphological field that the incongruities are greatest. Research into the skull formations and other characteristics of individuals or groups regarded as authentic 'Aryans', 'Teutons', 'Anglo-Saxons' and 'Celts' shows considerable variation alike in earlier ages and in our own. It is a proven fact that there have been both brachycephalics and dolichocephalics in Europe since the earliest ages. The work of von Holder, Lissauer, and Virchow (1870-80) demonstrated that the primitive population of the Baltic was morphologically heterogeneous with a large percentage of brachycephalics. In 1889 Virchow asserted: 'The typical Aryan postulated in theory has never been discovered' and even expressed the opinion that the brachycephalic was superior to the dolichocephalic. However, this was not enough to check belief in the superiority of the 'blond dolichocephalic', which had taken strong root in the popular imagination.

A moment came, however, when even the creators of the Aryan racial myth began to realize little by little that the physical types for which they claimed superiority and the 'inferior' non-Aryan were non-existent figments of the mind. Ammon himself admitted that he had never met a pure Alpine brachycephalic: 'Some brachycephalics were blond, others tall, others with narrow noses or with some other trait which they should not have had.'

However, the contradictions under this head reach their worst when Chamberlain, who had described the 'blond Teuton' type, concluded by denying all worth to anthropometry because it could give no indication of superiority. He admits that 'the Teutons of antiquity were not all dolichocephalic giants', but . . . 'a tentative examination of them would show us that all of them present the specific characteristics of the German people both physically and mentally'. He then asserts that this subjective appreciation 'teaches more than can be learnt in a congress of anthropology'. At one point he asks: 'In fact what type of man was the Aryan?' explains that philosophy, anthropology and ethnology cannot give an exact and detailed description of the Aryan people, and adds: 'Who knows what will be taught about the Aryans in 1950?'

He has no hesitation in asserting that 'the noble visage of Dante is indisputable proof of his Teutonic origin' (despite which Waltmann—as we have seen—thought Dante a product of miscegenation). Luther is also regarded as of Teutonic type although his traits are quite unlike Dante's (Luther was dolichocephalic while Dante was brachycephalic), but that does not prevent our author writing: 'Dante and Luther are at the two extremes of the noble range of physiognomy of the great men of the German race.' He concludes with another coruscating phrase: 'He who proves himself German by his deed is German, whatever his genealogy.'

In view of the physical heterogeneity of the supposed 'Nordic' or 'Aryan' (a good example of this would be an individual 'as tall as Goebbels, as blond as Hitler and as slim as Goering'), Nazism cast aside every pretence of biological justification for its imperialistic doctrine of the economic subjugation of other peoples and reached the conclusion that 'a Nordic soul may be joined to a non-Nordic body', and that 'the Nordic man may be recognized by his deeds and not by the length of his nose or the colour of his eyes' (*Nationalsozialistische-Korrespondenz,* June 1936).

The inference is clearly that in racism the physical criterion is a mere smokescreen, abandoned as useless when the circumstances of the moment require: 'The differentiation of the human races is not a matter of science; it is by immediate perception that we recognize emotionally the differences we call racial.' In the view of Dr. Gross (1934): 'Politics cannot wait until science has worked out a racial theory; politics must outstrip science with the intuitive basic truth of the diversity of blood between peoples and with its logical consequence, the principle of rule by the most gifted.'

Thus the origin of racism is not scientific but political. It is used by enemies to justify their fighting each other although they may be of similar racial composition, or by allies to discover a 'racial brotherhood' even when they are morphologically distinct. For instance Aryans should logically have regarded the Japanese people as inferior, a race of sub-men, on account of their colour. However, political pacts make compromise necessary, and the explanation was given that the white Ainus of Japan had interbred considerably with the yellow races and hence the Japanese today, while presenting the aspect of yellow men, 'nevertheless possess all the moral and intellectual qualities of an Aryan and even of a Nordic people'. On the strength of a theory so adaptable, Alfred Rosenberg (1935) was able to state officially that 'the Japanese leaders are as biologically reliable as the German'.

Ruth Benedict is in the right of it in saying: 'No distortion of anthropomorphic facts is too absurd to be used by propaganda backed by force and the concentration camp.'

CONCLUSION

The existence of individual somatic and psychic differences is a fact; in every race, nation, class or community, better and worse endowed individuals can be found. This is a biological fact to which there are no exceptions. The variations in question are however completely unconnected with the alleged superiority or inferiority of specific human groups.

That one's own family or race is better than any other is a belief of long standing. What is relatively new is the attempt to justify this alleged 'superiority' scientifically on the grounds of innate biological characteristics.

The growing discontent of the peoples of India, the development of racial feeling among the Negroes, and the self-confidence displayed by the Japanese, Chinese and Indonesian peoples, are among many proofs that the races hitherto despised for their supposed inferiority are every day less ready to accept the judgement on their qualities passed by certain elements in the white races.

Democracy recognizes the existence of differences between

men, but considers that *all men* possess the same inalienable rights and seeks to afford *all men* equal political, social and economic opportunities.

Totalitarianism also accepts the differences between men and peoples as inevitable but holds that they imply the principle of obedience to the will of a 'master' race expressed through 'superior men'. Its concern is to enslave all who are capable of falling-in with the will of the 'masters' and to exterminate all those unable to make themselves units in the totalitarian world.

As scientific discoveries and technological progress have largely destroyed the effectiveness of myth pure and simple among the masses, contemporary racism is accordingly forced to adopt a scientific disguise. Hence the racist myths of the twentieth century must seem to be based on science although, according to Prenant, it may be 'at the price of the most shameless falsifications and contradictions'. Racism has sought to capture and use for its own ends anthropology, the physiology of the blood, the laws of heredity, etc. But without success.

In 1918 the victorious allies rejected the proposal of the Japanese delegation to the Paris Conference of 1919 for the inclusion in the Charter of the League of Nations of a declaration proclaiming the equality of all races. Since 1945, however, the work of the United Nations Organization and its Specialized Agencies has been shared by tall blond dolichocephalics, short dark dolichocephalics, brachycephalics, yellow men, Negroes, halfbreeds and representatives of many nations differing in culture and morphology. All these varied elements drafted and unanimously approved in December 1948, the Universal Declaration of Human Rights, the second Article of which lays down that: 'Everyone is entitled to all the rights and freedoms set forth in the Declaration, without distinction of any kind, such as race, colour, sex, language, religion, political or other opinion, national or social origin, property, wealth or other status.'

The amazing assertion of Burgess (1890) in justification of German colonial policy—that the Germans 'are fully entitled to annex the territory of recalcitrants (the reference is to the native peoples) and transform it into the dwelling place of civilized man'—is a revealing instance of how the 'superiority' of the racist leads him to accept without concern for morality or law the criterion of power as the source of law where 'inferior' peoples are concerned.

There are two questions the answers to which will go far towards banishing racial myths. What degree of difference is possible between individuals of similar heredity living in unlike settings? And again, what are the differences between individuals differing in heredity and living in the same setting?

Differences between human beings should be regarded as facts requiring understanding and interpretation and not as qualities meriting blame or praise. Major Morton writes: 'Much of the friction between races, as between nations or individuals, is due to misunderstanding; if the peoples were willing to devote a little of their time to understanding each others' points of view they would often realize that things are not going as badly as they think' (1920).

Racial prejudice may spring from economic and political causes, from a particular race's superiority or inferiority complex, from biological differences, from hereditary instinct or from a combination of several of these causes. In every case matters are greatly aggravated by the tendency to accept theories and hypotheses without the slightest critical examination.

Doctrines of racial superiority have played an unprecedented role in the high policy of States. They have been the excuse for cruelty and inhumanity, they have served as a pretext for the colonial expansion of Europe and for modern imperialism, sharpened race hatred, carried patriotism to absurd lengths and promoted war.

Nothing will be achieved by promulgating new laws or enforcing compliance with the present laws, since the effectiveness of those laws is in direct proportion to the conviction of the majority of citizens of the need for them and their intrinsic rightness. More can be done against racial prejudices and myths by endeavouring to amend the conditions which give rise to them.

Fear is the first of these: fear of war, fear of economic insecurity, fear of loss of personal or group prestige, etc. Racial prejudice in one form or another will continue in the world as long as there is not a greater sense of personal security.

It is necessary to demonstrate the absurdity of regarding human groups en bloc as 'completely good' or 'completely bad'. Science, democratic beliefs and humanitarian feeling are at one in rejecting the condemnation of any man on the grounds of his race or colour or of his chancing to be in a state of slavery.

Racism is quite different from a mere acceptance or scientific and objective study of the fact of race and the fact of the present inequality of human groups. Racism involves the assertion that inequality is absolute and unconditional, i.e., that a race is inherently and by its very nature superior or inferior to others quite independently of the physical conditions of its habitat and of social factors.

The last half century has seen the development of a hypertrophied nationalism. The horrors of war and the anxieties of an armed peace are doing much to maintain it. The elimination, through individual and group conviction, of racial myths can exert a powerful influence and bring about a better spirit and better understanding in the relations between man and man.

BIBLIOGRAPHY

BENEDICT, Ruth. *Race, science and politics.* New York, 1941, 209 p.

BURNS, Alan. *Colour prejudice.* London, 1948, 171 p.

COMAS, Juan. *Existe una raza judía?* Mexico, 1941, 29 p.

—. *El mestizaje y su importancia social.* Mexico, 1944, 12 p.

—. *La discriminación racial en América.* Mexico, 1945, 27 p.

COUNTS, Earl W. *This is race.* An anthology selected from the international literature on the races of man. New York, 1950, 747 p.

DUNN, L. C. and DOBZHANSKY, Th. *Heredity, race and society.* New York, 1950, 165 p.

HANKINS, Frank H. *The racial basis of civilization: a critique of the nordic doctrine.* New York, 1926.

HUXLEY, Julian S. and HADDON, A. C. *We Europeans: a survey of 'racial' problems.* New York and London, 1936, 246 p.

KLUCKHOHN, Clyde. *Mirror for man.* New York, 1949, 313 p.

MONTAGU, M. F. Ashley. *Man's most dangerous myth. The fallacy of race.* New York, 1942, 304 p.

ORTIZ, Fernando. *El engaño de las razas.* La Havana, 1946, 428 p.

PARKES, James. *An enemy of the people, anti-semitism.* New York, 1946, 151 p.

PRENANT, Marcel. *Raza y racismo.* Mexico, 1939, 172 p.

RACE AND SOCIETY

by
KENNETH L. LITTLE

Department of Social Anthropology
University of Edinburgh

INTRODUCTION

In any discussion of race and society, it is essential to have a clear understanding of the terms employed. It is history rather than race which is the main factor in producing the differences between the cultures and cultural attainments of the world's population. The fact that such differences exist is not sufficient reason for believing that there are underlying disparities in innate capacity for intellectual and emotional development.

Why, then, if 'racial superiority' is only a myth and lacks any real substance, does 'race' play such a large part in the affairs of modern life? In many parts of the world racial differences are the basis for discriminatory legislation and social practices which signify a flat denial of the scientific view. Moreover, many people—for instance both in the southern part of the United States and in the Union of South Africa —continue to argue that the Negro is biologically inferior to the white man. Many white Southerners claim that he is quite a different being, and many South Africans that he is unfit to live as a member of a white civilization. Australia prohibits the immigration of coloured races, and in a number of other countries black and white are separated, either by law or by custom. Can it be simply that the various fallacies of race are not yet known and understood by the governments and peoples concerned?

The plain answer, of course, is that superstitious and ill-informed thinking is not the primary cause of racial prejudice and of the innumerable laws and customs which govern relations between races. Harmony between persons of different racial origin does not depend upon their being properly informed about the latest findings of modern anthropology! If racial amity did so depend, it would be necessary to explain why racial differences are tolerated in one country and not in another; why they are virtually ignored in, say, Brazil or Hawaii, and why so much attention is paid to them in, say South Africa or the United States. Brazil has far fewer schools per head of the population than white South Africa, and until the present century many Hawaiians were illiterate.

The fact is that race itself, in the biological sense, is irrelevant to racial attitudes and thinking. No doubt, there are many people with a deep and unreasoning repugnance to an individual of different colour who cannot bear the thought of any kind of physical contact with him. But this does not mean that they were born with such feelings or that such feelings are instinctive. The more likely explanation is that inhibitions of this kind are acquired, for the most part unconsciously, during early childhood. Children tend to take on the attitudes of those in charge of them at home and in school, and they learn to react emotionally in the same way as those about them. If their parents and friends strongly hold certain beliefs that the members of a particular racial group are unclean, unhealthy, etc., it is not surprising that, growing up in that environment, they come to have the same sort of feeling about that racial group as they do about dirt and disease. In any case, what is much more convincing than any psychological explanation is the fact that although such racial aversions are very common in some places, notably the southern United States and South Africa, they are almost unknown in certain other countries. If feelings of repugnance *were* innate, it would obviously be very difficult to explain how millions of men and women manage to work and to mix together without the slightest difficulty on this score. It would be even harder to account for the fact that miscegenation frequently goes on even in the face of severe penalties against it. The truth is that people can get along together without attributing peculiar qualities to each other, despite wide differences in complexion and variability in the shape and size of noses and heads.

The last point should help us to realize that it is not the existence of racial differences *per se* which gives rise to the problem of racial relations, but the fact that such differences are singled out by the members of a given society. What is important, therefore, is not whether groups of individuals *do,* or *do not,* differ in actual biological terms, but the fact that they conceive themselves as racially different. As it happens, there are national and cultural groups in all parts of the world which are not proper races in the anthropological meaning of the term. This does not prevent their members regarding themselves and other similar groups as races. Without this consciousness of group differences, race relations in the strict sense of the word cannot be said to exist, *however* biologically mixed the given society may be. Race relations depend fundamentally upon the recognition and treatment of individuals as the representatives of a given biological, or supposed biological, group; and in the absence of that kind of recognition a relationship between persons of different race is no different from any other kind of relationship occurring in human society.

The problem of race and society is psychologically complicated. Racial attitudes and feelings do not exist *in vacuo.* As they are not biological in origin, they can only be social. This means that they must be the product not only of existing circumstances, but of the kind of contact which the groups concerned have had with each other in the past. This latter point is important because of the varying extent, as between one society and another, to which racial consciousness is fostered. In some countries the fact that people differ from each other in racial appearance passes unnoticed; in others it is a matter of constant attention. In some cases, it gives rise to special laws against intermarriage; in others it has no social consequences. What is the explanation of this paradox —has culture anything to do with the matter? Can it be that conflict in race relations occurs because the groups concerned have different ways of life? There are many people, indeed, who assert that this is the main factor and that there will always be friction so long as racial differences are linked with differences in language and custom among the members of the same society. But the fact is that there are instances of groups with dissimilar cultures getting along amicably with each other, just as there are examples of hostility between races with similar cultures. And there are examples of racial groups with similar cultures living together in amity, just as there are instances of friction between races with dissimilar cultures. A few illustrations will clarify this point.

Jamaica, in the British West Indies, contains a population which is racially mixed in terms of whites, coloured (i.e. people of mixed blood), and blacks, but has a common religion and language, and is governed by a single system of laws. The wealthier and more prominent people are mainly white or near-white; there is a middle class composed mainly of coloured; the labouring and peasant section is mostly black. A great deal of attention is paid to gradations in colour and it is a considerable social and economic asset for an individual to be light in skin. This is because colour differences are largely linked with class differences. But there is no discrimination on grounds of race (as distinct from colour), and race is no bar to any official position on the island. The children attend the same schools, and at any important social gathering there will be persons of black as well as white complexion.

As in Jamaica, whites and Negroes in the southern United States also have the same general habits and customs, speak the same language, and have the same general outlook on life, but there a rigid separation of the races exists in nearly every sphere. Negroes have separate schools, churches, recreational centres, etc., and are not allowed to mix publicly with white people in any form of social activity. Recently, however, the United States Supreme Court has ruled that segregation in public schools is unconstitutional. School segregation is already disappearing in some of the states chiefly affected, and some Southern states universities, too, have admitted Negro students within recent years. Segregation is upheld partly by law and partly by strong social mores on the side of the whites. It is strictly enforced by legal means, by intimidation or even by physical force. Violent action, such as dynamiting a house, may be taken against Negroes who infringe the code of racial etiquette by trying to improve the subordinate status assigned to them.

These are examples of racially dissimilar groups with similar cultures. In South Africa, the groups concerned are culturally as well as racially and ethnically dissimilar. There are the Europeans, who speak English or Afrikaans and are Christians; the Cape Coloured (people of mixed blood), who speak pidgin-English or Afrikaans and are Christians; the Indians, who speak mainly Hindustani and are Hindus or Muslims; and the native Africans, who speak mainly Bantu languages and follow mainly tribal customs and religions. As will be explained below in more detail, these various groups are socially segregated from each other, and the non-European sections of the population are kept completely subordinate. There is considerable friction and hostility between Europeans and non-Europeans in areas where they meet. In contrast, again, is New Zealand, which also has a racially and culturally mixed population. The majority are people of European descent, mostly British. They are known locally as Pakehas. The minority consists of Maoris, a people of Polynesian descent. The larger part of the Maori population still follows tribal customs, but there is no discrimination. Maoris have full equality under the laws of the Dominion and share the benefits of a social security act in common and equally with white New Zealanders. They are also eligible for, and sit as members of, the House of Representatives. A certain amount of racial mixture goes on, mainly with Pakehas belonging to the lower economic class, and a number of Maoris have settled in the towns. White New Zealanders tend to look down on the latter group, but the more general attitude is tolerant of racial differences, and the average Pakeha takes pride in his Maori compatriots.

An alternative to examining racial attitudes in terms of their cultural context is to compare the *antecedents* of each case with those of others. For example, in the Southern states, it was the institution of plantation slavery which firmly ingrained the notion of Negro subordination in the minds of the white population. In South Africa, it was the social and religious exclusiveness of the early Boer farmers which was largely responsible for native Africans and other non-Europeans being regarded and treated as an 'out-group'. But history is not a conclusive factor. Jamaica also had the institution of Negro slavery, and most of the slaves worked on plantations under conditions similar to those in the Old South. Brazil provides another example. Yet, both in Jamaica and in Brazil, race relations took a very different, and more liberal, course than in the United States. Again, the complete subordination of the coloured races of South Africa, which followed their wars with the European settlers, lacks its counterpart in New Zealand. Wars were also fought there between settlers and the native population less than a hundred years ago, but they have resulted in racial parity, not subjugation.

Thus, at first sight it appears as if cultural and historical considerations throw very little light upon the problem. However, if we extend our review of culture and history beyond the area of Western civilization in its modern form, we are confronted by a very significant fact. This is the virtual absence of racial relations as we define the term, before the period of European overseas expansion and exploration. In no other civilization, either ancient or modern, do we find the kind of legal and customary recognition of group differences which characterizes the contact of European peoples with other races. In the Muslim world, for example, the important differences today, as in the past, are those of religion. Muslim people are traditionally 'colour-blind', and Islam insists on the equality of believers, whatever their race or colour. According to Koranic law, all members of a conquered population who embrace Islam become the equals of the conquerors in all respects. Racial considerations are also lacking in the Hindu caste system although some writers claim that it originated in racial diversity. They argue that classical Hindu society was divided into four original *varna,* or colours, and explain this as racial differentiation. However, the word *varna* has quite a different meaning from *caste,* and the basis of exclusion in the caste system is not racial. It is religious and ritual, and both excluders and excluded assent to it and play their part in enforcing it. This is unlike any modern form of racial relations regulated by law and by social pressure on the subordinated group.

In other older civilizations, such as those of Egypt and Greece, the relationship between races was that of captor and captive, or master and slave. There is little evidence of aversion or special prescription on the grounds of race or colour. The Egyptians, for example, spoke scornfully of the Negroes to the south of them, and Egyptian artists sometimes caricatured the Negro's thick lips and woolly hair. But the Egyptians looked upon other foreigners, including blue-eyed Libyans, with equal disdain. Like other earlier peoples, the Egyptians mixed freely with their captives, whatever their colour, and some of the Pharaohs showed in their features signs of their partially Negroid ancestry. The Greeks also knew Negroes as slaves, but most of the slave population of Greece were of the same race as their masters, and there was no occasion to associate any physical type with the slave status. In any case, the kind of distinction which the Greeks made between people was cultural, not racial. They looked down on all barbarians but, provided the barbarian took on Hellenistic characteristics, he does not seem to have been subjected to social exclusion on account of his physical appearance.[1] In Rome, too, the situation was similar. The slave population was drawn from North Africa, Asia Minor, and Western Europe, and it included Nubians and Ethiopians as well as Germans and Britons. Roman citizens thought poorly of the peoples they conquered and spoke disparagingly of them, and of non-Romans in general, irrespective of race. It was considered disgraceful for a Roman soldier to take a barbarian wife, but this was not from any objection to racial differences: it was because such a union disregarded the custom of marriage between citizens. Nevertheless, it is said that nine out of every ten free plebeians at the end of the first century A.D. had foreign blood, and citizenship was given to every free-born man in the empire early in the third century. This conception of common humanity was widened further by the teaching of the Stoics and, above all, by the spread of Christianity.

In the period following the downfall of Rome, the Catholic Church emerged as a powerful political as well as religious institution. The Church fostered the spiritual unity of Christendom, teaching that all who were Christians were the same kind of men. As time went on the Church was more and more conceived as an instrument of international order, the glory of God demanding that the whole world be brought under its sway. With this purpose in view wars were fought against Muslims and 'pagans', the basis of antagonism being entirely religious. Jews were persecuted and Muslims enslaved because they were enemies of the faith, not because they were considered racially different from Christians. Nevertheless, Jews, Muslims, and pagans, in their unlikeness from Christian Europe, serve as forerunners of the modern concept of alien races. In other words, this period between the First Crusade and Columbus' discovery of America was characterized by the religious view of world order, and it established a pattern of dealing with non-Christian peoples which was to be continued —lacking only its religious motivation—to the present day. In the meantime, Italian, Spanish and Portuguese merchants were making their voyages of discovery and meeting new peoples and cultures. The Moors and heathens whom the Portuguese encountered down the African coast were inferior to them as fighters, but this led to no conclusions about racial superiority. Nor was there, as yet, any idea of perpetuating the servile status of black people captured in such raids and

---

1. cf. Ina C. Brown. *Race Relations in a Democracy*, Harper, 1949.

forays. On the contrary, their conversion to Christianity was sought with enthusiasm, and this transformation was supposed to make the Africans the human equals of all other Christians. In this way, many of the Africans taken by the Portuguese were assimilated in the general population and a number of them rose to important positions in the Portuguese State.

What changed this easy-going attitude to men of different race was the development of capitalism and the profit-motive as a characteristic feature of Western civilization. The new lands discovered in America provided ideal opportunities for economic exploitation and their native inhabitants were too weak to withstand the well-armed European settler-business man. Tobacco, indigo, rice, cotton, and sugar cane, which could be produced on a large scale and at a considerable profit, were grown for sale in Europe. The difficulty was to recruit the workers required. There was a lack of free labour, and so it became necessary to use slaves. Slavery in the Spanish colonies was at first limited to the aboriginal Indians, but long before the end of the colonial era a large part of the native population was wiped out by harsh treatment or by European diseases. Also, Indian slavery was severely criticized on religious grounds by the Jesuit and other missionaries, including the celebrated priest, Las Casas; and so it was decided to introduce Negroes from Africa. They made better workers and were less restive in captivity.

The first African Negroes were landed in the New World about 1510. As already mentioned, trade in African slaves, including Negroes, was not new in commerce; but before the middle of the fifteenth century it was limited to the Mediterranean. In West Africa, there was not the same excuse for war, but if Christian men had any misgivings, they were allayed by a bull of Pope Nicholas V which authorized the Portuguese 'to attack, subject and reduce to perpetual slavery the Saracens, Pagans, and other enemies of Christ southward from Capes Bajador and Non, including all the coast of Guinea'. The usual condition was attached: all captives must be converted to Christianity.

These elementary methods of securing slaves sufficed while the trade was local, but the rapid exploitation of fresh settlements in the West Indies and on the American mainland greatly stimulated the demand and brought a more elaborate system into being. All along the West African coast trading-stations sprang up, which were stocked by African purveyors, and at which slaves could be procured by barter. The Africans offered for sale were, or were supposed to be, war-captives, condemned criminals, or persons who had sold themselves into slavery. By this convenient rationalization, the Europeans were relieved of moral responsibility, and the supporters of the slave trade even took credit for saving their victims from death. However, the scale of the commerce was too large to escape public attention, and as time went on there was increasing knowledge of the harsh and inhuman conditions on the plantations as well as of the horrors of the Middle Passage. The slave owner and trader had to find some way of justifying themselves or run the risk of losing both property and business. At first, they argued on the grounds of the economic necessity of slavery to national prosperity, and then, as the humanitarian attack was pressed, they offered the ingenuous theory that Negroes were sub-human and incapable of moral feelings; hence there was no obligation to treat them like ordinary human beings.

Mr. Long, in his *History of Jamaica,* published in three volumes in 1774, wrote:

'We cannot pronounce them *unsusceptible of civilization since even apes* have been taught to eat, drink, repose and dress *like men.* But of all the human species hitherto discovered, their *natural baseness of mind* seems to afford the least hope of their being (except by miraculous interposition of Divine Providence) so refined as to think as well as act like *men.* I do not think that an Orang Outang husband would be any dishonour to an Hottentot female.'

What this amounted to was a deliberate attempt to depersonalize a whole group of human beings—to reduce them to mere articles of commerce or economic 'utilities'. The extent to which it was successful may be illustrated by the case of the slave ship *Zong,* when one hundred and thirty slaves were thrown overboard on the plea of lack of water. The law took its course, but the trial was not for murder. It was to decide whether the throwing overboard of the slaves was a genuine act of jettison, for which the insurance company would have to pay, or a fraud on the policy.

However, what is significant about this earlier development of racial prejudice is the fact that efforts to impersonalize human relations in order to exploit men more effectively for economic purposes were not confined to the African slave. The capitalist-entrepreneur of the day was just as ready to use people of his own race in the same way. Indeed, part of the early demand for labour in the West Indies and on the mainland was filled by white servants, who were sometimes defined in exactly the same terms as those stereotyping the Negro. Plantation owners bid eagerly for supplies of convicts from the London prisons, and hundreds of children were kidnapped and shipped from Scotland. But the white servants were allowed to work off their bond, while the Negro was gradually pushed into chattel slavery. His servile status was established by substituting a racial reason for the previous religious one—by characterizing a whole race as degenerate, degraded, immoral, lacking in intelligence, etc. The religious argument proved insufficient when it came to be a question of continuing slavery for the convert.

This, then, as Dr. Oliver Cromwell Cox has pointed out, marks the beginning of modern race relations.

'It was not an abstract, natural, immemorial feeling of mutual antipathy between groups, but rather a practical exploitative relationship with its socio-attitudinal facilitation —at that time only nascent racial prejudice. Although this peculiar kind of exploitation was then in its incipiency, it had already achieved its significant characteristics. As it developed and took definite capitalistic form, we could follow the white man around the world and see him repeat the process among practically every people of colour.'[1]

Dr. Cox goes on to quote Earl Grey's description in 1880 of the motives and purposes of the British in South Africa.

'Throughout this part of the British Dominions the coloured people are generally looked upon by the whites as an inferior race, whose interest ought to be systematically disregarded when they come into competition with our own, and who ought to be governed mainly with a view to the advantage of the superior race. And for this advantage two things are considered to be especially necessary: firstly, that facilities should be afforded to the white colonists for obtaining possession of land heretofore occupied by the native tribes; and secondly, that the Kaffir population should be made to furnish as large and as cheap a supply of labour as possible.'

Dr. Cox's thesis is that racial exploitation is merely one aspect of the problem of the proletarianization of labour, regardless of the colour of the labourer. Hence, racial antagonism is essentially political class conflict. The capitalist exploiter, being opportunistic and practical, will utilize any convenience to keep his labour and other resources freely

---

1. Oliver C. Cox. *Caste, Class and Race,* Doubleday, 1948.

exploitable. He will devise and employ race prejudice when that becomes convenient. The reason why race relations are 'easier' in most countries colonized by the Latin nations, viz. Portugal and Spain, is partly because neither Spain nor Portugal ever attained the industrial development of Northern Europe. They remained longer under the political and economic authority of the Church. Also, the capitalist spirit, the profit-making motive among the sixteenth-century Spaniards and Portuguese, was constantly inhibited by the universal aims and purpose of the Church. This tradition in favour of the old religious criterion of equality is in contrast to the objective, capitalistic attitude of Anglo-Saxon and Germanic countries, such as Britain, the Netherlands, and the United States.[1] It might be compared in some respects, however, with the assimilative aims of French colonial policy—to absorb colonial and coloured subjects as part of a 'greater France' on a common basis of culture and citizenship.

What this implies is a direct relationship between racial attitudes and society—*that race relations are, in effect, a function of a certain type of social and economic system.* The best way to consider the matter further is to take a number of societies with varying attitudes towards race and colour. South Africa is a convenient example to start with because racial consciousness and feeling is probably more intense there than in any other part of the world and is most explicitly confessed as a code of official opinion. Brazil and Hawaii represent the opposite extreme, and Great Britain will be considered as intermediate in this respect. The British situation will be described at some length, because it is less well known to students of racial problems, and because it illustrates quite strikingly the somewhat paradoxical fact that both racial discrimination and racial toleration sometimes exist alongside each other in the same society.

THE SOUTH AFRICAN CASE

The South African situation is the outcome of European colonization, which commenced when the Dutch made their initial settlement in 1652, in and near what is now Cape Town. When the British took over the colony in 1806, its population

---

1. ibid., p. 174.

numbered some 76,000 souls, including 30,000 slaves from Madagascar, India and the East Indies; 20,000 native Hottentots; and about 26,000 whites. Factors of race and colour were not so important as were religious considerations. Thus, if a freed slave woman were baptized she frequently married a white man, and she and her children would become absorbed in the white community. Marriage between white and Hottentot, as distinct from co-habitation, was extremely rare. The marriage of Eva, a Hottentot woman, and van Mierhoff, a white explorer, celebrated at Government House, was an exception and will be quoted as such in all books referring to this period. As the colony expanded, a growing divergence of outlook and way of life developed between the town and country folk. The lack of racial consciousness, and hence prejudice, in the town was largely due to the freer and less conventional mode of life. The population was in a constant state of flux, the town acting chiefly as a port of call, and refreshment and provision station for visiting ships. In the country, on the other hand, a more homogeneous, independent, and stable community was developing. Composed chiefly of farmers whose main concern was to flee interference by the administration, it developed a stricter and more rigorous mode of life. This group lacked all those elements of class differentiation which existed among many of the earlier pioneers of European colonies in the New World. They were people with a common code and ideology deeply rooted in the Calvinistic tradition of seventeenth-century Europe. The doctrine of predestination and the concepts of the eternally damned and the elect were a part of their social heritage to which they clung tenaciously. The frontier farmer thus came to regard membership of his religious group as an exclusive privilege which distinguished and separated him by an immeasurable distance from those who did not share it with him. This belief in the exclusiveness of his group and its privileges justified his right to dominate the 'out-group' which surrounded him, viz. the heathen Bantu whom he fought, and the primitive Bushmen whom he hunted as vermin. Any conception of the equality of human beings was foreign to him, and 'liberty' and 'fraternity' held no validity for him outside his closed circle.

This awareness of group exclusiveness found expression in a consciousness of racial and social superiority which coincided with the distinctions of creed and colour. Thus, colour became a mark of a separate breed, and for the first time in the history of South Africa group colour prejudice was accepted as a social fact. The attempts of missionaries to spread Christianity within the ranks of the 'out-group' threatened this group exclusiveness and the Boer farmers met evangelical efforts to improve and regularize interracial relations with strong suspicion and hostility.

The growing influence of the administration and its machinery of control, were, together with the above considerations, a main reason for the movement eastwards and northwards known as the *Great Trek,* during the first half of the nineteenth century. This movement marked the opening up of the South African interior. Eventually, the trekkers managed to appropriate all the land north of the Vaal and Orange rivers, and a large number of Africans became employed on European-owned farms. A labour tax was introduced and the practice of employing African child labour was highly favoured. For the first time in their history these early pioneers were able to rule as they wished and deemed right— a policy of complete domination was apparent in its most extreme form. By contrast, in the Cape, a more liberal policy was in force. The 1853 Cape constitution had granted the right of franchise to all men over 21, with property or land worth £25, or earning a yearly salary of £50, irrespective of colour or creed. In Natal, a policy of separation had been established. Thus, completely divergent racial policies found expression and formulation within the same country.

The discovery of diamonds and gold in 1870 and 1886 respectively brought about radical changes in an economy which, till then, had been entirely agricultural. In the wake came an unprecedented growth of communications, the establishment of towns, and the employment of a rapidly increasing African labour force. The discovery and development of these new primary industries led to the growth of other enterprises, all requiring additional labour, and these also opened up new types of employment for the large untapped African labour source. African women came to be employed in the European economy as domestic servants, washerwomen and cooks. In turn, this expansion of industry and growth of urban centres stimulated agriculture, and Africans continued to provide the majority of farm labourers. Their work was largely seasonal, and many would move into the towns in search of work during slack agricultural periods. Never in the history of South Africa had there been such a large scale migration of non-Europeans, in particular of Bantu, from the country to the larger European centres.

This introduced a new factor into the South African problem—Europeans and non-Europeans living next door to each other. Almost up to the time of the first world war, there was, in fact, virtual separation, the vast bulk of the African population being out of sight on reserved land in the southeast, or in distant Natal. Transformation of the predominantly subsistence farming economy into a more complex industrial system with different standards of living brought large numbers of Africans into close contact with Europeans; it also produced the 'poor white'. This category of European failed to find a secure foothold in the new economy, partly owing to the quick adaptation of the African to heavy manual and unskilled work, and the contempt with which Europeans came to regard such labour. It included farmers who had reacted slowly to the expanding demand for their products and failed to benefit from the urban markets. These, and the landless Europeans congregated on the periphery of the towns, living largely on public and charitable assistance. Their numbers were increased by the depression which followed the Boer War, and the growth of European poverty became a matter of public concern. A policy of protecting Europeans from non-European competition attracted political support and a series of colour bar acts were passed.

The first of these (in 1911) prevented Africans from obtaining certificates of competency necessary to certain skilled types of work, and laid down certain categories of work as exclusively for whites. A second act consolidated existing laws of recruitment and employment established in the gold and diamond industries, and made it a criminal offence for an African to break his work contract or to strike. In 1918, the South African Industrial Federation came to a *Status Quo* Agreement, which as its name implies, aimed at preserving the existing position of white and black employment. An attempt to repudiate this agreement and to dismiss some 2,000 white miners led to the 1922 miners' strike. The strike itself was unsuccessful but its importance lies in the fact that it showed the lengths to which European labour was prepared to go to protect its position.

This factor has greatly influenced subsequent industrial legislation including the civilized labour policy, heralded by the 1924 Industrial Conciliation Act and the 1925 Wage Act. The former introduced machinery to promote industrial peace on a basis of collective bargaining but the statutory definition of 'employee' in the Act debarred the majority of African workers from benefiting. The purpose of the Wage Act was to enable minimum wages and conditions of work to be laid down for industries in which labour is organized. Somewhat illogically, however, agriculture and domestic service, the two industries in which labour is most difficult to organize and in which non-Europeans predominate, were excluded from the operation of the Act. Neither Act permits differential rates to be laid down on racial grounds, and this means that where non-Europeans are employed as artisans they are subject to the same statutory minimum rates as Europeans. Wage legislation of this type has tended to restrict the openings for the less capable workmen and particularly for non-Europeans as they are prevented from off-setting lack of skill by accepting lower wage rates.[1]

A further important aspect of the industrial situation is the extensive nature and use of African migrant labour, which is mostly of a temporary kind. The wants of Africans have multiplied as they have come into contact with an increasing range of European goods, and they have a general desire to improve their economic circumstances by moving from the rural areas to earn wages in mining and other industries. The effect of migration is to increase the supply of labour in the areas to which the migrants move and so, in the absence of wage fixation, to depress wages and incomes in different parts of the country. In other words, the existence of a plentiful supply of cheap African labour and of restrictive labour laws and customs tends to constitute a vicious circle. On the one hand is the fear of the European worker of his wage-scale being under-cut; on the other hand, the African worker is debarred from the very means which, by raising his economic standard, would make him less of a competitor on the labour market.

In the mining industry, a statutory colour bar was created by restricting Africans to unskilled or semi-skilled categories, whilst skilled and supervisory occupations were preserved for the Europeans. This tendency to restrict the participation of non-European peoples in the life of South African society has been a significant feature ever since Union. The result is a caste-like system of human relations in which Europeans invariably occupy the superior, and non-Europeans the inferior place. One of the clearest illustrations of this is revealed

---

1. cf. Sheila T. van der Horst in *Handbook on Race Relations in South Africa*, ed. Ellen Hellmann, Oxford University Press, 1949.

in salary and wage figures. Not only do the Africans provide the bulk of the unskilled workers, which means that they receive the lowest wages; but even those who attain high professional status never receive as much as their European counterpart. For example, in the teaching profession scales will vary according to the qualifications, but even where these are similar in the case of a European and a non-European teacher, the salary scales differ. Thus, a non-European teacher possessing a university degree and professional certificates is on the scale £210-£390, and a European teacher with a degree and one year's training is on the scale £300-£700. In social work, the European male starts at £260 p.a., and an African male at £96 p.a.

Also characteristic of caste is the close relationship in economic life between occupation and social group. In the South African situation, as Dr. van der Horst points out, the greatest occupational gulf is between Europeans and Africans. 'Coloureds and Asiatics, in the districts in which they live, occupy an intermediate position. Professional, supervisory, and skilled work is performed mainly by Europeans; to a lesser extent by coloureds and Asiatics, and to an almost negligible extent by Africans. This is true of all branches of economic activity, viz. agriculture, manufacturing, transport, public administration, and professional work, with the exception of teaching, nursing, and religion where non-Europeans serve their compatriots.'[1]

A further characteristic of the system is the rigid separation of European and non-European in nearly every sphere of social life. Recent legislation enacted under the present Government's policy of *apartheid* decrees that non-Europeans are to be residentially segregated from Europeans, and separate areas are also to be provided for the various non-European groups. This means that only persons belonging to the group for which the area is proclaimed can occupy land there, though employees belonging to another group can reside with their employers. In other words, Africans who work for Europeans can live near their homes and farms. In urban areas there are different forms of segregation. The most important of these is the establishment of locations, villages or townships administered by the local or municipal authority. All towns have one or more of these, and in these areas Africans may be permitted to lease lots for the erection of houses and huts.

---

1. ibid., p. 109.

Other Africans live in mine compounds, as domestic servants, and the remainder in tribal reserves and on European-owned farms.

This type of residential segregation forms the basis of other types of segregation. For example, all non-European primary and secondary schools are separated from the European school system, and there is a tendency for the different non-European groups to have separate schools. While a number of universities open their doors to non-Europeans, the Government has provided a separate university for them in Durban.

Generally, both Europeans and non-Europeans enter public buildings and shops by the same entrance and are served at the same counters. In post offices separate counters are provided: otherwise separate queues are formed, and in such cases the non-European will generally have to wait until all Europeans have been attended to. In certain new buildings special lifts are set aside for non-Europeans. Separate waiting- and cloakrooms are to be found at all railway stations, even at small sidings along subsidiary lines of communication. In Cape Town, the bus service for Cape Town and greater Cape Town is used by all racial groups without discrimination as to seating. More generally in South Africa, however, the African section of the non-European group has separate buses and street cars, manned by Europeans or Indians in most instances. Coloureds and Indians may use European means of transport, but of late public opinion has been so explicitly disapproving that they have themselves preferred to use non-European transport. Third classes on all main, subsidiary and suburban lines are reserved for non-Europeans, whites using only first and second class. Where non-Europeans use first and second class, these are separated from the European coaches. In the Cape, coloureds were allowed to share coaches with the whites, but this was changed soon after the Nationalist Party came into power. Despite protest, the coloureds now have to travel in separate coaches.

Libraries are run only for Europeans, though separate branches have been set up in some of the larger cities, e.g. in Johannesburg the Public Library has established a travelling library which visits each municipal location once a week. Hospitals are run separately, and staffed by European doctors. European doctors may practise amongst white and black, whilst non-European doctors only practise amongst their own people. In reformatories, juvenile delinquents' homes, non-European social workers are employed under the direct supervision of a European. In the prisons, which are also separate for whites and non-whites, warders are all European. Non-European policemen may only serve in non-European areas and may only handle non-European offenders.

These measures and the whole system of racial relations in South Africa derive mainly, of course, from the political supremacy of the European group. Only persons of European descent are eligible for either House of Parliament. Most of the political rights the non-Europeans at some time enjoyed on a common roll have been successively withdrawn. In 1936, Africans on the common roll at the Cape were transferred to a separate voters' roll with the passing of the Representation of Natives Act. More recently, attempts have and are being made to transfer the Cape coloured from the common roll to a separate voters' roll. Political representation is at present as follows. In the Lower House, there are three European representatives, elected by individual vote by Africans in the Cape. There is no special Cape coloured or Indian representation. In the Upper House four senators, elected by a system of electoral colleges, represent Africans of the four provinces; there are also four senators nominated for their special knowledge of non-European affairs. There are no elected coloured or Indian representatives.

What this racial situation in South Africa amounts to is, in large part, an adjustment to the circumstances created by the impact of a technically advanced civilization upon a primitive one. The industrial revolution begun at the end of the last century has continued, and its social results are analogous to the upheaval experienced by Britain during the late eighteenth and early nineteenth centuries. To serve the new industries of the Union, Africans have been recruited and have settled in numbers which far outstrip housing accommodation. The consequence is insanitary slums, shacks and shanties knocked up by the occupants out of bits of wood, corrugated iron, and old rags sprawling alongside new housing estates. The Africans are underfed and have inadequate medical services, their standards of living being extremely low. Most of them, moreover, are fresh from tribalism and have had no time to accustom themselves to the different rules and conditions of an urban life.

From the angle of the Nationalist Party, therefore, *apartheid* may be seen as a planned attempt to solve these problems by avoiding the friction of races living and working in close contact with each other. In furtherance of these aims, the present Union government spends a good deal more *per capita* on the welfare of its Bantu people than other territories on the continent. Its supporters also point out that the Union is the pioneer in Africa of a service such as pensions for Bantu blind; that its Bantu housing is efficient enough to have become a model for low-cost building in other countries in and out of Africa; that its Bantu education services, from kindergarten to university, though still inadequate, are nevertheless far in advance of those elsewhere on the continent; and that each year thousands of Africans from neighbouring territories illegally cross the Union's borders in quest of the higher wages to be earned in South Africa. It is also claimed that *apartheid* envisages the Bantu people expressing themselves politically in their own institutions; hence legislation, such as the Bantu Authorities Act.

In these respects, *apartheid* does not signalize any radical change in the older policy. What it does stress, however, is that the real factors of racial cleavage lie very deep and are psychological as well as economic. Ostensibly, the position of the 'poor white' is the main reason for colour bar legislation. Yet, behind the resistance to non-European encroachment on the living standards of the European working class lies the fear of virtually the entire white population of being politically and culturally submerged by a coloured race. This is the basic reason why equal rights are denied to the non-Europeans, and particularly the Africans, who comprise nearly 70 per cent of the total South African population. This explains the European reluctance to allow non-Europeans to develop culturally in a European direction, and to allow them comparable opportunities of education and training. The ever present fear is that as ever larger sums are spent on the uplift of the African, ever increasing numbers will demand enfranchisement and the time will therefore come when power will have passed into African hands.

It must be realized that this opposition to non-European advancement is felt almost as a moral obligation for many whites. It is not merely political or economic. Indeed, many of the most ardent exponents of *apartheid* acknowledge that their country would benefit economically and industrially through fuller use of its reserves of non-European man-power. However, the fact is that a large proportion of the white population, particularly amongst the Afrikaner element, have attitudes which are quite non-rational towards the subject of 'colour'. They have feelings about meeting and mixing with coloured individuals which are irreconcilable with any notion of racial equality. These feelings go back to the earlier Boer farmers—the pioneers of modern South Africa. In other words, it is still the latter group's sense of exclusiveness, based on the doctrine and teaching of predestination, in a racial homogeneity, which constitutes the hard core of resistance and which rules out any solution not based on racial separation.

THE BRAZILIAN AND HAWAIIAN CASES

In striking contrast to South Africa is the situation in Brazil and in Hawaii. Though obviously not comparable in many other respects, these two countries have at least two things in common—an extremely heterogeneous population and a highly tolerant attitude towards racial mixture. In both cases, this attitude was present from the start of European colonization.

BRAZIL

The first people with whom the Portuguese settlers of Brazil came into contact were the aboriginal Indians. Most of these early settlers, and, in particular, the garrison men, had no family ties, and though white women were encouraged to come to the country, they were insufficient in number to provide the necessary mothers for a new generation. Consequently, there were widespread relations with Indian women, who were absorbed into the Portuguese community as concubines, and later, as wives. The Portuguese had already had a prolonged history of contact and marriage with the Moors, and thus, long before the discovery of Brazil, were accustomed to mixed unions and their offspring. Any repugnance to intermarriage among these early colonizers was overcome by the Roman Catholic Church which firmly sanctioned it.

Intermixture was continued with the Negroes brought over as slaves to replace the Indians. The economy of the plantations was patriarchal and the Portuguese masters and the Negro slaves lived in a type of close intimate association which, to quote an American author, 'excels the most sentimental and romantic accounts of the social solidarity existing between master and slave in the Southern States'. The children of slaves were in close contact with the children of their masters, and came almost exclusively to speak Portuguese, to wear European clothes, and to take part in the religious life of the family. The master recognized a common religious bond with his slaves. They were regularly instructed in Roman Catholic ritual and, in the eyes of God, were treated as equals.

Mulatto children of the plantation owner were frequently taken into his family, and it is also a fact that even when there were sufficient white women for marriage, extra-marital relationships with coloured women were condoned. Such women and their children were housed, supported, and cared for by their white fathers. In addition, many of the later Portuguese immigrants from Europe were too poor and ill-educated to obtain a white wife, and therefore set up with coloured women. There was also prestige for her in having a 'white' child, and this encouraged miscegenation.

It is believed that this social selectivity has resulted in a tendency for whites to absorb lighter mixed-bloods, and mulattoes to absorb blacks, and the Brazilian population claims that it is undergoing a 'lightening' process. However, the discovery of ancestral Negro blood does not alter the social standing of the individual. The fact is that if a dividing line were drawn according to conventional racial distinctions, it would often mark out members of the same family from each other.

These circumstances, particularly the last, help to explain why, in Brazil, racial tolerance has become a kind of philosophy which seeks to bind together a wide variety of groups. A popular slogan is, 'We Brazilians are rapidly becoming one people. Some day, not far distant, there will be only one race in our country'. Consequently, there has always existed a great pride in amalgamation, and racism is vigorously attacked. Racial mixture is accepted as inevitable and no attempt is made to go counter to this process. There is a wide range in skin colour in the Brazilian population and the higher up the scale one goes, the lighter the complexion tends to be. In other words, colour is associated with class differentiations, but it is not a principal factor. A popular saying in Bahia (the oldest city in Brazil) is that 'a rich Negro is a white man, and a poor white man is a Negro'. This is merely another way of saying that class (one criterion of which is wealth), not race, is the primary consideration.[1]

In the early days, when Brazil was still a Portuguese colony, there seemed to exist in both town and country three social classes: the whites as slave-owners at the top; the mixed-bloods as an intermediary class; and the blacks at the bottom of the scale. As the plantation system broke down, the mixed-bloods emerged as a more important social element. Their rise was helped by a conviction which, since at least the late eighteenth century, had been crystallizing in the minds of Brazilian intellectuals—to the effect that the Negroes, whose strong arms and broad backs had long furnished the country's labour supply, were the economic builders of Brazil. Among the mixed-bloods who contributed in large measure to the cultural history of Brazil were men of letters, painters, sculptors, musicians, and scientists. The list is a long one. It should, however, be noted that though the light mulattoes set the pace in the struggle to rise and constituted the bulk of the advancing individuals of colour, they did not completely monopolize the field. They were followed, and in some cases, out-distanced by individuals from the darker sections of the population.

A picture, therefore, of the present social stratification of Brazilian society shows a concentration of whites in the upper level, diminishing sharply as one descends the occupational scale and appearing in small percentages in the lower levels. Thus, analysis of class composition, based on indices such as occupation, tax returns, automobile ownership, etc., indicates that blacks and the darker mixed-bloods generally occupy the lower economic levels; the medium and light mulattoes the middle position; and whites the upper stratum. The upper classes consist mainly of the descendants of the original Portuguese settlers, but there are some black people among them, just as there are some whites, among the recent immigrants, at the base of the social pyramid.

Absence of racial legislation does not, of course, rule out the possibility of unofficial forms of discrimination; but the fact that most dark skinned persons belong to the poorer economic classes means that it is difficult to draw a sharp distinction between class and racial prejudice. For example, in many Brazilian cities coloured people live apart, but this is because residential segregation easily establishes itself on grounds of economic differences. Like white persons of equally

---

1. cf. Donald Pierson. *Negroes in Brazil*, Chicago University Press, 1942.

limited means they usually avoid hotels, restaurants, and the smarter dance halls.

A university inquiry carried out in the state of Sao Paulo found that Negroes of the middle class had ambivalent attitudes towards white people. They felt frustrated for two reasons: firstly, because in the competition for jobs and positions employers required more from them than from white candidates; secondly, because though they were at the same social level as white middle-class persons and though many of them had friends among the whites, they felt strongly that they were not taken as equals. In such places as fashionable clubs and high-class hotels, Negroes are not welcome, and there are few whites who dare to introduce Negro friends or relatives into such places. It was also found that Negroes are excluded from quite a large number of formal associations maintained by the upper-class families of the city, although the club statutes do not contain any reference to Negro members. On the other hand, some exclusive clubs have Negroes and dark mulattoes as members, and the explanation usually given to those who are puzzled by this contradictory behaviour is that these persons are not regarded as Negroes. In other words, social class as a factor of integration seems to be somewhat stronger than the segregating influence of racial differences.[1]

The Sao Paulo evidence further suggests that possibilities of social advancement are connected with skin colour and other Negroid traits, i.e. the more Negroid the physical features, the more probable become attitudes of rejection on the part of white people. The mulatto's own concern about his appearance is expressed in the saying that 'to be good-looking' means to look like white people.

However, in so large a country as Brazil, a good deal of regional variation in racial behaviour is to be expected. Sao Paulo, for example, contains many recent immigrants from Europe and the bulk of the darker population lives elsewhere, in northern states like Bahia—but the more general position seems fairly explicit. It is that if a coloured person has ability and shows evidence of personal worth, his racial origin will, at least to some degree, be disregarded. Whether black or mulatto, he can win prestige and esteem, both locally and nationally, for his qualities. Colour prejudice is probably felt

1. cf. Emilio Willems. 'Race Attitudes in Brazil', *American Journal of Sociology*, Vol. 54, 1948-49, pp. 402-8.

among many Brazilians and in certain social circles, but it is generally not overt, and public opinion is opposed to any form of open discrimination on racial grounds.

In the Hawaiian Islands, a still more remarkable amalgamation of many different races and cultures is taking place, though on a much smaller scale. In addition to the native Hawaiians, there are the Chinese, the Japanese, and the Koreans, whose outlook is influenced by Buddhism, and Confucianism. There are the people of North American and North European origin whose moral standards have been conditioned by Protestant Christianity, and those from Southern Europe whose background is Roman Catholic. There are the Filipinos who have also been brought up as Catholics. Racial mixture takes place mainly through intermarriage. There is no law against such intermarriage and no public disapproval of it. The islands are now an integral part of the United States and under the federal laws Latin immigrants sometimes cannot qualify for naturalization because of illiteracy. But the Hawaiian-born children of all immigrants are citizens by birth. School education, which is compulsory up to the age of 15, is open to all, and there are no formal limitations to political and economic opportunity on the grounds of race.

The reason for this racial freedom in Hawaii lies largely in the very heterogeneity of the population which is racially so distributed that no politician, business man, or newspaper proprietor could afford to affront any of the more important groups of his followers or customers with race prejudice. Moreover, so numerous are the Hawaiians of mixed blood, so influential, so closely related to influential white or Chinese families that one cannot in any large group speak against mixed marriage lest he offend people of prominence who have relatives of mixed ancestry. However, these remarks describe, rather than account for, Hawaii's unorthodox character as regards race relations.

There was little foreign settlement in Hawaii until the middle of the nineteenth century and the population has grown to its present proportions mainly through immigration. The earliest foreign contact was chiefly a trading one. The islands were not discovered until 1778, and in the beginning the masters of ships engaged in the fur trade would round Cape Horn on the way to the north-west Pacific, and call at Hawaii for water, fruit, and fresh meat. It was a haven for scurvy-ridden mariners. After 1820 Honolulu and other island ports were visited by the vessels engaged in whaling in the North Pacific. They, too, needed foodstuffs and Honolulu became a centre for the refitting of ships.

A number of castaways and deserters from this traffic found their way ashore and there were always a few foreign men after 1790 but no resident foreign women until 1820. This resulted in there being nearly three times as many white men with native wives as with wives of their own race at as late a date as 1849. There were also more than twice as many persons enumerated as 'half caste' as there were Hawaiian-born children of foreign parentage. It is probable that only the children acknowledged by their fathers were counted as 'half caste'. Such mixed-bloods as may have survived from transient and irregular unions between sailors and Hawaiian women were apparently counted as Hawaiians.

There was no opposition to mixed marriage during this early period of contact. In fact, conditions on both sides favoured it. Some of the few white men who came to Hawaii in the eighteenth or early nineteenth century rendered important services to the native monarchy as advisers in military and civil affairs. In order to bind these men to Hawaii and to his service, the King gave them Hawaiian women of high rank. The absence of white women thus meant that the resident whites had the choice of a Hawaiian mate or remaining single. A good many found the native women attractive, married them and had families. Some secured status and landed property by such marriage. These interracial relationships were also facilitated by the Hawaiian family system which permitted a married woman to consort with more than one man. Their equalitarian nature was maintained by the continued independence of Hawaii and the continuation of a system in which the native King was a personage of authority and dignity. Hawaii was not annexed by the United States until 1898, and throughout most of the nineteenth century foreign enterprise depended very largely on the King's good will. The fact that planters, traders, and missionaries alike found it necessary to treat him with respect prevented any sharp drawing of racial lines.

However, Hawaii did not become a 'racial melting-pot' until well on in the nineteenth century. In the 'fifties there was a considerable development of sugar production under foreign control. The Hawaiians had sufficient land for their own needs. They were not attracted by the kind of monotonous labour required on the plantation and so it was decided to import Chinese under indenture. The experiment was continued and from the 'seventies onwards there was a heavy influx of immigrants of many nationalities to serve directly or indirectly the expanding economy. This was based on only one form of employment—agriculture—and for most of the period of Hawaii's modern development, on only one important crop—sugar cane. Some 46,000 Chinese, chiefly men, came to the islands, mainly before 1898, but nearly half of these later returned to China. Japan and the Philippines sent the largest contingents, but more than half the Japanese and Filipinos who came to Hawaii have emigrated. Other immigrant groups include Portuguese, Spaniards, Galicians, Germans, Poles, Russians, and Puerto Ricans.[1] According to the 1940 census, the population of Hawaii includes some 14,000 Hawaiians, 50,000 part-Hawaiians, 112,000 Caucasians ('whites'), 20,000 Chinese, 158,000 Japanese, 53,000 Filipinos, and 6,900 Koreans.

The various immigrants came widely in touch with the native Hawaiians. Many of them worked only a few years on the plantations before seeking other sorts of economic opportunity in the islands, and contacts were established nearly everywhere. Many of the newcomers were without wives and some of them married native women. As the immigration population increased the rate of out-marriage for Hawaiian women became higher. Conversely as the number of immigrants became larger and as there came to be more women among them, their rate of out-marriage with Hawaiians decreased, even though the absolute number so marrying increased. What is interesting in this matter is that out-marriage between various immigrant groups and Hawaiians and part-Hawaiians has been determined, not so much by racial preference or prejudice, as by numbers, length of residence, and sex ratios. It is also interesting that white people of American and North European ancestry have played the most important role in amalgamation—by reason, not only of their numbers, recently augmented by servicemen but also their long period of contact—and next come the Chinese, who have

1. cf. Romanzo Adams. *Interracial Marriage in Hawaii*, Macmillan, New York, 1937.

been numerous for a long time. The Portuguese sex ratio was more normal and hence there has been less intermarriage with Hawaiians. The Japanese were able to obtain wives from their homeland without much difficulty, and only a few have married outside their group. Intermixture has gone on fairly freely between Filipinos and Hawaiians.[1]

Out of this amalgamation have come a great many types, chiefly Caucasian (white)-Hawaiians and Chinese-Hawaiians, or a three-way mixture. Today, the part-Hawaiians greatly outnumber the 'pure' Hawaiians, and the trend of marriage suggests that individuals of mixed blood will constitute a majority of the population by the end of the century. By 1920-24 the ratio of out-marriages had increased to 22.6 per cent and by the early 'forties (1940-41) somewhat less than a third of all marriages were interracial in the Hawaiian sense.

However, it is significant that since the overthrow of the Hawaiian kingdom the ratio of marriages between Hawaiians and *haole* has declined. *Haole* is the term applied in Hawaii to white persons of superior social and economic status. The strong social connexions of the *haole* with the United States have established their cultural and political domination of Hawaiian life. Nowadays, in Honolulu, members of this class maintain a degree of segregation, particularly as regards more intimate contact with the other racial groups. There are residential areas in which houses and building lots are not sold to others. There are schools in which most of the pupils are *haole,* and there are churches mostly attended by *haole.* The rural *haole* and the whites who are newcomers to Hawaii are less aloof, and they marry out of their group much more freely.

Closer contact with the United States and the making of Honolulu into a great naval and military base has affected the cultural development of the Hawaiian. It is making him more and more of an American. It is also tending to diffuse the traditional American attitude towards race relations into the islands. Thus, in spite of the doctrine and practice of racial equality, the race and nationality groups are not equal in terms of cultural status, social prestige, and economic power and political influence. Racial etiquette does not permit public forms of racial discrimination. Nevertheless, in some fields the Oriental learns that he may advance so

1. ibid., pp. 22-3 *et seq.*

far and no further. For example, the positions of greatest responsibility in the plantations and in certain non-political enterprises controlled by *haole* are open only to whites. In fact, the attitude of the *haole* is somewhat ambivalent. On the one hand, there is a sentimental attraction towards the Hawaiian and a paternalistic impulse which would push him into a prominent position just because he is a Hawaiian, and not because of merit. On the other hand, there is a desire to maintain social distance from him and a subtle prejudice and discrimination against Hawaiians when, for example, they seek employment in business.

This dual pattern of racial relations has psychological repercussions on the other racial and cultural groups, particularly the part-Hawaiians. The social position of the mixed-bloods is as complex as their biological heritage. Some of them are leading university graduates, and those who are descendants of important white and Hawaiian ancestors have a relatively high status. But their position among Hawaii's social elite is at best equivocal, and they feel the private condemnation of mixed marriage. The Chinese-Hawaiian tends to compensate for the insecurity of this cultural position by blaming his Hawaiian blood and heritage. Those mixed-bloods who are closer to Hawaiian parentage and are rejected by the white side identify themselves with other part-Hawaiians.

Thus, there is a tendency to create social groups made up of similarly constituted members of the different groups. This is strongest among the Chinese. Most of the original Chinese immigrants were people of humble position in their old homes. Now the sons and daughters, born in Hawaii, have had a good education, and as they have come to know more about China and its civilization they have developed a new sense of their own dignity as its representatives. Organizations have been started for the perpetuation of Chinese culture in Hawaii, and one of the consequences of the increasing respect of the Chinese of things Chinese is a raising of status in the community. It has also produced a certain degree of group exclusiveness in relation to marriage. Among those Chinese who have achieved high social standing there is severe parental disapproval when a son or a daughter is married to a non-Chinese.

Nevertheless, the more general trend in Hawaii is in the direction of a common cultural and national sentiment rather than towards the drawing of strict social lines on the basis of culture and race. Closer and closer ties with the mainland and an educational system modelled on American lines are rapidly adapting the Hawaiian community to American ideals of thought and conduct. So far as racial relations are concerned, perhaps the most significant comment on the contemporary situation is the one made by the small Negro minority, now resident in the islands. Although there is far from a 'complete absence of Negrophobia in Hawaii', Negroes find there 'the closest approach to real democracy available under the Stars and Stripes'.[1]

THE BRITISH CASE

From Hawaii we may now turn to a lesser known and quite different racial problem—that of Britain. A number of factual considerations distinguish race relations in the United Kingdom from the countries considered above, South Africa and Brazil in particular. In the first place, the coloured group forms a very small proportion of the total British population, and is largely the result of recent immigration into the British Isles. Secondly, the expression 'coloured' is used very loosely in Britain; its popular application is wide enough to include almost any person not of European origin. It tends, therefore, to denote not only African and New World Negroes, but Arabs, Indians, Chinese and North Africans. This means that when English people speak of the 'colour problem', they may have in mind practically any type of racial or ethnic contact which involves persons or groups of persons darker, or believed to be darker, in skin colour than themselves.

There is no official or reliable estimate of this 'coloured' population of the British Isles, it may be put tentatively at 60,000-80,000. The majority are males from the British colonies, principally the West Indies and West Africa. There are also relatively large numbers of Indians and Pakistanis, and Somalis and Arabs, the latter groups coming mainly from Aden. Most of these people live in the seaport cities of Liverpool, Cardiff, Newcastle, Manchester, and Hull, and also in London and Birmingham. They have well-established homes and households of their own in many cases, but for the most

---

1. cf. F. M. Davis. 'A Passage to Hawaii', *The Crisis*, 56, pp. 296-301, November 1949.

part their wives and consorts are white women drawn from the poorest and least educated sections of British society. Their living is gained mainly by seafaring. They serve as boilermen, firemen, stokers, and greasers on ocean-going steamers and tramps. An increasing number work in factories and various branches of industry.

Apart from this working class element, but included in the general total, are more than 5,000 students attending British universities or training in hospitals and technical institutes. Most of them are also from the West Indies and West Africa, but unlike the working class group, which is for the most part permanently domiciled, the majority of the students return home when their period of three or four years in college is over. A further number of coloured residents earn a living as doctors, or in other types of professional employment; others are occupied in clerical work, in trading, and in the theatrical and entertainment industry.

London had a relatively large population of Negroes during the eighteenth century, and during the nineteenth century other non-Europeans came in small numbers to settle in Britain. But the present coloured community originated largely in the circumstances of World War I. During 1914-18, many of the ships on the West African and other routes on which Negroes and other coloured seamen are usually employed, were requisitioned by the Government for transport service, and their crews left behind. Coloured labour battalions were formed for service abroad, and the men were subsequently demobilized in Britain. Coloured men were also recruited for work in chemical and munitions factories and were brought over to Manchester and other cities. All this meant the domiciling of considerable numbers of Negroes, and, when the war industries and other forms of employment were closed down, very many of them flocked to seaports such as Cardiff and Liverpool, where there was opportunity of work, in connexion with seafaring and the shipping industry. The recent war led to further immigration. Men from the British colonies were again recruited for industry and the armed services. Several parties of West Indians were brought over as skilled and semi-skilled workers, and other West Indians, serving in the Royal Air Force, were stationed in Britain. Although most of these latter were subsequently repatriated, many of them have since paid their own fares back to look for work they could not find at home. During and since the war, there has also been an extra influx of students from the colonies and, in addition, quite large numbers of West Indians and West Africans have found their way into the United Kingdom by less orthodox means. In many cases they have boarded ship at a colonial port and stowed themselves away for the voyage; others have signed on as members of the crew for the trip to a British port and 'jumped the ship' on arrival. Since World War II, there has been a fairly substantial influx of further immigrants from the West Indian islands.

The fact that nearly all these coloured people in the United Kingdom possess British nationality through having been born in a British colony or protectorate, or in Britain itself, means that they are entitled to the same rights and privileges as any other British subject irrespective of race or colour. There is a complete absence of any kind of legislation affecting race relationships in Britain. There are absolutely no regulations of any statutory or official kind, such as exist in South Africa, decreeing where a person of colour shall live or the kind of employment he may or may not take up. This does not mean that unofficial forms of racial and colour discrimination are lacking, or that relations between white and coloured people are entirely amicable. When it comes to employment, for example, there are frequent difficulties in persuading an employer to engage a coloured man and white employees to work alongside him. As mentioned above, a large part of the coloured population lives in seaports and depends upon the shipping industry for a living; this has meant difficult times for many of them because in the periods of economic depression between the two wars, coloured workers have suffered more severely from unemployment than other sections of the community. For example, on 11 June 1936, out of a total of 690 unemployed firemen on the Cardiff Docks Register, 599 were coloured men. A more recent estimate in respect of Liverpool suggests that one in every six coloured colonials is unemployed, compared with one in every 20 in the total insured population.

In particular, there has been widespread prejudice against the employment of coloured juveniles both in Liverpool and in Cardiff. In 1929 one juvenile employment committee noted:

'Little difficulty is experienced (in regard to the coloured children) during school-days, as they mix quite freely with the white children, and usually belong to homes which are at least equal in condition and parental supervision and care to those of white children. It is when they leave school and desire to enter industry that the difficulties arise. . . . The industrial problem is much more acute in relation to girls, for though the boys are not so easily placed as white boys, there is not the same prejudice shown to the coloured by male workers as by female workers. A fair proportion of the boys eventually go to sea after an interval of some months after leaving school. In regard to the girls, the committee are faced with a serious difficulty, as they are not usually acceptable in factories and there is only the poorest type of domestic service open to them.

'An industrial survey is being conducted at the present time, and employers are being approached with a view to the absorption of some of these girls into their works and factories, but the response is far from reassuring. The difficulty is not with the employers, but with the white girls employed, who strongly object to the suggestion of the introduction of half-castes. It is a very sad commentary on the Christian spirit shown, and indicates that the Colour Bar is still very strong in this country.'[1]

Difficulties in placing West Indian technicians have been reported more recently from Liverpool; and coloured seamen have complained since the war that shipping companies have shown an increasing reluctance to sign them on, especially in ships where they may have to work alongside a white crew. More generally, the situation is variable and often difficult to disentangle. Certain firms, for example, have employed coloured workers for many years and speak highly of their services. Some employers refuse to engage a coloured man on the grounds that their staff will go on strike; others complain that the coloured worker does not 'stick' at the job, or is unwilling to do unskilled labour because, he says, it is beneath his dignity. The coloured worker's own explanation is that he is the victim of deliberate discrimination and is relegated to menial work, such as cleaning floors.

The resident coloured communities usually live on quite friendly terms with their white neighbours in the immediate locality except during times of general unemployment and economic uncertainty. On such occasions, there have been instances of racial antagonism which have sometimes led to violence. For example, in 1919, after World War I there

---

1. I am indebted to Messrs. Routledge and Kegan Paul, Ltd., for permission to include this quotation and other quotations referring to the British situation, from my book, *Negroes in Britain*.

were racial riots in a number of cities. In Liverpool, many Negro families did not venture out of doors for some ten days, and there is at least one Negro there today who recalls having been given a police escort to his work every day, for fear of lynching. The rioters are said to have numbered several thousands and the police were obliged to make a number of baton charges on the crowd. In Cardiff, shops and houses in which Negroes lodged were attacked and one shop was completely demolished. Exchanges of revolver fire and fighting with razor blades resulted in 10 people being admitted to hospital, where one of them died. Eventually, soldiers were called in to assist the police, but not before a number of unlucky Negroes had been chased by the mob, to find sanctuary just in time, either in a house, or behind the horses of mounted police. Further serious disturbances, including fights between white people and coloured people, occurred in Liverpool, in 1948, and the police made 60 arrests.

Public protests about the presence of the coloured men and their families have also been made periodically in Cardiff, in Liverpool, and in parts of London. There have been complaints in the press, in speeches from public platforms, and even in the House of Commons about their 'moral undesirability', and about the 'dangers' of racial mixture. A good deal of this opprobrium was the result of disputes in the shipping industry, it being felt by the white seamen that the ship owners were deliberately substituting coloured for white crews in order to save on the wages bill. The following is a fairly typical outburst. Speaking in a Parliamentary debate in 1934, Mr. Logan, M.P., said:

'Is it a nice sight as I walk through the south end of the city of Liverpool, to find a black settlement, a black body of men—I am not saying a word about their colour—all doing well, and a white body of men who faced the horrors of war, walking the streets unemployed? Is it a nice sight to see Lascars (East Indians) trotting up the Scotland Road, and round Cardiff, and to see Chinamen walking along in the affluence that men of the sea are able to get by constant employment, while Britishers are walking the streets and going to the public assistance committees?'

This kind of feeling has also given rise to attempts to secure 'repatriation' of the coloured population on the grounds of their being a charge on the public purse. The idea was to transport them, adults and juveniles alike, to the West Coast of Africa. In reply to one of these proposals made at a public meeting in Liverpool, a coloured man arose and asked the speaker in a broad local accent where the latter thought he ought to go!

Legislation for the benefit of the shipping industry has also affected the colour problem. For example, both in Liverpool and in Cardiff the operation of the Special Restrictions (Coloured Alien Seamen) Order, 1925, obliged many coloured seamen who were really British colonial subjects to register as aliens unless they could produce clear documentary evidence of their nationality—and even then pressure was often brought to bear upon the man to comply with the regulations and to register with the police as if he were an alien. In Cardiff, for instance it is estimated that the effect was to force some 1,500 men to carry alien cards. The original object of the order was to prevent British crews being replaced by coloured alien crews, but the actual operation of the order caused considerable hardship to British subjects who were coloured. It meant their exclusion from employment by firms for whom most of them had worked regularly. An additional hardship, in Liverpool, was that Englishwomen married to coloured seamen were also to all intents and purposes, treated as aliens and were even deprived of the opportunity to vote. It is difficult to say how much of this situation was deliberately engineered by the local branches of the seamen's unions, and how much of it was inadvertent.

Coloured people in Britain also meet difficulty over housing and accommodation. There are instances of special clauses in the leases of houses and flats excluding a coloured person, and quite often a coloured family will have to pay a higher rent than a similar white family. Houseowners are reluctant to let because they fear that the presence of coloured tenants will cause a lowering of assessments in the districts concerned, and hence a depreciation in the value of their property. Residents in the area are afraid that their peace will be disturbed and the neighbourhood acquire a bad name. Antipathy is even stronger when it comes to sharing the same house, or lodgings. The effect is to cause a fairly definite concentration of coloured families in less desirable parts of the town because of the difficulty of finding rooms elsewhere.

This means that the cities concerned—notably, Cardiff, Liverpool, and Manchester—all have specific localities, known as the 'coloured quarter', which produce to some extent the social and other features of the so-called 'black belts' of American cities like Chicago and New York. The comparison, it must be admitted, is not a complete one; partly because the coloured aggregation in the British case is numerically very much smaller, and partly because it is limited almost entirely to persons of the same low economic class. At the same time, the white inhabitants of these British cities have much the same kind of feeling as the white inhabitants of American cities, of their own racial and social separateness from the coloured areas. This attitude, in turn, creates special psychological barriers to normal methods of social intercourse and communication between the two groups. It means, for example, that any matter attracting police attention in the coloured quarter is given special notice in the press and that the unfavourable comment aroused tends to be extended beyond the individual concerned to all the inhabitants. It means that the kind of stereotype gained of the coloured man is based on the relatively poor educational and economic traits of the local coloured community.

The fact that many people are reluctant to live at close quarters with a coloured person creates a special problem for colonial students seeking lodgings. The attitude of landladies and boarding house keepers is governed very largely by the prejudices of their customers, and if the latter object to a coloured lodger, business interests may dictate a policy of exclusion. In some cases a student is promised accommodation, by correspondence or over the telephone, before his racial identity is known, only to be turned away when he presents himself in person. It is difficult to gauge the exact extent of discrimination of this kind, but it is certainly widespread, particularly in London. Thus, from inquiries made before the war it was estimated that up to some 60 per cent of lodging, guest and boarding house keepers and of private individuals normally in the habit of taking paying guests, refuse a coloured lodger, even of 'good class'. Difficulties of this sort have led the Colonial Office to institute a number of special hostels for colonial students. In recent years, additional hostels have been provided and are now managed by the British Council. The idea is to provide comfortable surroundings and social centres where the coloured residents can meet other people and where general amenities are available. These hostels are also open to white students from the colonies, but the actual result is segregation, and the British Council has therefore tried the policy of dispersing students in approved lodgings.

What all this amounts to is that a fairly strong body of colour prejudice exists in Britain, despite its lack of sanction or support by the law. Indeed, the attitude of the courts, as a rule, is definitely to deprecate it. For example, in a case in Liverpool, Mr. Hemmerde, the Recorder, commented critically on the Government's failure to protect its colonial subjects from discourtesy, and in another case, involving an Indian, a juryman who raised 'the question of colour' was ordered to leave the box, and another juror sworn in.

The fact that there is no specific legislation against racial or colour discrimination makes it very difficult to contest alleged instances of it. All that a person who has been promised accommodation can do is to sue the hotel management for breach of contract. By refusing to accommodate coloured persons when room is available the innkeeper commits a legal offence. Cases have been taken to the courts and, in each instance, the verdict, when favourable to the coloured plaintiff, has been on a purely technical point. It has hinged in no way on race or colour.

The question of legislation has been raised in the House of Commons, in respect both to the position of lodging houses and hotels, and the licensing of dance halls. In each case, however, the reply has been that such matters are not under the control of the legislature, and in the case of dance halls, are under local control. If it can be shown that a hall which is licensed for a given purpose is, in fact, discriminating against a section of the community, it is a matter for local appeal against the holder of such a licence. Fairly recently, an attempt on the part of Mr. Reginald Sorenson, M.P., to introduce a Private Member's Bill failed owing to there being insufficient time for it to be debated.

While there are many people who favour legislative action in Britain, there is also a strong feeling that coloured people— or Jews—are as much citizens as anybody else with equal rights and equal obligations. Many feel that the introduction of protective legislation would tend to delimitate too clearly the groups concerned, a position which would run counter to the policy favoured on behalf of Jews, i.e. that of assimilation.[1]

The fact that racial discrimination exists in Britain without any backing from the law or the constitution means that colour prejudice has developed as part of the heritage of British society. It is relevant to recall that it was the British

---

[1]. I am indebted to Mr. L. G. Green of the Faculty of Laws, University College, London, for guidance on the above matters.

who played a major part in the slave trade and that a large proportion of African slaves were transported in British ships. During the course of the trade 'left-overs' from these human cargoes were frequently landed at English ports and publicly auctioned. Other Negroes were brought into the country by returning West Indian planters whom they served as slaves and body-servants. It is estimated that at one time there were some 20,000 of these Negroes in London alone. In this way, no doubt, English people became accustomed to seeing and hearing of black men in servile and menial positions, and the ground was laid for the ideas and arguments which, as mentioned above, were used in England and other Western countries to combat Abolition. How far these circumstances were psychologically conclusive cannot be measured today, 200 years after the event, but it is evident that the myth of Negro inferiority was firmly entrenched among most classes of Englishmen by the nineteenth century. This is the impression conveyed by the novels of the day. In Thackeray's *Vanity Fair,* George, the son of an ambitious middle-class family, is invited to propose marriage to a coloured heiress from the West Indies. George's response is: 'Marry that mulatto woman? I don't like the colour, sir. Ask the black that sweeps opposite Fleet Street, sir. I'm not going to marry a Hottentot Venus. . . .' And in Jerrold's *St. Giles and St. James,* Miss Canary, the genteel vendor of fruit and snacks at the Covent Garden Theatre, shrinks away in horror and disgust from Gumbo, the Negro coachman.

By the middle of the nineteenth century, Britain's possessions overseas were very extensive, and included India and large parts of Africa. This seems to have convinced many English people of their superiority to the coloured man and to have produced an attitude of mind which, in terms of arrogant and harsh treatment of native individuals of rank, was responsible—to take one example—for the situation leading up to the Indian Mutiny. 'The most scrubby mean little representative of *la race blanche* . . .' (wrote the correspondent of *The Times*) 'regards himself as infinitely superior to the Rajpoot with a genealogy of 1,000 years.'

Probably this habit of looking down on coloured races was also strengthened by a widely awakened interest in evolution and man's relationship to other members of the animal kingdom. As early as 1796, a paper read to the Manchester Philosophical Society was entitled 'An Account of the Regular Gradations in Man, and in Different Animals and Vegetables, and from the Former to the Latter'. Its thesis was that the Negro 'seems to approach nearer to the brute creation than any other of the human species'. Later, nineteenth-century biology was interpreted popularly in a similar way and the Darwinian theory was also misused. It seems to have largely taken the place of previous arguments justifying the dominance of the white races. Since the latter had survived and had been more successful than the other races, they must be superior to them, not only in organization and efficiency, but in every other field, including the mental and moral.

Theories of biological evolution were accompanied by theories of social evolution. Thus, Lewis Morgan, who paid special attention to kinship, marriage, and property, divided all history into three main stages—savagery, barbarism, and civilization—and correlated each with intellectual and economic achievements. As civilization was correlated with literacy, it meant that all non-literate peoples, including all Negro peoples in Africa, were lower and more primitive than Europeans.

The later nineteenth century was notable, too, not only for the parcelling out of black Africa amongst the European powers, but for the readiness with which the imperialist tendencies of those powers were rationalized. Extensive use, in which the British joined, was made of racial myths like Aryanism, Nordicism and Teutonism, which affirmed the superior race to be white and attributed biological inferiority to the coloured races. Since the new colonial territories brought under control were inhabited almost entirely by coloured peoples with cultures wholly different and technically more primitive than Western society, these ideas are not surprising. Evolutionary theories had already prepared the ground. Moreover, the immense achievements of Western civilization—unprecedented development of machines, technology, efficient organization, scientific inventions, etc.—provided a convincing contrast with the meagre material equipment of Africans and Melanesians. And many of the returning travellers, traders, and missionaries had horrific tales to tell of native customs which, taken outside their proper context, were barbarous and repellent to English ears.

This complicated background of overseas exploration, slave trading, colonial expansion, and scientific rationalization helps us to understand the ambivalent nature of modern racial attitudes in Britain. They are a mixture of apathy and toleration because a large number of British people have never had

personal contact with a coloured person and have little interest
in or concern with the colonies. They also include a good deal
of friendly curiosity and paternalism, which are as much a
part of the social heritage as feelings of repulsion and condescension. Long before the Abolitionist movement, individual
writers and philanthropists were pleading the cause of the
Negro slave and striving for his freedom. Abolition itself largely
originated in England among the Nonconformist sects and
started a tradition of philanthropy and liberalism which is
still a great force in British dealings with colonial peoples.
But this British toleration of racial differences tends on the
whole to be idealistic rather than real. The reason is that it
arose out of the abstract idea of freedom for the Negro, and
in the absence of actual necessity to treat him as an equal in
the ordinary give and take of social life. Consequently, though
many English people are favourably disposed and sympathetic
towards the coloured man, their desire that he should be given
a 'square deal' is largely an abstract one, partly because the
other psychological elements in the matter, though less conscious, are actually as strong.

In contrast with the idealistic trend, there is the fairly general feeling that coloured people are in some way 'inferior',
not merely because they are 'alien' or 'foreign' but because
of their pigmentation and other physical characteristics. Along
with this go the culturally derived associations of colour and
physiognomy with horror and repulsion. The result is that
for some people it is as if the 'blackness' of the Negro diffuses
itself over persons or objects around. Some of them speak of
being 'contaminated' by his physical proximity and women,
in particular, express special aversion to the idea of his hand
coming into contact with their white skin.

What this amounts to is that skin colour has a definite
significance for many English people, a darker complexion
making a person socially less acceptable. It means that there
is a tendency for Africans and darker West Indians to be
eschewed not merely because they are racially different from
the English men and women who might consort with them,
but because of the likelihood of social stigma from such association. In other words, colour prejudice is to some extent
linked with class prejudice, and this means the frequent exclusion of even well-educated persons of colour from British
middle-class homes. Though many of the individuals concerned may lack personal prejudice, they feel that their social
reputation will be jeopardized if they are known to have

coloured friends or acquaintances. To introduce a Negro into their social circle would cause embarrassment because it would lower prestige in much the same kind of way as bringing the milkman or grocer's boy into the house. As an example of this, a bank manager, with whom I discussed the application of two African students to occupy the house next door to him (his own property), strongly objected to the idea. He added, partly in parenthesis, partly in apology, 'Oh, I know these days we are all supposed to be equal'. The belief that having coloured guests will get one's house a 'bad name' is also often mentioned. 'Colour' has the same socially inferior connotation as English spoken ungrammatically, or without the 'correct' accent, or of wearing a muffler instead of a collar and tie.

Nor is this feeling of racial and social superiority confined to self-conscious members of the middle classes. Much, no doubt, depends on the political or ideological attitude of the person concerned, but working class people can be equally colour-conscious, when it comes to being seen calling on or talking to a coloured person. The point is particularly evident whenever any kind of contact or mixture between the sexes is involved. A good many people will declare that they have absolutely nothing against a coloured person 'so long as he leaves the girls alone', and one of the most frequent objections made to inviting an African or West Indian home is through fear of its leading to some kind of liaison with a female member of the household. The emotional effect of seeing a white girl in the company of a coloured man is often very great, and sometimes insulting remarks are addressed to the couple. Consequently, when intermarriage takes place, it is often in the teeth of opposition from the girl's parents and she may be estranged from most of her friends. In the relative absence of women of their own race, the result is that many coloured men are virtually debarred from female companionship, or their opportunities of it are limited to prostitutes. Thus, a 'vicious circle' is set up. It means that a girl of 'good' class may have to consider whether she is prepared to risk her reputation before she decides to associate with a coloured man.

The ordinary coloured individual reacts to the racial situation in Britain with a good deal of bitterness—not always expressed on the surface. Those born in the country naturally feel that they are entitled to the same rights and privileges as any other citizen, and they particularly resent being regarded or treated as 'foreigners'. Those arriving from the colonies feel that British professions of racial equality are insincere so long as discrimination can be practised without interference from the Government. What they find specially galling is the British pretence of the same treatment for all races.

Quite a large number of colonials coming to Britain have been brought up under strong missionary and Christian influence. It is the conflict between the ideals of brotherhood and a common humanity they have been taught and the experience of being cold-shouldered on account of their colour which affects them most deeply. Hardly less disturbing to both West Indians and Africans than any overt display of colour prejudice, is the fairly constant battery of curious questions to which they are subjected. These have mainly to do with the supposed abundance of wild animals, the climatic conditions, and the 'uncivilized' behaviour of the 'natives'. West Indians particularly resent being asked if they speak English, which is their native language. African students sometimes remark that they are asked if they wore clothes before they came to England, and complain that they are regarded as savages, even by persons who beg alms of them in the streets.

Whether or not such attitudes imply actually colour prejudice, the important point is that many coloured persons live in constant expectation of it. The result is that the ordinary coloured man is very wary in his relationship with British people. Sometimes, he is so afraid of humiliation that he will deliberately keep out of their way and hold himself aloof rather than run the risk of it.

Paradoxically, the very fact that racial relations are not officially regulated in Britain exacerbates these feelings. Unlike South Africa or the United States, the public authorities in Britain have no responsibility for the colour bar, and so any disabilities which the coloured person suffers are felt, not as something impersonal and unpremeditated, but rather as a deliberate and personal piece of discrimination. Again, the fact that colour prejudice is not limited to, or necessarily associated with, any particular kind of social institution, but may crop up in virtually any field of social intercourse, only increases his uncertainty and doubt about personal relations. How is he to know, for example, when a disregarded greeting or proffered clasp of the hand is unintentional, and when it is a sign of racial rejection? The easier way is to give up speculation and simply assume that all one's English acquaintances are insincere at heart, whatever their professed attitude.

For example, a West Indian technician, who was asked his opinion of the foreman in charge of his work, replied that the latter's behaviour was always 'correct' but he knew, nevertheless, that 'inside' the foreman looked down on him as an inferior.

Additional reasons for racial friction and misunderstanding arise out of the coloured person's own background. Quite a large number of colonials arrive in Britain without much knowledge of the subtleties of European social custom and etiquette. They do not realize how much importance is attached to punctuality in personal as well as business relationships; they are unaware of the conventions of home visiting; the Western attitude to relations between the sexes is strange to them. Many of the newly arrived immigrants not only lack the ability to read and write, but do not possess sufficient English or the kind of industrial skill necessary to earn a satisfactory living. The fact that they are refused a job or are debarred from higher paid work because they lack the experience or training for it, not because they are coloured, is not always apparent to them. Their experience of Europeans in the colonies, all engaged in relatively highly paid, 'white collar' occupations, has led them to expect that in the European's own country the same conditions will apply to everyone.

Again, some colonials mistake for racial ostracism and aversion the 'normal' impersonality of life in a large European city. Coming straight from African or West Indian communities, characterized by warm kinship and neighbourly ties, they find the relative anonymity of the English environment almost intolerable, and suffer from an acute sense of isolation. Other colonials, particularly those studying, have problems of finance, are doubtful about their prospects of employment on returning home, or fail to pass a crucial examination. In such cases, there is usually some feeling of personal insecurity and frustration for which the existence of 'colour bar' provides a convenient form of compensation. It serves as a means of explaining, and even excusing, personal difficulties and failures.

Thus, there is a variety of reasons why the race question should be a subject of considerable and intrinsic interest for coloured people in Britain. With so much diversity in cultural background and experience, and in personal aspirations, it is the one thing binding them together as a group and creating a common sentiment.

Yet the development of an active sense of racial consciousness is less frequent than might be imagined. Its lack can be explained by the fact that the majority of permanently resident coloured people are poorly educated, and the small size and scattered nature of the population offers little opportunity for racial leadership on a national scale. Students from the colonies constitute the only articulate section with any influence, and they, as temporary migrants, have only a transient interest in the matter. They are concerned far more with what is going on in their own countries than with Britain. Only on rare occasions of crisis in race relations, such as the Seretse Khama affair, is a 'common front' created.

Consequently, there are but few organizations of Negro, or coloured 'protest', and there are none at all comparable in terms of function or effectiveness with, say, the National Association for the Advancement of Coloured People in the United States. Indeed, politically the significance of the racial situation in Britain lies mainly in its relation to the British colonies. The colonial young men and women, who study in Britain, belong to the class leading public opinion in their own countries, and there is no doubt that student experiences and reactions to life in Britain are instrumental in the rapid growth of colonial nationalism. A good deal of the dissatisfaction felt with conditions in Britain is 'drained off' to swell the demand for speedy self-government in the colonial countries themselves.

The race problem in Britain, in itself comparatively unimportant, is indeed mainly a function of the relationship between the United Kingdom, as mother country, and the other members of the Commonwealth and empire. A number of 'coloured' countries—India, Pakistan, and Ceylon—have remained within the Commonwealth after becoming self-governing, and it is the expressed desire of the British Government that the present colonial dependencies shall follow suit when they, too, gain the right to self-determination. Logically, this policy has two implications. In the first place, it means that the British Government has to retain and, if possible, increase the feelings of loyalty and goodwill among its colonial subjects. This will obviously necessitate something more than political progress and constitutional reform abroad. It will also require positive measures at home among the British public to arouse sympathy and interest in the colonial peoples and countries. This, in turn, should lead to greater exertion, educationally, to correct confused thinking about racial and similar matters. Secondly, the achievement of self-government by one or more of the African or West Indian colonies should have the result of elevating not only the political status of the countries concerned, but the personal status of their nationals. And this, in turn, should lead to an improvement in the status of all persons of Negro origin, since, from the point of view of the man in the street, all Negroes are the same, whether they come from Jamaica, Trinidad, the Gold Coast, or Nigeria.

As already mentioned, the British Council endeavours to provide, or to obtain, accommodation for colonial students who need it; a special department of the Colonial Office also deals with problems of welfare in general. There are also signs of increasing interest in the matter on the part of churches and of the trade union movement, and numerous voluntary associations offer hospitality to students, and hold meetings, 'socials' and conferences of an interracial kind. Evening institutes, intended to provide opportunities for study and recreation for both coloured and white people have been opened in several cities. On the local plane, relations between the resident coloured community and their white neighbours are generally amicable. The student's personal connexion with the wider public is also growing, and he is generally accepted with little or no reservation in most university circles.

Thus, it is possible to foresee the development of a fresh trend in race relations in Britain. It must be emphasized, however, that the 'problem' there consists not only in certain traditional attitudes, but in the fact that the coloured individual so often exhibits traits such as poor education and low living standards, which apparently confirm the familiar stereotype of racial inferiority. There are signs that the coloured population in Britain is increasing and that it may continue to increase through immigration. This will make assimilation, in a biological sense, an unlikely solution. The best remedy seems to lie in getting rid of existing educational and cultural disparities. It is these which mainly hold up the economic advance of the resident coloured group and restrict the social opportunities of those of its members who desire a better status in British society.

CONCLUSION

From these four examples of race relations which we have considered certain conclusions may be drawn relevant to the thesis propounded on page 175. All four situations are the direct or indirect outcome of white colonization. In very few cases have such colonies been established out of philanthropic motives. Priests and missionaries, it is true, have gone to America, India, Africa, and the Pacific to spread the gospel; but the majority of Europeans who moved to lands overseas between the fifteenth and the twentieth centuries went to earn a living, to trade, to make profits. The way of life of these migrants was strongly opposed to the cultural systems which they encountered; therefore, the native inhabitants had to be suppressed whenever they obstructed, or threatened to obstruct, the European purpose. This suppression was frequently carried out in the early days with rapidity and with but few scruples on the ground that the native people constituted an 'out-group' from the point of view of Christianity.

But religious arguments gradually lost their importance, and it became necessary to seek some other reason more compatible with the scientific and rational spirit of the times. This was found in the notion that coloured races were mentally retarded, childlike, and incapable of looking after themselves in a modern, economically specialized age; hence they were the 'white man's burden'. The white man is responsible for the welfare of the coloured races; therefore he has the right to order and control their affairs as he deems fit. If he considers that contact with his own civilization is inimical to them, then racial segregation and exclusion from Western education and skills is the right as well as the logical policy.

This kind of reasoning is best illustrated by South Africa, but the British experience also shows how rationalization of the exploitation of India and other colonial territories has shaped the attitude of the man in the street. It is obvious that the British sense of racial superiority is inherited mainly from the days when Britain was the world's mightiest political and military power. Rationalization is necessary in such cases because of the wide gap, which frequently occurs in race relations, between ideology and practice. Peoples like the British, the North Americans, and the South Africans, who have a traditional attachment to Christianity, democracy, and egalitarianism, are also those who have made the sharpest distinction between races; hence the rationalizing tendency. It avoids serious moral and intellectual conflict amongst members of the prejudiced group by providing them with an explanation of what is incongruous. The belief, for example, that racial separation is ordained by God makes it possible for the believer to exclude people of another colour from his church without giving up his faith in the Fatherhood of God.

The examples of Brazil and Hawaii, however, suggest a somewhat different explanation from the exploitation one. In Brazil, the Portuguese never erected any barriers between themselves and the coloured population. Intermixture and intermarriage made it impossible for the whites to retain an exclusive monopoly of power and privilege as a racially distinctive group. Moreover, the Portuguese remained industrially undeveloped compared with the colonizing peoples of northern Europe, and the growth of capitalism was retarded by the attitude of the Roman Catholic Church. Perhaps the part played positively by the Church in encouraging and supporting the institution of the family was even more significant. The fact that the family was maintained as a solid unit, fulfilling its patriarchal functions and obligations, inhibited distinctions which would have interfered with the loyalty of its members to each other.

In Hawaii, effective white control was only secured at a comparatively late date. The initial circumstances of racial contact created a liberal attitude towards intermarriage which was also compatible with the nature of later immigration into the islands. In addition, the rise among the non-white population of a number of relatively influential and economically important cultural groups, differing but little in their racial traits, has prevented the development of any simple basis for discrimination.

The conclusion of this essay, then, is that the phenomenon of race relations is part of a special era in human history, that it arose out of the earlier European attempt to exploit overseas territories, and that it later became an integral part of colonialism, as an economic and imperial policy. In fact, a study of Western politics during the nineteenth century reveals a very close connexion between racial myths and national and imperial ambition. Racial attitudes and antagonisms can be described, therefore, as functions of the wider organization of Western society, and as the product of those social movements which have been shaping its development for the past five or six hundred years.

If this analysis is correct, it means that there is nothing permanent about the race problem. Human society is essentially dynamic, and there are already signs that several of the countries primarily involved are taking up a fresh attitude. For example, the British conception of the welfare state is being extended to Britain's colonial possessions in terms of large annual grants and interest-free loans for local development. The British have also promised their colonial peoples the right of self-government: one West African territory, the Gold Coast, has already advanced far along that road, and others close behind her. The French, whose principal colonial possessions are also in Africa, have similarly instituted important constitutional and legal reforms. The status of French citizen is now applicable to all Africans. This means that a Muslim, or a pagan, are accorded the same public liberties. They also enjoy certain political rights, very similar to, and sometimes even identical with, those of a French citizen. Penal law for major offences is the same for all and is no longer administered by special courts for non-Europeans different from those reserved for Europeans, although due consideration is given to religious and traditional customs. In a wholly different sphere of race relations, in the United States, there has been a steady growth in liberal opinion. Laws forbidding discrimination in industry have been passed in a number of states, and some cities also have local laws. Segregation has been declared illegal on inter-state forms of transportation, and recent judgements in the courts make it increasingly difficult for the Southern states to keep Negroes from attending the same schools and universities as whites. A large number of Southern cities now employ Negroes in the public services, including the police; and the Negro is beginning to play an effective part in politics. One of the obstacles—which has recently been removed—was the restriction of primary elections in the South to whites. The South is still firm on social segregation, but a substantial proportion of white Southerners thoroughly condemn all practices of violence, and a large number favour the Negro having full political and economic opportunities.

Taking the long view, therefore, we can look forward with some confidence to the day when race and colour distinctions will have ceased to plague mankind. Indeed, to future generations it may seem unbelievable that a slight difference in the chemical composition of their skins should have caused men to hate, despise, revile, and persecute each other. But, in the meantime, the danger remains—and it is a very grave one, and may become a major issue in world affairs. There are already signs that the fears and tensions which underlie South African race consciousness are spreading to the central and eastern part of the African continent, and are threatening to transform a previously cultural division of peoples into a narrowly racial one.

A fundamental aspect of the problem is the enormous disparity in relative prosperity between Western peoples and the rest of the world. North Americans, and most Europeans, have a standard of life which is many times higher in material comforts and social security than that of most Asians and Africans. There is also, in large part, the same kind of psychological gap as obtained between rich and poor at the time of the agrarian and industrial revolutions. Writers like J. L. and Barbara Hammond have described the attitude of the ruling class towards the English labourer in terms which could be duplicated in several modern situations of race. The English common people were conceived solely as hewers of wood and drawers of water. They should receive only vocational and industrial education, and they should not be encouraged or permitted to obtain employment outside their menial station in life.[1] The analogy, moreover, does not stop here. Just as the workers of England organized themselves as a body and broke the tyranny of the employer and landlord class, so colonial peoples today are in revolt against what they regard as the oppression of alien rule. The new factor is that the underprivileged are now of different ethnic or racial stock from the privileged, and the struggle has in most cases assumed a nationalist or racial complexion, rather than a class one. India, Indonesia, and more recently, colonial peoples in Africa, all exemplify in various ways, and to a varying extent, these new social movements. Politically and psychologically relevant, moreover is the fact that a major world power—Soviet Russia—claims that it has no colour problem. The constitution of the U.S.S.R. guarantees its citizens equal rights, no matter what their race may be, and, according to the Russians, there is no such thing as racial segregation among them: neither in education nor in anything else is any difference made between races and colours.

Seen in this kind of perspective, the future of race relations is bound up with the whole reorganization of world affairs

---

1. For further discussion of this point, see Cox, op. cit., p. 338 *et seq.*

and is a world responsibility. Something much more imaginative and realistic than armaments is needed to meet the practical and psychological requirements. The race problem is no longer a matter to be settled by parochial politics. What happens to people of colour in South Africa or in the United States is felt by non-Europeans nearly everywhere as their personal concern. It should be equally the concern, therefore, of the white peoples of other nations, and particularly those with coloured citizens or subjects of their own.

What is needed, primarily, is an international effort to liberalize racial attitudes. This must not stop short at admonition: racial harmony is not, unfortunately, a simple matter of goodwill. Fundamental political and economic issues are also involved. A nation like South Africa, for example, is confronted not only with the psychological problem of prevailing racial attitudes, but with the vast costs of urbanization, of coping with a disintegrated tribal society, and the urgent need for rural rehabilitation. In other words, many of the immediate difficulties to be overcome have nothing whatever to do with what people think about race.

Again, the 'coloured countries' are handicapped by illiteracy and malnutrition, and by general poverty and under-production. Part of the task of remedying this is already being performed by Unesco and those related organizations which are conducting health and literacy campaigns, distributing educational and cultural literature, and so on. The United States has a plan for economic aid to 'backward' territories, and MSA exists to provide them with finance and technical assistance. The colonial powers have their schemes for general development. But a very great deal more will have to be done; not only to 'iron out' existing economic inequalities, but to convince the coloured peoples of the sincerity of European and white society. There is no use disguising the fact that this will call for sacrifice as well as understanding on the part of European communities. It will mean forgoing some of the privileges hitherto regarded as essential to the continuation of their special cultural and racial heritage.

BIBLIOGRAPHY

ADAMS, Romanzo. *Interracial marriage in Hawaii*. Macmillan, 1937.

BENEDICT, Ruth. *Race, science and politics*. Viking Press, 1945.

BROOMFIELD, A. W. *Colour conflict*. Edinburgh House, 1943.

BROWN, Ina C. *Race relations in a democracy*. Harper, 1949.

COX, Oliver C. *Caste, class and race*. Doubleday, 1948.

DINGWALL, E. J. *Racial pride and prejudice*. Watts, 1946.

DOLLARD, J. *Caste and class in a southern town*. Yale University Press, 1937.

FRAZIER, E. F. *The negro in America*. Macmillan, 1950.

FREYRE, G. *The masters and the slaves*. Knopf, 1947.

HANKINS, F. H. *The racial basis of civilization*. Knopf, 1927.

HELLMAN, Ellen (ed.). *Handbook on racial relations*. Oxford University Press, 1949.

JOHNSON, C. S. *Patterns of negro segregation*. Harper, 1943.

LITTLE, K. L. *Negroes in Britain*. Routledge and Kegan Paul, 1948.

LOCKE, A. and STERN, B. J. *When peoples meet*. Ninds, Hayden and Eldredge, 1946.

MACCRONE, I. D. *Race attitudes in South Africa*. Oxford University Press, 1937.

MACMILLAN, W. M. *Africa emergent*. Faber, 1938.

MACWILLIAM, Carey. *Brothers under the skin*. Little, Brown and Co., 1944.

MYRDAL, Gunnar. *An American dilemma*. Harper, 1944.

PIERSON, Donald. *Negroes in Brazil*. Chicago University Press, 1942.

REUTER E. B. *Race and culture contacts*. McGraw-Hill, 1934.

THE JEWISH PEOPLE

A Biological History

by
HARRY L. SHAPIRO

*Chairman, Department of Anthropology
American Museum of Natural History
New York*

THE TRACES OF THE PAST

Not the least remarkable thing about the Jews is their antiquity. Most of the nations and peoples that preceded or were coeval with them have long vanished or have been absorbed into newer ones. The Sumerians, the Akkadians, the Hittites, the Assyrians, the Babylonians, the Phoenicians and a host of lesser nations and of peoples scarcely more than tribes have all disappeared from history. For 4,000 years the Jews, however, have preserved a cohesion that has bound them together and has enabled them to maintain a continuous identity. As a people conscious of their distinct tradition and of their existence as an entity, only the Egyptians are older than they.

The survival of the Jews is all the more remarkable because during at least half of their history they have had neither a formal corporate structure nor an established homeland. The fact is the Jews are difficult to classify in our current system of socio-political categories. They are not a clan, a tribe, or in a strict sense, a nation. At various periods in their history they were all these things, having begun as scarcely more than an extended family and having attained nationhood about 3,000 years ago—the highest and most complex form of socio-political estate. And like most other nations they then had acquired the usual attributes associated with this stage of political organization. They possessed a common tradition, a mutually intelligible language, a unified political structure, a feeling of common descent and a land of their own. By all

107

expectation when they lost their national independence and were subsequently dispersed over the earth and among the nations on it, they should have disappeared as Jews. This certainly must have been the expectation of the Assyrians and later of the Romans who were among the agents of the Diaspora. Most nations subjected to such an experience—the destruction of a common life together and the loss of political co-ordination, the strains of fragmentation arising from physical dispersion and from a loss of linguistic unity, and above all the removal from the land of birth—never recover and end in anonymity. This, however, did not happen to the Jews. That they lost many of their people was an acknowledged fact and has remained to them a lamentable tragedy. But despite the loss of the attributes of a nation and the disruption of exile and division, they nevertheless managed to continue their identity by evolving into somewhat of an anomaly—a people held together by ties of a common tradition and a common religion, the language of which provided a means of communication even where the adoption of mutually unintelligible vernaculars might have created irreparable fissures.

Thus the Jews of today enjoy an unbroken continuity exceeded in length of time by only one other people. If, for no other reason, such an unbroken history makes the Jews an exceptionally interesting people for the study of the dynamics of population. The biological fortunes of the Jews over a period of 4,000 years, if we knew them in their entirety, would offer extraordinarily valuable information of the greatest significance for other populations as well. But more specifically the history of the Jews invites the questions: what are the racial origins of these peoples, how have they changed in time, what effect has residence among and contact with a variety of people during the past 2,000 years—since their dispersal—had upon them, and what is their present racial and biological status? These and similar questions are the subject of this book. Although I do not expect to be able to answer definitively all these queries, it is worthwhile trying to establish what can be said about them from the evidence at hand. Moreover, so much nonsense has been written and promulgated along these lines about the Jews that some clarification may not be amiss.

Since this is a biological history of the Jews—an attempt to understand the racial history of a population over the course of four millennia—one might reasonably inquire what objective evidence is available for such a reconstruction. Indeed, one might go further and ask, in the light of the complexities involved, is such an enterprise possible? It must, of course, be admitted at the outset that the information for such an undertaking for any people is never and nowhere completely adequate. Peoples or nations in the past did not collect or deliberately leave for this purpose the kind of data we are only now beginning vaguely to recognize as necessary for such a task. Indeed such investigations as this would not even have occurred to them.

But this need not leave us altogether discouraged since some clues to what has happened in the past are recoverable from the ancients themselves. Their remains, literary and material, represent sources of information that become more and more valuable as the excavations of modern archaeologists continue to accumulate the means of validation and interpretation. Perhaps one of the major sources of the early history of the Jews is the Bible itself. For some time now the Bible has suffered an eclipse as a trustworthy historical document. It became the fashion during the last century to belittle the Old Testament as a reliable archive of the past, while its literary merits were extolled. The demonstration of science that the biblical account of Genesis was a myth served to undermine the reliability of the entire text. It was unfortunately overlooked that Genesis and similar passages represented the conception of a cosmogenesis that prevailed among the Jews when the Old Testament was set down and is valid as an historical, if not a scientific, fact. It does not minimize the historical value of Herodotus or Thucydides to discover in them explanations that appear naïve or unscientific to us. We recognize that contemporary explanations have significance aside from their accuracy as truth. If this were not the case, we should have to discard much, if not all, of the history of the past since it is permeated by the myths of the time. And who can vouch that our own histories written today may not be declared unsound if our current beliefs, even those based on science, prove invalid in the future.

But the crucial point is not the reliability of the biblical cosmogenesis or any other interpretation; these are always subject to change from one age to another. It is the fact that the Bible is more than that. It is a complex document made up of explanations of natural phenomena, political narrative, poetry, exhortation, moral codes, attitudes, statements of belief, theology, reflections on life, anecdotes, myths, and all the varied threads that make up the life and conviction of a people. It is a saga, a self-portrait, a diary of the Jews at one stage of their spiritual and secular development as a people. And if its 'science' must be rejected, its observations on contemporary life and its value as history are in no way affected by this. These are on another level and demand other standards of critical evaluation. The Bible as history should, therefore, be treated seriously. It contains both historical reconstruction and contemporary observation that are probably no more distorted than similar accounts in other places and times. What survives critical scrutiny can be of the greatest significance.

More conventional historical sources are also available for our purposes. Among others, the accounts of Josephus and Philo provide rich detail for the period when the Jews were being dispersed and adjusting themselves to the Roman world.

Wherever people live, they leave behind them a deposit of the things they used and made. They even leave themselves— their bones or ashes. And the longer they live in an area the thicker the debris or deposits grow. It used to be thought that that was about all they left behind. We now know from recent investigations that mixed with these bare relics, called artifacts, are a variety of other remains, such as pollen, seed and food, that also help to reconstruct the life of the past. From such things, both artifacts and other remains, the skilled archaeologist is able to draw a variety of inferences. From the techniques and styles of manufacture and decoration, he can establish the cultural relationship of one people with another. From objects of specific origin he can determine routes of trade; from the architectural remains, the size of population, the social, political and religious organization of a community. In this way the remains of a people are made to yield up an unsuspectedly rich amount of information. If this is never so fully clothed as are literary remains, or as furnished with a *dramatis personae*, it frequently has other virtues. It speaks with an objectivity that written remains rarely provide. Stripped of the beguiling influence of personalities and situations, archaeological remains generally reflect, on the contrary, the anonymous trends and currents of a society. And if archaeological reconstructions are often used merely to corroborate history, it must also be said, and with particular point here, that they frequently illuminate aspects of life that written records neglect or overlook.

For the purposes of this inquiry archaeological activity is especially important since in addition to the debris of living, it also turns up the skeletal remains of those who accumulated the debris. And from these bones and crania much valuable evidence can be salvaged. Comparative studies of these remains make it possible to establish the variability of the population they represent and to determine their affinity with other populations. From these skeletons one can obtain data on certain types of disease and pathology, derive information on the vital statistics of the population and recover the so-called A-B-O blood types which are of special importance since their heredity and distribution are known and thus of value in an inquiry such as this.

If from these sources we can obtain some conception of the biological characteristics of the ancient Hebrews, it is of course in the living descendants that we may trace the effect of their four thousand years of history as a people. Studies of several kinds exist on living Jewish populations. There is, for example, some information on the Samaritans and other groups surviving in proximity to the ancient homeland. The question here is to what extent such survivals actually represent the original population. If it turns out that they do, then their importance is obvious in amplifying our knowledge of the ancients by providing data unobtainable from skeletal remains and in setting up a kind of standard by which changes in the rest of the Jewish people can be measured.

Fortunately, there are also a considerable number of reports on various Jewish groups settled not only in diverse parts of Europe, but also in North Africa, Asia, and even in the New World. Most of the older publications of this sort are anthropometric, that is to say, concerned with the physical attributes and racial traits of these groups. But in addition there are also demographic and medical studies that are pertinent to our purpose.

More recently, Jewish groups, along with all sorts of other populations, have been examined for the frequency of their blood types and for other genetic traits. And from such data certain inferences may be drawn.

If the total of these various types of evidence is far from complete, their value when combined is very considerable. My purpose will be to determine what kind of pattern these data provide and what inferences may be reasonably drawn from them.

THE GENESIS OF THE JEWS

An inquiry into the biological and genetic origins of any population should properly begin at the beginning. For the Jews, this has always meant going back to Abraham,[1] the traditional founder of their line. According to the narrative in Genesis, Abraham was a native of Ur of the Chaldees, a city in Mesopotamia, a land where his kindred continued to dwell in the vicinity of Haran and Nahor and whither he sent his son Isaac to find himself a wife. Abraham, however, had been directed by the Lord to abandon his people and the country of his birth and to settle in the land of Canaan. Accompanied by his nephew, Lot, and their households, he migrated to the west and entered Canaan which was promised to him and to his descendants. Here, the narrative continues, Abraham's offspring increased in the course of generations and formed the band of Israelites that followed Joseph, one of their members, into Egypt where he had prospered. Although they continued to multiply under the Pharaohs, their servitude in Egypt grew heavy and eventually under the guidance of Moses they fled, in their thousands, seeking refuge in the Wilderness of Sinai. After a period of wandering and hardship, but united under the Mosaic Law, a formalized religion, and in a Covenant with the Lord, they re-entered Canaan and conquered it. This was the long-awaited and deeply desired fulfilment in the Land of Promise—a people in Israel—a nation of Hebrews.

So, in its barest outline, runs the biblical account of the birth of the Jews as a people. It is an origin tradition that traces their lineage to a single patriarchal founder of a family that subsequently by its own increase burgeoned into a nation. It is not uncommon to find this kind of origin myth to account for the existence of a whole tribe or people, but it is nowhere more appropriate and natural than in a primitive, nomadic, herding society like that of the early Israelites, where every circumstance of their way of life would encourage this view of their own as well as their neighbours' origins. The Old Testament is full of references to tribes and people whose beginnings are similarly traced to founding fathers: the Ishmaelites were the descen-

---

1. Recent archaeological investigations combined with modern biblical studies have led scholars to place Abraham as far back as the beginning of the second millennium B.C. For this reason I have taken 4,000 years as a rough approximation to the length of Jewish history.

dants of Ishmael, and similarly from Japheth, Shem, and Ham, the sons of Noah, were sprung the races of mankind.[1]

In a nomadic herding economy the extended family, consisting of the patriarch surrounded by his sons and their wives and children, and his servants, was everything and survived as a kind of entity in the successive generations. It is a tightly integrated and self-sufficient economic unit that bound each member closely to it so that together they could face the rigours of the country and the hostility of their enemies, but apart from which they were lost and without status. Their ties with other nomadic family groups were tenuous and traditional rather than organized and highly structured. In such a family unit power and prestige were lodged in the patriarch who controlled its destinies and who was consequently a figure of awe and respect. The children of the house could submit to him or rebel against him, but they could not ignore him. The sons, the grandsons and their descendants were the issue of his loins and descent was traced through the male line to him. This patrilineal descent was cherished and the genealogical sequences from male to male were carefully preserved, as the long and often tedious recitals that occur frequently in the Old Testament bear witness. Under these circumstances it was natural for the nomadic Israelites to envisage their origin in terms of family descent back to Israel (né Jacob) the patriarch, and through him to his grandfather Abraham who, in their traditions, had gone out from his own people to establish his house in Canaan. To the Jews, then, they were literally the descendants of Father Abraham.

Although this explanation of the origin of the Jews has the virtue of simplicity and served to reinforce the early Hebrews in their belief that they were the chosen people by emphasizing the purity of their descent from a patriarch signalled out especially by God, there is evidence in the Bible itself that the story was more complicated than the traditions of Genesis made it appear. When these folk beliefs came to be written down, centuries after the events described, they had like most myths an element of truth. But the nuclear facts were interwoven with details borrowed from a familiar world and with interpretations and interpolations to make the whole fabric consistent and harmonious. And as in most legendry, it is not difficult to find overlooked inconsistencies.

---

1. Even today among Arabic and Berber tribes, descent is counted from a common male ancestor and their designations carry 'beni' or 'bani' or 'ait', meaning 'sons of'.

The mistake would be to ignore the embedded truths because of the detected elaborations. In the past it was difficult to distinguish truth from accretion and to recognize that accretion, too, is a kind of truth—as a reflection of the times and of the speculation of men. Now, with the aid of archaeology, comparative linguistics, literary and textual analyses, it is possible to confirm many things that formerly had to be taken on trust. And more than this, these studies have uncovered a contemporary world the Israelites knew only dimly, if at all, and a past that had become totally lost to them, but to both of which they belonged and by both of which they were influenced. It is as though time and archaeology had elevated us onto a peak that enables us to see on the plains of the past something of the patterns and the relationships that were imperceptible to those who dwelt there.

Hazy as these vistas must necessarily be until more is known, it is already possible to discern that the early history of the Israelites and their origins are part of a larger story. They emerged out of one of the population movements that periodically swept across the Fertile Crescent like drifts of fallen leaves set in motion by gusts of wind. And having come to rest in the Land of Canaan they conquered it and developed a way of life and, in particular, an entity that has continued down to our time.

The country in which the Israelites settled and where they arose as a nation was already populated with people destined to establish a variety of relationships with them. It is, therefore, of more than passing interest in the history of the Israelites to discover what we can about their neighbours and their predecessors in Canaan.

The occupation of the region goes back to the early Palaeolithic and continued down to our own time without interruption. It is not, however, until the mid-Palaeolithic, the Mousterian, that we can obtain any idea of the kind of men who made the stone tools that mark their cultural progress. In this period—some 100,000 to 125,000 years ago—Neanderthal and related people dwelt in Canaan. Their remains have been discovered by Turville-Petre near Galilee, by McCown in the caves of Et Tabun and Mugharet el Skhul on the slopes of Mount Carmel, and by Neuville and Stékelis in the cave of Jebel Kafzeh near Nazareth. They range from types scarcely to be distinguished from contemporary Neanderthal men in Europe, with heavy brows and massive chinless jaws, to individuals transitional to modern man; but all of them became extinct in the sense that their characteristic features were no longer visible in those of their successors that we know anything about. This, in fact, is not until we reach the Mesolithic, perhaps 10,000 years ago.

The Natufian culture is a late phase of the Mesolithic in Palestine and was first identified from Miss Garrod's excavations. The Natufians dwelt in caves, hunted and fished for a livelihood, and continued to use stone tools. Although by our standards they were still a primitive people culturally speaking, they had, nevertheless, come a long way from Palaeolithic levels of technology. Among other interesting developments, they had evolved tools for cutting wild grains and for milling their seeds. Childe even suggests that they might already have been experimenting with a very crude form of agriculture. The population itself is represented by a relatively abundant series of remains: about 132 exhumed from caves at Shukba and at Mount Carmel, and six or seven found by Neuville at Erq-el-Ahmar, south of Bethlehem. Unfortunately, the bones are extremely fragmentary and, such as they are, have been only summarily described, except for one skull reported by Vallois. The descriptions available, however, leave little room to doubt that the Natufians were *Homo sapiens* in type, that is to say, modern men. They were extremely short, the men averaging scarcely 5 feet 3 inches and the women about 5 feet. Their crania, according to both Sir Arthur Keith and H. H. Vallois who have examined them, conform to what might be called a primitive or emergent Mediterranean type that has parallels in the Near East, North Africa, Malta, among pre-dynastic Egyptians, and among the Mesolithic population of Mugem in Portugal. Both authors noted a certain degree of facial projection and a low vaulted nose suggestive of negroid affinities. These characters have also been found in Palaeolithic skulls in Europe and attributed to the same racial source. But other explanations for these morphological characters cannot yet be ruled out.

The population of Palestine comes into view again at Jericho in the early Neolithic. Part of this town, the earliest yet found in Palestine and perhaps in the whole Near East, has been systematically excavated by Miss Kathleen Kenyon who has laid bare its Neolithic origins and has demonstrated that the first settlers already possessed a knowledge of agriculture. Although a favourable concentration of marine supplies of food may permit moderate concentration of settled populations greater than the more primitive hunting and/or gathering stages of human economy can support, yet even these are limited in their expansion. Jericho, therefore, illustrates the fact that once agriculture became the established means of obtaining food, it not only required a settled life but permitted the foundation and growth of true city organization with all that may imply for human evolution.

Jericho has also yielded evidence that pottery, formerly regarded as virtually coeval with the Neolithic, need not be so. For no pottery is to be found in the earliest levels of the Neolithic at Jericho. This confirms Childe's frequent assertion that the significant event in ushering in the 'Neolithic revolution' was an economic one, namely, the shift from hunting or gathering economies to agriculture.

It is fortunate that in these very early pre-ceramic Neolithic levels at Jericho, datable to about 7500 B.C., a relatively abundant series of human skeletons was discovered. Although within their limitations these human remains will eventually yield precious information obtainable from no other source, it is as yet not fully available. Up to the present, the only description of them in print is by G. Kurth,[1] who assisted in their extraction and published brief but interesting observations that can only be tentative until he is able to assemble and analyse all the material.

Kurth was able to distinguish in this pre-ceramic Neolithic population (82 individuals, subsequently increased to about 200) two distinct types which he regards, for various archaeological reasons, as having separate origins. The predominant one, at least in this period, is a short-statured people of about 5 feet 3 ½ inches (163 cm.). They were delicate in bone structure and had long, narrow or dolichocephalic skulls. These characters are suggestive of the Natufian people we have already encountered earlier in the preceding Mesolithic. Indeed, Kurth observes that this Jericho component does resemble these antecedents. But he attributes some of the special features of the short Neolithic people to a kind of 'domestication' phenomenon. Presumably this might be induced by their new agricultural-urban environment and the effect of selective factors now brought into prominence.

If this population element should prove to represent a continuity from the Natufians and to resemble them as much as has been suggested, their emergence as a response to the urban conditions of Jericho may need to be reappraised; in any

---

1. G. Kurth, various articles in *Homo*, 1955, vol. 6; 1957, vol. 8; 1958, vol. 9.

event it is probable from the age at death established for the various skeletons that a severe degree of selection was affecting them. The infant mortality was very high and the average length of life was extremely low—around 21 to 22 years. At that time survival past maturity was virtually non-existent. These demographic conditions prevailed not only among these people but were also characteristic of the second population element of Neolithic Jericho.

It is of considerable significance that the short, long-headed people of Jericho had counterparts in other areas of the Neolithic world of the Near East. Similar types have been excavated and described in early levels of the Mesopotamian civilization as well as in Egypt. Although it is still too early to draw firm conclusions on the continuity of the population of the Fertile Crescent at this stage of emergent urban civilization, some degree of relationship between the people scattered over this stretch of territory is becoming increasingly evident despite the existence of some local variation.

The second element identified in the population of pre-ceramic Jericho is quite different. Its representatives were taller, reaching in the males an average of about 5 feet 8 inches (175 cm.). Their bony structure was heavy and massive in contrast with the delicately modelled skeletons of the predominant type. The distinction between the two population elements is also evident in the proportions of the skull and face. This second type had massive, broad, and relatively low faces with cranial vaults only moderately narrow and long. In all these features they recall the Cro-Magnon people of the upper Palaeolithic in Europe. Kurth, in fact, refers to them as 'Cro-Magniform' and suggests that they were perhaps derived from a herding people who joined the small agricultural settlement of Jericho. Their burials revealed peculiarities that also serve to distinguish them as a culturally distinct population element. The skull was usually severed from the body which suggests some kind of ancestor cult. Moreover, the skulls themselves were frequently artificially deformed. These types, at least at Jericho, continued to exist all through the Neolithic and the following Copper Age without fundamental modifications or any additional accessions of new people.

At Megiddo, in northern Palestine and at some distance from Jericho, we encounter another population that can be dated to the Chalcolithic or Copper Age, thus overlapping the early Jericho people. This was a period—about 4000 B.C.—when cities were developing out of earlier agricultural hamlets, not only in Palestine but all through the Fertile Crescent. Presumably agriculture has spread widely among the indigenous population. It is interesting, therefore, to find from the evidence of a small series of 28 skulls described by Hrdlička that the prevailing type at Megiddo is similar in certain respects to the long-headed, short-statured component at Jericho which apparently was the indigenous sub-stratum there. Hrdlička assigned 'all of the specimens to the Mediterranean type of people, except for the skull of a young female with negroid features'.[1] My own statistical analysis of the published data confirms this general attribution, if the term 'Mediterranean' is taken in a very broad sense. This Copper Age population had long, quite narrow and low vaulted heads, producing an extreme degree of dolichocephaly. The facial structures that have survived are relatively narrow with narrow noses, features that agree with the assignment of these crania to a basic Mediterranean stock. As among the contemporary Jerichoans of similar type, the bony structure was light and gracile. Hrdlička states that they, too, were relatively short in stature.

In discussing the type these crania from Megiddo represent, Hrdlička speaks of their being remarkably 'pure', by which he obviously means that the individual crania showed little variation one from another. This may mean that the population of Megiddo at this time was relatively isolated and possibly inbred, although Hrdlička's implication was, I think, intended to suggest that the population was racially unmixed. Our knowledge of population genetics would, however, it seems to me, favour the former interpretation.

Apart from the series from Jericho and Megiddo only a couple of skulls have been reported elsewhere from this general period, inclusive of the Neolithic and Copper Ages. These were discovered in a cave at Ain Jebrud in Judaea by P. H. Hansler, O.S.B. in 1912. In so far as their defective condition permits comparison, they do not appear to depart significantly from the type at Megiddo.

The racial characteristics of the population show no fundamental change in the succeeding early Bronze Age—that is, down to approximately 2000 B.C. The prevailing type remains Mediterranean, as far as can be determined from the still inadequately reported data from Gezer, Megiddo, and Jericho. Kurth, who has examined the Jericho crania, has characterized

---

1. A. Hrdlička, 'Skeletal Remains', In: *Megiddo Tombs,* edited by P. L. O. Guy and R. M. Engberg (*Papers,* Oriental Institute, Chicago, vol. 33, 1929).

them as prototypes of the 'Orientalid' type, apparently on the basis of the frequency of convex nasal profiles. But since the alleged distinctions between 'Mediterranean' and 'Orientalid' are largely expressed in the missing soft parts, it might at this stage be premature to attempt to make too fine a differentiation.

In the Bronze Age, however, the population lived notably longer lives. This can be inferred from the appearance of definitely senile skulls and the higher average age of the skeletons of this period discovered at Jericho. Whether this can be laid to an amelioration of living conditions or to the effect of rigorous selection over several thousand years cannot be determined from the available evidence.

These, then, are the people, as far as their physical remains bear witness, who inhabited the land that the Hebrews were to know as Canaan and whom they were to call Canaanites. They were part of a much larger group of mankind that extended from beyond Mesopotamia to Egypt. Despite local variations, the people of the Fertile Crescent who were associated with the beginnings of civilization in this region were prevailingly of the racial type identified as Mediterranean. The subordinate Cro-Magniform type, identified by Kurth in the Neolithic, had apparently become absorbed in the population of the Bronze Age or had at least become reduced to an insignificant element. The ultimate distribution of the predominant Mediterranean type in the Neolithic and early Bronze Age is not completely known. Similar types have been found in the Mediterranean, in Anatolia, in Egypt, and at such trans-Mesopotamian sites as Tepe Hissar and Sialk. Indeed, in view of the enormous range of territory represented, the resemblances are very striking and suggest a broad diffusion, possibly from the Fertile Crescent itself. For it was here that agriculture, towns, and civilization first evolved, imparting an expansive and a centrifugal force to the population associated with these developments.

It is this similarity in racial origins that explains why no fundamental change appears in the population of Canaan from the Neolithic to the end of the early Bronze Age (2100 B.C.), although the archaeological record reveals considerable cultural diffusion and even migration. Beginning, however, with the middle Bronze Age, roughly from 2100 B.C., some modifications in the population of Canaan can be clearly traced. In the cranial remains from Gezer, Megiddo, and Jericho, a perceptible increase in the cranial width becomes apparent, and brachycephaly, which had previously been absent or rare, now is not infrequent. Unfortunately, both the fragmentary condition of much of the remains and the inadequate reports on them make more penetrating analyses and comparison impossible. Nevertheless, this change bespeaks some fundamental readjustment going on. We may postulate either some kind of selective adjustment leading to brachycephaly—a process some students have claimed to be able to trace in other places and at other times—or the addition of invading racial elements. At this stage of our knowledge the former hypothesis must remain an inference based on analogy. The latter has at least some historical confirmation and offers a biologically less complex explanation.

Although it is rather difficult at present to equate racial events in various parts of the Fertile Crescent, it is striking that in Anatolia, Syria, and Mesopotamia a strong shift towards brachycephaly appears at roughly the same time and that the archaeological evidence suggests that these changes were associated with new cultural influences, invasions, and conquests. The overthrow of old empires by invading conquerors and the establishment of new ones like the Hittite and the Mitanni on the fringes of the older centres strongly support the interpretation that new people on the outskirts of the older civilized areas were making successful incursions at this time. It was an economic and historical process not very different fundamentally from what happened later in Greece and Rome. The Mycenaean civilization and people were an attractive target for the predatory and mobile Dorians who pillaged and then took over the rich centres of Greece. In our own era, the Germanic tribes found the rich, settled European provinces of Rome equally attractive for conquest and settlement. There can be little doubt that gene interchange took place in those two instances and that the older populations were genetically profoundly affected by it.

There is no reason to believe that similar gene exchanges did not modify the older population of Mesopotamia and Anatolia by similar invasions of surrounding people. That such racial and genetic influences should eventually percolate to Canaan and modify to some extent the indigenous people seems inevitable. As in the earlier periods of its history, Canaan continued to be exposed to cultural influences from the north and east and to the incidental contacts that this implies. But, perhaps more important, the combined literary and archaeological evidence can only be interpreted to mean that during the middle Bronze Age Canaan was exposed to massive invasions.

It is significant that in the preceding early Bronze Age, Canaan was relatively secure, prosperous, and settled with flourishing communities. By the beginning of the middle Bronze Age towns were being abandoned throughout the land and nomadism as a way of life had become highly characteristic. Such a combination can only mean that the urban and social structure had collapsed. In the Execration Texts, found in Egypt and dating to this period, the reference to Canaan confirms this picture of an unsettled, disturbed country.[1] The archaeological remains themselves reveal a marked falling off of skill and refinement, reflecting a technological regression and cultural deterioration.

Such troubled conditions, coeval with the historic rise of new empires north and east of Canaan, suggest that the disturbances incident to the transfer of power to conquering usurpers and the expansiveness of a newly organized people, were resolved in the dislocation and migration of older populations. There is, indeed, good reason to believe that fresh invasions of Semitic people from the eastern empires were moving into Canaan during the period of unrest, and perhaps these anonymous folk were in part responsible for the decay of early Bronze Age culture and settled life in Canaan. These displaced Semites were followed in the first half of the second millennium B.C. by a series of invasions by people who are no longer anonymous —we have such identifying names as Hyksos, Hittites, Hurrians, etc.—but who are racially little known. It has been frequently assumed that they carried, at least in part, elements of the new populations that had been invading and infiltrating the older population strata of Mesopotamia and Anatolia. Some Indo-European influence is certainly suggested by the notable increase in names of this origin that suddenly appear in this period. Since these people are contemporaneous with a series of racial modifications, it is not unreasonable to infer that they brought new strains into Canaan and contributed to the observed changes in the people among whom the Hebrews were to arise and with whom they were to establish close relations.

1. W. F. Albright, *The Archaeology of Palestine*, Harmondsworth, Penguin Books, 1956.

THE CHOSEN PEOPLE

Neither the mortal remains nor the dwellings of the earliest Israelites, neither the things they made nor the objects they used are available for the kind of studies by which scholars determine the cultural and racial origin and relationship of the peoples of the past. As nomadic herdsmen their debris, from which an archaeology might have been salvaged, could only have been extremely thin, widely scattered, and difficult to recover. And even if their traces might have been excavated and be in hand, how would one be able to recognize them among the comparable remains of non-Israelitish tribes of herdsmen roaming the same areas and living in a way that was probably not very different? How, then, can we ever know what they were really like, what their genetic relationships were with the people among whom they lived or to what origins they may be ultimately traced? The Bible itself is strangely barren of the kind of detail we should now like to know. For example, there are virtually no details about the physical appearance of the persons who play important roles in the narrative. Later in their history, identifiable remains—skeletal, architectural and manufactured—in varying abundance have provided confirmation of written records and even furnished information on matters about which the written records are themselves silent. But when they first emerged from anonymity and began their distinct and corporate existence we can rely at present only on such indirect sources as the Bible, linguistic evidence, and the inferences that our knowledge of the contemporary world might permit us to draw. These are admittedly less satisfactory than more direct kinds of evidence, but it would be unwarranted to dismiss or underrate the value of what is available.

The historicity of the biblical tradition of the origin of Abraham and his followers is now generally accepted by virtually all scholars. The reference to Ur of the Chaldees as the city from which Abraham departed is quite explicit. Similarly, both Haran and Nahor are mentioned as the towns where Abraham's kin continued to live long after his departure. These places are all now located in Mesopotamia where the early civilizations of Sumer and Akkad flourished. Consistent with such an origin, at least for Abraham and his immediate followers, is the language the early Israelites spoke. In Deuteronomy xxvi. 5, according to the modern version, it was written: 'a wandering Aramaean was my father'. And again, in Genesis xxviii. 5 there is this reference: 'And Isaac sent away Jacob; and he went to Paddan-Aram [Mesopotamia] unto Laban, son of Bethnel the Aramaean, the brother of Rebekah, Jacob's and Esau's mother.' Aramaic is a dialect of western Semitic, the same branch to which the language of the Canaanites belonged. Support of such an identification also comes from the analysis of given names in the early genealogies. They fall overwhelmingly into the same language group, which linguists have traced back to the Mesopotamian region.

That the homeland of the founders of the Hebrew line was Mesopotamia is also supported by recent studies of the literary remains from that area. In particular, the cosmogonical views of Genesis are too strikingly similar to those in such Mesopotamian epics as Gilgamesh to be indicative of any explanation other than a common tradition.

Since there is no reason to believe that the founders of the Hebrew people were a distinctive group in their homeland— linguistically, religiously,[1] or culturally—it would place too great a strain on probability to assume they were, in any significant way, genetically or racially differentiated from the general population to be found there. Any such assumption would, indeed, demand circumstances not known to have existed there. Experience among better known people quite clearly demonstrates that where barriers of culture, religion, or language do not exist, even genetically distinct groups living in one area tend to interbreed, thus maintaining a gene flow that would lead to eventual amalgamation.

In any event, what is known of the racial characteristics and their variations among the Mesopotamian population contemporaneous with the Terachid migration does not suggest the existence of any distinctive racial group that might have given rise to the Israelites. Thus if the founding fathers of Israel were in effect representative of their contemporaries in Mesopotamia in the vicinity of Ur, Haran, and Nahor, inferences concerning their racial affiliation would depend on our knowledge of the general population at the time when the migration occurred.

Albright,[2] although admitting the difficulty of precisely dating

---

1. 'Your fathers dwelt of old time beyond the River, even Terah, the father of Abraham and the father of Nahor; and they served other gods.' Joshua xxiv. 2.

2. W. F. Albright, *The Archaeology of Palestine*, Harmondsworth, Penguin Books, 1956; *From Stone Age to Christianity*, Philadelphia, Johns Hopkins Press, 1946.

this migration, has offered the opinion, based on his evaluation of the available evidence, that it may have taken place in the twentieth and nineteenth centuries B.C. Allowing some slight variation, such a date would, I think, receive general support from current scholarship. We have already seen that much of the Fertile Crescent, and in particular Mesopotamia and the Land of Canaan, was occupied by a predominantly Mediterranean racial type at least down to the end of the early Bronze Age, or roughly to about 2100 B.C.

Subsequently, as I have already indicated, some modification can be detected in the physical characteristics of the population, probably traceable to the invasion of new people and the rise of their empires. Since the emergent Hebrews were not known to have been part of the expansive conquering armies of these new states, it might be argued that neither were they representative of the new population that was eventually established. Instead, they might well have come from the older elements that were being displaced and forced to move. It is also very probable from cognate data that Canaan, as well as other coastal regions, had been overrun for some time by such dislocated people from the east. Since non-Semitic languages appear with the new population elements, the Semitic speech of the early Israelites reinforces the view that they are derived from the older population stratum. If this be a tenable inference, the first Israelites would have to be reckoned as principally Mediterranean in their origins. It should, however, be admitted as a possibility that some of the adherents to Abraham's cohort, or some of those who might have subsequently joined the coalescing group of Hebrews, were representative of the more recent additions to the racial complex evolving in this area. Thus one might, as an alternative, reconstruct the Hebrews as basically Mediterranean with some minor addition of the broad-headed element that was beginning to become manifest in some localities.

Proximity provides the opportunity for intermarriage, and intermarriage is the means by which genetic exchange occurs. An appraisal, therefore, of the biological elements that contributed to the formation of the early Israelites can scarcely afford to overlook the people among whom they had come to dwell. Although at various times in the long history of the Jews men spoke out against miscegenation with non-Jews, the fact remains that the practice can be documented and its very existence is amply bespoken by the prohibitions against it. It is true that both the minatory and monitory utterances against out-marriage were written long after the formative stage we are considering and at a time when religious distinctions had become formalized and traditional and therefore vulnerable to corruption from other religious systems. Indeed, the real fear behind the prohibitions is often explicit enough. If the sons of Israel marry daughters outside the faith, they will become influenced to practise rites and worship gods that were abominations in the eyes of the faithful. This, one must admit, is sound observation and, if one is a believer, a source of real threat. Endogamy, therefore, within the nation—a natural enough tendency under normal circumstances—can be seen in this context as virtually a dogma and as a means of protecting the purity of the religion of the Israelites.

But in the beginning when Israel was not as distinctive and perhaps as self-conscious as it was to become, intermarriage might not have seemed so dire as it did in later times. Thus one might anticipate greater freedom in this regard in the early days. It is, of course, impossible to determine with any assurance whether intermarriage with neighbouring tribes was greater or less in these early days than it was subsequently. But in general one would expect that if the practice were not too uncommon, its effect, genetically speaking, would be greater when the population was small, as it must have been compared with its magnitude in later periods.

The Bible itself contains numerous references to intermarriage, both during this early phase of Israel's history and later. Abraham himself, for example, had a son Ishmael by Hagar, the Egyptian handmaiden of his wife Sarah. And since concubinage was practised in his day, it is not improbable that some of his concubines were also of diverse origin. The same theme reappears in the lives of Isaac and Rebekah. Esau, one of their sons, married a Hittite woman, and Rebekah became concerned for her second son, Jacob. 'I am weary of my life,' she declared, 'because of the daughters of Heth. If Jacob take a wife of the daughters of Heth, such as these, of the daughters of the land, what good shall my life do me.' [1] And Isaac charged Jacob, 'Thou shalt not take a wife of the daughters of Canaan'.[2] These injunctions may well represent the fears of later generations put in the mouths of the patriarchs. For by the witness of

---

1. Genesis, xxvii. 46.
2 Genesis, xxviii. 1.

sacred tradition which could not be altered, the revered fathers had done frequently enough what was to be condemned.

Even Moses apparently went twice to outside sources for a wife. In Numbers (xii) he is said to have married a Cushite woman, and in Exodus (ii. 21) he is reported to have taken to wife, Zipporah, a daughter of a Midianite. And among the Israelites who were wandering under the guidance of Moses, there was 'the son of an Israelitish woman, whose father was an Egyptian'. [1] How many other children of Israel had inter-married with Egyptians during the sojourn in Egypt we cannot even surmise.

These, indeed, are only a few of the instances of intermarriage cited specifically in the Bible. Many more direct references to miscegenation could be listed and to these could be added the opportunities for genetic exchange provided by the capture of women from defeated enemies. The virgins of Midian that were spoils of war were counted by thousands. We can only infer that some of them became mothers of Israelites. For the practice of taking captured women as wives was recognized as customary and permissible. In Deuteronomy it was sanctioned in this fashion:

'When thou goest forth to battle against thine enemies, and the Lord thy God delivereth them into thy hands, and thou carriest them away captive, and seest among the captives a woman of goodly form, and thou hast a desire unto her, and wouldst take her to thee to wife; then thou shalt bring her home to thy house; and she shall shave her head, and pare her nails; and she shall put the raiment of her captivity from off her, and shall remain in thy house, and bewail her father and her mother a full month; and after that thou mayest go in unto her, and be her husband, and she shall be thy wife. And it shall be, if thou have no delight in her, then thou shalt let her go whither she will; but thou shalt not sell her at all for money, thou shalt not deal with her as a slave, because thou hast humbled her.' [2]

These contacts of the children of Israel with their neighbours included virtually all the principal tribes and peoples mentioned in the Bible as inhabiting the region of Canaan and the surrounding areas. Unfortunately, the names for the most part are meaningless for our purposes since they cannot be identified with actual remains except in the case of the Egyptians. The important point, however, is that the Israelites

---

1. Leviticus, xxiv. 10.
2. Deuteronomy, xxi. 10-14.

were not isolated genetically from the rest of the population. In fact, the evidence is beyond question that the early Israelites were freely mingling with their neighbours who were in most cases closely related to them by language, culture, and racial origin. From this we are obliged to conclude that biologically they had absorbed elements from the surrounding people and that they approximated the prevailing type.

That type, as far as the remains from Gezer[1] go (the only considerable corpus of contemporary material), seems from the published data to be comparable with the Mediterranean type we found to be characteristic of Mesopotamia. Thus we would have to conclude from existing evidence that the Israelites encountered and mixed with tribes in Canaan that did not differ racially very much from them to begin with.

During the period we are considering, namely the middle and late Bronze Age—roughly from the twentieth to the fifteenth century B.C.—the Hittites are frequently mentioned in the Bible. The Hittites are known from other evidence to have invaded Canaan during this period. but whether the archaeological definition of these people is precisely the same as the biblical one is difficult to assess. The reasons for bringing them forward are that the Hittites spoke a non-Semitic language, an Indo-European one in fact, that Indo-European names appear in Canaan during this era, and especially that the Hittites are often considered to represent one of the newer racial elements introduced into the general area around this time. In the centres of Hittite influence to the north, brachycephaly is correlated with their ascendancy in the archaeological record. And according to some authorities the broad-headedness they are thought to have introduced is of a particular form associated with the Armenoid people. The evidence, however, on this is not specific enough to permit firm conclusions, although some modification towards brachycephaly does seem tied in with the appearance of these people on the scene.

Since, however, we do not know the numerical strength of the people known as Hittites in Canaan, nor whether they represented the original stock of Hittites in Anatolia or were merely part of the population conquered by them and endowed with their name, it is obviously impossible to evaluate their significance, if any, in affecting the Israelites and the other people living in Canaan. At the most, it is probable that some

---

1. R. A. S. Macalister, *Gezer*, London, published for the Committee of the Palestine Exploration Fund by J. Murray, 1912.

influence of the Hittite racial type did percolate through to Canaan, since there is some evidence of a slight tendency toward brachycephaly. The shift, however, is not overwhelming or decisive. But in the light of the frequency of intermarriage of all kinds during this period, it would be unlikely that the Israelites would have escaped this influence.

In cuneiform texts, found in Mesopotamia and Syria, and dated to this period, reference has been found to a class of people known as 'Apiru (Khapiru) which Albright,[1] among others, has suggested had some connexion with the Hebrews. They were landless soldiers, raiders, and slaves. When they appear in Canaanite documents of the fourteenth century B.C., they are rebels against Egyptian authority, sometimes in alliance with native princes. Ethnically they are apparently of diverse origin, drawn originally from various sources resident in Mesopotamia. The issue is still unresolved, but if the Hebrews or Israelites prove to be in part sprung from this source, there would still be little reason to suggest that racially they were different from the contemporary population among which they were interspersed.

Egypt loomed large in Canaan during the middle and late Bronze Age, but mostly as the seat of imperial power. Egyptian governors, officials, and traders, and no doubt soldiers, servants and other followers, resided there. But colonists were not known to have migrated there in large numbers. The Israelites, however, who were still dwelling in and moving their flocks and herds about Canaan and its vicinity, would not have much opportunity for intermarriage with such a relatively small ruling class.

But during their sojourn in Egypt, which modern scholarship indicates was of considerable duration, the opportunities, at least, for miscegenation were vastly increased and some were known to have been realized. Joseph had married the daughter of an Egyptian priest and his sons Manasseh and Ephraim, therefore, would be reckoned as half-Egyptian. I have already cited the son of an Israelitish woman and an Egyptian father. How many more instances of this kind occurred during the long years in Egypt can no longer be determined, but certainly they must have been numerous. The Israelites before their arrival in Egypt had already mingled fairly freely with their Canaan neighbours. It would be remarkable if they had ceased

---

1. W. F. Albright, *From Stone Age to Christianity*, Philadelphia, Johns Hopkins Press, 1946.

to do so once they reached the land of Egypt. The barriers to intermarriage that religious separatism might have raised could not at this time have been effective, since neither in Canaan earlier nor in Egypt had the Israelites fully evolved the religious system and the self-consciousness that adherence to it would impart.

This appraisal of the formative years of Israel leads us to see the Israelites as a composite people, derived originally from the population of north-western Mesopotamia, but subsequently absorbing adherents from and intermarrying with the various related tribal groups with whom their wanderings brought them into contact.

The biblical account of the world in which the early Israelites lived, moving among the various tribes and groups that shared the land with them, with the intimate relationships that this kind of life created, leaves little room to doubt that these years and this kind of existence must have been critical ones. Their migration from Haran, Nahor, and Ur, all the way to Egypt via Canaan, meant that they had traversed, in the five or six hundred years of this stage of their development, virtually all the Fertile Crescent and had absorbed racial or ethnic elements from every part of this great expanse of the civilized world. They were a kind of synthesis of the population elements living there at that time.

THE PROMISED LAND

The Children of Israel re-entered the Land of Canaan—their promised land—sometime at the beginning of the Iron Age in the thirteenth century B.C. The exact date remains a matter of controversy. They, themselves, as we have already seen, were most probably a composite group—a blend of the local ethnic strains with which they had mingled not only earlier in Canaan but also during their long settlement in Egypt. Since the basic element in the population of which they were a part was Mediterranean, with an overlay of newer racial elements characterized by brachycephaly, the Israelites cannot have departed significantly from it.

They found on their return a Canaanite population probably not very different from themselves and a people closely related to them. These were the Israelites who had not participated in the migration to Egypt.[1] They had settled in the more thinly occupied hill country east of the plains occupied by the Canaanites and were apparently well established in north central Palestine when the conquest of Canaan began. Some scholars have interpreted biblical sources, combined with other bits of evidence, to mean that the Israelites, returning from Egypt, quickly, completely, and peacefully absorbed their cogeners.[2]

The Canaanites, however, entrenched in their towns and cities and occupying the richer lands of the coastal plain, were not to be absorbed in this fashion. The Israelites could enter the land and settle there only by conquest, and settlement and possession of the land were a prime motivating force among them. The old days of nomadism, a wandering life following the sheep and their requirements of pasturage, were gone. Cultural pressures and the adoption of sedentary life during the years in Egypt had created different needs. These demanded for their fulfilment ownership of the land.

The Bible records with remarkably accurate detail the conquest which the Israelites undertook in the thirteenth century B.C. and the immediately subsequent centuries. The impression one receives from reading this account is that the conquest was not at all like what one would expect in the modern world when one nation is arrayed against another in warfare. Conquest in such a case involves taking the seat of central authority and with it the total area. Canaan, on the contrary, was not fully organized as a State. Rather, it was a series of cities and towns, many of them at certain periods under the hegemony of a foreign empire, such as the Egyptian or the Hittite; but at other periods independent of each other or grouped in small principalities under powerful native chieftains. The Canaanites were, therefore, not a population identifying itself with a political entity whose fall might involve the entire nation, but a series of autonomous chieftaincies, any one of which might succumb without necessarily carrying the others down with it. Their community was based largely on a common language,

1. W. F. Albright, *From Stone Age to Christianity*, Philadelphia, Johns Hopkins Press, 1946.
2. The drama of the Egyptian sojourn and exodus and the subsequent crystallization of the religious framework of the Israelites in the Wilderness have quite naturally dominated the tradition preserved in the Bible. Thus the narrative has centred on the principal actors, leaving in obscurity the segments of Israel that were not participants in the main events of the epic of Israel. Only recently have scholars been able to reconstruct a number of episodes significant to us by careful analysis of the biblical text itself against the background of newly discovered contemporary documents.

a common culture, and the possession of a number of widely spread religious concepts and practices.

Since there was no integrated political centralization, the Israelites consequently were not obliged to conquer the whole land at once and, in any event, could not do so decisively. They could and did capture over a long period of time single cities, holding them or resettling them with their own people, while neighbouring towns might continue as Canaanite centres. It was, in other words, a slow process of infiltration and gradual conquest. And even when Israel had eventually taken a large number of settlements and had become the dominant power, there remained islands of Canaanite control not yet overcome or incorporated into the nation that Israel was becoming.

This kind of conquest has obvious consequences which are both implicit and, often enough, explicit in the biblical account. The conquest of a city, as far as the fate of its population was concerned, might lead to: (a) complete displacement either by the destruction of the entire population or by a forced resettlement; (b) the co-existence of the original population with an addition of Israelite settlers; or (c) a partial survival of the Canaanite occupants, usually the women and children, among the Israelite conquerors. Although it is not always manifest precisely what happened in each instance, it is clear enough that all these eventualities occurred at one time or another. In the light of practices widely current in those days, and indeed in our own as well, it is not unexpected to encounter these consequences of conquest. In any event, history itself makes it quite clear that the conqueror, with few exceptions, eventually absorbs or is absorbed by the conquered. One might conclude that whatever amalgamation or approximation to the Canaanite population the Israelites had failed to achieve during their genesis in an earlier age must have been completed as a result of their invasion of Canaan.

And if the incorporation of Canaanite women or the absorption of surviving segments of conquered cities was not enough to create a thorough intermingling, the continuation of unconquered Canaanite centres provided additional sources for gene flow between the two peoples. For despite the emphasis in the Scriptures on the hostilities that existed between the two camps, there is abundant reference to intimate cultural relationships and to actual intermarriage.

The use both by Canaanites and by Israelites of dialects of the same Semitic language provided a means of communication that must have enormously facilitated contact and cultural interchange. The proof of this is the fact that the Israelites were constantly having to be reminded that they were falling into practices anathematic to the purity of their religious faith. The reproaches are specific and thundering, with the vengeances of Jehovah invoked. The images of Canaanite gods, their apparently orgiastic rites, continued to exercise a fascination as long as the Canaanites survived as a people. We hear nothing more of these particular abominations once the Canaanites disappear.

Such cultural and religious borrowing might be also expected to encourage intermarriage. Again, the Bible records the fact that such miscegenation did take place. Genetic exchange of the magnitude suggested by this evidence can, of course, lead only to the conclusion that any racial or genetic distinctions that might have arisen would inevitably disappear. The forces which we can infer were in operation could have led to no other resolution, and even in the absence of a detailed documentation, which incidentally we are not very likely to discover, these issues appear inevitable.

The only published data on the population of Palestine or Canaan that can be assigned to this period from the re-entry of Israel to its effective dispersion 1,200 or 1,300 years later are far from adequate to the task of fully documenting this generalization. As far as they go, however, they do confirm it.

To begin with, the series of crania excavated by Macalister at Gezer includes one lot that can be dated to the early part of this period. In general, Macalister reported that they resembled the immediately preceding people, dating to the late Bronze Age. The tabular summations bear out the continuity of the earlier population. In the later period about 10 per cent of the skulls are brachycephalic. There is a reduction in the number of extremely long and narrow vaulted skulls, but the bulk of the individuals represented have retained the characteristic cranial proportions of the Mediterranean type. In other anatomical details this identification is borne out by a consistent assemblage of traits. The nose, for example, is fairly narrow and quite prominent. The orbits are characteristically high, with their horizontal axes tilted downward at their outer margins. Faces were generally narrow. Facial protrusion or prognathism was absent in both sexes except in a couple of crania.

Megiddo also has yielded some evidence on the Iron Age

population of Palestine. Although the data are meagre and fragmentary, Hrdlička has provided some details useful for comparative purposes. The few skulls that were relatively complete resemble the Gezer series in most traits, but Hrdlička noted some tendency in the total group toward brachycephaly, and, in particular, observed one individual with what he called an 'Assyroid' face. I am not at all clear what he meant by this since what are generally taken to be Assyroid traits are developments in the fleshy parts of the face which obviously are not available for observation in these crania.

The only other series of crania, aside from scattered individual ones, comes from Lachish and can be dated to about 700 B.C. Since this is the largest sample of a Palestinian population on record and comes besides from a city in the possession of the Israelites for over 500 years, it should help establish what the Israelites were like in this era of their history. But even so it must not be forgotten that Lachish represents only a single community and although Palestine was a small country with fairly easy access to all parts of it, some slight local differentiation may have survived from an earlier age or, indeed, have developed in the course of its complex history of invasion and conquest.

The sample of the inhabitants of Lachish in 700 B.C. was found in a series of underground chambers or tombs. The bones were disposed in unordered heaps and some of them were calcined from burning. Risdon[1] has concluded from this and from the peculiar age distribution of the individuals represented that they must have died in some kind of catastrophe or holocaust and were interred in this fashion.

Altogether, 695 crania were collected which means that there were at least that many individuals, although additional individuals may be uncounted in the miscellaneous disarticulated bones. The series, unfortunately, does not include all the skeletal fragments encountered, since the archaeologists reported that 'less attention was paid to the skulls of children owing to their supposed smaller anthropometrical value'. One might assume from this that had all the remains been available the series would have shown an even younger average age than it does. As it is, the age distribution reveals a remarkable scarcity of mature and senile individuals, with a heavy concentration on the young adult categories. Although the discrepancy when compared with comparably large samples,

---

1. D. L. Risdon, *Biometrika*, 1939, vol. 31, pp. 99-166.

ancient or modern, is great, its meaning is difficult to assess because the circumstances surrounding the origin of the sample itself are unknown.

Judging from Risdon's report of the series, these remains show little evidence of pathology or disease traceable in the bony or dental structures. The teeth appear to have been relatively free from caries and dental anomalies were infrequent.

Eight of the skulls, including male and female, had been artificially deformed during life. The practice of deliberately moulding the skull during infancy or childhood, when it is most malleable and easy to reshape either by bandages or by the use of pads or boards, is a cultural phenomenon. Risdon states that it was excessively rare if it occurred at all in Egypt, but was known in parts of western Asia, Crete, and Cyprus. Artificial deformation of the skull has also been reported by Kurth among the skulls found in Jericho as early as the Neolithic.

The deformed skulls of Lachish, therefore, suggest a survival in Palestine of an ancient cultural phenomenon, perhaps associated with a particular segment of the population. Certainly it is not an Israelite custom and its presence in over 1 per cent of the sample can scarcely be a chance inclusion of exotic individuals.

Although the osseous remains cannot be expected to tell us as much as would living organisms, they are the only direct evidence of ancient populations we have and we must extract what we can from them. One of the questions most frequently asked about any people, living or dead, is what is their origin and to what other known people are they related? The obvious way of answering this is by comparison. People who are so similar they cannot be distinguished from each other we consider in common practice to be related or identical in origin. Zoologists, with certain refinements of method, base their systems of classification on this same principle. The assumption, unless other evidence proves the contrary, is that an identity or close resemblance in a large number of morphological traits or developments must signify a genetic community. By the same token, a striking difference, or one that is significant by statistical measures, is regarded as arising from genetic difference.

Although modern genetic analyses and studies of organic plasticity have revealed to us that nature can be more complicated than this in certain circumstances, and that such assumptions are perhaps not tenable as an invariable rule, the fact is that degree of similarity of visible and measurable characteristics of organisms remains a fundamental tool for classifying and arranging organisms in many, if not most, situations. The reliability of this method increases with the number of items available for comparison, so that if two populations agree in a large galaxy of traits we can feel more confident in interpreting the result than when only one or two items are in question. In any event, the experience of generations of systematists who have used this method with conspicuous success cannot easily be set aside.

As far as human skeletal material is concerned, the problem is complicated beyond what faces the zoologist working with living, infra-human creatures. The soft parts and surface patterns so diagnostically useful in living men are either impossible or difficult to reconstruct from the bony structure that supports them. Comparative studies of the skeleton, therefore, are concentrated largely on the skull where the most significant differentiation seems to be concentrated. This means that the criteria for the classification of mankind, based on living subjects, is not always strictly identical or coterminous with systems based on cranial studies. Some errors of judgement and interpretation are accordingly possible and have to be carefully avoided.

It is fortunate in the case of the Lachish sample that the available crania were carefully examined and measured in far greater detail than most of the other ancient series from this region. By contrast, the other Palestinian samples are inadequate in size or in detail. Comparisons with them can, therefore, be only general. As far as it goes the Lachish series agrees with them quite well. The most ample, from Gezer in Israelite times, is very similar in the few items available for comparison. The Megiddo crania of comparable age also are reasonably like those from Lachish, allowing for the fact that the Megiddo population in the Iron Age is represented by only a few crania.

Of exceptional interest is the extraordinary identity of the Lachish crania with several of the fully documented and large series from Egypt. The resemblance was closest with a fourth-fifth dynasty series from Deshasheh and Medum in Lower Egypt and with eighteenth dynasty samples from Thebes and Abydos in Upper Egypt. On the basis of his statistical analysis, Risdon has concluded that the Lachish population of 700 B.C. might well represent an Egyptian colony: the similarity is so close for so many individual points of comparison.

The parallelism between Lachish and Egypt can scarcely be denied, but the conclusion drawn bears further scrutiny. The historical background for Israel around 700 B.C., the date assigned to the Lachish population, is fairly rich and reliable. There is no historical indication whatever that Egypt maintained a colony or a military garrison at Lachish at the time. If the population was descended from a much earlier colony, it is difficult to see how it might have preserved its genetic integrity through centuries of time. Intermarriage with the local Canaanite and Israelite people would have absorbed it into the local gene pool.

If, however, Canaan and Lower Egypt formed a racial continuum, perhaps of great antiquity, the similarity would fit into the picture I have presented here. The prevalence of what has been identified as a Mediterranean type, stretching at least from Mesopotamia to Canaan as late as the end of the Bronze Age, has already been stressed. The contemporary Egyptians, although sometimes differentiated as Hamites on linguistic grounds, share in fact the basic characteristics of the Mediterranean type.

The reasonableness of this view derives support from a comparison of the Lachish crania with a substantial group of others from Tepe Hissar III to the east of Mesopotamia in Iran. These were dated by Schmidt[1] who excavated them to the period between 3000 to 2000 B.C.,[2] and were reported by Krogman.[3] The Lachish crania compared with the Hissar III skulls[4] turn out to be as similar to them as they are with the Deshasheh and Medum series from Egypt. In fact, the Lachish means are rather more similar to the Iranians from Hissar in a number of items than they are to the Egyptians, with whom Risdon thought they were virtually identical. From this it would appear that as late as the Bronze Age the basic Mediterranean stock inhabiting the Fertile Crescent extended as far as Tepe Hissar. Smaller samples of population from Sialk and other Iranian sites bear out the existence of such a distribution. Thus a population, fairly homogeneous as these things go, occupied this vast stretch from Iran (and possibly beyond) to Egypt. Variously and at different times and places new elements began to appear and to merge with this old population. As the process continued with time, the evidence from a large number of sites

---

1. E. Schmidt, *Excavations at Tepe Hissar*, Philadelphia, The University Museum, 1937.
2. Some scholars place the period in question somewhat later.
3. W. M. Krogman, 'The People of Early Iran, etc.', *Amer. Journ. Phys. Anthrop.*, vol. 26, 1940.
4. It was necessary to regroup these crania into one pooled sample.

in Mesopotamia and in the fringing sites in Anatolia shows a complex pattern of modification which does not concern us here.

The interpretation, therefore, to which we are led is that in the time of Lachish the racial community which was once so widespread throughout the Fertile Crescent had survived at least between Egypt and Israel, and that the Israelites were still fairly representative of it.

According to the archaeological evidence, shortly after the Israelites had invaded Canaan from the hill country, the southern coast was overrun and settled by a people known in Scripture as Philistines. Their cultural remains, well known from excavations, link them with the world of Crete, Cyprus, and Asia Minor. It is very probable that they were so-called Pelasgians, the people who preceded the Classic Greeks and were absorbed by them. Little is known about the racial affinities of these newcomers, but the fact that they brought with them a Pelasgian kind of culture would suggest, but not necessarily prove, that they were biologically connected with them. The Pelasgians, however, were themselves not sufficiently homogeneous from place to place for this appellation to mean very much in identifying the Philistines. The Cypriotes, for example, were distinctly different from the Cretans, and those from Asia Minor, although not too well known, possessed still other marks of differentiation.

That the Israelites came into contact with the Philistines is too well known from Biblical sources to require underlining. As in the case of the Canaanites, the Amorites, and the other tribal groups the Israelites encountered, fought and later married; the Philistines also went through a similar cycle. Defeated and victorious by turn, they too intermarried with Israelites. The most celebrated union was Samson's with Delilah. Although one cannot now with our meagre recovered information hope to estimate how large or indeed what kind of contribution the Philistines made to the amalgam of local groups that Israel was and had become, they too added something.

From 700 B.C.—the date of Lachish—on down to the Roman times and the effective dispersion of the Israelites, we have only a handful of published records of crania that have either been positively identified as Jewish[1] or may be presumed to

---

1. After the conquest of the Kingdom of Israel by the Assyrians in the latter part of the eighth century B.C., the Kingdom of Judah alone survived. Hence the Hebrews became known as the Children of Judah, or Jews.

be.[1] Five were discovered at Wadi-en-Nar, in the vicinity of Jerusalem and were dated at around 200 B.C. Two others came from the Mount of Olives and are assigned to the time of Christ. An eighth specimen was located at a site between Bethlehem and Helvan, but its age can be given only very approximately as first millennium B.C. These eight skulls are far from being an adequate sample of the Jewish population of Palestine during these centuries but, nevertheless, it is worth noting that for so small a series they reflect a very considerable degree of heterogeneity. A couple of the crania depart distinctly from the Mediterranean type which appeared to be the prevailing one among the earlier inhabitants and suggest the appearance of a racial strain found more commonly in Anatolia and Asia Minor. The traditional type, however, continues to be well represented in the others.

This increasing physical variety in the population fits very well into the frame of a culture which we know, both from rich archaeological remains and from the historical evidence provided by the Bible, had become cosmopolitan in many ways. As Palestine grew prosperous, with flourishing cities and with an expanding trade and economy, it became attractive to traders, merchants, and artisans. Its very geographic position made it in times of peace and prosperity a natural route between the two powerful centres of contemporary civilization and wealth—Egypt and Mesopotamia. Thus being drawn into world economy, it inevitably received currents of population movement which, although minor in relative numbers, would have contributed to an increasing heterogeneity.

Potentially of far greater significance were the foreign elements introduced by the Assyrian policy of reshuffling conquered populations. Expanding from the nucleus of their empire in Mesopotamia, the Assyrians were to become the dominant force in the middle years of the first millennium B.C., and eventually to overrun virtually all of the Near East. It was inevitable that Palestine, like other small and relatively weak States that stood in the path of this colossus, should be confronted with its might. The ineffectual resistance that the tiny Kingdoms of Israel and Judah[2] could muster quickly collapsed before the superior power of the Assyrians.

1. See H. Virchow, 'Ein Schädel aus altpalästinischen Grabkammern', *Zt. Ethnol.*, vol. 60, 1929; K. D. Henckel, 'Zur Kraniologie Palästinas', *Zt. Morph. u. Anthrop.*, vol. 28, 1930.
2. The original united kingdom that flourished under David and Solomon had become split into two related but separate kingdoms: Israel with its capital in Samaria, and Judah with its capital in Jerusalem.

First to feel the devastation of Assyrian conquest was the Kingdom of Israel. Sargon, the King of Assyria, commemorated his victory in 721 B.C. with an inscription found at his palace at Khorsabad. The text runs:

'I besieged, and conquered Samaria, led away as booty 27,290 inhabitants of it. I formed from among them a contingent of 50 chariots and made the remaining inhabitants assume their social positions. I installed over them an officer of mine and imposed upon them the tribute of the former King. . . . The town I rebuilt better than it was before and settled therein people from countries which I had myself conquered.'

The Bible records the same event in 2 Kings xvii. 24 in the words: 'And the King of Assyria brought men from Babylon and from Cuthah, and from Avva, and from Hamath and Sepharvaim, and placed them in the cities of Samaria instead of the Children of Israel; and they possessed Samaria, and dwelt in the cities thereof.'

Earlier, in 738 B.C., Tiglath-pileser had made incursions which were recorded on stone slabs that Layard found at Nimrud.

'As for Menahem I overwhelmed him like a snowstorm . . . all its [Israel's] inhabitants and their possessions I led to Assyria.'

The parallel reference in 2 Kings xv. 29 is:

'In the days of Pekah, King of Israel, came Tiglath-pileser, King of Assyria, and took Ijob and Abel-beth-maacah, and Janoah, and Kadesh, and Hazor and Gilead and Galilee, all the land of Naphtali; and he carried them captive to Assyria.'

Sennacherib by his own account also deported a large contingent of the population from Israel.

'I drove out . . . 200,150 people, young and old, male and female, horses, mules, donkeys, camels, big and small cattle beyond counting and considered them booty.'

These references to ancient disasters have a peculiar poignancy by their very terseness, and the human tragedy and suffering they imply is heightened by their failure to mention them. If the value of the Bible as a source of history, moreover, remains in question, the extraordinary agreement between these independent records should serve to settle it. But of special interest to this inquiry is the indubitable evidence they present that profound replacements had taken place.

The Assyrians, more than any other ancient people, had developed a consistent policy of resettlement of conquered populations. This was a device by which potential rebellion could be discouraged. Obviously in this case, they had removed a large number of Hebrews—apparently a considerable if unknown proportion—from their homeland and replaced them with people drawn from other parts of the empire.

We can only infer what the consequences of this major event must have been. The Hebrews settled abroad have come to be known as 'lost'. I shall have some suggestions to make about them later. The foreign contingents brought in by the Assyrians to replace them were settled among the remaining Hebrews and apparently the process of acculturation began.

'And so it was, at the beginning of their dwelling there, that they feared not the Lord [of the Hebrews]; therefore the Lord sent lions among them, which killed some of them. Wherefore they spoke to the King of Assyria, saying: "The nations which thou hast carried away and placed in the cities of Samaria, know not the manner of the God of the land; therefore he hath sent lions among them, and, behold, they slay them, because they know not the manner of the land."

'Then the King of Assyria commanded, saying: " Carry thither one of the priests whom ye brought from thence; and let them go and dwell there, and let him teach them the manner of the God of the land." So one of the priests whom they had carried away from Samaria came and dwelt in Beth-el, and taught them how they should fear the Lord.'[1]

Although the chronicler adds that the new nations 'feared the Lord' but continued to 'serve their graven images', we need not conclude from this that their Hebraicization was totally ineffective. It would have been remarkable if some of them were not absorbed into the Hebrew community, the dominant element in Israel and, as the record shows, one with considerable capacity for assimilation. But although concordance in religious belief and practice might certainly encourage intermarriage, it was, as we have already seen, not essential.

We are again faced with a similar paucity of reliable evidence, but with the same probabilities, when we consider the contacts which the Jews made during the following centuries when they were under the political control of the Ptolemies, Seleucids, and subsequently the Romans. In many ways the Seleucid influence penetrated most deeply and was more lasting. Under the dynasty founded by Alexander's general, Greek civilization, which had already begun to affect much of the

1.   2 Kings xvii. 17-25 ff.

eastern Mediterranean, Palestine included, now as the official civilization of the nation's rulers achieved an ascendancy that attracted to it in particular the wealthier Jews. The extent of Palestine's Hellenization in secular things emerged beyond question in the unprejudiced remains of that era. Public buildings reflect Greek architectural style; pottery and decoration copied Greek models. Arenas were built for Greek games played by naked youths—certainly a revolutionary change in traditional Jewish attitudes and customs. Greek inscriptions on tombs and elsewhere testify to the adoption of Greek as a common language. And many, most frequently among the more susceptible upper classes, also took Greek names in preference to their ancient Hebraic ones.

Undoubtedly much of this kind of assimilation was merely cultural. But considering the increased mobility that the richer Jews and the merchants were able now to enjoy as members of the larger Seleucid empire, and, conversely, the greater freedom with which foreigners from Asia Minor and elsewhere could enter Palestine, this cultural situation could scarcely fail to bring into the Jewish community representatives of the larger world. Both during the era of the Seleucids and under the Romans, these absorptive tendencies existed. To what extent, unfortunately, cannot yet be determined.

Finally, to illustrate the continuing accretions of the Jewish community, two historical episodes are worth mentioning because they demonstrate in a specific fashion the forces at work. The first one involves the Herodian line that ruled around the time of Christ. Although Herod was a Jew, his family was of Edomite origin. In fact, the Herods, along with other Edomites in the Idumaea which was situated south of Judaea, had been forced about a century earlier to adopt formally the Jewish religion. The conversion had already been partially accomplished through the natural assimilative processes of Edomite contiguity with Jewish foci of influence and by their previous acceptance of the Israelite patriarchs.

The other concerns the archaeological discovery at Marisa in Judaea of a series of tombs cut out of limestone rock. They are dated to the latter part of the third century B.C. and are especially notable for their elaborate painted decoration. But they have another implication for us. The tombs were prepared for the reception of the leaders of a Sidonian colony that had been established here in the heart of Judaea. In other words, foreign trading communities were still being established in

Palestine during the Hellenistic period and introduced new stocks among the established people.

The synthesis which the early Israelites had become by virtue of their origin, their mobility ranging from Mesopotamia to Egypt via Canaan, and their conquest and absorption of a variety of local tribal groups in Canaan, had not frozen into an isolated population entity. All during the centuries, down to their dispersion on a wider world stage, they continued to absorb new elements brought into the country as a result of world events and expanding economies. Unconsciously they were functioning as one of the active centres of gene redistribution for the part of the world to which they belonged. Although undoubtedly much remained of the older population that conquered Canaan a millennium or more earlier, it had altered in certain significant ways.

THE DIASPORA

The final dispersion of the Jews from the land where they had lived as Jews for 2,000 years, and where some of their ancestors had lived before for unknown millennia, is commonly dated from the destruction of Jerusalem by the Romans in 70 A.D. The fact is, however, that the dispersion was a protracted movement that actually began long before this and continued long after. By the sixth and seventh centuries A.D., it was virtually complete. The Jewish population in Palestine was by then reduced to a small, unimportant remnant clinging to its ancient seats and monuments. The vast majority was now settled in almost every civilized area from Mesopotamia to the Atlantic.

The Diaspora may be said to have begun with Nebuchadnezzar in 586 B.C. who had carried off into Babylon a large portion of the population of Jerusalem after destroying the city itself. Even earlier his predecessors had also resettled Jews from the Kingdom of Israel in Mesopotamian cities. Although these earlier victims of Assyrian aggression have long been counted lost, it is not unlikely that some if not all of them survived to be absorbed by the later captives from Jerusalem.

Forced upon them as it was, the Babylonian captivity however turned out to be more than this. It also became an independent settlement, yet remaining a part of Judaism—a fragment geographically separated from the main body. Because it was the first permanent major division of the Jewish people after they had achieved a fully developed national self-consciousness and also because issues characteristic of later stages of the Diaspora became manifest here, it is in a very real sense the prototype of the many disparate colonies in which the Jews were to live down to the present time. Since the Diaspora has had a profound affect on virtually every aspect of the life of the Jews and on their biological history, it is of some value to examine the Babylonian story.

The later books of the Old Testament provide invaluable details for the reconstruction of the significant aspects of the Captivity. It was a period that exerted a formative influence on Judaism. And if this is little known or appreciated outside scholarly circles, the psychological significance of the exile itself in creating a favourable milieu for such developments has passed virtually unnoticed.

The attitudes that evolve in a group of people severed from their homeland and from their culture fall into a pattern that almost seems to conform to laws of social dynamics. Among other things, such a detached colony tries to reconstitute initially as best it can a simulacrum of its inherited civilization and way of life. Anything less seems a grievous loss and a deprivation. Objects, manners, customs and ideas associated with the home country acquire an enhanced value as though group survival depended upon them—as perhaps it does. In any case, these items of culture or belief easily take on symbolic meaning and serve as a focus for the maintenance of a group spirit. Frequently enough, common origin and tradition also serve, at least for a time, to hold such groups together when they find themselves set down in an alien population. They prefer to live close to one another, to rebuild a cultural milieu in which they can feel at home, and thus to derive what support and comfort they can from it.

History and our own living world are full of expressions in varying degree of this universal reaction. The fixation on England and English civilization as a source of inspiration and as an example to emulate was once characteristic of the American colonies and now is to be found in such outlying British communities as those in New Zealand, Australia, and Kenya. Even after generations of residence abroad, England is still 'home' to the inhabitants of her settlements abroad. And the visiting Englishman, because he symbolizes the ascendancy of English values to the colonists, enjoys a special prestige among them. The highest compliment to pay anything in a British colony is to say it is typically British.

In nineteenth-century America, little Italies, Germanies, Irelands, etc., emerged wherever settlers from European countries established themselves in number. Here the language and traditions of the home country were cherished and preserved. Lest one imagine that this is a phenomenon confined to more highly evolved civilizations, many illustrations could also be cited from among simpler cultures.

The Jews, carried away to Babylonia 2,500 years or more ago, cannot have reacted differently to the loss of community with their homeland. And indeed, I think the desire to surround themselves with as much of their tradition as they could must have served as a powerful stimulus, if not the prime motivating force, that saw during the Babylonian Captivity a special reverence for the 'Torah' as a symbol of the traditional law of the people. The emergence of a class of scribes who by writing down the 'Torah' could preserve it and make it available to the exiles must have been enormously influenced by this psychological need of a people bereft of the normal sources of cultural support. Thus one can discern in this situation a reaction that led to developments of fundamental importance to the history of Judaism. The later prophets like Ezekiel, as well as such leaders as Ezra and Nehemiah, reflect all this, both explicitly and implicitly.

When Cyrus, 50 years after the destruction of Jerusalem by Nebuchadnezzar, allowed the Jews to return to Palestine, 42,462, according to Josephus,[1] elected to return. Although among those who had been led away were many of the priests and leading men, leaving the original community bereft of its natural leadership, it is not without significance that the population that had remained in Jerusalem had done nothing whatever to repair the damaged Temple. And it is relevant that for the returning exiles, on the contrary, this was their first and most burning desire, for the Temple had meant much to them during the years of their separation. We shall probably never know to what extent the experience of the Babylonian Captivity, with all its psychological overtones, gave force, direction, and form to the Jewish faith. There can be little doubt that it was profound.

But if it is characteristic of first generation exiles and

---

1. Josephus, *The History of the Jews.*

colonists to feel deeply the severance from home and to cherish fiercely the symbol of their lost world, there is another side to the colonial coin. For as the colony continues, the ties with home and the values of the symbol tend to weaken progressively in the succeeding generations born abroad. If there is no competing culture, the process takes the form of a slow growth of an indigenous, locally adapted civilization with its own peculiar character, although related to the original one. But if on the other hand the exiles are planted in the midst of a foreign civilization, the process takes the form of assimilation to it. There are countless instances to illustrate the inexorability of this assimilative pressure. When it does not occur or develops only partially, there are always special circumstances that have interfered with the expected outcome. In the general picture these are the exception rather than the rule.

In the Babylonian colony, only 50 years had elapsed when Cyrus allowed the Jews to return to Jerusalem. Despite the relatively brief span of time a very considerable number of Jews did not elect to go. The slow, subtle adjustment to the new world had grown strong and overt in the generation born abroad.

The children born in Babylon, not knowing life in Jerusalem save at second-hand from their parents, conditioned by the life and customs around them, learning the language of the people among whom they lived, inevitably were at home there. It is evident enough from the Bible that many of the Babylonian Jews had made just this kind of adjustment and had become natives in their new country. Their careers, some highly successful, were inevitably intertwined with the country of their birth and not with that of their heritage. The simple fact was that they had become Babylonian by nationality. Even Nehemiah after visiting Jerusalem and aiding in the reconstruction of the Temple eventually returned to Babylon.

The colony continued there down to modern times as an active centre of Jewish faith, and at various periods when Judaism was weak and threatened elsewhere it served as a veritable tower of strength. It is pertinent to ask why it did survive when experience would lead one to expect the more usual dissolution of a culturally detached community like this. And because this once unique phenomenon was repeated over and over again in the subsequent history of the Diaspora, it is all the more central to understanding the underlying process that made the biological survival of the Jewish people possible. An analysis, however, of the conditions mainly responsible for

145

it may be more appropriate after we have surveyed briefly the course of the dispersion down to our own times.

If the Babylon colony represents the first major settlement of Jews outside Palestine, it was not long before others began to appear. The prevailing direction of movement was, as one might expect, controlled by political, cultural, and economic factors which were reorientated after the fall of the Persian Empire. Under the attacks of Alexander in 333-331 B.C., that great Mesopotamian Empire established by the Assyrians and inherited by the Persians completely collapsed. Greek civilization and trade, which had already been penetrating Asia Minor, the Black Sea, and the eastern half of the Mediterranean, now had a clear road with no obstacles from any rival power. The Persian Empire and the additional conquests of Alexander fell to his generals who eventually divided the enormous area into separate spheres. Palestine fell initially to Ptolemy, seated in Egypt, although his rival, Seleucus, with his Syrian domains bordering it to the north, disputed his claim. In 198 B.C. the Seleucid Dynasty finally took possession and held it, with a brief interlude of Jewish resurgence under the Maccabees until it was engulfed in the irresistible advance of the Roman Empire.

The set of historical events during the centuries between Assyria and Rome had shifted the centre of the civilized world westward from its earlier site in Mesopotamia. To accommodate the growing importance of the eastern Mediterranean, new foci of political, economic, and cultural energy arose. Even Egypt, which was enjoying a renewed but final burst of glory, built Alexandria to face the Mediterranean which now was the centre of everything.

To help found his new city, soon to become one of the most brilliant of the Hellenistic world, people from various parts of his empire were encouraged by Ptolemy to settle there. Among others, he brought in Jews who participated in the founding and development of it. Under its favourable regime they expanded in number until they formed a large proportion of the total population. As in Babylon, they maintained their own worship and by this were held together as a group. Nevertheless, they quickly became Alexandrian in their attachments and in their culture. And because they had become Greek in speech as well, the Septuagint version of the Bible, written in that language, became necessary. The synagogue, however, a new feature in Judaism developing among Jews parted from Palestine and the Temple, served as a focus for religious life. And until the Temple was again and finally destroyed by the

Romans, the Alexandrian Jews, as did Jews in other colonies, made annual contributions to it as an expression of loyalty to their faith. This custom curiously suggests the later practice in Christendom of regular support of Rome by the provincial churches.

Less dramatic than Babylon and less notable than Alexandria, numerous other settlements of Jews continued to spread within the Hellenistic world. As conditions in Palestine worsened with population pressure and unemployment mounting drastically, and as technological opportunities opened up in various parts of this world, Jews emigrated as have other people before and since for similar reasons. Artisans with negotiable skills, landless labourers, business men and even soldiers as mercenaries were forced to seek a livelihood abroad. They settled in Crete, Cyprus, various ports on the coast of Phoenicia and Asia Minor, in Syria, in the trading towns on the Black Sea, and in new cities like Antioch with their demand for labour, skills, and settlers. Some of them went to the Mediterranean shores of North Africa and when the Romans replaced the Seleucids, they went to Rome too. In the time of Josephus a sizeable colony was already not only there but in such Roman provinces as Spain and Gaul. The distribution among the smaller communities was probably a secondary movement from such major foci as Rome, Alexandria, and Antioch.

Most of those colonies, except in the large metropolises like Babylon, Antioch, Alexandria, and Rome, were probably relatively small. It is impossible now to know how many of them there actually were before the destruction of Jerusalem by the Romans. But their number must have been considerable, to judge by the estimates of Jewish population settled in the various parts of the Roman Empire. These population figures are, of course, estimates only and lack the accuracy of a modern census, but they are of interest if only for the general idea they convey of the extent of Jewish distribution at that time.

In the year 70 A.D., one estimate[1] enumerates a total of about 4.5 million, of whom 3.5 million lived in various parts of the Roman Empire and 1 million in Palestine. Although these figures are only roughly approximate, they do indicate the extent to which Jews had already spread throughout the Roman

---

1. Arthur Ruppin, 'The Jewish Population of the World', in: *The Jewish People, Past and Present*, New York, Jewish Encyclopedic Handbooks, Central Yiddish Culture Organization, 1946, vol. 1.

world so that more of them were now established outside than inside Palestine.[1]

One plausible explanation for the large number of Jews outside Palestine is based on the active proselytism that existed at that time. It is known, for example, that conversion to Judaism was common enough to lead many communities of Jews to create a special class of adherents with full recognition being reserved for their children. Among the converts was the ruling family of the Kingdom of Adiabene, a fragment of the ancient Assyrian Empire. It was perhaps the existence of these Jewish communities abroad that was one of the reasons the Apostles wandered as widely as they did preaching the Gospel. They were carrying to their co-religionists in their far-flung settlements the new word from the Holy Land. One wonders what might have been the course of Christianity if this settlement pattern of the Jews had not existed.

Under Roman rule the situation of the Jews in Palestine continued to deteriorate. Official corruption, heavy taxation and, perhaps most intolerable of all, interference with religious freedom, deposited on many people a burden of hopelessness that could be eased only by emigration. The destruction of Jerusalem by Titus in 70 A.D., and the defeat again sixty-odd years later under Hadrian, accelerated the decline. From then on, the Jewish community in Palestine was a dying branch. During the following centuries its intellectual leadership was vigorous enough to produce the Mishna, but with the passage of time it slowly but inevitably slipped away to be assumed by the Babylonian and other offshoots. Its economy fell to a level that was unable to support the population. Gradually, except for a tiny remnant, the country was emptied and the land became a blighted area given over once more to nomadism and precarious living in the few surviving towns. When Obadiah of Bertinoro visited Jerusalem in the fifteenth century he found a mere 4,000 families, of which only 70 were Jewish.

In the later Roman Empire, the distribution of Jewish settlements continued to expand, not only in its eastern section but also in the western. Along the southern shore of the Mediterranean they reached the region of present-day Algiers and Morocco; on the northern side, Spain and Gaul (France); and

---

1. Again we see here an interesting parallel with modern times in the similar results of recent migration patterns in certain European countries. There are, for example, more people of Irish, English, Portuguese, and Spanish descent settled abroad than are to be found in the home countries.

as early as 321 A.D., Jews were resident in the Rhine country of Germany.

After Constantine (306-337 A.D.), however, the situation of these settlements and the position of the Jews generally began to deteriorate significantly. Pagan Rome had been tolerant and permissive toward religious variation and in general the Jews had not been penalized in their rights as citizens for their religious separation. With the adoption of Christianity, however, as the State religion by Constantine, repressive legislation against Judaism was enacted. And after the division of the empire into an eastern and a western branch, there was little to choose between them as far as religious persecution and disabling measures were concerned.

The irruption of the barbarian hordes into the West, however, eventually made the empire based on Rome far more hazardous for Jewish survival. Having been gradually restricted in their economic activities, they found themselves in a decidedly precarious position with the general collapse of the imperial economy. Their numbers at any rate declined sharply. How much was the effect of economic pressure and how much was the result of the gradual dissolution of isolated communities during a period of increasing deterioration and despair is difficult to establish.

Mounting religious intolerance played some part, for the record of Visigothic Spain is sufficiently documented to disclose that violence and the threat of forceful conversion drove many Jews from the country. Some apparently went to North Africa where there were communities of Jews that gave them refuge. Others went north into southern France where old settlements also existed.

As the tide of the Diaspora ebbed away in the West, it came to a flood in the East, particularly in Babylonia. Under the Sassanian Empire the Jewish population increased there to the point of embracing the majority of Jewry, who were organized in a semi-autonomous way under a hereditary exilarch. Here once again spiritual leadership flourished as the communities in the West entered a period of harassment and decline.

With the seventh century a new tide in the affairs of the Jews swept in with the rise of Islam as a world power.[1] Inevitably,

---

1. The reader will find in A. Steinberg's 'The History of the Jews in the Middle Ages and Modern Times', in: *The Jewish People, Past and Present*, New York, Jewish Encyclopedic Handbooks, Central Yiddish Culture Organization, 1946, an excellent summary of this complex period.

since the bulk of the Jews were concentrated in the Meso-potamian area and in Asia Minor, they entered into intimate contact with Islam, first as the dominant political power and later in the economic and cultural spheres. On the whole the relationship between them was marred by relatively few serious repressions. In fact, they became so intimate that Jews participated very fully in the Arabic cultural renaissance. The cultural interpenetration also reached a point where it engendered a profound psychological receptivity on both sides: Moslem sects incorporating Judaic ideas were balanced by Jewish sects recognizing Mohammed as a true prophet.

As the Moslem Empire expanded to take in the huge territory from India to Portugal, the Jews also participated in the economic life that opened up as a result. The spread of Islam to the west in particular brought in its train an active resettlement of Jews in North Africa and Spain. Minor lines of migration also diverged toward Italy as commercial intercourse between the Christian and Moslem world began to open up with the revival of Italy's economy.

In its effect on the future development of European Jewry this numerically secondary stream was highly significant. From it came settlers who moved north into the Frankish Empire, reviving some of the older communities dating to, Roman times and also establishing many new ones in what was to become France and Germany. But it was the contemporary settlements in Spain that formed the major nucleus in Europe, both in size and in the brilliance of their achievements. Under the Moors, the Jews enjoyed an era of fairly steady development and growth. And even when the Spaniards began the slow replace-ment of the Arab Kingdom, they continued at first the tolerant attitude of their predecessors. All this came to a tragic end in 1492 with the expulsion of the Jews from Spain. The complex motivations for it, compounded of religious, economic and his-torical causes, lie, however, outside the purposes of this account. Although some Jews had been forced into the adoption of Christianity, many of them were refugees to various Jewish communities in North Africa, the eastern Mediterranean, Italy, and Western Europe.

The Jews, however, who had preceded them to Western Europe in several waves of migration had had their own his-tory of ups and downs. The tolerant and happy conditions during the pagan Roman Empire were followed by harsh, repressive actions under Christian Rome. In Carolingian times there was again a return to more favourable circumstances that were rudely shattered during the period of religious tension symbolized by the Crusades. As in other episodes of deteriorating relations, the fundamental cause was not a single one but a mixture of factors, not the least of which was economic. Driven by restrictive legislation in their choice of occupation and dispossessed of a landed status by the rise of feudalism, the Jews were increasingly forced into commercial activities peculiarly antipathetic to the values of contemporary society.

The combination of social, economic, and historical events culminated in the twelfth and thirteenth centuries in the renewed displacement of ancient establishments of Jews. Many began to move eastward as Hungary, Poland, Lithuania, and the Ukraine began to emerge from their long benighted conditions and to offer inducements to attract Jewish settlers. Here and in Russia they met another stream of Jews, new and old ones, coming up from the Balkans and other parts of the Byzantine Empire and from the Crimea.

The Jews from this latter region were apparently a mixture derived from colonies whose origins are lost in antiquity with newer Jews from the former Kingdom of the Khazars. Between the Caspian and the Black seas, from the Volga to the Dnieper, this area of southern Russia had been overrun and conquered by an Asiatic people related to the Turks. In the eighth century their rulers and nobility had adopted the Karaite version of Judaism.[1]

Although conversion among their people was not obligatory, many followed their leaders and when the Kingdom was overthrown in 1240 A.D., they joined their co-religionists in the Byzantine Empire. Of these mixed groups some moved north where they encountered European Jews moving eastward; others remained in southern Russia.

With the advent of modern times, the Jews found themselves concentrated in Europe. Their ancient centres in the Near East and North Africa were either stagnant or decayed. And of their communities in Europe the western ones, although prosperous and making substantial advances in their cultural integration with their native countries, were relatively small. As they progressed in their increasing secularization they became subject to erosion through intermarriage and conversion to

---

1. Karaism, like various later Christian sects, considered orthodox Judaism to be distorted by its accretions and advocated a return to the Scriptures, with every man taking his guidance directly therefrom without the aid of Rabbinical interpretation.

Christianity. Numerically the principal settlements were now in Eastern Europe—Poland, the Baltic provinces, Russia, the Balkans—with secondary areas in Central Europe, particularly in Germany, Bohemia, Hungary, and Austria. Economic, political, cultural, in short historical, watersheds, had combined to collect in this region of Europe a substantial reservoir of the Jewish population of the world. These were the Ashkenazi, in distinction to the Sephardic Jews who had formerly developed a local tradition in Spain. Into their hands now had passed the principal guardianship of Jewish tradition, which during the long Diaspora had at various times been lodged in Babylonia, Alexandria, and Spain.

Speaking Yiddish, a dialectical form of German, which they had carried with them from their earlier homes in German-speaking countries, marked by customs that had become stabilized in their segregated settlements, these mainly are the Jews that were to become familiar to much of the Western World in recent times. For the great Jewish migrations that have once more redistributed these people in our own times came from these areas. It is true that some Sephardic Jews had joined older communities in the Netherlands, England, France, and other European countries in the sixteenth century. And some during the same epoch had also reached the New World, both South America and the United States. But by and large the great recent accession of Jewish population to the New World and to Western Europe occurred during the last one hundred years or so. Beginning around the middle of the nineteenth century with a moderate emigration from Germany that spread westward and crossed the Atlantic (mainly however for economic and political reasons) it gathered momentum within a generation as the Jews farther east began to participate in it. The conditions of the Jews in Polish lands and Russia had by the nineteenth century reached such a point of degradation and oppression that the rest of the world was justly appalled. Economic restrictions had imposed dire poverty on the mass of the Jewish people, population increase was pressing heavily on their limited resources, and murderous attacks were periodically let loose on their defenceless settlements. When, therefore, the industrial revolution in the West and the un-paralleled economic expansion in the New World, especially the United States, opened up the need and opportunity for immigrant settlers, the Jews in Eastern Europe responded with an overwhelming desire to escape to the freedom they saw there. The greatest number went to the United States, but considerable groups also settled in England and her various colonies. Even Germany became a receiving country as her industrial development expanded in the late nineteenth and early twentieth century.

If we count the present-day movement back to Israel as a return to the homeland from which it all began, then the last considerable redistribution of the Diaspora must be reckoned as the flight from Germany and Austria during Hitler's ascendancy. Although a large number of German and an even larger number of Polish Jews were murdered outright, some escaped. By the standards of Jewish migration in the latter part of the nineteenth and early twentieth centuries, it was only a trickle. But despite its numerical unimportance it was a significant migration in that it contained a high proportion of outstanding leaders in every kind of intellectual pursuit and it was widely distributed.

From this summary account of the odyssey of the Jewish people one might derive the notion that despite their peregrinations they had surmounted all their trials more or less intact as a people. The common conception, indeed, is one in which Jewish settlements either survived intact through the ages, holding their populations firmly within their religious bounds or, when dislodged, moved on to more suitable locations where they continued their existence. This is only partially true. The fact is that any simple generalization can scarcely cover the fortunes of so many individual communities exposed to such a diversity of conditions. Although there is a kind of pattern to all this, it is not a simple or a single one for the thousands upon thousands of colonies in scores of countries during twenty centuries and more.

One aspect of the Diaspora, frequently overlooked, is the attrition suffered by the Jews through cultural and religious assimilation. Aside from the losses in numbers that were common both to them and to the general population as a result of the protracted economic decline after the fall of the Roman Empire, they also lost members during times of general prosperity. The Italian community for example, although an ancient establishment, has failed to keep pace with the growth of the general population. The losses through acculturation and abandonment of ties with Judaism has kept it small. Similarly, many ancient colonies of Jews in France have disappeared as such, but not because they were oppressed. In the nineteenth century the rate of intermarriage between Jews and Christians in Germany had attained proportions that threatened to reduce the older communities drastically by this process. In England, too, the tendency of upper-class Jews to become Christian and intermarry outside the faith had drained off a considerable number of older families. Even in the United States the relatively large group of Jews living in Philadelphia during colonial days has virtually disappeared by absorption into the general population. Although the evidence is less well documented for non-European countries, particularly during earlier times, it is plain something of the same kind also happened in Moslem countries, where Jews were often highly acculturated to Arabic civilization. There are instances of voluntary assimilation. Equally effective were the forced conversions such as those in Spain where an unknown but apparently sizeable group was lost to Judaism.

That this assimilation of Jews took place need not surprise us. It is, if anything, what one might expect of families long settled in a country, speaking its language, sharing its culture, and feeling themselves through long residence to be natives. The subtle pressures to abandon Judaism and the unpredictable disabilities of a minority group are powerful agents.

These losses, if they were random ones from among a homogeneous people, would perhaps have little significance biologically. There is, however, some indication, as we shall see, that the dispersed Jewish population was not homogeneous. These losses, therefore, may well have had consequences on the gene frequencies now found among Jewish populations.

The question that inevitably suggests itself in connexion with the extraordinary history of the whole Diaspora is one that was indicated early in this chapter. If the general tendency is for detached groups of people to be absorbed into the population of the country where they settle, why have the Jews managed to survive even in part after 2,500 years of dispersion? The answer is too complex to document fully here. But since the continuity of the Jewish people is part of their biological history, I am offering a brief interpretation.

It is usual to say in this connexion that religion played the determining role. There is no doubt that it certainly was a highly significant factor. But without distorting its influence, other factors, particularly cultural ones, must also be given due importance. To appreciate this point the nature of adherence to Judaism must be understood. Judaism is more than a religious system regulating man's spiritual relations with God. It also prescribes rules of conduct between man and man, and between man and his natural environment. Every aspect of daily life is covered in the total system of Judaic belief. The dietary laws that govern the kinds and classes of food are only the better known of many similar regulations for other types of behaviour. This ethical content of Judaism is not, of course, unique. It may be found also in Christianity, but in its extent and pervasiveness it forms a sharp contrast with Christianity. Mohammedanism is in this respect rather more similar. The cultural, ethical, and spiritual are all so interwoven in Judaism that the effect of all this is that an orthodox Jew faithfully practising his religion is also conforming to what is a cultural norm. Thus a Jewish community established in a Gentile world differs not only in religious practices but also in cultural behaviour. The Jew observes the Sabbath, he requires special methods of processing his food supply, and in other ways organizes his life and values in a recognizably distinctive way. And to ease the business of providing these necessities he often prefers to live with other Jews. This has given an aspect of separatism to Jewish communities and has posed for them one of their major problems: how to preserve their traditions while participating in the general life of their country. When they have emphasized the latter, they have run the risk of losing their members; when they have insisted on rigid observance of tradition, they have run the risk of alienating their non-Jewish neighbours.

In the pagan days of the Diaspora, and later during periods of less marked religious intolerance, it was this cultural aspect of Judaism that served to segregate Jewish colonies and thus make them targets for oppression when social tensions required some form of release. Religion itself, whatever it may have meant to the Jews, was curiously ambivalent in Rome and Babylon for example. The pagan religions, although they differed from one another in their deities and rites, were remarkably receptive. The Greeks, Romans, and Egyptians like other pagans borrowed quite freely from each other. And a pagan might follow the religious customs of the nation where he happened to live without feeling that he had violated some sacred injunction to which he was committed.

At the same time, political power and religion were embodied in the head of the State, so that a failure to submit to the worship of the king or emperor as god could seem to mean a repudiation of his political authority as well.

The Jews, however, were the first people in the pagan world to evolve a monotheistic religion that explicitly forbade the worship of other gods and the use of alien rituals as abominations and sins. They were enjoined to maintain the purity of their faith. Any departure from the canon or any accretion of foreign beliefs was counted as an abandonment of Judaism. This extraordinary strictness, this refusal to accept other gods seemed to their contemporaries odd, stiff-necked, and even suspicious of evil intent. Nowadays, when other monotheistic religions enjoin on their adherents a similar devotion to their beliefs, this behaviour is admissible and respected. The Romans, in particular, who had encountered no such resistance to their official pantheon elsewhere were astonished at, perplexed by, and resentful of such an attitude. When they, for example, took steps to suppress Jewish religious practices it was, however, less for religious reasons than for political ones.

During periods, however, of intense religious feeling in later Christian times, religion as such undoubtedly contributed more strongly to the repression of Jewish groups and the violence toward them. Although even then cultural and economic factors were also deeply involved.

Thus because the Jews in practising their religion inevitably created a kind of sub-culture, they were exposed to the suspicion that any cultural difference evokes, particularly in immature societies. This, when combined with economic or religious factors brought on by historical events, often led to measures of repression. But repression has a tendency to evoke a corresponding resistance and to fill its objects with a burning faith to adhere to their principles. Jewish communities have often dissolved under benign and tolerant conditions and have closed ranks when malevolent forces were directed toward them.

Among other conditions contributing to Jewish survival are the absence of a highly centralized hierarchical structure of religion, and a distribution throughout so wide a range of Asiatic and European countries. Had Judaism been organized as a world religion, with a central authority like the Pope, and a closely intermeshed system of administration and control, any destruction of its central source of power might have left its communities helpless and easily subject to dissolution. The strength of Judaism lay in its extreme flexibility in the face of disaster. Each congregation was virtually independent, relying on the authority of the Torah, Mishna, and other sacred writings. The destruction of one congregation consequently did not inevitably bring down the others with it.

The distribution of the Jews through many different countries and civilizations also provided a sort of insurance. At times when conditions were particularly severe in one country, as for example in Visigothic Spain, they were favourable elsewhere. And when Western European Jews were scarcely holding their own or were declining, those in Eastern European countries were increasing and able to replenish them.

IN THE FULLNESS OF TIME

For 2,000 years, more or less, the Jews have maintained themselves as a strange anomaly: a people with a continuing identity but divided into discontinuous and often isolated populations between which communications were only intermittent at best and sometimes completely non-existent. This was an anomaly all the stranger, as the rest of the world became more and more committed to highly centralized States and fully organized national entities. As far as mere physical dispersion is concerned, the Jews in their colonization had been earlier than but no different from various other people. The Chinese, for example, established trading centres throughout South-East Asia and the adjacent islands; the Indians settled in the Malay Peninsula, Indonesia and even Fiji; the Arabs founded commercial stations in East Africa and in other areas bordering the Indian Ocean; the European countries dotted the entire earth with their settlements. Where the Jews differed from these not unusual expansive migrations was in the loss of a permanent centre—a homeland. The situation in which the Jews consequently found themselves has no close parallel among other peoples. It can only be likened to such a hypothetical one as might arise if Britain were to cease being British, leaving all its dominions, colonies and people of British descent connected only by a shared language and a cherished tradition. Perhaps a closer analogy would be the Chinese, Arabic, or Indian colonies, because they were mostly relatively small groups in much larger native populations, whereas many of the British colonies are almost exclusively British. That some Jewish communities survived is, as we have already seen, the result of the complex interplay of cultural, social, economic, and religious factors. But having survived, the thread that held them together was their adherence to the Torah and the Judaic regulations inscribed in the Mishna.

The historical knowledge of common origin and the feeling of belonging to a distinct tradition gave to Jewish groups throughout the world a sense of unity that has masked the diversity that had arisen among them—a diversity in part cultural but also genetic and, by extension, racial. Despite their community of origin the various settlements diverged from one another in a number of ways. They spoke the language of their countries; they adopted prevalent styles of dress; they followed the modes of behaviour and were influenced by the ideas and values with which they came into contact. Thus by the natural process of cultural assimilation and by varying degrees of adaptation, each group accumulated differences from the others which their isolation only intensified. Such a development is not inconsistent with the preservation of a kind of sub-culture or minority status which, it must be remembered, varied from highly tenuous to fairly conspicuous degrees of recognizability. Membership in such a group need not and did not automatically prevent assimilation in the cultural areas not already defined by it. Indeed, the degree of integration may reach a virtually complete unity with the dominant culture. And in no instance would such a group be impervious to the subtle and profound influence of the country where it had become native.

The rise, however, of cultural diversity need not necessarily imply any corresponding biological effects. And yet some of the conditions responsible for the one have to be considered for possible influence on the other. I propose now to examine the biological consequences to the Jewish people that have come from their long and peculiar experience as a highly fragmented population living under a considerable range of cultural and geographical conditions and reacting to possible selective factors to which their history might have exposed them.

It is odd, in the light of their past, that the Jews are often considered, and much effort expended to prove them to be a distinct race. The documentation of their own writings, if nothing else were available, should convince us that during their residence in Palestine they had absorbed elements of every tribal and ethnic strain that had entered the country. Through this accretion they had in effect become a kind of synthesis of the populations existing in the area surrounding Palestine. Because Palestine is a small country, with all its parts readily accessible, it is quite unlikely that there would have been opportunity for the development of any significant local differentiation within its population. One might expect such a biological development only where the population history differed from one region to another and the resulting differences were confined by isolation, either geographical or cultural, or where environmental conditions varied sufficiently to exert differential pressures on the population. Since conditions in Palestine were not favourable for this kind of regionalism it is a fair assumption even in the absence of adequate data to conclude that the Jews, whatever their diversities, were fairly uniform in them from one end of the country to the other.

The Diaspora had the effect of distributing such a population over an enormous area in relatively small groups (with some notable exceptions). Isolation between the various sections of the people now became the rule. Whatever in a biological way happened to one of these groups need not now be transmitted to the others by the operation of gene flow from one group to the other, as would have been the case if they had continued to live in proximity to one another. Of course, some groups separated for a time did rejoin others and no doubt under these circumstances genetic differences that might have evolved would have been exchanged and evened out in the normal course of intermarriage. But the historical evidence is clear that at no time did all the distributed colonies come together. The exigencies of geography operated in such a way as to keep various areas more or less segregated from each other. Thus the North African colonies expanded and contracted but had no contact whatever with the remote branches of the Jewish people long settled in the Caucasus, for example. Nor for the same reasons did the European settlements maintain contact with those in North Africa or the Near and Middle East. And, of course, the still more removed colonies in Arabia, Ethiopia, India, and—according to some reports—those in China, were isolated from all the others.

Isolation by itself does not necessarily create differences. It is merely the mechanism that preserves within the population those that have already arisen by mutation or genetic change or through intermarriage with neighbouring people. For despite the isolation of various Jewish colonies from each other, they were not cloistered from the populations among whom they settled.

The question, therefore, becomes this. What evidence do we have in the existing populations that indicates that they do or do not form a race? Since I am using the concept of race in a biological sense, some identification of its meaning becomes necessary, particularly as it is a much misused term.

Although a Churchill, for example, may with great effect

speak of the 'English race' where 'English people' would not do for literary reasons, too many writers and, alas, too many readers do not clearly differentiate the biological and the literary usage. We encounter, therefore, constant references to the French, Italian, or Spanish race, to the Semitic or Aryan race, to the Anglo-Saxon race, as though attributes of nationality, language, or culture were primary criteria of racial distinction. None of these actually has any value in differentiating mankind into biological racial groups, since they are acquired by residence or learning and are not directly the consequence of genetic processes. The zoological concept of race is founded, on the contrary, primarily on the physical inheritance of anatomical or physiological characteristics. Acquired traits are not permissible.

In the zoological scale of classification, a race is a subdivision of a species. And since it is almost the ultimate subdivision that zoologists can recognize with any degree of assurance, the criteria used are necessarily the most superficial of all those available for zoological classification. They have to do with minor variations and not the more basic ones that have already been exhausted in distinguishing the broader categories of genus, order, and other groupings. Also, since racial differences can appear only after the species has been evolved, they are necessarily late in the history of an organism. The commoner traits, for example, that serve over and over again as racial criteria in the higher vertebrates are such things as colour of fur or feathers, patterns of pigmentation, variations in size or proportion, form of hair or fur. Besides such criteria as these there are also specialized developments that are sporadic and peculiar or even unique.

It is not commonly understood that the tendency of a species to form races is an inextricable part of evolution. Race is possible, just as evolution is possible, only because of the same fundamental tendency of all organisms to vary. To paraphrase an axiom of physics: Nature abhors absolute uniformity. Change from some pre-existing form is the essence of evolution as it is of racial differentiation. And without variation among the organisms of a population neither could occur.

The significant variation in both these aspects of change arises from genetic sources, the best known and perhaps most important being through the mutation of the genes that control the hereditary component of developed characters. It is because the environment acts as a selective agent on these variations that evolution advances and races differentiate.

If a species occupies a narrowly constricted area in a uniform environment and interbreeds freely, the chances are minimal that subspecies or racial differentiation would develop. The reasons are these. Any genetic variation appearing in the population would be selected by a uniform agent and consequently one section of the population would change in the same way as all others. Moreover, with interbreeding freely available to all members of the population, any genetic change would soon be distributed throughout the entire group. On the contrary a species dispersed widely, inhabiting a variety of contrasting environments and with each population completely isolated from the other would provide ideal conditions for the emergence of subspecies or races. In this case, the normal genetic variation provided by mutation would be variously selected by the differing environments and the accumulated genetic differences would be confined to the respective populations; the impossibility of their interbreeding with each other would prevent what is called gene flow.

Man shares with other organisms the tendency to vary genetically. And, as is the case among other organisms, these variations when exposed to diverse environments are selected differentially. The extent to which the adaptations that evolve by this process become fixed into racial subdivisions depends primarily, but perhaps not entirely, upon the degree of isolation that segregates the accumulated differences in each emergent race.

The racial process is not a static affair. On the contrary, it is obvious from what has been said that it is a highly dynamic one. It arises in the beginning by change and it is subject to change subsequently. I am referring not only to the continuation of trends implicit in the first emergence of racial differentiation, but also to the modifications that come from contact between various groups as they become defined. For isolation, although complete from time to time in human groups, is not infrequently violated by neighbouring populations, producing highly diverse genetic consequences. The interbreeding resulting from these contacts serves to break down racial distinctions or at least to create intergrades and transitional forms. The racial classification, which is at best a convenient abstraction, never perfectly fits nature. And this in the human situation has created many of the misunderstandings of the racial problem, which in mankind is peculiarly complex.

Of all the higher animals, man is by far the most mobile and capable of changing from one environmental zone to another.

The acquisition of culture has given him a means of rapid extra-organic adaptation to environment which, in turn, has allowed him enormous geographical freedom. As a result, human history and archaeology are witness to the constant ebb and flow of human population. While geographically remote groups were until just recently protected by distance from immediate influence upon one another, those nearer together have repeatedly had more or less direct contact through migration, war, trade, and other forms of intercourse. The result is a highly complicated interrelationship and overlapping between more or less contiguous populations that have blurred racial differences that were in various stages of definition. If the major divisions of mankind are relatively clear because of geographical distance, the minor ones are frequently not.

One final point about race that needs clarification concerns the common error that pure races exist. The standard descriptions of racial classifications and the writings of earlier investigators have created the impression that races were or should be uniform. We have already seen that through interbreeding virtually all human populations represent various amalgams of local varieties. But even if racial entities could have been completely isolated from their very inception and kept inviolate thereafter from genetic contamination with any other group, genetic theory requires that variation within the group inevitably be present. This polymorphism would be expected to arise simply through the process of genetic mutation to which all populations, isolated or not, are subject. In other words, uniformity of race never existed in the past and is an impossible conception except under a kind of artificial and rigorous control that has never prevailed in the affairs of men.

These generalities about race suggest a 'now you see it, now you don't' situation. And indeed this is not too far from the truth. The fact remains, however, that race is a fundamental biological expression of the interaction of genetic variation and environmental selective pressure. That the results of this process are sometimes obscured by interbreeding and gene exchanges makes classification difficult, but does not diminish the biological realities.

The method adopted by students of race to determine affiliation and relationships between diverse populations is basically similar to those employed by zoologists. It is a comparative method, using morphological criteria that from experience seem to have value in distinguishing one group from another. In the case of human groups, pigmentation of skin, hair and eyes, hair form, eye folds, shape of lips and nose, and various dimensions of the head, face, and body together with their respective proportions are among some of the more commonly used traits. Identity or similarity in these characters between two groups is taken to indicate a close racial relationship; diversity or difference indicates the opposite. The assumption, subject to serious reservations for some of these traits, is that their expression as we see it in living men or in their skeletal remains is fundamentally a matter of genetic endowment and any deviations are to be traced to corresponding genetic differences.

In the past generation blood-group frequencies, finger-prints, and other characters have also been used to establish racial or genetic relationships. The blood groups, in particular, appeared to offer a more precise, objective and strictly genetic method, since the exact gene frequencies for the various blood groups can be determined for a population. An added advantage claimed for their use was their supposed freedom from environmental influence.

When we examine the morphological characteristics of various contemporary Jewish populations in order to ascertain what we can of their biological history, several significant facts become obvious. In the first place, they are not identical with each other in the conventional racial criteria. If they were, as has often been claimed, all members of a distinctly Jewish race, they should, allowing for the fluctuations inherent in the sampling process, be approximately alike in the traits that are cited in proof. In Table I some of the more recent and reliable studies have been assembled to demonstrate this lack of identity. Particularly striking is the extremely wide variation in the cephalic index. The Jewish group (Mzab) settled in Ghardaia in the Sahara has an average index of 72.0, which is near the minimum for any living people, while the Jews from Galicia stand at the opposite extreme of broad-headedness with a mean of 83.4. Even this is exceeded by ancient Jewish communities in the Caucasus (not listed), with averages around 85 and over. In stature the groups cited here range from 162.8 cm. to 171.7 cm., a difference of roughly 9 cm (3 1/2 inches). This diversity is also evident in rather extreme differences in the cranial dimensions and in various diameters of the face. Even in the proportions of the nose considerable deviation exists, for example, between the Syrian Jews and the Saharan sample from Mzab.

Comparing these same Jewish groups for pigmentation of skin, hair and eyes, and for hair form and nose form is rather

TABLE I. Comparative series of Jewish groups—males.

	Mzab[1]	Morocco[1]	Spaniol[2]	Syrian[3]	Iraq[4]	Polish[5]	Galicia[5]	Baltic[5]	German[6]	East European[7]
Stature, cm.	166.10	164.90	165.90	165.80	164.50	163.60	162.80	164.90	—	171.70
Span, cm.	171.60	—	172.00	—	—	—	—	—	—	177.30
Relative span	103.30	—	103.50	—	—	—	—	—	—	103.30
Sitting height, cm.	88.60	—	—	—	87.25	—	—	—	—	89.70
Relative sitting height, cm.	53.40	—	—	—	53.24	—	—	—	—	52.20
Shoulder width, cm.	37.00	—	37.5	—	—	—	—	—	—	39.10
Relative shoulder width	22.20	—	22.60	—	—	—	—	—	—	22.80
Head length, mm.	195.50	188.20	189.10	183.00	181.05	188.00	186.60	191.90	188.00	193.00
Head width, mm.	140.70	141.70	147.60	148.00	148.20	156.20	155.60	155.20	152.00	157.10
Cephalic index	72.00	75.00	78.10	80.90	82.05	83.20	83.40	80.90	80.80	81.40
Head height, mm.	124.90	127.40	123.10	—	—	—	—	—	—	128.00
Length-height index	63.90	67.70	65.10	—	—	—	—	—	—	66.40
Breadth-height index	88.80	89.90	83.50	—	—	—	—	—	—	81.50
Minimum frontal, mm.	105.80	110.50	—	—	113.46	—	—	—	—	107.30
Fronto-parietal index	75.40	78.00	—	—	76.48	—	—	—	—	68.40
Bizygomatic, mm.	132.90	132.40	135.70	136.00	137.55	140.00	139.0	141.60	—	141.30
Cephalo-facial index	94.50	93.40	—	—	—	—	—	—	—	90.00

	1	2	3	4	5	6	7				
Zygo-frontal index	79.60	83.50	—	—	82.74	—	—	—	—	—	—
Bigonial, mm.	105.40	—	104.70	—	107.06	104.80	104.60	107.40	—	—	104.80
Zygo-gonial index	79.30	—	—	—	79.33	74.90	75.30	75.90	—	—	—
Face height, mm.	123.40	125.20	121.40	126.00	123.70	—	—	—	—	—	120.30
Face index	93.00	94.00	89.50	92.60	90.00	—	—	—	—	—	85.70
Upper face height, mm.	74.00	—	—	—	72.85	—	—	—	—	—	—
Upper face index	55.70	—	—	—	52.91	—	—	—	—	—	—
Nose height, mm.	55.80	58.00	58.20	56.00	54.98	—	—	—	—	—	57.70
Nose width, mm.	37.60	34.00	35.60	33.00	33.89	—	—	—	—	—	35.90
Nose index	68.1	64.70	61.50	58.90	62.78	—	—	—	—	—	62.30

1. L. Cabot Briggs, *The Living Races of the Sahara Desert* (*Papers*, Peabody Museum, Harvard University, vol. 28, no. 2, 1958).
2. F. Wagenseil, 'Beiträge zur Physischen Anthropologie der Spanioli-schen Juden', *Zt. Morph. u. Anthrop.*, vol. 23, 1925.
3. J. Weissenberg, 'Die Syrischen Juden Anthropologisch betrachtet', *Zt. Ehnol.*, vol. 43, 1911.
4. Henry Field, *The Anthropology of Iraq* (*Papers*, Peabody Museum, Harvard University, vol. 46, nos. 2-3, 1952).
5. W. Dornfeldt, 'Studien über Schädelform und Schädelverände-rung, etc.', *Zt. Morph. u. Anthrop.*, vol. 39, 1941.
6. S. Weissenberg, 'Anthropologie der Deutschen Juden', *Zt. Ehnol.*, vol. 44, 1912.
7. K. Saller, 'Beitrag zur Anthropologie der Ostjuden', *Zt. Morph. u. Anthrop.*, vol. 32, 1933.

more difficult because the standards of judgement are less objective than direct measurements, and the data in any case are less ample for the purpose (Table II). Nevertheless, wide differences are apparent in this class of racial characteristics too. The Jews of East European ancestry as represented by Saller's series are characterized by a relatively high frequency of light coloured eyes which is strongly in contrast with the group from Iraq, where less than 2 per cent have blue eyes and 80 per cent have brown. It is interesting that in the Mzab group, in an area not notable for blue eyes, the frequency of that colour is appreciable. And, in fact, one can find in the older literature summarized by Fishberg[1] that the percentage of blue eyes is very high in European Jews inhabiting areas where this feature is common.

For hair colour the recent data are still more restricted. The four groups represented here agree fairly well, but unfortunately

TABLE II. Comparative series of Jewish groups—males (percentages).

	Mzab	Spaniol	Syrian	Iraq	East European
Eye colour					
Blue (light)	11.10	6.40	10.00	1.88	14.00-20.00
Mixed	11.10	13.30	—	16.03	32.00-48.00
Light brown	5.60	80.30	25.00	—	—
Brown	72.20		65.00	80.19	48.00
Hair colour					
Blonde	—		—	—	—
Light brown	2.80	2.20	5.00	3.50	—
Red brown	11.10		—	—	—
Medium brown	5.60				
Dark brown and black	80.50	97.80	95.00	96.50	—
Hair form					
Straight	30.60	9.10	—	—	—
Low waves	30.60	67.90	—	100.00	—
Tight waves	—	0.80	—	—	—
Deep waves	27.70	19.10	—	—	—
Curly	11.10	2.30	—	—	—
Frizzly	—	0.80	—	—	—

1. M. Fishberg, *The Jews,* New York, Charles Scribner's Sons, 1911.

do not include any European samples. Supplementing again from Fishberg's data, the evidence shows that the lighter shades of hair rise to about 25 per cent among English Jews and are only somewhat lower (15-20 per cent) in various Eastern European countries. Hair form has not been as frequently recorded in these studies as other characters, but the three groups for which we have observations show a striking difference. The Mzab sample has the highest percentage (30 per cent) with straight hair. The Spaniol group from Turkey has only 9 per cent with straight hair, but 68 per cent with low waved types. The Iraq sample was apparently uniform in this character, with 100 per cent showing low waved hair.

Much has been made of the so-called Jewish nose as a distinguishing racial feature. Considering the origin of the Jews from a population identified as Mediterranean in its fundamental affiliation, and its early absorption of various local strains found in the Near East, it is not surprising that the convex nasal bridge and the depressed nasal tip be found among them. It is a common enough type of nasal development among these people and in that part of the Mediterranean. Moreover, these features are also to be found in varying degree in some European populations as well.

The data available for the assembled series show that considerable variation occurs even in this 'typical' feature. Although it is difficult to equate the diverse samples because of different subdivisions of nasal profile employed, it is obvious the Syrians, for example, differ noticeably from the Iraq group (Table III). And it is worth noting that convexity is far from universal among Jews. Fishberg, who took the attempts to fasten a specific type of nose on all Jews far too seriously, collected a considerable body of data to demonstrate that this claim could be refuted by statistics. As a matter of fact, the observations on

TABLE III. Nasal profiles—Jewish males (percentages).

	Mzab	Spaniol	Syrian	Iraq	East European
Concave	5.50	13.40	—	2.80	—
Straight	38.90	37.30	50.00	25.23	—
Undulating	11.10	—	—	1.87	—
Concavo-convex	2.80	—	—	4.67	—
Recto-convex	25.00	—	—	—	—
Convex	16.90	49.30	50.00	65.42	57.00

nasal form are not always easy to compare. Observers differ in their judgements; the various elements that go to make up the total form of the nose are not always given and in any event figures on the frequency of the 'Jewish nose' among Jews have little value when we scarcely know the frequency of the same feature among non-Jewish groups more or less comparable to them.

These comparisons, typical of many more extensive ones that could be made, prove that the fundamental requirement for any claim that the Jews form a racial entity cannot be met, at least by those traditional standards of racial classification. The various communities differ from each other too significantly to be grouped together as a single race. In any case, the variations among individuals within these populations are often so great that they suggest by themselves a considerable degree of inter-mixture.

In recent years the use of blood types has been prominent in racial studies. Jews among other populations have also been surveyed for their characteristic blood types. In the following tables I have assembled typical samples from Western and Eastern Europe, the Near and Middle East, Arabia, and North Africa. In Table IV the ABO series are compared. From these frequencies it is evident that the various samples vary almost as widely as samples of non-Jewish groups from a corresponding geographical range would be expected to do.

Because the B group is relatively rare in Western Europe, roughly 10 per cent or slightly less, and high in Asia, reaching 30 or 40 per cent or more in various Asiatic populations, this type is often critical in wide geographical comparisons. The Jewish samples show pretty much the same distribution; group B is low in Western European and high in Asiatic Jewish groups. In the German and Dutch series of Jews, the frequency of group B is comparable with the corresponding non-Jewish population. As one moves toward Eastern Europe and into the Near East, the frequency of group B increases, attaining 35 per cent in a sample of Samarkand Jews. This represents approximately three times the frequency found among Berlin Jews.

Thus these ABO groups clearly demonstrate the same heterogeneity among Jewish populations that was found to exist in their morphological racial traits. They also clearly reflect a gradient of change in frequency well known for non-Jewish populations. This can only suggest: (a) that Jews and non-Jews have been exposed to the same influences, or (b) that the Jews have through intermarriage approximated the frequencies

TABLE IV. Comparison of various Jewish groups for ABO blood group series (percentages).

	Size of sample	*O*	*A*	*B*	*AB*	
Holland	705	42.60	39.40	13.40	4.50	(Herwerden)
Berlin	230	42.10	41.10	11.90	4.90	(Schiff & Ziegler)
Czechoslovakia	144	23.60	50.00	22.20	4.20	
Poland	818	33.10	41.50	17.40	8.00	(Halber & Mydlarski)
Minsk	99	35.20	43.60	17.00	4.20	(Raskina)
Minsk	257	34.50	45.00	16.60	3.90	(Rachowsky & Sukhotin)
Rumania	211	26.10	38.80	19.80	15.30	(Manuila)
Rumania	1 135	38.20	39.00	17.50	5.30	(P. & E. Jonescu)
Ukraine	384	28.00	42.30	23.50	6.20	(Rubaschkin & Dörrman)
Balkans	500	38.80	33.00	23.30	5.00	(Hirszfeld & Hirszfeld)
Samarkand	541	28.90	31.40	32.70	7.00	(Libman)
Samarkand	616	32.30	29.20	35.50	7.90	(Vishnevski)
Iran	431	33.50?	32.50	25.00	9.20?	(Younovitch)
Iran	116	19.80	46.60	25.00	8.60	(Milkikh & Gringot)
Morocco	642	36.90	35.90	19.90	7.30	(Kossovitch)
Yemenites	1 000	56.00	26.10	16.10	1.80	(Younovitch)

characteristic of the countries where they have long been established.

The MN series, for which the literature is far less extensive, repeats the evidence of heterogeneity among the Jewish samples I have been able to assemble (Table V). Group M fluctuates from 27.5 to 57 per cent; N from 5.8 to 26.5 per cent.

TABLE V. Percentage of MN blood types among Jews.

	M	*MN*	*N*	
Yemenite	57.00	37.20	5.80	(Brzezinski *et al.*)
Iraq	40.74	39.51	19.75	(Gurevitch & Margolis)
Kurdistan	51.60	29.60	18.80	(Gurevitch *et al.*)
Kurdistan	30.63	44.17	25.00	(Gurevitch & Margolis)
Tripolitania	27.50	46.00	26.50	(Gurevitch *et al.*)

The Rh series of blood types is also unfortunately not as abundant for comparison between diverse samples of Jews as is the ABO, but enough is available to indicate general trends. Among the array of Rh groups, the one known as Rh negative has a peculiarly European centre of distribution. The highest frequency is to be found among the Basque people of north-western Spain and south-western France where over 30 per cent of some populations have been found to possess this particular blood reaction type: almost as high a frequency has been reported for isolated and ancient Berber groups in Morocco. Elsewhere in Western Europe it fluctuates moderately around 15 per cent. Outside Europe, Rh negative becomes relatively rare or absent. For example, only about 5 per cent of a sample of African Negroes gave this reaction. Japanese and Chinese vary from 1 to 2 per cent. It appears to be completely unknown, or exceptional, among American Indians, Indonesians, Filipinos, Pacific Islanders, and Australian aborigines. Among Jews the frequency of Rh negative varies from 3.85 in one sample of Yemenites to 18.67 in Oran (Table VI). Samples of

TABLE VI. Percentage of Rh negative in Jewish samples.

	Rh positive	Rh negative	
Oran	81.33	18.67	(Solal & Hanoun)
Jerusalem	90.43	9.57	(Gurevitch *et al.*)
Canada	91.83	8.17	(Lubinski *et al.*)
Sephardi	87.70	12.30	(Gurevitch *et al.*)
Ashkenasi	86.47	13.53	(Gurevitch *et al.*)
Kurdistan	94.80	5.20	(Gurevitch *et al.*)
Yemenite	96.15	3.85	(Dreyfuss *et al.*)

Jews native to various European countries are not significantly different from the corresponding non-Jewish populations. Mourant,[1] who has recently assembled most of the data on all types of blood groups, comments: 'These results are what would be expected in a Mediterranean population which had acquired a considerable local component during residence in central and northern Europe.'

The wide range of variation between Jewish populations in their physical characteristics and the diversity of the gene

1. A. E. Mourant, *The Distribution of the Human Blood Groups*, Oxford, Blackwell, 1954.

frequencies of their blood groups render any unified racial classification for them a contradiction in terms. For although modern racial theory admits some degree of polymorphism or variation within a racial group, it does not permit distinctly different groups, measured by its own criteria of race, to be identified as one. To do so would make the biological purposes of racial classification futile and the whole procedure arbitrary and meaningless. Unfortunately, this subject is rarely wholly divorced from non-biological considerations and despite the evidence efforts continue to be made to somehow segregate the Jews as a distinct racial entity.

I suppose that one of the reasons, aside from political and cultural ones, that incline many people to accept readily the notion that the Jews are a distinct race, is the fact that some Jews are recognizably different in appearance from the surrounding population. That some are not to be identified in this way is overlooked and the tendency, naturally enough, is to extend to all the stereotype of a part. This process occurs in so many other situations it is scarcely surprising that it does here too.

It has been the fortune of the Jews, like so many other people in human history, to have migrated into a variety of areas and among a broad range of racial groups. The particular racial amalgam they represented originally was, of course, distinctive to the degree that the people among whom they settled differed from it. In the countries neighbouring Palestine the contemporary people were probably not especially or strikingly different in their origins or in their appearance from the Jewish contingents that joined them. But as the Jewish colonists increased the radius of their dispersion, they inevitably found progressively wider differences from themselves. Although as we have already seen many of even these differences have diminished with time, some have remained to reinforce stereotypes.

Thus in the Mediterranean countries and in various Near Eastern regions Jews are more likely to be recognized by cultural than by biological attributes. In some of the northwestern and eastern countries of Europe, on the contrary, the local racial history has been compounded of elements that played only a relatively insignificant part in the Mediterranean area. Under the circumstances one might expect as a result that Jewish settlers in these areas would display obvious differences, springing from their diverse racial components, and some overlap where certain strains were common. Although centuries, even millennia, of contact have established an unknown but appreciable amount of gene flow between Jewish colonies and the surrounding population, as the corresponding gene frequencies suggest, these initial differences have not been completely eliminated. Jewish populations in these areas still retain some elements of genetic difference, while they have departed from the standards of the original population from which they were derived. It is likely that these subtle and residual deviations would have remained principally of interest only for the light they throw on the process of biological differentiation and the mechanics of group contact and group continuity, were it not for the fact that they have frequently enough served as symbols of cultural and religious conflicts and been used as expressions of complex antagonisms arising from a variety of causes.

There still remains the problem of explaining the distinct heterogeneity that now characterizes the Jewish population of the world and the direction of the changes that can be identified. The theoretical possibilities available from our current knowledge of the subject are three. One has already been implied in the preceding discussion—namely, the intermixture of Jewish populations with the people of the countries where they became established. Obviously it is impossible at this late date to determine from records the extent of this process. Although some Jewish communities, often as a result of factors already outlined, tended to maintain a subcultural identity, long residence in an area could not have failed to provide opportunities for intermarriage. At various times in the early history of the Christian Church, concern was expressed in one form or another at the amount of intermarriage that was current. Even restrictive measures were promulgated to lessen the danger. I have already referred to the actual loss of many Jewish communities through intermarriage. In a recent monograph on the people of the Sahara, Briggs[1] refers to the custom of Jewish men in the Mzab group to maintain Arab concubines whose offspring in some cases might become part of the Jewish community. This kind of evidence might fill many pages, from the records of proselytization in the early centuries of the Christian Era to the demographic evidence in Germany and Austria in the early twentieth century, when for certain Jewish segments of the population intermarriage with Christians was virtually as frequent as

---

1. L. Cabot Briggs, *The Living Races of the Sahara Desert* (*Papers*, Peabody Museum, Harvard University, vol. 28, no. 2, 1958).

marriage within the Jewish population itself. But for long periods of time and for some areas marriage was probably fairly restricted. Otherwise amalgamation would have been complete. The reality, however, of some degree of assimilation, if not of the precise extent, is measured by the tendency of the gene frequencies of the blood groups in Jewish populations to approximate to those characteristic of their native countries.

The modification of Jewish population units in the course of time may also be illustrated by an interesting series of crania described by Matiegka,[1] the Czechoslovak anthropologist. These remains came from a seventeenth-century Jewish cemetery in Prague. I have compared in Table VII the standard measurements of this Jewish sample with (a) the Lachish population, an earlier Palestinian group that lived some

TABLE VII. Prague Jews compared with Christian contemporaries and ancient Palestinians.

	Lachish	17th-century Prague Jews	17th-century Prague Christians
Head length, mm.	184.30	180.51	178.70
Head width, mm.	137.10	147.81	149.00
Head height, mm.	133.80	131.18	132.50
Minimum frontal, mm.	95.40	97.82	98.50
Nasion opishion arc, mm.	375.90	365.00	367.60
Transverse arc, mm.	308.70	308.06	320.90
Horizontal arc, mm.	518.10	520.30	518.90
Basion-nasion, mm.	100.60	100.36	99.60
Bizygomatic, mm.	128.40	134.46	130.50
Nasion alveon, mm.	70.10	67.71	67.79
Nose height, mm.	51.30	52.21	49.30
Nose breadth, mm.	25.20	25.29	25.00
Orbital breadth, mm.	41.40	40.42	37.20
Orbital height, mm.	32.80	33.25	32.30
Cranial index	74.50	81.97	83.53
Length-height index	72.70	72.58	74.39
Breadth-height index	102.50	112.17 *	112.50 *
Nasal index	49.60	48.63	50.94
Orbital index	79.30	82.35	85.36

* Calculated.

1. J. Matiegka, 'Příspěvky ku Kraniologii Zidu', *Anthropologie*, Prague, vol. 4, 1926.

2,300 years before, and (b) a group of contemporary Christians from Prague. It is clear that the Prague Jews are far more like their contemporaries from Prague than their ancestors in Palestine. In fact, the differences between the two Prague groups are minimal and show the extent to which the Jews have departed from a Palestinian group that cannot have been radically different from the population that participated in the Diaspora.

Another factor to be taken into account in the geographical differentiation of the Jews is the modification in physical development and ultimately in developed characters that can occur through migration from one geographical area to another or from one economic milieu to another. This has to do with the plasticity of the human organism and its ability to respond to such changes and adapt itself accordingly. That populations do become modified in their dimensional characters can no longer be denied. The first significant study on this aspect of man's adaptability grew out of the investigation of Boas of the children of immigrants to the United States.[1] He found particularly that Italian and Jewish children born and bred in the United States surpassed their immigrant parents in stature and, together with this, exhibited a change in the cephalic index. Some twenty years after the report by Boas, I had an opportunity to examine Japanese immigrants to Hawaii and their children born and raised there.[2] This investigation was designed to meet certain criticisms that had been directed toward the findings of Boas and the data were collected to provide a genetic control. Samples were obtained in Japan from the same families that had furnished the immigrants. I found that not only were the Japanese born in Hawaii taller than their immigrant parents, with altered bodily and cephalic proportions, but that the immigrants themselves were in certain features statistically different from their relatives who remained in Japan. These results are now supported by a number of other studies yielding similar conclusions.

Considering the climatic and geographical changes alone that Jewish migration has encountered, some modification in physical development appropriate to the various areas of settlement must be admitted. It is, however, impossible from any

---

1. F. Boas, *Changes in Bodily Form of Descendants of Immigrants*, Washington, Government Printing Office, 1910.
2. H. L. Shapiro, *Migration and Environment*, New York, Oxford University Press, 1939.

existing corpus of data to determine the relative importance of genetic changes brought about by intermarriage and those that have come from adaptation to diverse environments. Both, of course, have undoubtedly played their part.

Finally, the possibility that selection has also been contributing to this complex and dynamic situation cannot be altogether ignored, even though direct evidence for this is lacking. Although most of us have become accustomed to the concept of evolution and admit readily enough that man has attained his present biological status through some form of natural selection, it is not as widely understood that the operation of selection and evolution has not ceased with the emergence of *Homo sapiens*. Not only does the physical environment in which we live continue to exert a selective effect on the genetic variety presented to it, but human culture itself has come to play a determining role in human evolution. Jewish populations, along with all other human aggregations living under specific environmental and cultural conditions, are bound to be affected by the selective pressures inherent in the milieu. This is of course an inescapable inference from well established theory. That it cannot at present be documented satisfactorily in a measurable way is ultimately to be assigned to the difficulties of technique and method.

As a theoretical force, then, in producing the existing differentiation among Jews and in contributing to their approximation to the people of their respective countries, selection must also be added to the interplay of factors that have changed and modified these people over the millennia we have been surveying. But raising the problem of selection brings forward a special aspect of the problem as it relates to the Jews. As we have already seen, this people has repeatedly been in the forefront of events that subsequently became common enough, and by its very position has been exposed to the penalties that often fall on advance guards. With certain notable exceptions, the various colonies of Jews have been subject to the selective pressures of urbanization more universally and over a consistently longer period of time than any other people. Even before the Diaspora the growth of an urban structure of society had already made considerable headway in Palestine. As a result of the dispersion, the Jews, when they migrated, settled principally but not universally in cities. There were, of course, a number of reasons that directed this tendency. Land tenure systems were not, generally speaking, favourable to small contingents or family groups taking up land, even if the Jewish migrants had been financially able to do so. Cities, moreover, because of their cosmopolitanism, their trade and industries, also provided more accessible opportunities for livelihood and a more tolerant situation for new settlers. The economic and social history of the Jews that served to maintain them as an urban people through all the intervening years is too well known to bear repeating here. The restrictions by the church and government, limiting Jews to typically urban occupations, kept them in such environments.

Thus whatever selective factors might be characteristic of highly urban conditions would have been particularly effective on the Jews, since they could scarcely leave them for centuries on end. The devastating epidemics that swept medieval cities and towns, to take one example, would in the long run have been more selective on Jewish populations than any others, leaving them with progressively greater immunity as time went on. The Jews lived only in the city so that all of them would have been exposed to such effects and their modern descendants would, therefore, represent the survivors of a rigorous and specific selective process. The non-Jewish population on the other hand was only to a relatively small extent resident in cities and their modern counterparts would be drawn constantly from fresh rural recruits. Perhaps it is this long continued experience that accounts for some of the special immunities and medical characteristics that have been reported for Jewish populations. Tuberculosis, for example, has often been cited as relatively rare in Jewish populations compared with rates found in their countries generally. Other medical idiosyncrasies may well have a similar basis.

Although many of the puzzling peculiarities of disease rates found in some Jewish demographic units can be accounted for by selection, there are others, particularly inherited pathologies like amaurotic idiocy, that suggest another factor. Inbreeding, which in small isolated groups must have occurred frequently, could well account for such variations in the rate of occurrence. By the same token, a breakdown of old, relatively inbred groups should lead to an amelioration of the rate. Indeed, the fluctuation of many medical statistics confirms such an interpretation.

In many ways the biological fortunes of the Jews through the millennia of their existence as a people typify the complex forces that are exerted upon any, indeed all, peoples. The continuities, the changes, the adaptations to varying conditions, the interplay of cultural and historical currents affecting biological developments are to be found wherever man exists.

The resultants may differ but the process is universal. The Jews, in particular, have as a consequence of their history displayed some of those forces with enough clarity to enable us to discern their course. If the details have faded here and there, the grand masses of the picture still loom up. We have seen how the Jews evolved as a people from a fragment of an ancient Mesopotamian stock, gradually absorbing elements of the various related stocks they encountered in their wanderings in Canaan and Egypt and subsequently incorporating foreign peoples deposited in Palestine by invasion. As a result of these interminglings the Jews emerged in the restricted civilized world of the centuries just before Christ as one of the syntheses typical of that time and place.

The Diaspora that followed had a profound biological effect on the Jews. Had it not occurred they might well have remained a people something like the living Samaritans of today, relatively untouched by the population movements of an expanding world. The Diaspora did for the Jews what the vast population movements did to European people in creating new combinations and syntheses. But instead of the Jews undergoing these changes by invasion and conquest, they achieved similar results by their own migrations. Through their dispersion they remained a world people, enormously expanding their geographical and racial contacts. Few other peoples in modern times have had consequently so varied a biological history. As a result they have contributed something of their genetic heritage to perhaps more different people than any other group and have, in return, absorbed an equal number of new genetic strains, enriching and diversifying themselves.[1]

And now, having been through such a process, representing in their diversity a great range of the racial elements characteristic of Europe, North Africa and Western Asia, they are reassembling once more in Israel where all these elements may be pooled in a fresh synthesis. Although only a small part of

---

1. The latest statistics on the Jewish population of the world, as compiled by the American Jewish Committee for 1958, give a total of slightly more than 12 million. This figure is an estimate, since many groups of Jews have not been accurately counted for some time and others have never been included in a proper census. The geographical breakdown of the total is as follows: New World, 6,200,000 (nearly 5,000,000 in the United States); Europe, including the U.S.S.R., 3,500,000; Asia, including Israel, 1,950,000; Africa, 560,000; Australia and New Zealand, 65,000.

   If the estimate of 4.5 million Jews in Roman times is adjudged not unreliable, then the increment over the last 2,000 years would be roughly threefold. This is scarcely comparable with the enormous growth of various European populations during the same period.

World Jewry may ever return to the ancestral homeland, it is representative of the whole gamut of the differentiation that has evolved, since the departure some 2,000 years ago, through intermixture, adaptation, and selection. We may witness now in Israel the beginnings of a new chapter in the biological history of the Jews.

BIBLIOGRAPHY

In English

ABRAHAMS, Israel, *Jewish life in the Middle Ages,* Philadelphia, Jewish Publication Society, 1920.
 Although first published more than sixty years ago, this is still a useful book.

ALBRIGHT, W. F., *The archaeology of Palestine,* Harmondsworth, Penguin Books, 1956.
 An excellent survey of the archaeological record of the Jews and their precursors by a scholar who has himself contributed substantially to our archaeological knowledge of the area.

ALBRIGHT, W. F., *From Stone Age to Christianity*, Baltimore, Johns Hopkins Press, 1946.
 An interpretation of the development of Judaism.

BARON, S. W., *A social and religious history of the Jewish people,* Philadelphia, Jewish Publication Society, 1937 and 1952-58.
 The earlier edition has been revised and greatly expanded; eight volumes have so far appeared. It is a standard work of the highest scholarship.

FISHBERG, M., *The Jews,* New York, Charles Scribner's Sons, 1911.
 In spite of the fact that this classic book has become somewhat dated, it contains valuable insights and information. It is one of the few available books that covers the biological characteristics of the Jews.

GLUECK, Nelson, *Rivers in the desert,* New York, Farrar, Strauss & Cudahy, 1959.
 A fine popular book on the anthropology of the Negev by one of the most active investigators in this field.

GRAYZEL, S., *A history of the Jews,* Philadelphia, Jewish Publication Society, 1947.
 A useful popular history.

JOSEPHUS, Flavius, The Works of (various editions); in particular, *A history of the Jewish wars.*
 Although not always a reliable guide, Josephus was nevertheless contemporary with many of the events he describes and thus provides a unique and valuable picture of the Jews during Roman times.

ROTH, Cecil, *A short history of the Jewish people,* London, East & West Library, 1948.

An excellent account for the general reader.

ZBOROWSKI, Mark, and HERZOG, Elizabeth, *Life is with people: the Jewish little town of eastern Europe,* New York, International University Press, 1955.

This reconstruction of the traditional life of Jewish communities in eastern Europe illuminates one aspect of the social and cultural dynamics of the Jews as a minority group in a hostile environment.

In French

BARON, S. W., *Histoire d'Israël. Vie sociale et religieuse.* I: *Des origines jusqu'au début de l'ère chrétienne,* Paris, 1956. (Further volumes in preparation.)

Translated from the English. Standard work of modern Jewish historiography.

CATANE, Mosche, *Des Croisades à nos jours,* Paris, Bibliothèque juive, les Editions de Minuit, 1956.

A short, popular account of the history of French Jewry.

CHOURAQUI, André, *Marche vers l'Occident: les Juifs d'Afrique du Nord,* Paris, 1952.

A survey of the history, sociology and demography of Jews in North Africa.

ROTH, Cecil, *Histoire du peuple juif (des origines à nos jours),* Paris, 1957.

An excellent introductory survey of Jewish history translated from the English.

ROTH, Léon, *La pensée juive, facteur de civilisation,* Paris, Unesco, 1954.

An assessment of the Jewish element in the world's civilization.

SCHWARZFUCHS, Simon, *Brève histoire des Juifs de France,* Paris, 1956.

A short review of 2,000 years of Jewish history in France.

In German

DUBNOW, Simon, *Weltgeschichte des jüdischen Volkes,* Berlin, Jüdischer Verlag, 1925-29, 10 vols.

GRAETZ, Heinrich, *Geschichte der Juden von den ältesten Zeiten bis auf die Gegenwart,* Leipzig, Leiner, 1873-1900, 11 vols.

Standard works on Jewish history.

HERRMANN, Hugo, *Palästinakunde,* Wien, Fiba Verlag, 1935.

The descriptive and statistical parts of this book are out of date but it still remains a valuable compendium on the geography and history of the Jews in Palestine and contains an exhaustive bibliography.

RUPPIN, Arthur, *Soziologie der Juden,* Berlin, Jüdischer Verlag, 1930, 2 vols. (Bd. 1: *Die soziale Struktur der Juden*; Bd. 2: *Der Kampf der Juden um ihre Zukunft*).

A pioneering work on the sociology of the Jewish people. Outdated but still a useful introduction to the subject.

ZOLLSCHAN, Ignaz, *Das Rassenproblem unter besonderer Berücksichtigung der theoretischen Grundlagen der jüdischen Rassenfrage*, Wien, 1925.

A well-known study of racial problems.

Jüdisches Lexikon: ein enzyklopädisches Handbuch des jüdischen Wissens, Berlin, Jüdischer Verlag, 1927-30, 5 vols.

An excellent reference work containing a wealth of material on Jewish history.

Die Juden und wir, Göttingen, Arbeitskreis für angewandte Anthropologie, 1957. (Schriftenreihe Wissenschaft und Menschenführung.)

Contains a number of valuable papers on various aspects of anti-Jewish persecution in Germany.

RACE AND CULTURE

by
MICHEL LEIRIS

*Chargé de recherches at the
Centre National de la Recherche Scientifique
and Staff Member of the Musée de l'Homme, Paris*

> The nature of men is identical; what divides
> them is their customs.
> CONFUCIUS, 551-478 B.C.

After causing innumerable casualties, World War II ended with the defeat of Nazi Germany and her allies. The National Socialists had gained power on the strength of their racist ideology, and more particularly of their anti-Semitism, and it was in the name of that ideology that they went to war to 'unite all Germans in a greater Germany' and force recognition of German superiority on the whole world. Thus the fall of Adolf Hitler lent colour to the assumption that racism was dead. However, such a view both assumes the non-existence of forms of racism other than the Hitlerite, admittedly the most extreme and virulent of them, and overlooks the strong conviction of most white people—even those who do not on that account consider themselves racists—of their congenital superiority.

Admittedly, the white man has something to be proud of in his great inventions and discoveries, his technical equipment and his political power. It is questionable, however, whether these achievements have yet brought a greater sum of happiness to mankind as a whole. For instance, it can hardly be claimed that the pigmy hunter of the Congo forests lives a life less well adjusted than a European or American factory worker. Nor should we forget that, though science has brought us undeniable progress in such fields as sanitation, for instance, it has also enabled us to perfect the means of destruction to such a point that for some decades past, armed conflicts have been truly cataclysmic in their effects. Be that as it may, and despite his consciousness that the civil-

181

ization he regards as the only one worthy of the name is increasingly threatened with overthrow from within and without, the Western white man still claims the right of passage at the great cross roads to which his means of communication have reduced the world. A lack of historical perspective prevents his realizing not merely how recent is his privileged position, but how transitory it may prove, and he regards it as a sign that he is predestined to create the values which men of other races and other cultures are at best merely capable of receiving from him. Though he will readily admit that a number of inventions have come to him from the Chinese (to whom he is willing to concede a modicum of 'brains' and wisdom), and that such things as jazz have been given to him by the Negro (whom he nevertheless persists in regarding as an overgrown child), he is persuaded that his culture is of his own exclusive making and that only he can claim to have received—by right of blood and character—a 'civilizing mission'.

In an article published in *the Unesco Courier,* July 1950, Dr. Alfred Metraux (an ethnographer whose work has covered perhaps more of the world than that of any other) wrote: 'Racism is one of the most disturbing phenomena of the great revolution of the modern world. At the very time when industrial civilization is penetrating to all points of the globe and is uprooting men of every colour from their age-old traditions, a doctrine, speciously scientific in appearance, is invoked in order to rob these men of their full share in the advantage of the civilization forced upon them.

'There exists in the structure of Western civilization a fatal contradiction. On the one hand, it wishes and insists that certain cultural values, to which it attributes the highest virtues, be assimilated by other people. But, conversely, it will not admit that two-thirds of humanity is capable of attaining this standard which it has set up. Ironically, the worst sufferers from racial dogma are usually the people whose intellect most forcibly demonstrates its falseness.'

By an irony as strange, the more capable the so-called inferior races prove themselves of attaining emancipation, the more emphatic grows the assertion of racial dogma, stiffened by the coloured races' acquisition of a minimum of political rights or by their emergence as competitors. And the crowning paradox is that, to provide a rational justification for their blind prejudice, appeal is made to our age's gods—science and scientific objectivity.

It is true, as the writer of the article points out, that there has been no lack of anthropologists to condemn the arbitrary basis adopted for the classification of the human species into different groups and to maintain the proposition that a pure race is an impossibility. Moreover, it may today be taken as proved that 'race' is a purely biological concept, from which —at least in the present stage of our knowledge—it is impossible to draw any valid conclusion whatever as to the disposition or mental capacity of a particular individual. Nevertheless, racism, overt or covert, continues to be a baneful influence, and the majority of people still regard the human species as falling into distinct ethnic groups, each with its own mentality transmissible by heredity. It is accepted by them as basic truth that, despite the faults which must be recognized in the white race and the innate virtues they are prepared to concede to other races, the highest type of humanity is, if not the whole, at least the best, of the white race.

The error vitiating this apparent scientific justification of race prejudice lies in the failure to distinguish between *natural* and *cultural* traits, i.e., innate characteristics traceable to a man's ethnic origin, and those deriving from background and upbringing. All too often we fail, ignorantly or wilfully, to distinguish this social heritage from the *racial* heritage in the shape of physical peculiarities (for instance, pigmentation and other less striking characteristics). While there are undoubtedly very real psychological differences between individuals, which may be due in part to the subjects' individual biological ancestry (though our knowledge of the subject is still very vague), they can in no instance be explained by what is commonly called the individual's 'race', i.e., the ethnic group of which he is a member by descent. Similarly, while history has seen the development of distinctive civilizations and there are differences of varying degrees between contemporary human societies, the explanation must not be sought in the racial evolution of mankind (brought about by such factors as changes in the combination or structure of the genes—the elements determining heredity—by hybridization and natural selection) which has produced variations from what was probably an ancestral stock common to all humanity. The differences in question are cultural variations and cannot be explained either in terms of biological background or even of the influence of geographical setting, impossible though it is to overlook the importance of this last factor as at least one element in the situation with which a society must cope.

183

Although the source of race prejudice must be sought elsewhere than in the pseudo-scientific ideas which are less its cause than its expression and although these ideas are of merely secondary importance as a means of justifying and commending prejudices, they still continue to deceive many often well-meaning people, and it is thus important to combat them.

The object of the present paper, then, is to set forth what is generally acknowledged regarding the respective influence of race and culture. We have to show that, apart from his personal experience, a given individual is principally indebted for his psychological conditioning to the culture in which he was brought up, the latter being itself the product of history. We have to convince the world that, far from being the more explicit expression of something instinctive, race prejudice is a prejudice in the truest and worst sense—i.e., a preconceived opinion—cultural in origin and barely three centuries old, which has grown up and taken the form we know today for economic and political reasons.

SCOPE AND CONCEPT OF 'RACE'

The concept of race might at first sight be thought to be very simple and obvious: for instance an American office worker in Wall Street, a Viet-Namese carpenter building a junk, or a peasant of the Guinea Coast are men of three quite distinct races—white, yellow and black—whose ways of life are widely different, whose languages are not the same and who in all probability follow different religions. We accept without question that each of these three men represents a distinct variant of the human species, in the light of their differences not only in physique but in dress, occupation and (in all probability) in mentality, thinking, behaviour and, briefly, all that goes to make up personality. As our most immediate impression of a person is of his bodily appearance, we are quick to assume a necessary connexion between external physical appearance and manner of life and thought: we feel that in the nature of things, the white employee will pass his spare time in reading, the yellow man in gambling and the black in singing and dancing. We tend to see race as the primary factor from which all the rest follows, and the reflexion that today there are large numbers of men of the yellow and black races pursuing the same occupations and living under the same conditions as whites only makes us feel that there is something freakish or at best artificial about it, as though the real man had been given a kind of veneer making him less 'natural'.

We perceive clear-cut differences between the three major groups into which most scientists are agreed in dividing the human species, Caucasians (or whites), Mongols and Negroes. However, the question grows more complex the moment we consider the fact of interbreeding between these groups. An individual with one white and one black parent is what is called a 'mulatto'. But should the mulatto be classified as white or black? A white man, even if not an avowed racist, will in all probability regard the mulatto as a 'coloured man' and will tend to include him among the blacks, but this classification is glaringly arbitrary, since from the anthropological point of view, the heredity of the mulatto is at least as much white as black. We therefore have to realize that, while there are men who can be classified as white, black or yellow, there are others whose mixed ancestry prevents their due classification.

RACE DIFFERS FROM CULTURE, LANGUAGE AND RELIGION

In the case of the major racial groups, classification is relatively simple though there are doubtful cases (for instance, are Polynesians, Caucasians or Mongoloids?). There are peoples who indisputably belong to one of the three branches; no one could cavil at the statement that an Englishman belongs to the white race, a Baoulé to the black or a Chinese to the yellow. It is when we attempt to make subdivisions within the three main divisions that we begin to see how equivocal is the commonly held idea of race.

To say that an Englishman is a member of the white race, obviously admits of no argument and is indeed the merest common sense. It is, however, absurd to talk about an English 'race' or even to regard the English as being of the 'Nordic' race. In point of fact, history teaches that, like all the people of Europe, the English people has become what it is through successive contributions by different peoples. England is a Celtic country, partially colonized by successive waves of Saxons, Danes and Normans from France, with some addition of Roman stock from the age of Julius Caesar onwards. Moreover, while an Englishman can be identified by his way of dressing, or even by his behaviour, it is impossible to tell that he is an Englishman merely from his physical appearance. Among the English, as among other Europeans there are both fair people and dark, tall men and short, and (to follow a very common anthropological criterion) dolichocephalics (or long-headed people) and brachycephalics (or people with broad heads). It may be claimed that an Englishman can readily be identified from certain external characteristics which give him a 'look' of his own: restraint in gesture (unlike the conventional gesticulating southerner), gait and facial expression all expressing what is usually included under the rather vague term of 'phlegm'. However, anyone who made this claim would be likely to be found at fault in many instances, for by no means all the English have these characteristics, and even if they are the characteristics of the 'typical Englishman', the fact would still remain that these outward characteristics are not 'physique' in the true sense: bodily attitudes and motions and expressions of the face all come under the heading of behaviour; and being habits determined by the subject's social background, are cultural, not 'natural'. Moreover, though loosely describable as 'traits', they typify not a whole nation, but a particular social group within it and thus cannot be included among the distinctive marks of race.

Accordingly any confusion between 'race' and 'nation' must be avoided and there are sound reasons against the misuse of the terms, even in speech.

At first sight it might seem to make little difference to use the term 'Latin race' instead of the correct 'Latin civilization'. There never was a Latin race, i.e. (in Professor H. E. Vallois' definition) a *'natural group of men displaying a particular set of common hereditary physical characteristics'*, but there was a people of Latin speech and its civilization spread over the greater part of western Europe and even parts of Africa and the East, to include a wide variety of peoples. Thus 'Latinity' was not confined to Italy nor even to Mediterranean Europe and today its traces can be found in countries (e.g., England and western Germany) whose peoples do not regard themselves as being a part of the Latin world of today. Here the kinship with Latin civilization is as undeniable as the proportion of Latin blood is obviously minute.

There has been similar—and notoriously disastrous— muddled thinking about the 'Aryan' race. There never was an Aryan race and all we are entitled to infer is the existence in the second millennium before our era of a group of peoples inhabiting the steppes of Turkistan and Central Russia with a common 'Indo-European' language and culture, who over-ran or influenced a very wide area so that their tongue is the ancestor of many others including Sanskrit, ancient Greek, Latin and the majority of the languages spoken in Europe today. Quite obviously, the use of a common language does not mean that all individuals speaking it are of the same race, since the fact that one person speaks Chinese while another speaks English or Arabic or Russian is determined, not by biological heredity, but by what each has been taught.

A similar confusion, which unhappily appears far from being resolved today, concerns the Jews, who are also deemed to be a race whereas the only valid criteria for determining membership of the group are confessional (adherence to the Jewish faith) or at most, cultural, i.e., the survival of certain modes of behaviour not directly religious in origin, but common to Jews of different countries, as a result of the long segregation imposed by Christianity and still continuing to some extent. Originally the Hebrews were Semitic-language pastoralists like the Arabs of today, but at an early stage in their history, there was intermixture between them and other peoples of the Near East, including the Hittites, whose language was of the Indo-European group, as well as such major episodes as the sojourn in Egypt, terminated by the Exodus (second millenium, B.C.), the Babylonian captivity (sixth century B.C.), the Hellenization of Alexander's day (fourth century B.C.), and conquest by Rome. Thus even be-fore the Diaspora (dispersion) throughout the Roman Empire following the destruction of Jerusalem by Titus (A.D. 70), there was intensive interbreeding. In antiquity the Jewish people appears to have been made up of nearly the same racial elements as the Greeks of the Islands and Asia Minor. Today Jews are so little recognizable anthropologically—despite the existence of a so-called Jewish 'type', which itself differs as between the Ashkenazim or Northern and the Sephardim or Southern Jews—that the Nazis themselves were forced to use special badges to distinguish them and to adopt a religious criterion to determine who were Jews: those persons were considered as of Jewish race whose ancestry included a pre-scribed number of practising Jews. Such inconsistencies are typical of doctrines like racism, which have no hesitation in doing violence to the facts of science and even to common sense as their political needs require.

WHAT IS A RACE?

We have seen then that a national community is not a race and that race cannot be defined in terms of common culture, language or religion. Further, emigration by the white and yellow races and the slave trade in the case of the black, have made it impossible to draw clear lines of geographical demarcation between the three major racial groups. This means that we must approach the question of race from the standpoint of physical anthropology—the only one from which such a concept (essentially biological since it relates to heredity) can have any validity—and then go on to consider whether the fact of an individual's belonging to a particular race has psychological implications which might tend to differentiate him from the cultural point of view.

As we have seen, the concept of 'races' is in essence that the species *Homo sapiens* can be sub-divided into groups equivalent to botanical 'varieties' in terms of certain transmissible physical characteristics. Even from this angle the question is of some delicacy because no single characteristic can be selected as the criterion for the definition of a race (for instance, there are dark-skinned Hindus, but they are differentiated from Negroes in too many other particulars for it to be possible to place both in the same category). Moreover, each of the characteristics in question admits of a considerable degree of variation from the norm—so much so that, far from accurately reflecting the facts, any division into categories must be arbitrary. In practice, a race—or sub-race —may be defined as a group whose members' physical characteristics conform, on average, to those arbitrarily selected as differentials, and there will be overlapping between peoples: for instance, the lighter skinned individuals, in peoples classified as of the black race, will on occasion be no more—or even less—pigmented than the darkest skinned individuals in populations classified as white. Thus, instead of arriving at a table of races displaying clear-cut divisions, all that can be isolated are groups of individuals who may be regarded as typical of their races because they present all the characteristics accepted as distinguishing these races, but who have congeners lacking some of those characteristics or displaying them in a less marked form. Should we then conclude that these typical individuals are representative of the pure or almost pure stock of the race in question, whereas the remainder are mere mongrels?

Nothing entitles us to make such a statement. The Mendelian law of heredity shows the biological heritage of the individual as consisting of a long series of characteristics contributed by both parents which (to borrow the image used by Ruth Benedict) 'have to be conceived not as ink and water mingling but as a pile of beads sorted out anew for every individual'. Novel arrangements of these elements occur so constantly in new individuals that a multitude of different combinations is produced in no more than a few generations. Thus the 'typical specimen' in no sense reflects the former and 'purer' state of the race, but is merely a statistical concept expressing the frequency of certain distinctive combinations.

Hence, from the genetic point of view, it would appear impossible to regard the world population of today as other than more or less a hodgepodge, since the widest variety of types occurs from the prehistory epoch downwards and the indications are that folk migrations and considerable intermingling took place very early in the evolution of mankind. For instance, as far as Europe is concerned, in the lower palaeolithic period we already find distinct species.

Then a number of races succeed each other: in the middle palaeolithic epoch we have the Neanderthal Man (who may be either a very primitive variety of the species *Homo sapiens* or a separate species); in the upper palaeolithic age we first find representatives of *Homo sapiens* of today; the Cro-Magnon stock (of whom the Canary Islanders, descended from the ancient Guanches, may well be a modern remnant) and the quite distinct Chancelade and Grimaldi races (of a type reminiscent of the Negroid races of today). In the mesolithic period we find a mixture of races in existence from which there emerged in the neolithic period the Nordic, the Mediterranean and the Alpine types, who, up to our day, have constituted the essential anthropological elements in the population of Europe.

In the case of small societies, relatively stable and isolated (e.g., an Eskimo community living in an almost closed 'hunting' economy) the representatives of the various clans making up the community have approximately the same heredity. Here, it is possible to talk of racial purity, but not in the case of larger groups where crossings between families and the introduction of heterogeneous elements have occurred on an extensive scale. Applied to large groups with an eventful past and distributed over wide areas, the word 'race' means merely that it is possible to go beyond the differences between nations or tribes and identify groups characterized by the occurrence of physical features which are, to some extent temporary, since for demographic reasons alone, the groups concerned are in constant evolution and the historic process of contacts and blending continues.

WHAT DOES THE INDIVIDUAL MAN OWE
TO HIS RACE?

It may be taken, then, that from the point of view of physical anthropology, the species *Homo sapiens* consists of a number of races or groups differentiated by the frequency of particular physical traits which—be it remembered—represent only a mere fraction of a biological heritage otherwise common to all human beings. Although it follows that the similarities between men are much greater than the differences, we are inclined to regard as fundamental differences which are really no more than variations on the same theme, for, just as we are likely to notice much more difference between the faces of our immediate neighbours than between those of persons strange to us, so a quite false impression of great physical differences between the various races of men is reinforced by the fact of such differences between our own kind being more striking than those between varieties of other species.

The temptation to postulate psychological differences from such differences in external aspect is the stronger in that the men of different races in practice often have different cultures. There is not merely a physical but a mental difference between a magistrate in one of our great cities and a notable of the Congo. However, the mental difference between them is not a necessary corollary of the physical, but a consequence merely of their belonging to two different cultures and even so is not so great as to preclude the finding of certain resemblances between the two men arising from their roughly analogous positions in their respective societies, just as a Norman and a Mandigo peasant, both living off their own holdings, are likely to present some points of resemblance additional to those common to all men.

The assumption has often been made that what white men imagine to be the primitive features in the physique of coloured peoples are indicative of mental inferiority. Even the premise is vitiated by its *naïveté,* as the thinner-lipped, and hairier white man more closely resembles the anthropoid in these respects than does the Negro. As to mental inferiority, neither anthropological research on such subjects as the weight and structure of the brain in the different races nor psychologists' attempts at direct evaluation of relative intellectual capacity have produced any proof of it.

It has indeed been found that on average the Negro brain weighs a little less than the European, but the difference (considerably less than can be found between the brains of individual members of one race) is so minute that no conclusions can be drawn from it, while the fact that the brains of a number of great men have been found, after death, to be below average size shows that a greater weight of brain does not necessarily mean greater intelligence.

As regards psychological tests, in proportion as we have learned better how to make allowance for the influence of the physical and social environment (the influence of the state of health, social setting upbringing, standard of education, etc.) the results have pointed increasingly to a fundamental equivalence in the intellectual attributes of all human groups. In the present condition of science it is not possible to say of a particular race that it is more (or less) 'intelligent' than another. While it can undoubtedly be shown that a member of a poor and isolated group—or of a lower social class—is handicapped *vis-à-vis* the members of a group living under better economic conditions (e.g., better nourished, living under healthier conditions and with more incentives), this proves nothing as to the aptitudes which the less privileged individual might display in a more favourable setting. Similarly, in assuming the superiority of so-called 'primitives' over the 'civilized' as regards sensory perception—a superiority regarded as a kind of counterweight to their assumed inferiority intellectually—we are jumping to conclusions and failing to give proper weight to the former's training in observation: a member, say of a community living mainly by hunting and food-gathering, acquires notable superiority over the civilized man in the interpretation of visual, auditory and olfactory impressions, skill in finding his way, etc. . . . and here again, the operative factor is cultural rather than racial.

Lastly, research into character has not been able to show that it is dependent on race: the widest varieties of character are found in all ethnic groups, and there is no reason whatever for assuming greater uniformity under this head in any particular group. For instance, to assume a tendency to irresponsibility in the Negro and to contemplation in the average

191

oriental is to draw a false conclusion from incomplete data: probably white people would be less inclined to picture the Negro as irresponsible if these ideas of him were not based on individuals deprived by slavery or colonization of their natural background and forced by their masters to tasks to which they can bring no interest. Quite apart from its possibly debasing effect on its victims, such a life leaves them with little choice save between revolt and a resigned or smiling fatalism, which may indeed mask the spirit of rebellion. Similarly, even without the example of Japan's emergence as a full-fledged imperialist power after centuries of almost uninterrupted peace abroad and concentration mainly on questions of etiquette and aesthetic values, we should be less inclined to regard the yellow man as naturally contemplative if, from the beginning, we had gained our impression of China, not from her philosophers and the inventions for which we are indebted to her, but from the realistic literature which, like the licentious novel *Kin P'ing Mei,* first published in 1610, shows us a type of Chinese more inclined to riotous gallantry than to art and mysticism.

Accordingly, the conclusion to be drawn alike from the anthropological and the psychological researches of the last 30 to 40 years is that the racial factor is very far from being the dominant element in the formation of personality. This should be no cause for astonishment if we remember that psychological traits cannot be transmitted direct as part of the heredity (for instance, there is no gene governing mind-wandering or power of concentration) which in this sphere comes into play only so far as it affects the organs through which the psychological mechanisms operate, such as the nervous system and the endocrine glands. These, though of real importance in the determination of the affective make-up of normal individuals, obviously exercise a more limited influence on the intellectual and moral qualities compared with that of differences of environment. Under this head the major factors are the character and intellectual level of the parents (owing to the growing child's intimate contact with them), both social and academic training, religious teaching and training in self-mastery, source of livelihood and place in society, in other words elements in no respect traceable to the individual's biological heredity and still less to his race, but largely determined by the setting in which he grows up, the society of which he is a part and the culture to which he belongs.

MAN AND HIS CULTURES

It is a long-standing and widespread Western habit of mind to regard the converse of 'civilization' as 'savagery' (the state of life of the 'savage', in Latin *silvaticus,* the man of the woods), urban life being taken, rightly or wrongly, as a symbol of refinement in contrast to the supposedly cruder life of forest or bush, and to divide the human race into two categories in terms of these two opposing ways of life. It is accepted as true that parts of the world are inhabited by peoples classifiable on the above basis as savages and held to have risen comparatively little above the level of the beasts, while in other regions there are highly evolved or sophisticated 'civilized' peoples essentially differentiated from the first category as being *par excellence* the trustees and apostles of culture.

The colonial expansion which began with the maritime discoveries of the late fifteenth century introduced the Western stock even into the regions furthest from Europe in space and most unlike in climate, and temporarily at least, Western suzerainty was imposed there and Western culture imported. One consequence was the prevalence in the West until recently, of the view—naïvely egocentric notwithstanding their grounds for pride in their impressive technological progress—that civilization and culture were synonymous with the Western varieties, if only, in the latter case, the culture of the most privileged classes in the West. The exotic peoples with whom the Western nations made contact either as subject races in their colonies or in their search for products unobtainable in Europe, or new markets for their goods or incidentally to their dispositions for the safeguarding of their earlier conquests, were regarded either as untamed 'savages' ruled by their instincts, or, in the case of peoples deemed inferior but anyhow semi-civilized, as 'barbarians', the contemptuous name given by Ancient Greece to foreigners. The position today is that the majority of Occidentals, whether they regard the way of life of the so called 'uncultured' peoples as approximately that of the beasts or as 'primitive' in the sense of Paradisiac, believe that there are 'wild men' in the world—beings without civilization representing a phase in the history of humanity analogous to that of childhood in the life of the individual.

Either their noteworthy architectural remains or their close contacts with the classical world (Greece and Rome) fairly early enabled certain major Oriental cultures—or successive series of cultures—to secure acceptance by the West, and Egypt, Phoenicia and Palestine in the Near East, Assyria, Chaldea and Persia, in the Middle East were all sufficiently well known for swift acknowledgement of their title to be described as civilizations worthy of the name. Similarly, India, China, Japan and the great states of pre-Columbian America were not long in receiving their due and no one today would dispute their right to a place of high honour at the very least in any general history of humanity. However, it took the West much longer to realize that peoples little advanced technologically and with no written language as we understand it— like the majority of the black races of Africa, the Melanesians and Polynesians, the modern Indians of North and South America and the Eskimos—nevertheless have their own 'civilization', i.e., a culture which, even among the humblest of them, at some moment showed itself possessed of some power of expansion (even if that power is now lost or the culture is shrinking) and which is broadly common to a number of societies over a reasonably extensive geographical area.

The knowledge of anthropology (now a systematic discipline) possessed by Western science of the middle twentieth century warrants the assertion that there is no extant group of human beings today which can be described as being 'in the natural state'. For confirmation we need look no further than the elementary fact that nowhere in the world is there a people who leave the human body in an absolutely natural state, without clothing, adornment or some modification (tattooing, scarification or other forms of mutilation), as though —whatever the diversity of the forms taken by what the West calls modesty—the human body in its pristine state could not be tolerated. The truth is that 'natural man' is a figment of the mind and the note which distinguishes Man from the animal world is essentially that he has a culture, whereas the beasts have not, for lack of the capacity for abstract thought, needed for the development of systems of conventional symbols such as language, or the retention for future use of the tools made for a specific task. While it may not be an adequate definition of man to say that he is a *social animal* (since a very wide variety of other species are gregarious), he is sufficiently differentiated if described as *possessing culture,* since he is unique among living creatures in employing such artificial aids as speech and tools in his dealings with his fellows and his environment.

WHAT IS CULTURE?

Among human beings as among all other mammals, the general behaviour of the individual is determined partly by instinct (an item of his biological heritage), partly by his personal experience and partly by what he learns from other members of his species. In Man, however, with his unique powers of symbolizing, experience becomes more readily transmissible and in some sort 'storable', since all the acquisitions of a generation can be conveyed to the next through language, and can thus develop into a 'culture', a social legacy distinct from the biological legacy and from the acquisitions of the individual and definable in the terms adopted by Ralph Linton as 'a configuration of learned behaviour and results of behaviour whose component elements are shared and transmitted by the members of a particular society'.

Whereas race is strictly a question of heredity, culture is essentially one of *tradition* in the broadest sense, which includes the formal training of the young in a body of knowledge or a creed, the inheriting of customs or attitudes from previous generations, the borrowing of techniques or fashions from other countries, the spread of opinions through propaganda or conversation, the adoption—or 'selling'—of new products or devices, or even the circulation of legends or jests by word of mouth. In other words, tradition in this sense covers provinces clearly unconnected with biological heredity and all alike consisting in the transmission, by word of mouth, image or mere example, of characteristics which, taken together, differentiate a milieu, society or group of societies throughout a period of reasonable length and thus constitute its culture.

As culture, then, comprehends all that is inherited or transmitted through society, it follows that its individual elements are proportionately diverse. They include not only beliefs, knowledge, sentiments and literature (and illiterate peoples often have an immensely rich oral literature), but the language or other systems of symbols which are their vehicles. Other elements are the rules of kinship, methods of education, forms of government and all the fashions followed in social relations. Gestures, bodily attitudes and even facial expressions are also included, since they are in large measure acquired by the community through education or imitation; and so, among the material elements, are fashions in housing and clothing and ranges of tools, manufactures and artistic production, all of which are to some extent traditional. Far from being restricted to or identical with what is commonly implied in describing a person as 'cultured' or otherwise (i.e., having a greater or lesser sum of knowledge of a greater or lesser variety of the principal branches of arts, letters and science in their Western forms), that is, the ornamental culture which is mainly an outcrop of the vaster mass which conditions it and of which it is only a partial expression, culture in the true sense should be regarded as comprising the whole more or less coherent structure of concepts, sentiments, mechanisms, institutions and objects which explicitly or implicitly condition the conduct of members of a group.

In this context, a group's future is as truly the product of its culture as its culture is of its past, for its culture both epitomizes its past experience (what has been retained of the responses of its members in earlier generations to the situations and problems which confronted them) and also—and as a consequence—provides each new generation with a starting point (a system of rules and models of behaviour, values, concepts, techniques, instruments, etc.) round which it will plan its way of life and on which the individual will draw to some extent, and which he will apply in his own way and according to his own means in the specific situation confronting him. Thus it is something which can never be regarded as fixed for ever, but is constantly undergoing changes, sometimes small enough or slow enough to be almost imperceptible or to remain long unnoticed, sometimes of such scope or speed as to appear revolutionary.

CULTURE AND PERSONALITY

From the psychological point of view, the culture of a given society is the sum of the ways of thought, reactions and habits of behaviour acquired by its members through teaching or imitation and more or less common to them all.

Quite apart from individual variations (which by definition cannot be regarded as 'cultural', as they do not pertain to the community), there is no question of all the facets of a given society's culture being displayed in all the members of that society. While some of its elements can be described as general, there are others which the mere division of labour (found in all contemporary societies, if only in the form of the allocation of trades and social functions between the two sexes and the various age groups) makes the preserve of certain recognized categories of individuals, others again peculiar to a particular family or set and yet others (opinions, tastes, choice of specific commodities or furniture) which are merely common to a number of individuals between whom there is otherwise nothing particular in common. This uneven occurrence of the individual items making up a culture is a consequence, direct or indirect, of the economic structure of a particular society and (in the case of societies where even a slightly more advanced division of labour prevails) of its subdivision into castes or classes.

While culture may vary between groups, sub-groups and to a certain extent families, and while it is more or less rigid and contains elements of varying compulsive force, it is at the same time a paramount factor in the shaping of individual personality.

Since personality consists in the sum of the outward behaviour and psychological attitudes distinguishing the individual—he being unique, whatever the general type under which he is classifiable—it is affected by a number of factors: biological heredity, which affects the physical organs, and also transmits a range of the comportments which are instinctive or more accurately 'non-acquired'; the experience of the individual in his private life, at his work, and as a member of society—in other words, his life-story over the period (which may be lengthy) from birth until his character may be regarded as set; and his cultural background, whence he derives a proportion of his acquired behaviour by means of his social heritage.

Though biological heredity influences the personality of the individual (to the extent to which his bodily characteristics and more particularly his nervous and glandular make-up are inherited), this is true of the family, rather than of the racial ancestry. Even where individual pedigrees are concerned, we lack the requisite knowledge of the biological make-up of all ancestors, so that in any case our knowledge of what an individual may owe to his heredity is scanty. Furthermore, it can be demonstrated that all normal men, whatever their race, have the same general equipment of non-acquired behaviour (research into child behaviour brings out clearly the similarity of initial responses and shows that the explanation of subsequent variations in behaviour can be explained by differences in individual make-up or by early training); thus, it is not in the so-called 'instinct' that the differences between individuals reside. It must also be borne in mind that the true

197

category of unlearned behaviour is confined to the basic reflexes, and the common tendency to extend it is an error, much behaviour so classified being in fact the result of habits acquired, though never explicitly taught, at so early an age as to give the impression of something inborn.

While undoubtedly there are idiosyncrasies, in addition to those distinguishing individuals, which may be broadly regarded as differentiating the members of a particular society from the rest of the world, it is under the head of acquired behaviour that they will be found; they are thus, by definition, cultural.

To judge of the importance of his culture as a factor in the formation of the individual's personality, we need only remember that it is not merely in the form of the heritage handed down to him through education that his group's culture affects him: it conditions his whole experience. He is born into the world in a particular physical environment (what one might call the bio-geographical habitat) and in a particular social setting. Even the first is not a 'natural' but to some extent a 'cultural' environment, for the habitat of a settled population (agriculturalists or city dwellers) is invariably of its own making to a greater or lesser degree, and, even in the case of nomadic groups, the physical environment will include artificial elements in the shape of tents, etc.; in addition, the impact on the individual of both the natural and the artificial elements in his environment is not direct but is modified by the culture (knowledge, belief and activities) of the group. The influence of the social environment is twofold: direct, through the examples available to the newcomer in the behaviour of older members of his society and through the group's speech, in which the whole of its past experience is crystallized and which may therefore be likened to a concise encyclopaedia; and indirect, through the influence of the culture concerned on the personalities and the conduct towards the child of the individuals (e.g., parents) playing a prominent part in the subject's life, from early childhood—a crucial phase which will condition all later development.

In general, the individual is so thoroughly conditioned by his culture that even in the satisfaction of his most elementary needs—those which may be classified as biological because they are shared by man with the other mammals, e.g., feeding, protection and reproduction—he only breaks free of the bonds of custom in the most exceptional circumstances: a normal Western man will only eat dog if threatened with starvation, while many peoples would be utterly nauseated by foods which are a delight to us. Similarly, a man's choice of dress will be appropriate to his station (or to the rank for which he wishes to pass) and often custom, or fashion, will override practical considerations. Lastly, there is no society in which sexual life is absolutely free and, while the details may vary from culture to culture, there are rules everywhere against intercourse within prohibited degrees locally regarded as incestuous and hence criminal. It should also be noted that the individual is at least partially influenced by his culture even where he may seem furthest from the discipline of society: for instance, dreams are not, as was long believed, mere phantasies, but expressions of interests and conflicts which vary according to culture in terms of images drawn directly or indirectly from the cultural environment. Thus culture affects the life of the individual at every level and its influence is as apparent in the way in which a man satisfies his physical needs as in his ethics or his intellectual life.

The inference to be drawn from all this is that while obviously there are variations in the psychological heritage of individuals the fact of a man's belonging to a particular ethnic group affords no basis for deducing what are likely to be his aptitudes. On the other hand, the cultural environment is a factor of primary importance not merely because it determines what the individual learns and how he learns it, but because it is in the strict sense the 'environment' within which and in terms of which he reacts. For instance, it is a safe assumption that, if an African baby were adopted at birth by whites and brought up as their own child, there would be no marked psychological differences imputable to his origin between him and his foster parents' natural children of the same sex; he would express himself in the same idiom with the same accent; he would have the same equipment of ideas, feelings and habits and would differ from his brothers and sisters by adoption only to the extent to which the members of any group fall short of uniformity, however great and numerous the analogies between them. It should, of course, be realized that this example is purely hypothetical as, even in an adoptive family free of race prejudice in any form, such a child would in fact be in a different position from the rest. For the experiment to be valid, one would have to be able to eliminate the probable influence on the subject (of unforeseeable effect and importance) of his being regarded as different from others, if not by his immediate circle, at least by other members of the same society. The point however is that the special differentiating factor which might become operative would be not *race* but *race prejudice,* which, even without positive discrimination, puts its victims in a position differing in kind from that of persons whom no preconceived idea can cause to be regarded as not 'like everyone else'.

HOW CULTURES LIVE

Being identified with a way of life peculiar to a specified human society in a specified epoch, a culture, however slow its evolution, can never be entirely static. Insofar at least as it exists as an organized system, recognizable despite its variations, it is the apanage of a group which is constantly changing through the mere processes of death and birth. Its radius (i.e., 'membership') may increase or decrease, but at every stage in its history, it consists exclusively of elements socially transmissible (by inheritance or borrowing) and hence —though there are bound to be modifications or even major alterations, with the rejection of former elements and the addition of new—the culture itself is able to continue through all the transformations of the fluid group it represents, and share its hazards or disasters, assimilate new elements and export certain of its own, more or less replace the culture of a different group (through conquest or otherwise) or conversely be absorbed by another culture (leaving few, or no, visible traces behind it). Clearly, then, a culture is essentially a provisional and infinitely flexible system. Almost everywhere in the world we find the old comparing the way of life of the young unfavourably with 'the good old days', and that in itself amounts to an explicit or implicit admission that customs have changed and that the culture of their society has evolved further. The change may be brought about in either of two ways, by invention or discovery within the society, or by borrowing (spontaneous or under constraint) from outside.

Even when they result from an invention (a new application of existing knowledge of any kind) or a discovery (the appearance of new knowledge, scientific or otherwise), innovations in a culture are never entirely original in that they never 'start from scratch': for instance, the invention of the loom not merely implied prior knowledge of certain laws and of other simpler mechanisms, but also the response to a need arising at a particular moment in the evolution of modern industry.

Similarly, the discovery of America would have been impossible without the compass, while Christopher Columbus would never even have thought of sailing westwards if the march of events had not made a maritime trade route to the Indies a felt need. In the aesthetic sphere, the work of Phidias could never have come about without Polycletes, nor Andalusian folk music of today have developed without Arab music; and, as a last example, in the sphere of government, it was on Athenian life and aspirations already existing that Solon drew to endow his fellow citizens with a new Constitution, which in fact was no more than a codification of the existing social complex. Thus no invention, discovery or innovation can be ascribed exclusively to one individual. Inventors, or pioneers on other lines, are, indeed, found in all civilizations. However, an invention is not the result of a single flash of genius, but the last stage in a gradual advance, as the following sequence exemplifies: in 1663, the Marquess of Worcester devised a 'steam fountain' on his estate near London, based on principles suggested about 50 years earlier by a Frenchman, Salomon de Caus. Later came the invention of the pressure boiler by another Frenchman, Denis Papin, leading in turn to that of the reciprocating engine by James Watt and the final step was George Stephenson's construction of the 'Rocket' locomotive in 1814. Neither inventions nor discoveries are ever more than modifications, variable in their degree and their repercussions, which are the latest of a long series of earlier inventions and discoveries in a culture which is itself the work of a community and the product of indigenous innovations or borrowings from abroad by earlier generations. This is as true of innovations in religion, philosophy, art or ethics as of those in the various branches of science and technology. The work of great founders of religions (e.g., Buddha, Jesus or Mohammed) has never amounted to more than the more or less drastic reform of an existing religion or the combination of elements from a number of sources to construct a new creed. Again, it is traditional problems to which a culture's philosophers or moralists devote their time. The statement of the problems and the solutions propounded vary with the age, and divergent opinions on them may obtain concurrently, but nevertheless, the chain of tradition remains unbroken: each thinker takes up the question at the point where it was left by some predecessor.

It is not otherwise with works of literature or plastic art:

however revolutionary it may seem, such work always has its antecedents, as with the cubists claiming aesthetic descent from the impressionist, Paul Cézanne, and finding in African Negro sculpture, not lessons only, but a precedent to justify their own experiments. Lastly, even in social relations in the strict sense, non-conformists of every variety—and there are such in all peoples and all circles—normally claim a precedent for their views and, if they make innovations, confine themselves to developing further or more consciously what has elsewhere remained more or less rudimentary. Thus a culture is clearly the work neither of a 'culture hero' (as in so many mythologies) nor of a few great geniuses, inventors or law-givers; it is the fruit of co-operation. From a certain point of view, the earliest representatives of the human species might of all men be most legitimately described as 'creators'; but even here we have to bear in mind that they had behind them not a void but the example of other species.

Generally speaking, Western man of our own day is dazzled by the inventions and discoveries which can be credited to his culture and is almost ready to think that he has a monopoly in this field. To make this assumption would be to forget firstly that discoveries such as Einstein's theory of relativity or nuclear fission are the crown of a long process of evolution leading up to them and secondly that innumerable inventions, today out of date and their makers forgotten, showed in their age and place a degree of genius at least equal to that of the most famous of our own scientists. For instance, the primitive inhabitants of Australia made boomerangs which could return to the point from which they were thrown, with neither laboratories nor scientific research services to help them with the complex ballistic problems involved. Similarly the ancestors of the Polynesians of today, moving onward from island to island without compasses and with outrigger canoes as their only vessels, accomplished feats in no wise inferior to those of Christopher Columbus and the great Portuguese navigators.

FECUNDITY OF CONTACTS

Although no culture is absolutely static, it is indisputable that a high density of population furnishes more favourable conditions for new developments in the culture of the group concerned, as the multiplicity of contacts between individuals brings greater intensity to the intellectual life of each. Furthermore, in such numerous and thickly settled groups, a more extensive division of labour becomes possible—as noted years ago by Emile Durkheim, founder of the French Sociological School—and the increase in specialization results not merely in technological progress, but in the sub-division of the group into separate social classes between which tensions or conflicts of interests or self-esteem are bound to arise, this in its turn involving sooner or later a modification of the established cultural forms. In societies of this degree of complexity, the individual is on average confronted with a wider variety of situations which he must tackle along new lines and thus modify the traditional responses in the light of his numerous experiences.

Similarly the less isolated a people is, the more windows it has on the outer world and the more its opportunities for contact with other peoples, the more likelihood of its culture growing richer alike by direct borrowings and as a result of its members' diversified experience and increased need to meet new situations. Even war is a means of contact between peoples though far from the most desirable type, as all too often, only fragments of a culture, if anything, survive the trials of military conquest or oppression. A good example of cultural stagnation brought about by isolation is that of the Tasmanians who, being cut off from the rest of humanity by their island's geographical position, were still technologically at the middle palaeolithic stage when the English settled there at the beginning of last century. In fact, the ending of their isolation was far from advantageous to the Tasmanians, for today they are totally extinct, having perished piecemeal in their contact warfare against the colonists; hence the conclusion to be drawn is that, while in principle, contact, even through war, aids cultural evolution, it is essential, if such contact is to be fruitful, that it occurs between peoples whose technological levels are not too different (to avoid the mere extermination of one of them or its reduction to a state of near-servitude resulting in its traditional culture's extinction). It is also essential that armaments should not have achieved— as is unhappily the case with the great nations of the modern world—such a degree of effectiveness that both sides, even if they escape utter destruction, emerge from the conflict ruined.

We have seen, then, that the means, external or internal, whereby a culture is transformed include contact between individuals and between peoples, borrowings, the making of new combinations from existing elements and the discovery of new relationships or facts. So great is the part played by borrowings that we may say the same of cultures as of races, that they are never 'pure' and that there is none of them which, in its present state, is not the result of co-operation between different peoples. The civilization of which the Western world is so proud has been built of a myriad contributions, of which many are non-European in origin. The alphabet first reached the Phoenicians from the Semitic communities bordering the Sinai Peninsula, travelled from them to the Greeks and Romans and then spread through the western-most parts of Europe. Our numerals and algebra come to us from the Arabs whose philosophers and scientists incidentally played an important part in the various renaissances of mediaeval Europe. The earliest astronomers were Chaldeans; steel was invented in India or Turkistan; coffee comes from Ethiopia; tea, porcelain, gunpowder, silk, rice and the compass were given us by the Chinese who also were acquainted with printing centuries before Gutenberg, and early discovered how to make paper. Maize, tobacco, the potato, quinine, coca, vanilla and cacao we owe to the American Indians. The explanation of the 'miracle of Greece' is really that Greece was a crossroads, where vast numbers of different peoples and cultures met. Lastly, we should recollect that the wall paintings and engravings of the Aurignacian and Magdalenian ages (the most ancient works of art known in Europe, of which it may be said with truth that their beauty has never been exceeded) were the work of men of the Grimaldi type, probably not unlike the Negro races of today; that, in another aesthetic sphere, the jazz which plays so important a part in our leisure, was evolved by the descendants of Negroes taken to the United States as slaves, to whom that country also owes the oral literature on which the famous Uncle Remus stories are based.

RACE HISTORY AND CULTURAL DIFFERENCES

However numerous the exchanges between different cultures in the courses of history, and despite the fact that none of these cultures can be regarded as 'pure-bred', the fact is that differences do exist and it is possible to identify specific culture areas and periods: for instance, there was a Germanic culture described by Tacitus and of interest to him precisely because of its differences from Latin culture. In our own day, the task of the anthropologist is to study cultures diverging considerably from what with certain variants is the common culture of the Western nations. This must suggest the question whether there is a causal relationship between race and culture and whether each of the various ethnic groups has on balance a predisposition to develop certain cultural forms. However, such a notion cannot survive a scrutiny of the facts and it can be taken as established today that hereditary physical differences are negligible as causes of the differences in culture observable between the peoples. What should rather be taken into consideration is the history of those peoples.

The first point which stands out is that a given culture is not the creation of a particular race, but normally of several. Let us take as an example what we call 'Egyptian civilization', i.e., the cultural *continuum* found in Egypt between the Neolithic age (when wheat and the same type of barley as today were already being cultivated in the Fayum area) and the third century of our own era, when Christianity spread over the country; the excavation of tombs has shown that from the Polished Stone Age onwards the population of Egypt was Hamitic, while an entirely different strain is found in addition from the beginning of the dynastic epoch. At various times the country was invaded by the Hyksos (nomads from Asia who arrived in the second millennium B.C. and introduced the horse and the war chariot), by the Libyans, by the Peoples of the Sea (who may have included the Achaeans), the Assyrians, and the Persians (whose sway ended only with Egypt's annexation by Alexander in 332 B.C. and entry into the Greek orbit, in which she remained until the defeat of Antony and Cleopatra in 31 B.C.); while after a period of relative isolation there was sustained intercourse with the neighbouring countries of the Near East. The vicissitudes of Egypt's history appear to have had little effect on the physical type, which was stabilized at an early epoch, and although they altered her culture, she remained throughout the home of a civilization based economically on an oasis (in this case, the Nile Valley fertilized by the annual floods). Alexandria, capital of the Ptolemies, as a cosmopolitan city at the cross-roads of Asia, Africa and Europe, enjoyed a period of great brilliance during the Hellenistic Age. In Europe too, there is proof of the successive rise and decline of a number of races in the course of pre-history, while from the Neolithic Age onwards, the flow of trade points to true 'cultural relations' between different peoples. It is notable that in Equatorial Africa even the pygmies, who are exclusively hunters and food-gatherers, live in a kind of economic symbiosis with the settled Negroes who are their neighbours, and exchange game for agricultural products; this relationship is not without other cultural consequences and today the languages of the various groups of pygmies are those of the groups of Negro agriculturalists with whom they are thus linked.

Not only do all the indications point to there being no culture all of whose elements are due to a single race, but it is also apparent that no given race necessarily practises a single culture. In our own time, social transformations of considerable extent have taken place with no corresponding alteration in racial type of which the revolution engendered in Japan by the Emperor Mutsuhito (1866-1912) is the perfect example. To take another instance, the Manchus, who were a semi-civilized Tungus tribe when they conquered China in the middle of the seventeenth century, provided a dynasty which reigned gloriously over a country passing through one of the most brilliant periods of its civilization; and later China first overthrew the Manchu dynasty in 1912 in favour of a Republic and is now in the process of socialization. Again, when the expansion of Asia began after the death of Mahomet in A.D. 632, some Arab groups founded great States and built cities where the arts and sciences flourished, whereas other groups which had stayed in Arabia, remained simple pastoralists driving their flocks from grazing to grazing. Even before the total disruption of its ways of life first by the razzias of Muslim slavers, next by the seaborne traffic in human beings run by Europeans, and finally by European conquest, Negro Africa suffered the handicap of relative isolation. Nevertheless, its history tells us of such empires as the Ghana Kingdom in West Africa, roughly coeval with our own Middle Ages, which aroused the admiration of Arab travellers; and today, though many Negro tribes appear never to have achieved a political organization on a broader basis than the village, we find, as in Nigeria, great cities founded long before the European occupation. How then is it possible to claim that each physical type connotes a certain type of culture, especially if we look beyond the Negroes of Africa itself to those others, to the number of some 35 millions, who today form part of the population of the Americas and the West Indies? Though the descendants of Africans whose culture was utterly overset by the scourge of slavery, which robbed them of their freedom and their country, these people have nevertheless succeeded in adapting themselves to a cultural setting very different from that in which their ancestors were bred, and have since contrived (despite the prejudice of which they are the victims) to play a major role in many sectors in building and spreading the civilization of which Occidentals had believed themselves to be the exclusive representatives; in literature alone, a Negro, Aimé Césaire, of Martinique is among the major contemporary French poets, and another Negro, Richard Wright of Mississippi, may be accounted among the most talented of American novelists.

From the history of Europe as well, we can learn how much the customs of peoples can change without major alteration of their racial composition, and hence how fluid is 'national character'. Who would suspect that the peaceable farmers of modern Scandinavia were the descendants of the dreaded Vikings, whose long ships raided so much of Europe in the ninth century? Or would a Frenchman of 1950 recognize as his fellow-countrymen the contemporaries of Charles Martel, who conquered the Arabs at Poitiers if he had not learned it in the schools? It is also worth remembering that when Julius Caesar first landed in Great Britain in 52 B.C., the Britons struck the invaders as so barbarous that Cicero, writing to his friend Atticus, advised him against buying any of them as slaves because 'they are so utterly stupid and incapable of learning'. Nor should we forget that, after the fall of the Roman Empire, the inhabitants of Europe took many centuries to establish solidly organized and militarily formidable States; throughout the whole of the Middle Ages—conventionally taken as ending in 1453 with Mahomet II's capture of Constantinople—Europe had to defend itself alike against Mongol peoples such as the Huns (who nearly reached the Atlantic), the Avars, the Magyars (who finally settled in Hungary) and the Turks (to whom part of south-east Europe was subject for many centuries) and against the Arabs (who, after conquering North Africa, were settled for some time in Spain and the islands of the Mediterranean). At that epoch it would have been difficult to foresee that Europeans would one day found empires.

Analogous examples of variability in the aptitudes of a given nation are afforded by the history of the fine arts: the music, painting and sculpture or architecture of some country will pass through a brilliant period and then for some centuries at least nothing further of any note will be produced. Can it seriously be claimed that such fluctuations in artistic talent are due to changes in the distribution of the genes?

It is thus fruitless to seek in the biology of race an explanation of the difference observable between the cultural achievements of the various peoples. However, seeking to find the explanation, say, in the nature of the habitat is nearly as misleading and, just as North American Indians, despite a high degree of racial uniformity, display wide differences in culture (for instance the warrior Apaches of the South-West and the much more peaceable Pueblos who are racially identical), so a given climate does not imply a particular type of dwelling and costume (in the Sudan we find great variety in the types of house and heavily robed peoples living cheek by jowl with others almost naked). The life of a social group is of course conditioned by its biogeographical setting, agriculture is as out of the question in the Arctic zone as is cattle and horse breeding in the extensive areas of Africa infested by the tsetse fly; it is also indisputable that, as a general rule, a temperate climate is more favourable to human settlement and demographic development than one of extremes either way. However, varying techniques can secure very different results from similar biogeographical conditions: thus, as Pierre Gourou has pointed out, the practice of cultivating rice in flooded fields in tropical Asia has for ages past permitted a high density of population precluded in almost all other tropical areas, where land is cleared by fire and cultivated dry, by the poverty and instability of the soil. The explanation of the cultural diversity of the various peoples is accordingly more likely to be found in their past history than in their present geographical situation; the factors likely to be of preponderant importance are the knowledge acquired in the different areas they traversed during the wanderings (often long and complex) preceding their final settlement in the areas where we find them today, the degree of isolation in which they have lived or, conversely, their contacts with other peoples and the opportunities they have had of borrowing from other cultures—all of them explicitly classifiable as historical.

Franz Boas has written:

'The history of mankind proves that advances of culture depend upon the opportunities presented to a social group to learn from the experience of their neighbours. The discoveries of the group spread to others and, the more varied the contacts, the greater are the opportunities to learn. The tribes of simplest culture are on the whole those that have been isolated for very long periods and hence could not profit from the cultural achievements of their neighbours.'

The peoples of Europe—whose overseas expansion, be it remembered, is of very recent date, today restricted by the evolution of the very peoples they formerly surpassed in technique—owed their cultural lead to the opportunities they have long had of frequent contacts among themselves and with contrasting groups. The Romans, who may be regarded as the founders of the first major State to exist in Europe, borrowed from Asia in the construction of their Empire, and their only enduring successor, the Byzantine Empire, owed more of its administrative organization to Persia than to Rome. Conversely, the relative isolation of Africans for so many ages should be an added reason for admiring their success, despite these adverse conditions, in founding, before the fifteenth century, such a State as Benin (a prosperous kingdom which produced masterpieces in bronze and ivory in an age when Europe cannot have supplied the Negro artists with models), or making sixteenth century Timbuctoo, the capital of the Songoi Empire, one of the principal intellectual centres of the Muslim world. Not merely for Africa's sake, but for that of the rest of the world, it is regrettable that the rapid expansion of the European nations, at a period when the material equipment available to them was out of all proportion to those in the hands of other people, should have nipped in the bud a score of cultures whose full potentialities we shall never know.

CAN A HIERARCHY OF CULTURES BE ESTABLISHED?

Fundamentally, the cultures of the peoples reflect their past history and vary with their experiences. In peoples, as in individuals, the acquired qualities count for far more than the innate: their differing experience involves a corresponding difference in their acquired knowledge so that the world of today is populated by human groups of widely differing cultures, each having certain dominant preoccupations which may be regarded as representing (in Professor M. J. Herskovits' words) the 'focus of its culture'.

Main interest and scales of values may differ entirely between any two societies. The Hindus have gone deeply into the techniques of control of the self and meditation, but until recent days had devoted little attention to the material techniques on which their American and European contemporaries concentrated, and the latter in their turn show little inclination to metaphysical speculation and still less to the practice of philosophy. In Thibet the monastic life has always been preferred to the military interests which unhappily loom so large in our lives today. Among the Hamitic Negroes of East Africa, stock-raising is held in such esteem that their cattle are capital rather than food and we find a people like the Banyoro divided into two castes of which the higher concerns itself with stock-raising and the lower with agriculture; but conversely many societies of black agriculturalists in West Africa leave the care of their cattle to Fulani whom they despise. The existence of such degrees of cultural specialization should counsel caution in making value judgements of a culture; there is no culture which will not be found defective in certain respects and highly advanced in others, or which, on examination, will not prove more complex than the apparent simplicity of its structure had suggested. Although they used no draught animals and had not invented the wheel or discovered iron, the pre-Columbian Indian races have nevertheless left us impressive monuments which testify to the existence of a highly developed social organization and are among the finest works of man, while one such nation, the Mayas, arrived at the concept of zero independently of the Arabs. Again, no one will seek to dispute that the Chinese created a great civilization but for long ages they neither consumed their cattle's milk nor used the dung in agriculture. The Polynesians, though technologically only at the polished stone stage, developed a very rich mythology, while Negroes who had been thought to be, at best, suitable only as servile labour for the plantations of the New World, have made extensive contributions to the arts; incidentally, it was in Africa that the two varieties of millet, which have since spread throughout Asia, were first cultivated. Even the Australian aborigines, whose technology is rudimentary in the extreme, have marriage rules based on theories of consanguinity of the utmost subtlety. Lastly, our own civilization, despite its high technological development, is defective in many respects, as is proved by such facts as the high number of maladjusted persons found in the West, not to mention the social problems which the Western countries have still not solved nor the wars on which they periodically embark.

The truth is that all cultures have their successes and failures, their faults and virtues. Even language, the instrument and channel of thought, cannot serve as a yardstick to measure their relative worth; extremely rich grammatical forms are found in the speech of peoples without a written language and regarded as uncivilized. It would be equally vain to judge a culture by the criterion of our own ethical standards, for— apart from the fact that our ethics are too often no more than theoretical—many non-European societies are in certain respects more humane than our own. As the great African expert, Maurice Delafosse, points out: 'In African Negro society there are neither widows nor orphans, both alike being an automatic responsibility either of their families or of the husband's heir'; again, there are cultures in Siberia and elsewhere in which individuals whom we should shun as abnormal are regarded as inspired by the Gods and as such have their special place in social life. Men whose culture differs from our own are neither more nor less moral than ourselves; each society has its own moral standards, by which it divides its own members into good and evil, and one can certainly not form a judgement on the morality of a culture (or a race) on the strength of the behaviour, sometimes culpable from our point of view, of a proportion of its members living under the special conditions created by their status as a subject people or abrupt transplantation to another country as soldiers or labourers usually living under conditions of hardship. Lastly the argument of some anthropologists that, certain peoples are inferior on the grounds that they have produced no 'great men' is untenable. Apart from the desirability of an initial definition of what is meant by a 'great man' (a conqueror with innumerable victims to his credit; a great scientist, artist, philosopher or poet; the founder of a religion or a great saint), it is clear that, as the essential condition for classification as a 'great man' is the eventual widespread recognition of such 'greatness', it is impossible by definition for an isolated society to have produced what we call a 'great man'. It must however be emphasized that even in regions which were long isolated—in Africa and Polynesia for instance—we find strong personalities such as the Mandingue Emperor, Gongo Moussa (to whom is ascribed the introduction in the fourteenth century of the type of architecture still characteristic of the mosques and larger houses of the Western Sudan), the Zulu conqueror Chaka, the Liberian prophet Harris (who preached a syncretic Christianity on the Ivory Coast in 1913 and 1914), Finau, King of Tonga, or Kamehameha, King of Hawaii (a contemporary of Cook). These and a score of others may well have

211

been prevented merely by their too isolated and demographically restricted cultural environment from achieving recognition by a sufficient number of people to qualify—on quantitative as opposed to qualitative grounds—as 'great men' comparable in stature to our own Alexander, Plutarch, Luther or the Roi Soleil. Moreover, it is undeniable that even a relatively elementary technology implies a considerable background of knowledge and skill and that the development of a culture, however rudimentary, at all adapted to its environment, would be inconceivable if the community in question had never produced a mind above the average.

Our notions of culture being themselves integral elements in a culture (that of the society to which we belong), it is impossible for us to adopt the impartial point of view from which alone a valid hierarchy of cultures could be established. Judgements in this matter are necessarily relative and dependent on the point of view, and an African, Indian or Polynesian would be as fully justified in passing a severe judgement on the ignorance of most of us in matters of genealogy as we should on his ignorance of the laws of electricity or Archimedes' principle. What we are entitled to assert, however, as a positive fact is that there are cultures which at a particular point in history come into possession of technical resources sufficiently developed for the balance of power to operate in their favour and that such cultures tend to supplant other civilizations with inferior technical equipment with which they enter into contact. Today, Western civilization is in that position and—whatever the political difficulties and antagonisms of the nations representative of it—it is spreading over the world, if only in the form of its industrial product. The power of expansion conferred by technology and science might finally achieve recognition as the decisive criterion according to which each culture could be described as more or less 'great'; but it should be understood that 'greatness' must not be interpreted solely in what might be described as a *volumetric* sense and that it is moreover on strictly *pragmatic* grounds (i.e., in terms of the effectiveness of its recipes) that the value of a science can be assessed and that it can be regarded as living or dead and distinguished from a merely 'magical' technique. If the experimental method—in whose use the Western and Westernized nations of today excel—is an undoubted advance on *a priori* and empirical methods, it is essentially so because its results (unlike those of the other methods named) can serve as a starting point for new developments capable in their turn of practical application. Incidentally, it must be obvious that, since science as a whole is the product of a vast amount of experiment and development, to which all races have contributed for many thousands of years, it can in no respect be regarded by white men as their exclusive preserve and as indicating in themselves some congenital aptitude.

Subject to these explicit reservations, it is right to emphasize the capital importance of technology (i.e., the means of acting on the natural environment), not merely in the day to day life of societies but in their evolution. The chief milestones in the history of mankind are advances in technology which in turn have the widest repercussions in all other sectors of culture. The process begins with tool-making and the use of fire at the very beginnings of pre-history and even before the emergence of *Homo sapiens*; next comes the domestication of plants and animals for food, which raises the potential density of population and is the direct cause of the settlement of human groups in villages (a notable transformation of the natural environment), followed in turn by increasing division of labour and the emergence of crafts. At each stage the direct increase in economic resources leaves a sufficient margin for considerable development in other sectors. The latest such milestone is the development of power resources which marks the beginning of the Modern Age.

The earliest civilizations of any size, being based on agriculture, were restricted to areas made fertile by great rivers (the Nile, the Euphrates, the Tigris, the Indus, the Ganges, and the Blue and Yellow Rivers). They were followed by trading civilizations lying on inland seas or seas with frequent land masses (the Phoenicians and Greeks in the Mediterranean, and the Malays in the China Seas), which were later displaced by civilizations based on large-scale industry whose vital centres were the coal deposits in Europe, North America and Asia, and trading on a world-wide basis. Now that we have entered the Atomic Age, no one knows where—wars permitting—the principal centres of production will arise in the world nor whether the setting for the great civilizations of the future may not be regions today regarded as backward, whose inhabitants' only crime is that they belong to cultures less well equipped than our own with means of modifying their natural environment but possibly better balanced from the point of view of social relations.

THERE IS NO INBORN RACIAL AVERSION

The differences observable between the physiques of the different races (and we must remember that the only features
so far used by anthropologists as practical criteria or differentiation are purely superficial, such as colour of skin, colour
and form of eyes and hair, shape of the skull, nose and lips,
stature, etc.) afford no clue to the cast of mind and type of
behaviour characterizing the members of each of the human
varieties: outside the field of pure biology, the word 'race' is
utterly meaningless. Independently of their political division
into nationalities, men can undoubtedly be classified in groups
characterized by a certain community of behaviour, but only
in terms of their several 'cultures', in other words from the
standpoint of the history of their respective civilizations; the
groups thus delimited are quite distinct from the categories
which can be determined in terms of physical similarity, while
their relative worth can be determined in the light of pragmatic
considerations only, and such judgements lack all absolute
validity since they are necessarily conditioned by our own
culture. In any case, the scale of values thus arrived at might
well be relevant for a specific period only, since cultures, even
more than races, are fluid, and peoples are capable of very
rapid cultural evolution after centuries of near-stagnation. In
the light of this, it may be asked what is the origin of the
prejudice behind the attempt to classify certain human groups
as inferior on the ground that their racial composition is an
irremediable handicap.

The first point which emerges from any examination of the
data of ethnography and history is that race prejudice is not
universal and is of recent origin. Many of the societies investigated by anthropologists do indeed display group pride,
but while the group regards itself as privileged compared with
other groups, it makes no 'racist' claims and, for instance, is
not above entering into temporary alliances with other groups
or providing itself with women from them. Much more than
'blood', the unifying elements are common interests and a
variety of activities conducted in association. In the majority
of cases such groups are not in fact 'races'—if very isolated,
they may at most be homogeneous offshoots of a race—but
are merely societies whose antagonism to other societies,
whether traditional or arising from specific questions of
interest, is not biological but purely cultural. The peoples

whom the Greeks described as 'barbarians' were not regarded by them as racially inferior but as not having attained the same level of civilization as themselves; Alexander himself married two Persian princesses and 10,000 of his soldiers married Hindus. The main interest her subject peoples had for Rome was as a source of tribute and, since she did not pursue the same ends of systematic exploitation of the earth and its population as more recent imperialisms, she had no reason to practise racial discrimination against them. The Christian faith preached the brotherhood of man and, while all too often it fell short of its own principle in practice, it never evolved a racist ideology. The Crusades were launched against the 'infidels', the Inquisition persecuted heretics and Jews, and Catholics and Protestants exterminated each other, but in every case the motives alleged were religious and not racial. The picture only begins to change with the opening of the period of colonial expansion by the European peoples, when it becomes necessary to excuse violence and oppression by decreeing the inferiority of those enslaved or robbed of their own land and denying the title of men to the cheated peoples. (Differences in customs and the physical stigma of colour made the task an easy one.)

That the origins of race prejudice are economic and social becomes perfectly clear, if we bear in mind that the first great apostle of racism, Count de Gobineau, said himself that he wrote his two notorious 'Essays' to combat liberalism: the better to defend the threatened interest of the aristocratic caste of Europe, against the rising tide of democracy, he postulated their descent from a so-called superior race which he labelled 'Aryan', and for which he postulated a civilizing mission. We find the same motive yet again in the attempt by anthropologists such as Broca and Vacher de Lapouge of France and the German Ammon to demonstrate by anthropometry that class distinctions reflect differences in race (and hence are part of the natural order). However, the amazing intermingling of human groups which has taken place in Europe as in the rest of the world since prehistoric times, and the unceasing movements of population occurring in the countries of modern Europe are enough to demonstrate the fatuity of the attempt. Later, racism took on the virulent quality we know so well and, more particularly in Germany, appeared in nationalist guise, though still remaining in essence an ideology designed to introduce or perpetuate a system of caste economically and politically favourable to a minority, e.g., by cementing a nation's unity by the idea of itself as a master race, by inculcating in colonial populations the feeling that they are irremediably inferior to the colonizers, by preventing part of the population within a country from rising in the social scale, by eliminating competition in employment or by neutralizing popular discontent by supplying the people with a scapegoat which is also a profitable source of loot. There is bitter irony in the fact that racism developed parallel with the growth of democracy, which made an appeal to the newborn prestige of science necessary for the calming of consciences uneasy over flagrant violation of the rights of a section of mankind or refusal to recognize those rights.

Racial prejudice is not innate. As Ashley Montagu has noted: 'In America, where white and black populations frequently live side by side, it is an indisputable fact that white children do not learn to consider themselves superior to Negro children until they are told that they are so.' When a tendency to racism (in the form either of voluntary endogamy or the more or less aggressive assertion of one's own 'race's' virtue) is found in an 'outcast' group, it should be regarded as no more than the normal reaction of the 'insulted and injured' against the ostracism or persecution of which they are the victims and not as indicating the universality of racial prejudice. Whatever the role of the aggressive instinct in human psychology, there is no tendency for men to commit hostile acts against others because they are of a different breed and, if such acts are all too often committed, the reason is not hostility of biological origin; just as there has never, to the writer's knowledge, been an instance of a dog fight in which spaniels combined against bulldogs.

There are no races of masters as opposed to races of slaves: slavery is not coeval with mankind and only appeared in societies whose technology was sufficiently developed to make slave-owning profitable.

From the sexual point of view, there appears no evidence of any repulsion between race and race, and indeed all the facts so far collected demonstrate that there has been continual cross-breeding between races since the most ancient times. Nor is there the slightest evidence of such cross-breeding having given bad results since a civilization as brilliant as that of Greece arose in a human environment in which miscegenation appears to have been rampant.

Race prejudice is no more hereditary than it is spontaneous: it is in the strictest sense a 'prejudice', that is, a cultural value judgement with no objective basis. Far from being in the order of things or innate in human nature, it is one of the myths whose origin is much more propaganda by special interests than the tradition of centuries. Since there is an essential connexion between it and the antagonisms arising out of the economic structure of modern societies, its disappearance, like that of other prejudices which are less the causes than the symptoms of social injustice, will go hand in hand with the transformation of their economic structure by the peoples. Thus the co-operation on an equal footing of all human groups, whatever they be, will open undreamed-of prospects for civilization.

BIBLIOGRAPHY

BENEDICT, Ruth. *Race: science and politics*. The Viking Press, New York, 1945.

BOAS, Franz. *Racial purity*. 'Asia', XL, 1940.

Civilisation. Le mot et l'idée. Survey by Lucien Febvre, E. Tonnelat, Marcel Mauss, Alfredo Niceforo, Louis Weber. Discussion. Fondation 'Pour la Science'. Première semaine internationale de synthèse, vol. II. Alcan, Paris, 1930.

DELAFOSSE, Maurice. *Civilisations négro-africaines*. Stock, Paris, 1925.

DURKHEIM, Emile. *De la division du travail social*. 2nd edition. Alcan, Paris, 1902.

FINOT, Jean. *Le préjugé des races*. Alcan, Paris, 1906.

GOUROU, Pierre. *Les pays tropicaux*. Presses Universitaires de France, Paris, 1948.

HERSKOVITS, M. J. *Man and his works*. Alfred A. Knopf, New York, 1949.

HUXLEY, Julian S. and HADDON, A. C. *We Europeans: a survey of 'racial' problems*. Harper and Brothers, New York, 1936.

L'espèce humaine. Edited by Paul Rivet. *Encyclopédie française permanente*, vol. VII, Paris, 1936.

LESTER, Paul et MILLOT, Jacques. *Les races humaines*. Armand Colin, Paris, 1936.

LÉVI-STRAUSS, Claude. *Les structures élémentaires de la parenté*. Presses Universitaires de France, Paris, 1949.

LINTON, Ralph. *The study of man*. D. Appleton-Century Company, New York, London, 1936.

—. *The cultural background of personality*. D. Appleton-Century Company, New York, London, 1945.

MONTAGU, Ashley. *Man's most dangerous myth: the fallacy of race*. Columbia University Press, New York, 1942.

Scientific aspects of the race problem. By H. S. Jennings, Charles A. Berger, Dom Thomas Verner Moore, Aleys Hrdlicka, Robert H. Lowie, Otto Klineberg. The Catholic University of America

Press, Washington D.C., and Longmans, Green and Co., London, New York, Toronto, 1941.

The science of man in the world crisis. Edited by Ralph Linton. Columbia University Press, New York, 1945.

VALLOIS, Henri V. *Anthropologie de la population française.* Didier, Toulouse, Paris, 1943.

When peoples meet. Edited by Alain Locke and Bernhard J. Stern. Hinds, Hayden and Eldredge, New York, Philadelphia, 1942.

WHITE, Leslie A. *The science of culture.* Farrar, Straus and Co., New York, 1949.

RACE AND HISTORY

by
CLAUDE LÉVI-STRAUSS

*Director of Studies at the
Ecole pratique des hautes études*

RACE AND CULTURE

It may seem somewhat surprising, in a series of booklets intended to combat racial prejudice, to speak of the contributions made by various races of men to world civilization. It would be a waste of time to devote so much talent and effort to demonstrating that, in the present state of scientific knowledge, there is no justification for asserting that any one race is intellectually superior or inferior to another, if we were, in the end, indirectly to countenance the concept of race by seeming to show that the great ethnic groups constituting human kind as a whole have, as such, made their own peculiar contributions to the common heritage.

Nothing could be further from our intentions, for such a course of action would simply result in an inversion of the racist doctrine. To attribute special psychological characteristics to the biological races, with a positive definition, is as great a departure from scientific truth as to do so with a negative definition. It must not be forgotten that Gobineau, whose work was the progenitor of racist theories, regarded 'the inequality of the human races' as qualitative, not quantitative; in his view, the great primary races of early man— the white, the yellow and the black—differed in their special aptitudes rather than in their absolute value. Degeneration resulted from miscegenation, rather than from the relative position of individual races in a common scale of values; it was therefore the fate in store for all mankind, since all mankind, irrespective of race, was bound to exhibit an increasing intermixture of blood. The original sin of anthropology, however, consists in its confusion of the idea of race, in the purely biological sense (assuming that there is any factual basis for the idea, even in this limited field—which is disputed by modern genetics), with the sociological and psychological productions of human civilizations. Once he had made this mistake, Gobineau was inevitably committed to the path leading from an honest intellectual error to the unintentional justification of all forms of discrimination and exploitation.

When, therefore, in this paper, we speak of the contributions of different races of men to civilization, we do not mean that the cultural contributions of Asia or Europe, Africa or America are in any way distinctive because these continents are, generally speaking, inhabited by peoples of different racial stocks. If their contributions are distinctive—and there can be little doubt that they are—the fact is to be accounted for by geographical, historical and sociological circumstances, not by special aptitudes inherent in the anatomical or physiological make-up of the black, yellow or white man. It seemed to us, however, that the very effort made in this series of booklets to prove this negative side of the argument, involved a risk of pushing into the background another very important aspect of the life of man—the fact that the development of human life is not everywhere the same but rather takes form in an extraordinary diversity of societies and civilizations. This intellectual, aesthetic and sociological diversity is in no way the outcome of the biological differences, in certain observable features, between different groups of men; it is simply a parallel phenomenon in a different sphere. But, at the same time, we must note two important respects in which there is a sharp distinction. Firstly, the order of magnitude is different. There are many more human cultures than human races, since the first are to be counted in thousands and the second in single units; two cultures developed by men of the same race may differ as much as, or more than, two cultures associated with groups of entirely different racial origin. Secondly, in contrast to the diversity of races, where interest is confined to their historical origin or their distribution over the face of the world, the diversity of cultures gives rise to many problems; it may be wondered whether it is an advantage or a disadvantage for human kind, and there are many subsidiary questions to be considered under this general head.

Last and most important, the nature of the diversity must be investigated even at the risk of allowing the racial prejudices whose biological foundation has so lately been destroyed to develop again on new grounds. It would be useless to argue the man in the street out of attaching an intellectual or moral significance to the fact of having a black or white skin, straight or frizzy hair, unless we had an answer to another question which, as experience proves he will immediately ask: if there are no innate racial aptitudes, how can we explain the fact that the white man's civilization has made the tremendous advances with which we are all familiar while the civilizations of the coloured peoples have lagged behind, some of them having come only half way along the road, and others being still thousands or tens of thousands of years behind the times? We cannot therefore claim to have formulated a convincing denial of the inequality of the human *races,* so long as we fail to consider the problem of the inequality—or diversity—of human *cultures,* which is in fact—however unjustifiably—closely associated with it in the public mind.

THE DIVERSITY OF CULTURES

If we are to understand how, and to what extent, the various human cultures differ from one another, and whether these differences conflict or cancel one another out or, on the contrary, are all instrumental in forming a harmonious whole, the first thing to do is to draw up a list of them. But here we immediately run into difficulties, for we are forced to recognize that human cultures do not all differ from one another in the same way or on the same level. Firstly, we have societies co-existing in space, some close together and some far apart but, on the whole, contemporary with one another. Secondly, we have social systems that have followed one another in time, of which we can have no knowledge by direct experience. Anyone can become an ethnographer and go out to share the life of a particular society which interests him. But not even the historian or archeologist can have any personal contact with a vanished civilization; all his knowledge must be gleaned from the writings or the monuments which it or other societies have left behind. Nor must we forget that those contemporary societies which have no knowledge of writing, like those which we call 'savage' or 'primitive', were preceded by other forms of society of which we can learn nothing, even indirectly. If we are honest in drawing up our list, we shall have, in such cases, to leave blank spaces, which will probably be far more numerous than the spaces in which we feel we can make some entry. The first thing to be noted is therefore that, in fact in the present, as well as in fact and in the very nature of things in the past, the diversity of human cultures is much greater and richer than we can ever hope to appreciate to the full.

But however humble we may be in our approach, and however well we may appreciate our limitations in this respect, there are other problems to be considered. What are we to understand by 'different' cultures? Some cultures appear to qualify for this description, but, if they are derived from a common stock, they cannot differ in the same way as two societies which have had no contacts with one another at any stage of their development. For instance, the ancient Inca Empire in Peru and the Kingdom of Dahomey in Africa are more absolutely different than are, let us say, England and the United States today, although these two societies also are to be regarded as distinct. Conversely, societies which have been in very close contact since a recent date give the impression of representing a single civilization, whereas in fact they have reached the present stage by different paths, which we are not entitled to ignore. Forces working in contrary directions operate simultaneously in human societies, some being conducive to the preservation and even the accentuation of particularism, while others tend to promote convergence and affinity. Striking instances are to be found in the study of language for, while languages whose origin is the same tend to develop differences from one another—e.g. Russian, French and English—languages of different origin which are spoken in adjacent territories developed common characteristics: Russian, for example, has developed differences from other Slavic languages in certain respects and grown closer, at least in certain phonetic features, to the Finno-Ugrian and Turkish languages spoken in its immediate geographic neighbourhood.

A study of such facts—and we could easily find similar instances in other aspects of civilization, such as social institutions, art and religion—leads us to ask whether, in the inter-relations of human societies, there may not be an *optimum* degree of diversity, which they cannot surpass but which they can also not fall short of without incurring risks.

This optimum would vary according to the number of societies, their numerical strength, their geographical distance from
one another, and the means of communication (material and
intellectual) at their disposal. The problem of diversity does
not, in fact, arise solely with regard to the inter-relations of
cultures; the same problem is found within each individual
society with regard to the inter-relations of the constituent
groups; the various castes, classes, professions or religious
denominations develop certains differences, which each of
them considers to be extremely important. It may be wondered
whether this internal differentiation does not tend to increase
when the society becomes larger and otherwise more homogeneous; this may perhaps have been what happened in
ancient India, where the caste system developed as a sequel
to the establishment of the Aryan hegemony.

It is thus clear that the concept of the diversity of human
cultures cannot be static. It is not the diversity of a collection
of lifeless samples or the diversity to be found in the arid
pages of a catalogue. Men have doubtless developed differentiated cultures as a result of geographical distance, the special
features of their environment, or their ignorance of the rest
of mankind; but this would be strictly and absolutely true
only if every culture or society had been born and had
developed without the slightest contact with any others. Such
a case never occurs however, except possibly in such exceptional instances as that of the Tasmanians (and, even then,
only for a limited period). Human societies are never alone;
when they appear to be most divided, the division is always
between groups or clusters of societies. It would not, for
instance, be an unwarranted presumption that the civilizations
of North and South America were cut off from almost all
contacts with the rest of the world for a period lasting from
10,000 to 25,000 years. But the great section of mankind
thus isolated consisted of a multitude of societies, great and
small, having very close contacts with one another. Moreover,
side by side with the differences due to isolation, there are
others equally important which are due to proximity, bred
of the desire to assert independence and individuality. Many
customs have come into being, not because of an intrinsic
need for them or of a favourable chance, but solely because
of a group's desire not to be left behind by a neighbouring
group which was laying down specific rules in matters in
which the first group had not yet thought of prescribing laws.
We should not, therefore, be tempted to a piece-meal study of

the diversity of human cultures, for that diversity depends less on the isolation of the various groups than on the relations between them.

THE ETHNOCENTRIC ATTITUDE

Yet it would seem that the diversity of cultures has seldom been recognized by men for what it is—a natural phenomenon resulting from the direct or indirect contacts between societies; men have tended rather to regard diversity as something abnormal or outrageous; advances in our knowledge of these matters served less to destroy this illusion and replace it by a more accurate picture than to make us accept it or accommodate ourselves to it.

The attitude of longest standing which no doubt has a firm psychological foundation, as it tends to reappear in each one of us when we are caught unawares, is to reject out of hand the cultural institutions—ethical, religious, social or aesthetic which are furthest removed from those with which we identify ourselves. 'Barbarous habits', 'not what we do', 'ought not to be allowed', etc. are all crude reactions indicative of the same instinctive antipathy, the same repugnance for ways of life, thought or belief to which we are unaccustomed. The ancient world thus lumped together everything not covered by Greek (and later the Greco-Roman) culture under the heading of 'barbarian': Western civilization later used the term 'savage' in the same sense. Underlying both these epithets is the same sort of attitude. The word 'barbarian' is probably connected etymologically with the inarticulate confusion of birdsong, in contra-distinction to the significant sounds of human speech, while 'savage'—'of the woods'—also conjures up a brutish way of life as opposed to human civilization. In both cases, there is a refusal even to admit the fact of cultural diversity; instead, anything which does not conform to the standard of the society in which the individual lives is denied the name of culture and relegated to the realm of nature.

There is no need to dwell on this naïve attitude, which is nevertheless deeply rooted in most men, since this article —and all those in the same series—in fact refutes it. It will be enough, in this context, to note that a rather interesting paradox lies behind it. This attitude of mind, which excludes 'savages' (or any people one may choose to regard as savages) from human kind, is precisely the attitude most strikingly characteristic of those same savages. We know, in fact, that the concept of humanity as covering all forms of the human species, irrespective of race or civilization, came into being very late in history and is by no means widespread. Even where it seems strongest, there is no certainty—as recent history proves—that it is safe from the dangers of misunderstanding or retrogression. So far as great sections of the human species have been concerned, however, and for tens of thousands of years, there seems to have been no hint of any such idea. Humanity is confined to the borders of the tribe, the linguistic group, or even, in some instances, to the village, so that many so-called primitive peoples describe themselves as 'the men' (or sometimes—though hardly more discreetly—as 'the good', 'the excellent', 'the well-achieved'), thus implying that the other tribes, groups or villages have no part in the human virtues or even in human nature, but that their members are, at best, 'bad', 'wicked', 'groundmonkeys', or 'lousy eggs'. They often go further and rob the outsider of even this modicum of actuality, by referring to him as a 'ghost' or an 'apparition'. In this way, curious situations arise in which two parties at issue present a tragic reflexion of one another's attitude. In the Greater Antilles, a few years after the discovery of America, while the Spaniards were sending out Commissions of investigation to discover whether or not the natives had a soul, the latter spent their time drowning white prisoners in order to ascertain, by long observation, whether or not their bodies would decompose.

This strange and tragic anecdote is a good illustration of the paradox inherent in cultural relativism (which we shall find again elsewhere in other forms); the more we claim to discriminate between cultures and customs as good and bad, the more completely do we identify ourselves with those we would condemn. By refusing to consider as human those who seem to us to be the most 'savage' or 'barbarous' of their representatives, we merely adopt one of their own characteristic attitudes. The barbarian is, first and foremost, the man who believes in barbarism.

Admittedly the great philosophic and religious systems which humanity has evolved—Buddhism, Christianity or Islam, the Stoic, Kantian or Marxist doctrines—have constantly condemned this aberration. But the simple statement that all men are naturally equal and should be bound together in brotherhood, irrespective of race or culture, is not very satisfactory to the intellect, for it overlooks a factual diversity which we cannot help but see; and we are not entitled, either in theory or in practice, to behave as if there were no such diversity, simply because we say that it does not affect the essence of the question. The preamble to Unesco's second Statement on the race problem very rightly observes that the thing which convinces the man in the street that there are separate races is 'the immediate evidence of his senses when he sees an African, a European, an Asiatic and an American Indian together'.

Likewise, the strength and the weakness of the great declarations of human rights has always been that, in proclaiming an ideal, they too often forget that man grows to man's estate surrounded, not by humanity in the abstract, but by a traditional culture, where even the most revolutionary changes leave whole sectors quite unaltered. Such declarations can themselves be accounted for by the situation existing at a particular moment in time and in particular space. Faced with the two temptations of condemning things which are offensive to him emotionally or of denying differences which are beyond his intellectual grasp, modern man has launched out on countless lines of philosophical and sociological speculation in a vain attempt to achieve a compromise between these two contradictory poles, and to account for the diversity of cultures while seeking, at the same time, to eradicate what still shocks and offends him in that diversity.

But however much these lines of speculation may differ, and however strange some of them may be, they all, in point of fact, come back to a single formula, which might probably best be described by the expression *false evolutionism*. In what does this consist? It is really an attempt to wipe out the diversity of cultures while pretending to accord it full recognition. If the various conditions in which human societies are found, both in the past and in far distant lands, are treated as *phases* or *stages* in a single line of development, starting from the same point and leading to the same end, it seems clear that the diversity is merely apparent. Humanity is claimed to be one and the same everywhere, but this unity and identity can be achieved only gradually; the variety of cultures we find in the world illustrates the several stages in a process which conceals the ultimate reality or delays our recognition of it.

This may seem an over-simplification in view of the enormous achievements of Darwinism. But Darwinism is in no way implicated here, for the doctrine of biological evolution, and the pseudo-evolutionism we have in mind, are two very different things. The first was developed as a great working hypothesis, based on observations in which there was very little need for interpretation. The various types in the genealogy of the horse, for instance, can be arranged in an evolutive series for two reasons: firstly, a horse can only be sired by a horse; and secondly, skeletons varying gradually from the most recent to the most ancient forms are found at different levels in the earth, representing earlier and earlier periods of history as we dig deeper. It is thus highly probable that *Hipparion* was the real ancestor of *Equus caballus*. The same reasoning is probably applicable to the human species and the different races constituting it. When, however, we turn from biology to culture, things become far more complicated. We may find material objects in the soil, and note that the form or manufacture of a certain type of object varies progressively according to the depth of the geological strata. But an axe does not give birth to an axe in the physical sense that an animal gives birth to an animal. Therefore, to say that an axe has developed out of another axe is to speak metaphorically and with a rough approximation to truth, but without the scientific exactitude which a similar expression has in biological parlance. What is true of material objects whose physical presence in the earth can be related to determinable periods, is even more true of institutions, beliefs and customs, whose past history is generally a closed book to us. The idea of biological evolution is a hypothesis with one of the highest coefficients of probability to be found in any of the natural sciences, whilst the concept of social or cultural evolution offers at best a tempting, but suspiciously convenient method of presenting facts.

Incidentally, this difference, which is too often overlooked, between true and false evolutionism can be explained by the dates of their development. The doctrine of biological evolution admittedly gave sociological evolutionism a decided fillip but the latter actually preceded the former. Without going back to the views which Pascal took over from antiquity, and looking upon humanity as a living being passing through the successive stages of childhood, adolescence and maturity, we may see in the eighteenth century the elaboration of all the basic images which were later to be bandied about—Vico's 'spirals', and his 'three ages' foreshadowing Comte's 'three states', and Condorcet's 'stairway'. Spencer and Tylor, the two founders of social evolutionism, worked out and published their doctrine before the appearance of the *Origin of Species,* or without having read that work. Prior in date to the scientific theory of biological evolution, social evolutionism is thus too often merely a pseudo-scientific mask for an old philosophical problem, which there is no certainty of our ever solving by observation and inductive reasoning.

ARCHAIC AND PRIMITIVE CULTURES

We have already suggested that, from its own point of view, each society may divide cultures into three categories; contemporary cultures found in another part of the world; cultures which have developed in approximately the same area as the society in question, but at an earlier period; and finally, those earlier in time and occupying a different area in space.

We have seen that our knowledge of these three groups cannot be equally exact. In the last case, when we are concerned with cultures which have left behind no written records or buildings, and which employed very primitive techniques (as is true for one half of the inhabited world and for 90-99 per cent, varying according to region, of the time since the dawn of civilization), it may be said that we can really know nothing of them, and that our best efforts at understanding them can be no more than suppositions.

On the other hand, there is a great temptation to try to arrange cultures in the first category in an order representing a succession in time. It is, after all, natural that contemporary societies with no knowledge of electricity and the steam engine should call to mind the corresponding phase in the development of Western civilization. It is natural to compare native tribes, ignorant of writing and metallurgy but depicting figures on walls of rock and manufacturing stone implements, with the primitive forms of that same civilization, which, as the traces left behind in the caves of France and Spain bear witness, looked similar. It is in such matters that false evolutionism has mainly been given free reign. But the almost irresistible temptation to indulge in such comparisons whenever opportunity offers (is not the Western traveller wont to see the 'Middle Ages' in the East, 'the days of Louis XIV' in pre-1914 Peking, and 'Stone Age' among the aborigines in Australia or New Guinea?), is extraordinarily dangerous. We can know only certain aspects of a vanished civilization; and the older the civilization, the fewer are those aspects since we can only have knowledge of things which have survived the assaults of time. There is therefore a tendency to take the part for the whole and to conclude that, since *certain* aspects of two civilizations (one contemporary and the other lost in the past) show similarities, there must be resemblances in *all* aspects. Not only is this reasoning logically indefensible but, in many cases, it is actually refuted by the facts.

Until a relatively recent date, the Tasmanians and Patagonians used chipped stone implements, and certain Australian and American tribes still make such tools. But studying these teaches us very little about the use of similar tools in the palaeolithic period. How were the famous 'hand-axes' used? And yet their purpose must have been so specific that their form and manufacture remained rigidly standardized for one or two hundred thousand years over an area stretching from England to South Africa and from France to China. What was the use of the extraordinary flat, triangular Levalloisian pieces? Hundreds of them are found in deposits and yet we have no hypothesis to explain them. What were the so-called *Bâtons de commandement,* made of reindeer antler? What technical methods were used in the Tardenoisean cultures, which have left behind them an incredible number of tiny fragments of chipped stone, in an infinite variety of geometrical shapes, but very few tools adapted to the size of the human hand? All these questions indicate that there may well be one resemblance between palaeolithic societies and certain contemporary native societies; both alike have used chipped-stone tools. But, even in the technological sphere, it is difficult to go further than that; the employment of the material, the types of instruments and therefore the purpose for which they were used, were quite different, and one group can teach us very little about the other in this respect. How then can we gain any idea of the language, social institutions or religious beliefs of the peoples concerned?

According to one of the commonest explanations derived from the theory of cultural evolution, the rock paintings left behind by the middle palaeolithic societies were used for purposes of magic ritual in connexion with hunting. The line of reasoning is as follows: primitive peoples of the present day practise hunting rites, which often seem to us to serve no practical purpose; the many prehistoric paintings on rock walls deep in caves appear to us to serve no practical purpose; the artists who executed them were hunters; they were therefore used in hunting rites. We have only to set out this implicit argument to see how entirely inconsequent it is. It is, incidentally, most current among non-specialists, for ethnographers, who have had actual dealings with the primitive peoples whom the pseudo-scientist is so cheerfully prepared to serve up for whatever purpose happens to concern him at the moment, with little regard for the true nature of human cultures, agree that there is nothing in the facts observed to justify any sort of hypothesis about these paintings. While we are on the subject of cave paintings, we must point out that, except for the cave paintings found in South Africa (which some hold to be the work of native peoples in recent times), 'primitive art is as far removed from Magdalenian and Aurignacian art as from contemporary European art, for it is marked by a very high degree of stylization, sometimes leading to complete distortion, while prehistoric art displays a striking realism. We might be tempted to regard this characteristic as the origin of European art; but even that would be untrue, since, in the same area, palaeolithic art was succeeded by other forms of a different character; the identity of geographical position does not alter the fact that different peoples have followed one another on the same stretch of earth, knowing nothing or caring nothing for the work of their predecessors, and each bringing in conflicting beliefs, techniques and styles of their own.

The state which the civilizations of America had reached before Columbus' discovery is reminiscent of the neolithic period in Europe. But this comparison does not stand up to closer examination either; in Europe, agriculture and the domestication of animals moved forward in step, whereas in America, while agriculture was exceptionally highly developed, the use of domestic animals was almost entirely unknown or, at all events, extremely restricted. In America, stone tools were still used in a type of agriculture which, in Europe, is associated with the beginnings of metallurgy.

There is no need to quote further instances, for there is another and much more fundamental difficulty in the way of any effort, after discovering the richness and individuality of human cultures, to treat all as the counterparts of a more or less remote period in Western civilization: broadly speaking (and for the time being leaving aside America, to which we shall return later), all human societies have behind them a past of approximately equal length. If we were to treat certain societies as 'stages' in the development of certain others, we should be forced to admit that, while something was happening in the latter, nothing—or very little—was going on in the former. In fact, we are inclined to talk of 'peoples with no history' (sometimes implying that they are the happiest). This ellipsis means that their history is and will always be unknown to us, not that they actually have no history. For tens and even hundreds of millenaries, men there loved, hated, suffered, invented and fought as others did. In actual fact, there are no peoples still in their childhood; all are adult, even those who have not kept a diary of their childhood and adolescence.

We might, of course, say that human societies have made a varying use of their past time and that some have even wasted it; that some were dashing on while others were loitering along the road. This would suggest a distinction between two types of history: a progressive, acquisitive type, in which discoveries and inventions are accumulated to build up great civilizations; and another type, possibly equally active and calling for the utilization of as much talent, but lacking the gift of synthesis which is the hall-mark of the first. All innovations, instead of being added to previous innovations tending in the same direction, would be absorbed into a sort of undulating tide which, once in motion, could never be canalized in a permanent direction.

This conception seems to us to be far more flexible and capable of differentiation than the over-simplified views we have dealt with in the preceding paragraphs. We may well give it a place in our tentative interpretation of the diversity of cultures without doing injustice to any of them. But before we reach that stage there are several other questions to be considered.

THE IDEA OF PROGRESS

We must first consider the cultures in the second category we defined above: the historical predecessors of the 'observer's' culture. The situation here is far more complicated than in the cases we have considered earlier. For in this case the hypothesis of evolution, which appears so tenuous and doubtful as a means of classifying contemporary societies occupying different areas in space, seems hard to refute, and would indeed appear to be directly borne out by the facts. We know, from the concordant evidence of archaeology, prehistoric study and palaeontology, that the area now known as Europe was first inhabited by various species of the genus *Homo,* who used rough chipped flint implements; that these first cultures were succeeded by others in which stone was first more skilfully fashioned by chipping, and later ground and polished, while the working of bone and ivory was also perfected; that pottery, weaving, agriculture and stock rearing then came in, associated with a developing use of metals, the stages of which can also be distinguished. These successive forms therefore appear to represent evolution and progress; some are superior and others inferior. But, if all this is true, it is surely inevitable that the distinctions thus made must affect our attitude towards contemporary forms of culture exhibiting similar variations. The conclusions we reached above are thus in danger of being compromised by this new line of reasoning.

The progress which humanity has made since its earliest days is so clear and so striking that an attempt to question it could be no more than an exercise of rhetoric. And yet, it is not as easy as it seems to arrange mankind's achievements in a regular and continuous series. About 50 years ago, scholars had a delightfully simple scheme to represent man's advance: the old stone age, the new stone age, the copper, bronze and iron ages. But in this, everything was over-simplified. We now suspect that stone was sometimes worked simultaneously by the chipping and polishing methods; when the latter replaced the former, it did not simply represent a natural technical advance from the previous stage, but also an attempt to copy, in stone, the metal arms and tools possessed by other civilizations, more 'advanced' but actually contemporary with their imitators. On the other hand, pottery-making, which used to be regarded as a distinctive feature of the so-called 'Polished Stone Age', was associated with the chipping process of fashioning stone in certain parts of northern Europe.

To go no further than the period when chipped-stone implements were manufactured, known as the Palaeolithic Age, it was thought only a few years ago that the variants of this method—characteristic of the 'core-tool', 'flake-tool' and 'blade-tool' industries—represented a historical progression in three stages, known respectively as lower palaeolithic, middle palaeolithic and upper palaeolithic. It is now recognized that these variants were all found together, representing not stages in a single advance, but aspects or, to use the technical term, 'facies' of a technique which may not have been static but whose changes and variations were extremely complex. In fact, the Levallois culture which we have already mentioned, and which reached its peak between the 250th and 70th millenary B.C., attained to a perfection in the art of chipping stone which was scarcely equalled until the end of the neolithic period, 245,000 to 65,000 years later, and which we would find it extremely difficult to copy today.

Everything we have said about the development of cultures is also true of races, although (as the orders of magnitude are different) it is impossible to correlate the two processes. In Europe, Neanderthal Man was not anterior to the oldest known forms of *Homo sapiens*; the latter were his contemporaries and maybe even his predecessors. And it is possible that the most diverse types of *Hominidae* may have been contemporary even though they did not occupy the same parts of the world—'pygmies' living in South Africa, 'giants' in China and Indonesia, etc.

Once more, the object of our argument is not to deny the fact of human progress but to suggest that we might be more cautious in our conception of it. As our prehistoric and archaeological knowledge grows, we tend to make increasing use of a spatial scheme of distribution instead of a time scale scheme. The implications are two: firstly, that 'progress' (if this term may still be used to describe something very different from its first connotation) is neither continuous nor inevitable; its course consists in a series of leaps and bounds, or, as the biologists would say, mutations. These leaps and bounds are not always in the same direction; the general trend may change too, rather like the progress of the knight in chess, who always has several moves open to him but never in the same direction. Advancing humanity can hardly be likened to a person climbing stairs and, with each movement, adding a new step to all those he has already mounted; a more accurate metaphor would be that of a gambler who has staked his money on several dice and, at each throw, sees them scatter over the cloth, giving a different score each time. What he wins on one, he is always liable to lose on another, and it is only occasionally that history is 'cumulative', that is to say, that the scores add up to a lucky combination.

The case of the Americas proves convincingly that 'cumulative' history is not the prerogative of any one civilization or any one period. Man first came to that enormous continent, no doubt in small nomadic groups crossing the Behring Straits during the final stages of the Ice Age, at some date which cannot have been much earlier than the 20th millenary B.C. In twenty or twenty-five thousand years, these men produced one of the most amazing examples of 'cumulative' history the world has ever seen: exploring the whole range of the resources of their new natural environment, cultivating a wide variety of plants (besides domesticating certain species of animals) for food, medicines and poisons, and—as nowhere else—using poisonous substances as a staple article of diet (e.g. manioc) or as stimulants or anaesthetics; collecting various poisons or drugs for use on the animal species particularly susceptible to each of them; and finally developing certain industries, such as weaving, ceramics and the working of precious metals, to the highest pitch of perfection. To appreciate this tremendous achievement, we need only assess the contribution which America has made to the civilizations of the Old World, starting with the potato, rubber, tobacco and coca (the basis of modern anaesthetics), representing four pillars of Western culture, though admittedly on very different grounds; followed by maize and groundnuts, which were to revolutionize the economy of Africa before perhaps coming into general use as an article of diet in Europe; cocoa, vanilla, the tomato, the pineapple, pepper, several species of beans, cottons and gourds. Finally, the zero on the use of which arithmetic and, indirectly, modern mathematics are founded, was known and employed by the Maya at least 500 years before it was discovered by the Indian scholars, from whom Europe received it via the Arabs. Possibly for that reason, the Maya calendar, at the same period of history, was more accurate than that of the Old World. Much has already been written on the question whether the political system of the Inca was socialistic or totalitarian, but, at all events, the ideas underlying it were close to some of those most characteristic of the modern world, and the system was several centuries ahead of similar developments in Europe. The recent revival of interest in curare would serve to remind us, if a reminder were needed, that the scientific knowledge of the American Indians concerning many vegetable substances not used elsewhere in the world may even now have much to teach the rest of the globe.

'STATIONARY' AND 'CUMULATIVE' HISTORY

The foregoing discussion of the American case would suggest that we ought to consider the difference between 'stationary history' and 'cumulative history' rather more carefully. Have we not, perhaps, acknowledged the 'cumulative' character of American history simply because we recognize America as the source of a number of contributions we have taken from it, or which are similar to those we ourselves have made? What would be the observer's attitude towards a civilization which had concentrated on developing values of its own, none of which was likely to affect his civilization? Would he not be inclined to describe that civilization as 'stationary'? In other words, does the distinction between the two types of history depend on the intrinsic nature of the cultures to which the terms are applied, or does it not rather result from the ethnocentric point of view which we always adopt in assessing the value of a different culture? We should thus regard as 'cumulative' any culture developing in a direction similar to our own, that is to say, whose development would appear to us to be significant. Other cultures, on the contrary, would seem to us to be 'stationary', not necessarily because they are so in fact, but because the line of their development has no meaning for us, and cannot be measured in terms of the criteria we employ.

That this is indeed so is apparent from even a brief consideration of the cases in which we apply the same distinction, not in relation to societies other than our own, but within our own society. The distinction is made more often than we might think. People of advanced years generally consider that history during their old age is stationary, in contrast to the cumulative history they saw being made when they were young. A period in which they are no longer actively concerned, when they have no part to play, has no real meaning for them; nothing happens, or what does happen seems to them to be unproductive of good; while their grandchildren throw themselves into the life of that same period with all the passionate enthusiasm which their elders have forgotten. The opponents of political system are disinclined to admit that the system can evolve; they condemn it as a whole, and would excise it from history as a horrible interval when life is at a standstill only to begin again when the interval is over. The supporters of the régime hold quite a different view, especially, we may note, when they take an intimate part, in a high position, in the running of the machine. The quality of the history of a culture or a cultural progression or, to use a more accurate term, its *eventfulness,* thus depends not on its intrinsic qualities but on our situation with regard to it and on the number and variety of our interests involved.

The contrast beween progressive and stagnant cultures would thus appear to result, in the first place, from a difference of focus. To a viewer gazing through a microscope focused on a certain distance from the objective, bodies placed even a few hundredths of a millimetre nearer or farther away will appear blurred and 'woolly', or may even be invisible; he sees through them. Another comparison may be made to disclose the same illusion. It is the illustration used to explain the rudiments of the theory of relativity. In order to show that the dimensions and the speed of displacement of a body are not absolute values but depend on the position of the observer, it is pointed out that, to a traveller sitting at the window of a train, the speed and length of other trains vary according to whether they are moving in the same or the contrary direction. Any member of a civilization is as closely associated with it as this hypothetical traveller is with his train for, from birth onwards, a thousand conscious and unconscious influences in our environment instil into us a complex system of criteria, consisting in value judgements, motivations and centres of interest, and including the conscious reflexion upon the historical development of our civilization which our education imposes and without which our civilization would be inconceivable or would seem contrary to actual behaviour. Wherever we go, we are bound to carry this system of criteria with us, and external cultural phenomena can be observed only through the distorting glass it interposes, even when it does not prevent us from seeing anything at all.

To a very large extent, the distinction between 'moving cultures' and 'static cultures' is to be explained by a difference of position similar to that which makes our traveller think that a train, actually moving, is either travelling forward or stationary. There is, it is true, a difference, whose importance will be fully apparent when we reach the stage —already foreshadowed—of seeking to formulate a general theory of relativity in a sense different from that of Einstein, i.e. applicable both to the physical and to the social sciences: the process seems to be indentical in both cases, but the other way round. To the observer of the physical world (as the example of the traveller shows) systems developing in the same direction as his own appear to be motionless, while those which seem to move swiftest are moving in different directions. The reverse is true of cultures, since they appear to us to be in more active development when moving in the same direction as our own, and stationary when they are following another line. In the social sciences, however, speed has only a metaphorical value. If the comparison is to hold, we must substitute for this factor *information* or *meaning*. We know, of course, that it is possible to accumulate far more information about a train moving parallel to our own at approximately the same speed (by looking at the faces of the travellers, counting them, etc.) than about a train which we are passing or which is passing us at a high speed, or which is gone in a flash because it is travelling in a different direction. In the extreme case, it passes so quickly that we have only a confused impression of it, from which even the indicatons of speed are lacking; it is reduced to a momentary obscuration of the field of vision; it is no longer a train; it no longer has any *meaning*. There would thus seem to be some relationship between the physical concept of *apparent movement* and another concept involving alike physics, psychology and sociology—the concept of the *amount of information* capable of passing from one individual to another or from one group to another, which will be determined by the relative diversity of their respective cultures.

Whenever we are inclined to describe a human culture as stagnant or stationary, we should therefore ask ourselves whether its apparent immobility may not result from our ignorance of its true interests, whether conscious or unconscious, and whether, as its criteria are different from our own, the culture in question may not suffer from the same illusion with respect to us. In other words, we may well seem to one another to be quite uninteresting, simply because we are dissimilar.

For the last two or three centuries, the whole trend of Western civilization has been to equip man with increasingly powerful mechanical resources. If this criterion is accepted, the quantity of energy available for each member of the population will be taken as indicating the relative level of development in human societies. Western civilization, as represented in North America, will take first place, followed by the European societies, with a mass of Asiatic and African societies, rapidly becoming indistinguishable from one another, bringing up the rear. But these hundreds, or even thousands of societies which are commonly called 'underdeveloped' and 'primitive', and which merge into an undifferentiated mass when regarded from the point of view we have just described (and which is hardly appropriate in relation to them, since they have had no such line of development or, if they have, it has occupied a place of very secondary importance) are by no means identical. From other points of view, they are diametrically opposed to one another; the classification of societies will therefore differ according to the point of view adopted.

If the criterion chosen had been the degree of ability to overcome even the most inhospitable geographical conditions, there can be scarcely any doubt that the Eskimos, on the one hand, and the Bedouins, on the other, would carry off the palm. India has been more successful than any other civilization in elaborating a philosophical and religious system, and China, a way of life capable of minimizing the psychological consequences of over-population. As long as 13 centuries ago, Islam formulated a theory that all aspects of human life—technological, economic, social and spiritual—are closely interrelated—a theory that has only recently been rediscovered in the West in certain aspects of Marxist thought and in the development of modern ethnology. We are familiar with the pre-eminent position in the intellectual life of the Middle Ages which the Arabs owed to this prophetic vision. The West, for all its mastery of machines, exhibits evidence of only the most elementary understanding of the use and potential resources of that super-machine, the human body. In this sphere, on the contrary, as on the related question of the connexion between the physical and the mental, the East and the Far East are several thousand years ahead; they have produced the great theoretical and practical *summae* represented by Yoga in India, the Chinese 'breath-techniques', or the visceral control of the ancient Maoris. The cultivation of plants without soil, which has recently attracted public attention, was practised for centuries by certain Polynesian peoples, who might also have taught the world the art of navigation, and who amazed it, in the eighteenth century, by their revelation of a freer and more generous type of social and ethical organization than had previously been dreamt of.

In all matters touching on the organization of the family and the achievement of harmonious relations between the family group and the social group, the Australian aborigines, though backward in the economic sphere, are so far ahead of the rest of mankind that, to understand the careful and deliberate systems of rules they have elaborated, we have to use all the refinements of modern mathematics. It was they in fact who discovered that the ties of marriage represent the very warp and woof of society, while other social institutions are simply embroideries on that background; for, even in modern societies, where the importance of the family tends to be limited, family ties still count for much: their ramifications are less extensive but, at the point where one tie ceases to hold, others, involving other families, immediately come into play. The family connexions due to inter-marriage may result in the formation of broad links between a few groups, or of narrow links between a great number of groups; whether they are broad or narrow, however, it is those links which maintain the whole social structure and to which it owes its flexibility. The Australians, with an admirable grasp of the facts, have converted this machinery into terms of theory, and listed the main methods by which it may be produced, with the advantages and drawbacks attaching to each. They have gone further than empirical observation to discover the mathematical laws governing the systems, so that it is no exaggeration to say that they are not merely the founders of general sociology as a whole, but are the real innovators of measurement in the social sciences.

The wealth and boldness of aesthetic imagination found in the Melanesians, and their talent for embodying in social life the most obscure products of the mind's subconscious activity, mark one of the highest peaks to which men have attained in these two directions. The African contribution is more complex, but also less obvious, for we have only recently suspected what an important part the continent had played as the cultural melting pot of the Old World—the place where countless influences came together and mingled to branch out anew or to lie dormant but, in every case, taking a new turn. The Egyptian civilization, whose importance to mankind is common knowledge, can be understood only when it is viewed as the co-product of Asia and Africa: and the great political systems of ancient Africa, its legal organization, its philosophical doctrines which for so long remained unknown to Western students, its plastic arts and music, systematically exploring all the opportunities opened up by each of these modes of expression, are all signs of an extraordinarily fertile past. There is, incidentally, direct evidence of this great past in the perfection of the ancient African methods of working bronze and ivory, which were far superior to any employed in the West at the same period. We have already referred to the American contribution and there is no need to revert to it now.

Moreover, it is unwise to concentrate attention too much upon these isolated contributions, for they might give us the doubly false impression that world civilization is a sort of motley. Too much publicity has been given to the various peoples who were first with any dicovery: the Phoenicians with the use of the alphabet; the Chinese with paper, gunpowder and the compass; the Indians with glass and steel. These things in themselves are less important than the way in which each culture puts them together, adopts them or rejects them. And the originality of each culture consists rather in its individual way of solving problems, and in the perspective in which it views the general values which must be approximately the same for all mankind, since all men, without exception, possess a language, techniques, a form of art, some sort of scientific knowledge, religious beliefs, and some form of social, economic and political organization. The relations are never quite the same, however, in every culture, and modern ethnology is concentrating increasingly on discovering the underlying reasons for the choices made, rather than on listing mere external features.

THE PLACE OF WESTERN CIVILIZATION

It may perhaps be objected that such arguments are theoretical. As a matter of abstract logic, it may be said, it is possible that no culture is capable of a true judgement of any other, since no culture can lay aside its own limitations, and its appreciation is therefore inevitably relative. But look around you; mark what has been happening in the world for the past 100 years, and all your speculations will come to nought. Far from 'keeping themselves to themselves', all civilizations, one after the other, recognize the superiority of one of their number—Western civilization. Are we not witnesses to the fact that the whole world is gradually adopting its technological methods, its way of life, its amusements and even its costume? Just as Diogenes demonstrated movement by walking, it is the course followed by all human cultures, from the countless thousands of Asia to the lost tribes in the remote fastnesses of the Brazilian or African jungles which proves, by the unanimous acceptance of a single form of human civilization, such as history has never witnessed before, that that civilization is superior to any other; the complaint which the 'underdeveloped' countries advance against the others at international meetings is not that they are being westernized, but that there is too much delay in giving them the means to westernize themselves.

This is the most difficult point in our argument; indeed it would be of no use to attempt to defend the individuality of human cultures against those cultures themselves. Moreover, it is extremely difficult for an ethnologist to assess at its true value such a phenomenon as the universal acceptance of Western civilization. There are several reasons for this fact. In the first place, there has probably never before in history been a world civilization or, if any parallel does exist, it must be sought in remote prehistoric times, about which we know practically nothing. Secondly, there is very considerable doubt about the permanence of this phenomenon. It is a fact that for the past 150 years there has been a tendency for Western civilization to spread throughout the world, either in its entirety or by the development of certain of its key features, such as industrialization; and that, where other cultures are seeking to preserve some part of their traditional heritage, the attempt is usually confined to the superstructure of society, that is to say, to the least enduring aspects of a culture, which it may be expected will be swept away by the far more radical changes which are taking place. The process is still going on, however, and we cannot yet know what the result will be. Will it end in the complete westernization of our planet, with Russian or American variations? Will syncretic forms come into being, as seems possible so far as the Islamic world, India and China, are concerned? Or is the tide already on the turn and will it now ebb back, before the imminent collapse of the Western world, brought to ruin, like the prehistoric monsters, by a physical expansion out of proportion to the structure on which their working depends? We must take all these possibilities into account in attempting to assess the process going on under our eyes, whose agents, instruments or victims we are, whether we know it or not.

In the first place, we may note that acceptance of the Western way of life, or certain aspects of it, is by no means as spontaneous as Westerners would like to believe. It is less the result of free choice than of the absence of any alternative.

Western civilization has stationed its soldiers, trading posts, plantations and missionaries throughout the world; directly or indirectly it has intervened in the lives of the coloured peoples; it has caused a revolutionary upheaval in their traditional way of life, either by imposing its own customs, or by creating such conditions as to cause the collapse of the existing native patterns without putting anything else in their place. The subjugated and disorganized peoples have therefore had no choice but to accept the substitute solutions offered them or, if they were not prepared to do that, to seek to imitate Western ways sufficiently to be able to fight them on their own ground. When the balance of power is not so unequal, societies do not so easily surrender; their *Weltanschauung* tends rather to be similar to that of the poor tribe in eastern Brazil, whose members adopted the ethnographer, Curt Nimuendaju, as one of themselves and who, whenever he returned to them after a visit to civilization, would weep for pity to think of the sufferings he must have endured so far away from the only place—their village—where, in their opinion, life was worth living.

Nevertheless, this reservation merely shifts the question to another point. If Western culture's claim to superiority is not founded upon free acceptance, must it not be founded upon its greater vitality and energy, which have enabled it to compel acceptance? Here we are down to bedrock. For this inequality of force is not to be accounted for by the subjective attitude of the community as a whole, as was the acceptance we were discussing above. It is an objective fact, and can only be explained by objective causes.

This is not the place to embark on a study of the philosophy of civilization; volumes might be devoted to a discussion of the nature of the values professed by Western civilization. We shall deal only with the most obvious of those values, those that are least open to question. They would seem to be two: in the first place, to borrow Dr. Leslie White's phrase, Western civilization seeks continually to increase the *per capita* supply of energy; secondly, it seeks to protect and prolong human life. To put the matter in a nutshell, the second aspect may be regarded as a derivative of the first, since the absolute quantity of energy available increases in proportion to the length and health of the individual life. For the sake of avoiding argument, we may also admit at once that compensatory phenomena, acting, as it were, as a brake, may go with these developments, such as the great slaughters of world warfare and the inequalities in the consumption of available energy between individuals and classes.

Once this is admitted, it is immediately apparent that, while Western civliization may indeed have devoted itself to these forms of development, to the exclusion of all others—wherein perhaps its weakness lies—it is certainly not the only civilization which has done so. All human societies, from the earliest times, have acted in the same way: and very early and primitive societies, which we should be inclined to compare with the 'barbarian' peoples of today, made the most decisive advances in this respect. At present, their achievements still constitute the bulk of what we call civilization. We are still dependent upon the tremendous discoveries which marked the phase we describe, without the slightest exaggeration, as the neolithic revolution: agriculture, stock-rearing, pottery, weaving. In the last eight or ten thousand years, all we have done is to improve all these 'arts of civilization'.

Admittedly, some people exhibit an unfortunate tendency to regard only the more recent discoveries as brought about by human effort, intelligence and imagination, while the discoveries humanity made in the 'barbarian' period are regarded as due to chance, so that, upon the whole, humanity can claim little credit for them. This error seems to us so common and so serious, and is so likely to prevent a proper appreciation of the relations between cultures, that we think it essential to clear it up once and for all.

CHANCE AND CIVILIZATION

Treatises on ethnology, including some of the best, tell us that man owes his knowledge of fire to the accident of lightning or of a bush fire; that the discovery of a wild animal accidentally roasted in such circumstances revealed to him the possibility of cooking his food; and that the invention of pottery was the result of someone's leaving a lump of clay near a fire. The conclusion seems to be that man began his career in a sort of technological golden age, when inventions could, as it were, be picked off the trees as easily as fruit or flowers. Only modern man would seem to find it necessary to strain and toil; only to modern man would genius seem to grant a flash of insight.

This naïve attitude is the result of a complete failure to

appreciate the complexity and diversity of operations involved in even the most elementary technical processes. To make a useful stone implement, it is not enough to keep on striking a piece of flint until it splits; this became quite apparent when people first tried to reproduce the main types of prehistoric tools. That attempt—in conjunction with observation of the same methods still in use among certain native peoples— taught us that the processes involved are extremely complicated, necessitating, in some cases, the prior manufacture of veritable 'chipping tools'; hammers with a counterweight to control the impact and direction of the blow; shock-absorbers to prevent the vibration from shattering the flake. A considerable body of knowledge about the local origin of the materials employed, the processes of extracting them, their resistance and structure, is also necessary; so is a certain muscular skill and 'knack', acquired by training; in short, the manufacture of such tools calls for a 'lithurgy' matching, *mutatis mutandis,* the various main divisions of metallurgy.

Similarly, while a natural conflagration might on occasion broil or roast a carcass, it is very hard to imagine (except in the case of volcanic eruptions, which are restricted to a relatively small number of areas in the world) that it could suggest boiling or steaming food. The latter methods of cooking, however, are no less universally employed than the others. There is, therefore, no reason for ruling out invention, which must certainly have been necessary for the development of the latter methods, when trying to explain the origin of the former.

Pottery is a very good instance, for it is commonly believed that nothing could be simpler than to hollow out a lump of clay and harden it in the fire. We can only suggest trying it. In the first place, it is essential to find clays suitable for baking; but while many natural conditions are necessary for this purpose, none of them is sufficient in itself, for no clay would, after baking, produce a receptacle suitable for use unless it were mixed with some inert body chosen for its special properties. Elaborate modelling techniques are necessary to make possible the achievement of keeping in shape for some time a plastic body which will not 'hold' in the natural state, and simultaneously to mould it; lastly, it is necessary to discover the particular type of fuel, the sort of furnace, the degree of heat, and the duration of the baking process which will make the clay hard and impermeable and avoid the manifold dangers of cracking, crumbling and distortion. Many other instances might be quoted.

There are far too many complicated operations involved for chance to account for all. Each one by itself means nothing, and only deliberate imaginative combination, based on research and experiment, can make success possible. Chance admittedly has an influence, but, by itself, produces no result. For about 2,500 years, the Western world knew of the existence of electricity—which was no doubt discovered by accident—but that discovery bore no fruit until Ampère and Faraday and others set deliberately to work on the hypotheses they had formulated. Chance played no more important a part in the invention of the bow, the boomerang or the blowpipe, in the development of agriculture or stock-rearing, than in the discovery of penicillin, into which, of course, we know it entered to some extent. We must therefore distinguish carefully between the transmission of a technique from one generation to another, which is always relatively easy, as it is brought about by daily observation and training, and the invention and improvement of new techniques by each individual generation. The latter always necessitate the same power of imagination and the same tireless efforts on the part of certain individuals, whatever may be the particular technique in question. The societies we describe as 'primitive' have as many Pasteurs and Palissys as the others.

We shall shortly come back to chance and probability, but in a different position and a different role; we shall not advance them as a simple explanation for the appearance of full-blown inventions, but as an aid to the interpretation of a phenomenon found in another connexion—the fact that, in spite of our having every reason to suppose that the quantity of imagination, inventive power and creative energy has been more or less constant throughout the history of mankind, the combination has resulted in important cultural mutations only at certain periods and in certain places. Purely personal factors are not enough to account for this result: a sufficient number of individuals must first be psychologically predisposed in a given direction, to ensure the inventor's immediate appeal to the public; this condition itself depends upon the combination of a considerable number of other historical, economic and sociological factors. We should thus be led, in order to explain the differences in the progress of civilizations, to invoke so many complex and unrelated causes that we could have no hope of understanding them, either for practical reasons, or even for theoretical reasons, such as the inevitable disturbances provoked by the very use of mass observation methods. In order to untangle such a skein of countless filaments, it would in fact be necessary to submit the society in question (and the surrounding world) to a comprehensive ethnographical study covering every moment of its life. Even apart from the enormous scope of the undertaking, we know that ethnographers working on an infinitely smaller scale often find their opportunities for observation limited by the subtle changes introduced by their very presence in the human group they are studying. We also know that, in modern societies, one of the most efficient methods of sounding reactions—public opinion polls—tend to modify opinion at the same time, since they introduce among the population a factor which was previously absent—awareness of their own opinions.

This justifies the introduction into the social sciences of the concept of probability, which has long since been recognized in certain branches of physics, e.g. thermodynamics. We shall return to this question: for the time being we may content ourselves with a reminder that the complexity of modern discoveries is not the result of the more common occurrence or better supply of genius among our contemporaries. Rather the reverse, since we have seen that, through the centuries, the progress of each generation depends merely on its adding a constant contribution to the capital inherited from earlier generations. Nine-tenths of our present wealth is due to our predecessors—even more if the date when the main discoveries made their appearance is assessed in relation to the approximate date of the dawn of civilization. We then find that agriculture was developed during a recent phase, representing 2 per cent of that period of time; metallurgy would represent 0.7 per cent, the alphabet 0.35 per cent, Galileo's physics 0.035 per cent and Darwin's theories 0.009 per cent.[1] The whole of the scientific and industrial revolution of the West would therefore fall within a period equivalent to approximately one-half of one-thousandth of the life span of humanity to date. Some caution therefore seems advisable in asserting that this revolution is destined to change the whole meaning of human history.

It is nevertheless true—and this we think finally sums up our problem—that, from the point of view of technical inventions (and the scientific thought which makes such inventions

---

1. Leslie A. White, *The Science of Culture*, New York, 1949, p. 356.

possible), Western civilization has proved itself to be more 'cumulative' than other civilizations. Starting with the same initial stock of neolithic culture, it successfully introduced a number of improvements (alphabetic script, arithmetic and geometry), some of which, incidentally, it rapidly forgot; but, after a period of stagnation, lasting roughly for 2,000 or 2,500 years (from the first millenary B.C. until approximately the eighteenth century A.D.), it suddenly produced an industrial revolution so wide in scope, so comprehensive and so far-reaching in its consequences that the only previous comparison was the neolithic revolution itself.

Twice in its history, at an interval of approximately 10,000 years, then, humanity has accumulated a great number of inventions tending in the same direction; enough such inventions, exhibiting a sufficient degree of continuity have come close enough together in time for technical co-ordination to take place at a high level; this co-ordination has brought about important changes in man's relations with nature, which, in their turn, have made others possible. This process, which has so far occurred twice, and only twice, in the history of humanity, may be illustrated by the simile of a chain reaction brought about by catalytic agents. What can account for it?

First of all, we must not overlook the fact that other revolutions with the same cumulative features may have occurred elsewhere and at other times, but in different spheres of human activity. We have explained above why our own industrial revolution and the neolithic revolution (which preceded it in time but concerned similar matters) are the only groups of events which we can appreciate as revolutions, because they are measurable by our criteria. All the other changes which have certainly come about are only partially perceptible to us, or are seriously distorted in our eyes. They cannot have any meaning for modern Western man (or, at all events, not their full meaning); they may even be invisible to him.

Secondly, the case of the neolithic revolution (the only one which modern Western man can visualize clearly enough) should suggest a certain moderation of the claims he may be tempted to make concerning the pre-eminence of any given race, region or country. The industrial revolution began in Western Europe, moving on to the United States of America and then to Japan; since 1917 it has been gathering momentum in the Soviet Union, and in the near future, no doubt, we shall see it in progress elsewhere; now here, now there, within a space of 50 years, it flares up or dies down. What then of the claims to be first in the field, on which we pride ourselves so much, when we have to take into account thousands upon thousands of years?

The neolithic revolution broke out simultaneously, to within 1,000 or 2,000 years, around the Aegean, in Egypt, the Near East, the Valley of the Indus, and China; and since radio-active carbon has been used for determining archaeological ages, we are beginning to suspect that the Neolithic Age in America is older than we used to think and cannot have begun much later than in the Old World. It is probable that three or four small valleys might claim to have led in the race by a few centuries. What can we know of that today? On the other hand, we are certain that the question of who was first matters not at all, for the very reason that the simultaneity of the same technological upheavals (closely followed by social upheavals) over such enormous stretches of territory, so remote from one another, is a clear indication that they resulted not from the genius of a given race or culture but from conditions so generally operative that they are beyond the conscious sphere of man's thought. We can therefore be sure that, if the industrial revolution had not begun in North-Western Europe, it would have come about at some other time in a different part of the world. And if, as seems probable, it is to extend to cover the whole of the inhabited globe, every culture will introduce into it so many contributions of its own that future historians, thousands of years hence, will quite rightly think it pointless to discuss the question of which culture can claim to have led the rest by 100 or 200 years.

If this is admitted, we need to introduce a new qualification, if not of the truth, at least of the precision of our distinction between stationary history and cumulative history. Not only is this distinction relative to our own interests, as we have already shown, but it can never be entirely clear cut. So far as technical inventions are concerned, it is quite certain that no period and no culture is absolutely stationary. All peoples have a grasp of techniques, which are sufficiently elaborate to enable them to control their environment and adapt, improve or abandon these techniques as they proceed. If it were not so, they would have disappeared long since. There is thus never a clear dividing line between 'cumulative' and 'non-cumulative' history; all history is cumulative and the difference is simply of degree. We know, for instance, that the ancient Chinese and the Eskimos had developed the mechanical arts to a very high pitch; they very nearly reached the point at which the 'chain reaction' would set in and carry them from one type of civilization to another. Everyone knows the story of gunpowder; from the technical point of view, the Chinese had solved all the problems involved in its use save that of securing a large-scale effect. The ancient Mexicans were not ignorant of the wheel, as is often alleged; they were perfectly familiar with it in the manufacture of toy animals on wheels for children to play with; they merely needed to take one more step forward to have the use of the cart.

In these circumstances, the problem of the relatively small number (for each individual system of criteria) of 'more cumulative' cultures, as compared with the 'less cumulative' cultures, comes down to a problem familiar in connexion with the theory of probabilities. It is the problem of determining the relative probability of a complex combination, as compared with other similar but less complex combinations. In roulette, for instance, a series of two consecutive numbers (such as 7 and 8, 12 and 13, 30 and 31) is quite frequent; a series of three is rarer, and a series of four very much more so. And it is only once in a very large number of spins that a series of six, seven or eight numbers may occur in their natural order. If our attention is concentrated exclusively on the long series (if, for instance, we are betting on series of five consecutive numbers), the shorter series will obviously mean no more to us than a non-consecutive series. But this is to overlook the fact that they differ from the series in which we are interested only by a fraction and that, when viewed from another angle, they may display a similar degree of regularity. We may carry our comparison further. Any player who transferred all his winnings to longer and longer series of numbers might grow discouraged, after thousands and millions of tries, at the fact that no series of nine consecutive numbers ever turned up, and might come to the conclusion that he would have been better advised to stop earlier. Yet there is no reason why another player, following the same system but with a different type of series (such as a certain alternation between red and black or between odd and even) might not find significant combinations where the first player would see nothing but confusion. Mankind is not developing along a single line. And if, in one sphere, it appears to be stationary or even retrograde, that does not mean that, from another point of view, important changes may not be taking place in it.

The great eighteenth-century Scottish philosopher, Hume, set out one day to clear up the mistaken problem which has puzzled many people, why not all women, but only a small minority, are pretty. He had no difficulty in showing that the question means nothing at all. If all women were at least as pretty as the most beautiful woman of our acquaintance, we should think they were all ordinary and should reserve the adjective for the small minority who surpassed the average. Similarly, when we are interested in a certain type of progress, we restrict the term 'progressive' to those cultures which are in the van in that type of development, and pay little attention to the others. Progress thus never represents anything more than the maximum progress in a given direction, pre-determined by the interests of the observer.

COLLABORATION BETWEEN CULTURES

Lastly, there is one more point of view from which we must consider our problem. A gambler such as we have discussed in the preceding paragraphs, who placed his bets only upon the longest series (however arranged), would almost certainly be ruined. But this would not be so if there were a coalition of gamblers betting on the same series at several different tables, with an agreement that they would pool the numbers which each of them might require to proceed with his series. For if I, for instance, have already got 21 and 22 myself, and need 23 to go on, there is obviously more chance of its turning up if 10 tables, instead of only one, are in play.

The situation of the various cultures which have achieved the most cumulative forms of history is very similar. Such history has never been produced by isolated cultures but by cultures which, voluntarily or involuntarily, have combined their play and, by a wide variety of means (migration, borrowing, trade and warfare), have formed such *coalitions* as we have visualized in our example. This brings out very clearly the absurdity of claiming that one culture is superior to another. For, if a culture were left to its own resources, it could never hope to be 'superior'; like the single gambler, it would never manage to achieve more than short series of a few units, and the prospect of a long series turning up in its history (though not theoretically impossible) would be so slight that all hope of it would depend on the ability to continue the game for a time infinitely longer than the whole period of human history to date. But, as we said above, no single culture stands alone; it is always part of a coalition including other cultures, and, for that reason, is able to build up cumulative series. The probability of a long series' appearing naturally depends on the scope, duration and variation allowed for in the organization of the coalition.

Two consequences follow.

In the course of this study, we have several times raised the question why mankind remained stationary for nine-tenths or even more of its history; the earliest civilizations date back from 200,000 to 500,000 years, while living conditions have been transformed only in the last 10,000 years. If we are correct in our analysis, the reason was not that palaeolithic man was less intelligent or less gifted than his neolithic successor, but simply that, in human history, the combination took a time to come about; it might have occurred much earlier or much later. There is no more significance in this than there is in the number of spins a gambler has to wait before a given combination is produced; it might happen at the first spin, the thousandth, the millionth or never. But, throughout that time of waiting, humanity, like the gambler, goes on betting. Not always of its own free will, and not always appreciating exactly what it is doing, it 'sets up business' in culture, embarks on 'operation civilization', achieving varying measures of success in each of its undertakings. In some cases, it very nearly succeeds, in others, it endangers its earlier gains. The great simplifications which are permissible because of our ignorance of most aspects of prehistoric societies help to illustrate more closely this hesitant progress, with its manifold ramifications. There can be no more striking examples of regression than the descent from the peak of Levallois culture to the mediocrity of the Mousterian civilization, or from the splendour of the Aurignacian and Solutrian cultures to the rudeness of the Magdalenian, and to the extreme contrasts we find in the various aspects of mesolithic culture.

What is true in time is equally true in space, although it must be expressed in a different way. A culture's chance of uniting the complex body of inventions of all sorts which we describe as a civilization depends on the number and diversity of the other cultures with which it is working out, generally involuntarily, a common strategy. Number and diversity: a comparison of the Old World with the New on the eve of the latter's discovery provides a good illustration of the need for these two factors.

Europe at the beginning of the Renaissance was the meeting-place and melting-pot of the most diverse influences: the Greek, Roman, Germanic and Anglo-Saxon traditions combined with the influences of Arabia and China. Pre-Columbian America enjoyed no fewer cultural contacts, quantitatively speaking, as the various American cultures maintained relations with one another and the two Americas together represent a whole hemisphere. But, while the cultures which were cross-fertilizing each other in Europe had resulted from differentiation dating back several tens of thousands of years, those on the more recently occupied American continent had had less time to develop divergences; the picture they offered was relatively homogeneous. Thus, although it would not be true to say that the cultural standard of Mexico or Peru was inferior to that of Europe at the time of the discovery (we have in fact seen that, in some respects, it was superior), the various aspects of culture were possibly less well organized in relation to each other. Side by side with amazing achievements, we find strange deficiencies in the pre-Columbian civilizations; there are, so to speak, gaps in them. They also afford evidence of the coexistence—not so contradictory as it may seem—of relatively advanced forms of culture with others which were abortive. Their organization, less flexible and diversified, probably explains their collapse before a handful of conquerors. And the underlying reason for this may be sought in the fact that the partners to the American cultural 'coalition' were less dissimilar from one another than their counterparts in the Old World.

No society is therefore essentially and intrinsically cumulative. Cumulative history is not the prerogative of certain races or certain cultures, marking them off from the rest. It is the result of their *conduct* rather than their *nature*. It represents a certain 'way of life' of cultures which depends on their capacity to 'go-along-together'. In this sense, it may be said that cumulative history is the type of history characteristic of grouped societies—social super-organisms—while stationary history (supposing it to exist) would be the distinguishing feature of an inferior form of social life, the isolated society.

The one real calamity, the one fatal flaw which can afflict a group of men and prevent them from fulfilment is to be alone.

We can thus see how clumsy and intellectually unsatisfactory the generally accepted efforts to defend the contributions of various human races and cultures to civilization often are. We list features, we sift questions of origin, we allot first places. However well-intentioned they may be, these efforts serve no purpose, for, in three respects, they miss their aim. In the first place, there can never be any certainty about a particular culture's credit for an invention or discovery. For 100 years, it was firmly believed that maize had been produced by the American Indians, by crossing wild grasses; this explanation is still accepted for the time being, but there is increasing doubt about it, for it may well be, after all, that maize was introduced into America (we cannot tell when or how) from South-East Asia.

In the second place, all cultural contributions can be divided into two groups. On the one hand, we have isolated acquisitions or features, whose importance is evident but which are also somewhat limited. It is a fact that tobacco came from America; but after all, and despite the best efforts of international institutions, we cannot feel overwhelmed with gratitude to the American Indians every time we smoke a cigarette. Tobacco is a delightful adjunct to the art of living, as other adjuncts are useful (such as rubber); we are indebted to these things for pleasures and conveniences we should not otherwise enjoy, but if we were deprived of them, our civilization would not rock on its foundations and, had there been any pressing need, we could have found them for ourselves or substituted something else for them.

At the other end of the scale (with a whole series of intermediates, of course), there are systematized contributions, representing the peculiar form in which each society has chosen to express and satisfy the generality of human aspirations. There is no denying the originality and particularity of these patterns, but, as they all represent the exclusive choice of a single group, it is difficult to see how one civilization can hope to benefit from the way of life of another, unless it is prepared to renounce its own individuality. Attempted compromises are, in fact, likely to produce only two results: either the disorganization and collapse of the pattern of one of the groups; or a new combination, which then, however, represents the emergence of a third pattern, and cannot be assimilated to either of the others. The question with which we are concerned, indeed, is not to discover whether or not a society can derive benefit from the way of life of its neighbours, but whether, and if so to what extent, it can succeed in understanding or even in knowing them. We have already seen that there can be no definite reply to this question.

Finally, wherever a contribution is made, there must be a

recipient. But, while there are in fact real cultures which can be localized in time and space, and which may be said to have 'contributed' and to be continuing their contributions, what can this 'world civilization' be, which is supposed to be the recipient of all these contributions? It is not another civilization distinct from all the others, and yet real in the same sense that they are. When we speak of world civilization, we have in mind no single period, no single group of men: we are employing an abstract conception, to which we attribute a moral or logical significance—moral, if we are thinking of an aim to be pursued by existing societies; logical, if we are using the one term to cover the common features which analysis may reveal in the different cultures. In both cases, we must not shut our eyes to the fact that the concept of world civilization is very sketchy and imperfect, and that its intellectual and emotional content is tenuous. To attempt to assess cultural contributions with all the weight of countless centuries behind them, rich with the thoughts and sorrows, hopes and toil of the men and women who brought them into being, by reference to the sole yard-stick of a world civilization which is still a hollow shell, would be greatly to impoverish them, draining away their life-blood and leaving nothing but the bare bones behind.

We have sought, on the contrary, to show that the true contribution of a culture consists, not in the list of inventions which it has personally produced, but in its difference from others. The sense of gratitude and respect which each single member of a given culture can and should feel towards all others can only be based on the conviction that the other cultures differ from his own in countless ways, even if the ultimate essence of these differences eludes him or if, in spite of his best efforts, he can reach no more than an imperfect understanding of them.

Secondly, we have taken the notion of world civilization as a sort of limiting concept or as an epitome of a highly complex process. If our arguments are valid, there is not, and can never be, a world civilization in the absolute sense in which that term is often used, since civilization implies, and indeed consists in, the coexistence of cultures exhibiting the maximum possible diversities. A world civilization could, in fact, represent no more than a world-wide coalition of cultures, each of which would preserve its own originality.

THE COUNTER-CURRENTS OF PROGRESS

We thus surely find ourselves faced with a curious paradox.

Taking the terms in the sense in which we have been using them above, we have seen that all cultural progress depends on a coalition of cultures. The essence of such a coalition is the pooling (conscious or unconscious, voluntary or involuntary, deliberate or accidental, on their own initiative or under compulsion) of the wins which each culture has scored in the course of its historical development. Lastly, we have recognized, that, the greater the diversity between the cultures concerned, the more fruitful such a coalition will be. If this is admitted, we seem to have two conditions which are mutually contradictory. For the inevitable consequence of the practice of *playing as a syndicate,* which is the source of all progress, is, sooner or later, to make the character of each player's resources *uniform.* If, therefore, one of the first requisites is diversity, it must be recognized that the chances of winning become progressively less as the game goes on.

There are, it would seem, two possibilities of remedying this inevitable development. The first would be for each player deliberately to introduce *differences* in his own game; this is possible, because each society (the 'player' in our hypothetical illustration) consists of a coalition of denominational, professional and economic groups, and because the society's stake is the sum total of the stakes of all these constituent groups. Social inequalities are the most striking instance of this solution. The great revolutions we have chosen to illustrate our argument—the neolithic and the industrial—were accompanied not only by the introduction of diversity into the body of society, as Spencer perceived, but by the introduction of differences in status between the several groups, particularly from the economic point of view. It was noted a long time ago that the discoveries of the Neolithic Age rapidly brought about social differentiation, as the great cities of ancient times grew up in the East, and States, castes and classes appeared on the scene. The same applies to the industrial revolution, which was conditioned by the emergence of a proletariat and is leading on to new and more elaborate forms of exploiting human labour. Hitherto, the tendency has been to treat these social changes as the consequence of the technical changes, the relation of the latter to the former being that of cause and effect. If we are right in our interpretation, this causality (and the succession in time which it implies) must be rejected—as, incidentally, is the general trend in modern science—in favour of a functional correlation between the two phenomena. We may note in passing that recognition of the fact that the historical concomitant of technical progress has been the development of the exploitation of man by man may somewhat temper the pride we are so apt to take in the first of these developments.

The second remedy is very largely modelled on the first: it is to bring into the coalition, whether they will or no, new partners from outside, whose 'stakes' are very different from those of the parties to the original coalition. This solution has also been tried and, while the first may roughly be identified with capitalism, the second may well be illustrated by the history of imperialism and colonialism. The colonial expansion of the nineteenth century gave industrial Europe a fresh impetus (which admittedly benefited other parts of the world as well) whereas, but for the introduction of the colonial peoples, the momentum might have been lost much sooner.

It will be apparent that, in both cases, the remedy consists in broadening the coalition, either by increasing internal diversity or by admitting new partners; in fact, the problem is always to increase the number of players or, in other words, to restore the complexity and diversity of the original situation. It is also apparent, however, that these remedies can only temporarily retard the process. Exploitation is possible only within a coalition; there is contact and interchange between the major and the minor parties. They, in turn, in spite of the apparently unilateral relationship between them, are bound, consciously or unconsciously, to pool their stakes and, as time goes by, the differences between them will tend to diminish. This process is illustrated by the social improvements that are being brought about and the gradual attainment of independence by the colonial peoples; although we have still far to go in both these directions, we must know that the trend of developments is inevitable. It may be that the emergence of antagonistic political and social systems should, in fact, be regarded as a third solution; conceivably, by a constant shifting of the grounds of diversity, it may be possible to maintain indefinitely, in varying forms which will constantly take men unawares, that state of disequilibrium which is necessary to the biological and cultural survival of mankind.

However this may be, it is difficult to conceive as other than contradictory a process which may be summed up as follows:

if men are to progress, they must collaborate; and, in the course of their collaboration, the differences in their contributions will gradually be evened out, although collaboration was originally necessary and advantageous simply because of those differences.

Even if there is no solution, however, it is the sacred duty of mankind to bear these two contradictory facts in mind, and never to lose sight of the one through an exclusive concern with the other; man must, no doubt, guard against the blind particularism which would restrict the dignity of mankind to a single race, culture or society; but he must never forget, on the other hand, that no section of humanity has succeeded in finding universally applicable formulas, and that it is impossible to imagine mankind pursuing a single way of life for, in such a case, mankind would be ossified.

From this point of view our international institutions have a tremendous task before them and bear a very heavy responsibility. Both task and responsibility are more complex than is thought. For our international institutions have a double part to play; they have firstly, to wind up the past and, secondly, to issue a summons to fresh activity. In the first place, they have to assist mankind to get rid, with as little discomfort and danger as possible, of those diversities now serving no useful purpose, the abortive remnants of forms of collaboration whose putrefying vestiges represent a constant risk of infection to the body of international society. They will have to cut them out, resorting to amputation where necessary, and foster the development of other forms of adaptation.

At the same time, they must never for a moment lose sight of the fact that, if these new forms are to have the same functional value as the earlier forms, they cannot be merely copied or modelled on the same pattern; if they were, they would gradually lose their efficacy, until in the end they would be of no use at all. International institutions must be aware, on the contrary, that mankind is rich in unexpected resources, each of which, on first appearance, will always amaze men; that progress is not a comfortable 'bettering of what we have', in which we might look for an indolent repose, but is a succession of adventures, partings of the way, and constant shocks. Humanity is forever involved in two conflicting currents, the one tending towards unification, and the other towards the maintenance or restoration of diversity. As a result of the position of each period or culture in the system, as a result of the way it is facing, each thinks that only one of these two currents represents an advance, while the other appears to be the negation of the first. But we should be purblind if we said, as we might be tempted to do, that humanity is constantly unmaking what it makes. For in different spheres and at different levels, both currents are in truth two aspects of the same process.

The need to preserve the diversity of cultures in a world which is threatened by monotony and uniformity has surely not escaped our international institutions. They must also be aware that it is not enough to nurture local traditions and to save the past for a short period longer. It is diversity itself which must be saved, not the outward and visible form in which each period has clothed that diversity, and which can never be preserved beyond the period which gave it birth. We must therefore hearken for the stirrings of new life, foster latent potentialities, and encourage every natural inclination for collaboration which the future history of the world may hold; we must also be prepared to view without surprise, repugnance or revolt whatever may strike us as strange in the many new forms of social expression. Tolerance is not a contemplative attitude, dispensing indulgence to what has been or what is still in being. It is a dynamic attitude, consisting in the anticipation, understanding and promotion of what is struggling into being. We can see the diversity of human cultures behind us, around us, and before us. The only demand that we can justly make (entailing corresponding duties for every individual) is that all the forms this diversity may take may be so many contributions to the fullness of all the others.

BIBLIOGRAPHY

AUGER, P. *L'homme microscopique*. Paris, 1952.
BOAS, F. *The mind of primitive man*. New York, 1931.
DILTHEY, W. *Gesammelte Schriften*. Leipzig, 1914-31.
DIXON, R. B. *The building of cultures*. New York, London, 1928.
DE GOBINEAU, A. *Essai sur l'inégalité des races humaines*. 2nd ed. Paris, 1884.
HAWKES, C. F. C. *Prehistoric foundations of Europe*. London, 1939.
HERSKOVITS, M. J. *Man and his works*. New York, 1948.
KROEBER, A. L. *Anthropology*. New ed. New York, 1948.
LEROI-GOURHAN, A. *L'homme et la matière*. Paris, 1943.
LINTON, R. *The study of man*. New York, 1936.
MORAZÉ, Ch. *Essai sur la civilisation d'occident*. Vol. I. Paris, 1949.

PIRENNE, J. *Les grands courants de l'histoire universelle.* Vol. I. Paris, 1947.

PITTARD, E. *Les races et l'histoire.* Paris, 1922.

SPENGLER, O. *The decline of the west.* New York, 1927-28.

TOYNBEE, A. J. *A study of history.* London, 1934.

WHITE, L. A. *The science of culture.* New York, 1949.

PART TWO

RACE AND BIOLOGY

by

L. C. DUNN

Professor of Zoology
Columbia University, New York, U.S.A.

INTRODUCTION

Our era has often been called 'The Century of Science'. As we look back from our vantage point of 1960, we can see that few or none of the important questions of science have remained in the condition in which they were in 1900. In every field of science there have been fundamental changes in point of view, and this is a mark of progress, since science is in a sense a continuous adaptation to new knowledge.

In some cases the change in point of view is so great as to be 'revolutionary'. Future generations will probably so regard the changes in biology and its applications brought about by the establishment of the laws of heredity. It was the first half of the twentieth century that witnessed the rise of the science of genetics, responsible for a radical change in the way in which race and race differences in man are to be regarded.

The judgement of biology in this case is clear and unequivocal. The modern view of race, founded upon the known facts and theories of heredity, leaves the old views of fixed and absolute biological differences among the races of man, and the hierarchy of superior and inferior races founded upon this old view, without scientific justification. Biologists now agree that all men everywhere belong to a single species, *Homo sapiens*. As is the case with other species, all men share their essential hereditary characters in common, having received them from common ancestors. Other hereditary characters vary from person to person, and where marriages occur chiefly within local populations, isolated from other populations by geographic and similar barriers, some of these characters tend to become more concentrated in some groups than in other more distant ones. If these separations are long-continued in terms of hundreds or thousands of generations, such populations tend to differ from each other in the relative commonness or rarity of hereditary characters. Races arising in this way are thus seen to differ rather in degree than in kind. This change in biological outlook has tended to restore that view of the unity of man which we find in ancient religions and mythologies, and which was lost in the period of geographical, cultural and political isolation from which we are now emerging.

The way in which this radical change in view about race came about is intimately connected with the discovery of the mechanism of biological heredity. Biological heredity is what is transmitted over the living bridge of egg and sperm, which is the sole biological connexion between the generations. It is necessary to specify it as *biological,* since all humans are strongly influenced by *cultural* inheritance as well. This is what is transmitted outside the body, such as language, custom, education and so on.

Although the internal hidden stream of biological heredity passes continuously from parent to offspring only by means of the single reproductive cell, its effects or manifestations in the individual depend upon the conditions under which he lives. It is obvious that we cannot inherit characters as such, for physical traits such as height or skin colour and mental ones such as mathematical ability cannot be present as such in the minute single cell from which each human being takes his origin. What is transmitted by biological heredity is a set of specific potentialities to respond in particular ways to the environment. A person who has 'inherited' musical talent only exhibits this under certain conditions. The same is true for physical characters, but in less obvious ways, since the response may occur very early in development, as in the case of eye colour, hair form, and similar traits. Biological heredity thus consists in the passage from parents to child of a set of abilities to respond to a range of possible environments by developing a particular set of characters. A human being, like any other living thing, is always a product of both his heredity and his environment.

What is the physical means by which this transmission of heredity occurs? Before 1900 it was thought of as the passage of something from the parents which, like a fluid substance, could mingle and blend in the offspring. The contribution of each parent, popularly referred to as 'blood', was assumed to lose its own individuality in the blend which occurred in the child, and this blending process repeated itself in the children's children and in later descendants. Each person was supposed to have inherited half of his nature from each parent, hence one quarter from each grandparent and so on in decreasing fractions from remoter ancestors. If the parents differed in race or type the children were 'half-bloods', the grandchildren 'quarter-bloods', etc.

Although this blending or blood theory had some support from observation (for example, the descendants of parents differing in skin colour or in height are often of intermediate colour or size), it was based on an assumption which has been shown to be erroneous. This assumption was that the hereditary material was infinitely divisible and miscible like a solution. As early as 1865, Mendel, the founder of genetics, had shown that heredity consists in the transmission of discrete elementary particles, now known as genes. Genes are stable living units, perhaps the smallest units in which living matter can perpetuate itself; their peculiarity is precisely that they do not blend or lose their individuality in whatever combinations they take part.

As early as 1865, Mendel, whose experimental research gave rise to the modern science of genetics, had shown that the old theory was wrong. His results, confirmed by all subsequent studies of inheritance in all forms of life including man, proved clearly that what is transmitted by heredity from parent to offspring is a system of particulate living elements, now known as genes. Each cell in each living body contains in its nucleus hundreds or thousands of these tiny particles. When the reproductive cells—egg and sperm—are formed in man, each one contains all of the kinds of genes present in the person who produced the egg or sperm. The genes are too small to be seen. What permitted Mendel to discover them is the fact that each gene may occur in two (or more) alternative forms, known as alleles, and that these alternative forms may have different effects on the processes of growth and development of the individual. Thus if certain marriages between normally pigmented persons regularly produce two kinds of children—one normally pigmented, the other without dark pigment and with pink eyes (albinos) it can be shown that each parent transmitted two different forms (alleles) of a gene. We may call one form *A*, the other *a* and describe each parent, with reference to this one gene, as *Aa*. Mendel showed that such a parent always produces eggs or sperms of two, and only two kinds, again with reference only to this one gene. If half of the eggs transmit *A*, and half *a*, and half of the sperm transmit *A*, and half *a*, then if any sperm may fertilize any egg at random, the possible combinations would be:

Egg		Sperm		Child
A	×	*A*	=	*AA*
A	×	*a*	=	*Aa*
a	×	*A*	=	*aA*
a	×	*a*	=	*aa*

The possible outcomes occur in the proportions:

	Egg	Sperm	Child
	1/4 *AA*	1/2 *Aa*	1/4 *aa*
or	25% *AA*	50% *Aa*	25% *aa*
or	0.25 *AA*	0.5 *Aa*	0.25 *aa*

These are merely different ways of expressing the same proportion.

Now in fact repeated observation has shown that these are the proportions found among the offspring of such marriages. However, persons with two and with one *A* allele look alike, *AA* and *Aa* having normal pigment, while *aa* is albino. We say that the first two differ in genotype (gene constitution) but the third, the albino, differs from them in both genotype and in appearance. The latter distinction we refer to as the *phenotype* of the person, with respect to the difference in pigmentation. Where one of the two alleles determines the phenotype when received from only one parent, as is the case with persons of genotype *Aa*, Mendel referred to it as *dominant*, while when two like-alleles, one from each parent, are required to produce the phenotype (as in albinism) it is called *recessive*. This is not a constant rule since with many other genes, the effects of both affect the phenotype, *Bb* for example may be different in appearance from both *BB* and *bb*.

What is a universal rule, as proved in thousands of cases in animals, plants and man, is that heredity is transmitted by genes which do not blend or affect each other in any of the combinations through which they pass in the course of transmission from generation to generation. It is this which gives

266

Mendel's rule of disjunction of alternative alleles, or *segregation* (as it is usually called) its great importance.

This 'gene theory' is recognized by biologists as providing the most reasonable basis for explaining the facts of hereditary resemblances and differences. Although all of its implications for other scientific problems such as those of evolution and of individual development, and its practical uses in agriculture, medicine, and industry have not been completely worked out, it is already apparent that the gene theory is one of those basic ideas, like the atomic theory, which must underlie our attempts to understand the material phenomena of life.

It is not strange, therefore, that views about race differences in man should have been so much affected by the gene theory. Under the old blending or blood theory we should expect the descendants of parents showing hereditary differences to become more and more alike. We should thus expect pure races to arise and to become uniform, even though they had originated from a cross of two unlike races. Blending should obviously lead to the disappearance of variability, of differences between related individuals.

If, on the other hand, the biological characters are perpetuated through the transmission of genes which do not blend, then we should expect hereditary variability, once it has arisen, to persist indefinitely. The chief law which Mendel discovered tells us that the variety of genes which the parents received are shuffled and dealt out anew to each child, each gene remaining intact and unchanged, but entering into new combinations in the children. If, as in man, the number of kinds of genes is very high, then the number of different combinations, occurring at random, will be so great that no two people are likely to receive the same assortment. Each population, whether family, tribe, or racial group, should thus consist of individuals differing from each other, to a greater or lesser degree, in some of their hereditary characters. Consequently 'pure races' should not exist, in the sense of groups of identical individuals or even of individuals corresponding to some ideal racial type; and races might be expected to differ from each other in relative rather than in absolute ways, since the same elements (genes) might circulate through them because of occasional intermarriage either in the present or the past.

As we look upon the present human inhabitants of the earth, there is little doubt that what we see resembles closely what we should expect if the gene theory is true. All men are clearly alike in all the fundamental physical characters. Members of all groups may intermarry and actually do; this condition has apparently obtained for a long time, since different groups of primitive man were also races of one species. Yet every man is unique and differs in minor ways from every other man. This is in part due to the different environments in which people live and in part to the different combinations of genes which they have inherited.

Although genes are not changed by the company they keep and have been proved not to undergo blending or contamination, they do sometimes change spontaneously by a process known as *mutation*. An old gene which has been passed from parent to offspring for many generations may suddenly reproduce in a new form. An old gene which led to development of dark skin colour may give rise to a new gene which is unable to produce pigment, and colourless skin or albinism results. Instances of this have been known among the white, black and yellow kinds of men, so it seems to occur independently of race, skin colour, or environment. It is certainly not an adaptive change, that is, one that makes the person better fitted to his environment, since albinos, for example, are at a disadvantage, particularly in the tropics. The fact that mutations do not appear as adaptive responses to the environment indicates that the origin of new characters is not to be sought, as it was in the days before the rise of genetics, in the inheritance of acquired characters.

The origin of new genes by mutation is apparently the source of the hereditary variability by which individuals and groups of men are distinguished. How the common store of genes with which our species began was changed and distributed among the different groups of mankind will have to be examined in later chapters. Here it should be emphasized that the revolution in thinking about race which has resulted from twentieth-century studies in biology sprang from two main sources: (a) the proof of the gene theory of heredity and the disproof of the blending or blood theory; (b) the discovery that new genes arise by a random process of mutation, and not as adaptive responses to the environment.

WHAT IS RACE?

The chief purpose of this article is to make clear a modern biological view of race, which will necessarily be based on the evidence now available. This is certainly not complete and is sure to increase through the efforts of anthropologists, geneticists, and others who are actively studying the complex problems of human biology.

But although we do not know all about race, we are in the position in which scientific study often finds itself, of having good evidence that certain views once generally held are definitely wrong. (In the zig-zag process of learning, advance is often measured by the retreat from error.) We know now why certain views about race uniformity and purity and the fixity of racial differences were wrong; and why social and political views of race inequality were wrong. Since the former were often used as a justification for the latter, we should as reasonable beings like to believe that, if we get rid of our biological misconceptions, we should thereby cure the social and political ills of injustice and exploitation which appeared to be based upon wrong biology. Eventually we may expect this to happen, but we should not forget that the way in which human beings as individuals and as groups have acted with regard to race differences has more often stemmed from feelings and from prejudice than from knowledge. Knowledge eventually overcomes prejudice, but the delay may be long unless active steps are taken to implement the improvements in knowledge.

This is clearly illustrated by the fact that although there has been for some time a considerable measure of agreement amongst biologists about the concept of race in plants, animals and man, the word *race* as used in common speech has no clear or exact meaning at all, and through frequent misuse has acquired unpleasant and distressing connotations. Many people become confused when the direct question is put to them as it is in some official documents: 'To what race do you belong?' One has to stop and ask oneself: 'Now why do they want to know that?' The existence of that question is evidence of past misuse. Sometimes a question about race is intended to reveal one's national origin, and the answer to that question might be French or Lebanese or Brazilian or Japanese. But everyone knows that political entities are made up of people of many different origins. One has only to think of the U.S.A., in which persons from every part of the world are 'Americans', to see that race and national origin are quite different ideas.

Everyone in Germany in the Nazi period knew what a question about race was intended to reveal, for the nation was divided into two categories, Aryan and non-Aryan. Non-Aryans were persons with one or more grandparents who had been listed as Jewish. Aryans were the others, some of whose ancestors might have come from northern or eastern Asia or other non-Aryan regions. The intention of such a question was to facilitate a political classification and disfranchisement. What it actually did was to set up two 'races' and to define one by an ancient and outmoded linguistic term ('Aryan') and the other by the religion of some of one's forbears.

In some countries the immigration laws and the forms for sorting out applicants for schools or the professions still retain such questions.

Answers to them usually serve the purposes of racial discrimination rather than of providing reliable information, since it has proved extremely difficult to frame questions about individuals in such a way as to reveal their 'race'. Before such questions could have scientific value we should have to have a list of all of the 'races' of the world about which general agreement had been reached. Such a list does not exist, because anthropologists have not reached a general agreement on the exact racial classification of mankind.

Owing to its bad connotations and the absence of such an objective list, doubts have been expressed whether there is any valid and useful meaning of the word at all which would justify its retention in our vocabulary. It has been proposed for example to substitute for race the term 'ethnic group', meaning a people of one race or nation. Perhaps with sufficient use and general acceptance this may one day displace the old and misused word. But race has been found to be a useful category for describing the geographically separated varieties of a species of plants or animals. Although it is difficult to delimit the meaning of race, race-formation has been an important process in the evolution of man and as such it must be defined and understood. Thus it seems better to me to define it and explain how it should be used and thus to free it from false meanings than to evade the essential problem by excluding the word.

Nearly all peoples have the idea of blood-relationship and knowledge of biological kinship, and consequently nearly all languages require a word to express it. 'Race' is one of these words. We know that all men living today are descended from common ancestors and are thus blood relatives. The expression 'the human race' embodies this established fact. Sometimes we call ourselves 'the human family', and this is also sound usage. In many languages 'race' and 'family' are used more or less interchangeably.

The meaning of biological relationship is descent from common ancestors. In terms of genetics it means that related persons are those who have had access, through inheritance, to a common store of genes. The most useful biological definition of a population is that of a pool of genes from which each individual, through the egg and sperm from which he took origin, has received a sample from this common pool. A species is such a pool of genes. In the sense that all men are thus related, however distantly through intermarriage among their ancestors, the whole human race is one community of genes. It is biologically true that of the many thousands of hereditary units, genes, which any person inherits, the vast majority are the same as those in any other human being. These are the genes to which we owe our humanness. Many of them were derived from our animal ancestors; some of them, and particularly the combination in which they appear, are unique among animals and set us off as a species from all others; the species *Homo sapiens* keeps its peculiar inheritance because it does not exchange genes through crossing with any other species.

But within this great community of man there are smaller communities between which there is little or no intermarriage and this partial biological separation or isolation is accompanied by differences between the groups as regards the frequency with which certain biological characters appear in them. Thus, most of the inhabitants of Africa have dark skins, and since this persists in persons of African descent when they live elsewhere for many generations, as in America, it is biologically inherited. Negroes resemble each other in this trait and differ in it from persons of most other geographical areas. The Europeans, the mongoloid peoples of Asia, the aboriginal inhabitants of Australia are, as groups, recognizably different from each other. The characters by which they differ, as groups, are of the same sort as those by which individuals differ from each other.

Look for example at the kind of eyelid which we think of as Mongolian. It has a fold of fat which obscures the outer portion of each eye and makes the eye appear narrower and more slanted than the eyes of Europeans or Negroes.

271

Mongolians have no monopoly of this kind of eyelid. It appears in other peoples as well and is occasionally found as an individual variation in Europeans, especially in children. Or take the tightly curled hair which we think of as negroid. Hair almost exactly like this has been found in families in Norway and in Holland which are unrelated to each other and to Negroes, at least in historic times. In these two instances, a new gene which arose by mutation is probably responsible. We know that both the eye-fold and the woolly hair form depend upon a particular inheritance in which brothers and sisters of the same family may differ.

This illustrates an important fact. Racial differences, even those of the major 'races' above mentioned, are compounded of many individual inherited differences. This means that races are distinguished from each other, as *groups,* by the relative commonness within them of certain inherited characters. Thus the mongoloid eye-fold is very common in mongoloid peoples, but uncommon in Europeans. Woolly hair is very common in negroid peoples but uncommon in Europeans or Mongolians. It is more accurate to describe the difference in this way than to say of any one trait that it is present in all of one group and completely absent in the other. Most people would have said this of woolly hair—present in all Negroes, absent in all Europeans. But when the first woolly-haired Norwegian child was born, the statement became untrue, and this could happen for any one of the 'racial' traits. We are going to find out later how these *new* traits arise. In respect to any one 'racial' character, such as hair form, the relative commonness could change quite quickly. If it were of any advantage to Norwegians to have woolly hair, either biologically or aesthetically, the trait could spread from the small family which shows it now.

This illustrates another point about racial differences. Separate racial traits may change their frequency, that is to say, the 'race' is changeable, even in respect of heredity characters. Of course this is a slow process when many characters are involved, and races are usually distinguished from each other by many differences. But it is evident that if racial differences are particular collections or aggregates of the traits by which individuals may differ, and if these traits are subject to change by mutation, then 'race' is not a fixed or static category but a *dynamic* one. Biologically, a race is a result of the process by which a population becomes adapted to its environment. The particular array of traits which come to be the most frequent, and hence to characterize the group, are probably those which now or at some past time proved to be successful in a particular environment.

This then is the sense in which the word race may have a valid biological meaning. A race, in short, is a group of related intermarrying individuals, a population, which differs from other populations in the relative commonness of certain hereditary traits.

It is true that a definition like this leaves a good deal of latitude in deciding how big or how small a race may be, that is, how many people shall be included in it, and also in deciding how many races we shall recognize. These last are matters of convenience rather than of primary importance. What is important is to recognize that races, biologically, differ in relative rather than in absolute ways. The race gets its character from the commonness within it of hereditary characters which are not uniformly present in every member. Its stability depends on the durability of the genes responsible for the hereditary characters, and upon the habit of marrying within the race rather than outside it. When either of these changes, then the race changes. From this it must also be evident that there is in the human species no such thing as a pure race in the sense of one in which all members are alike; it is improbable that there ever has been or ever will be such a race of men.

HEREDITY AND ENVIRONMENT

The character of every human individual and of every human group is the joint product of its heredity and its environment. These influences have also been referred to as *nature,* that which is inherent, inborn, and *nurture,* the sum total of the external factors upon which the maintenance of life depends. There has been a strong tendency among most peoples to attribute the differences amongst themselves, and between their group and others, either to one or the other of these two influences. The influence of soil, climate, nearness to the sea and similar geographic variables are clearly apparent. But it is also evident that all people living under the same conditions are not alike, and that these differences are connected with the particular parents, family, tribe, or race from which they spring. Different people attribute different degrees of importance to environment and to heredity in shaping human individuals and groups such as races. They ask: 'Is heredity or environment the determining factor' tending to divide into two groups, environmentalists and hereditarians.

To the biologist this is a false and meaningless dichotomy. None of the reactions which a human being displays could occur without a particular environment, which can vary only within certain restricted limits; and no one is born except from particular parents. Heredity is what the new life starts with, environment is what makes its continuance possible. Both are essential. What we need to know is how they act together in shaping the traits of individuals or races.

Let us take a careful look at heredity. We called it the living link or bridge between the generations. Actually what goes over that bridge are thousands of tiny particles, packed away in the single cell which each of us received from each of our parents. These particles are called *genes*; they are the physical *beginnings* with which our parents endow each of us at conception. What we inherit are *genes*.

From these beginnings the new individual develops by taking in food, first from the mother's body, later directly from the outside world. The most remarkable part of this process by which a new individual develops is that, whatever he takes in, he converts into his own peculiar kind of substance. Lifeless food is not only made into a human being, it is made into a particular kind of person. The same food that is converted into a blond, blue-eyed, tall man who cannot distinguish between red and green colours of the rainbow and gets hay fever every August, is in his sister converted into a dark, brown-eyed, short person with good colour vision and no hay fever. This latter kind of difference seems to depend upon certain inside directors which determine how the body shall utilize its food and energy. In the brother and sister some of these directors are different. We have referred before to these internal directors as *genes* and later we shall see how they come to be different in brothers and sisters.

In spite of the fact that under certain conditions the brother and sister differ in complexion, one being light and one dark, under other conditions this may not be so. Let the sister spend a long illness in hospital, away from the sunlight, and let the brother work every day in the bright sun. The skin colour of one will get pale and the other will darken. Apparently the difference we saw first depends both upon genes and upon the sun; in fact we could say that the blond differs from the brunette in requiring more sunlight to reach a similar stage of darkness. They differ in responsiveness, and the internal directors or genes therefore do not settle the differences in an absolute way, but chiefly by deciding how the body will react to something in the environment. In the case of eye-colour the difference between brown and blue is settled chiefly by the genes before birth, and we know of no environmental difference that will change the eye colour, although we might find one by searching for it. On the other hand, the response which the brother expresses by sneezing and having a 'running nose', the symptoms of hay fever, can be avoided by keeping away from particular plants or kinds of food or by medication. Under these conditions we should not know he was different from his sister, who does not show this sensitiveness to the same plant or food. His heredity decides his reaction to a particular part of his environment, and in many cases this reaction can be changed by changing the environment. Many of us are susceptible to certain infectious diseases while others are not. Yet we all become alike when a drug is found which will kill the infection or the parasite.

Examples like this, together with the great body of biological research since 1900, show what heredity is. It is the pattern of genes, derived from the ancestry, which determines the possible kinds of response to the environment. Hereditary similarity is the rule throughout mankind, because that particular pattern of genes has been handed down to us which was found by the harsh test of natural selection to give the most successful response to the environments to which our ancestors were exposed. Hereditary differences, except those newly arisen by mutation and hence not tested by natural selection, are usually concerned with less crucial or critical responses. In every race there are not only some people who are colour-blind, like the brother in the example above, but others who are unable to taste certain substances, that is, are taste-blind; others who are smell-blind, and still others sound-blind, or as we say, tone deaf. These differences between people have been shown to be due to differences in single genes, which decide how much light or taste or sound it will take to register a certain sensation in the brain. The study of such relationships, which is still in its infancy, has led to the following analogy. Heredity determines the nature of the internal trigger which the stimulus from the environment may release to produce a given effect. Some triggers are so constituted as to resist most of the range of pressures which are possible in an ordinary environment; for example, they fail to respond to the stimulus of red or green light and hence result in colourblindness.

In elucidating the ways in which heredity and environment interact and estimating their relative roles in determining particular traits, nothing is more instructive than comparing a character in the two kinds of human twins. Whenever two babies are born at once, one of two things has happened. Either two eggs which happened to be present, instead of the usual one, were fertilized by two sperms and two different individuals thus got born at once; or else one egg, after fertilization by one sperm, separated into two parts and each part became one of the pair of twins. The first case is like the birth of ordinary brothers and sisters except for their being born at the same time. The second is like the duplication of a single individual. The difference is important, because ordinary brothers and sisters, coming from different eggs and sperm, may get different genes; while two individuals arising from a single egg and a single sperm, must perforce have the same genes. Any differences in the latter therefore cannot be due to heredity, and we have a measure of the degree to which heredity can control a particular trait; and conversely of the degree to which environment can modify a hereditary trait.

We have all been struck by the extreme similarity between the second kind of twins; they are always of the same sex, have the same kind of blood and the same bodily and facial and even mental features, and they react similarly to diseases and to education. These are the 'one-egg' or identical twins; and since they have the same heredity, any differences we see in them must be due to environment. They do show some differences in mental and emotional responses, and some physical traits such as weight may differ a little, but otherwise they remain extremely similar even when separated at birth and reared in different homes.

Members of the other kind of twin pairs, those arising from two eggs (often known as fraternal twins), are no more alike than ordinary brothers and sisters. They exhibit the usual gene differences to be found in any family, and as often as not are of opposite sex.

The greatest biological interest attaches to comparisons of the conditions of single traits in the members of the two kinds of twin pairs. Occasionally, one member of a twin pair is an albino. In all cases in which such a pair has been proved to have been derived from a single egg, then the other member is also an albino. In cases of fraternal twins the other member may or may not be an albino in about the same proportion as pairs of children from such parents born in separate births. In the classical blood groups (A, B, AB, and O, see Table I for details) and in all other blood factors so far studied, the members of all one-egg twin pairs are exactly the same, that is, they show 100 per cent concordance, whereas two-egg twin pairs may show discordance in the blood group. In the case of the AB group only about 25 per cent of the two-egg twin pairs are concordant. This alone would indicate that the blood group of a person is probably determined entirely by the genes which he has inherited, and that differences in environment encountered after birth are powerless to change it. The differences in this respect between two-egg twins and between brothers and sisters are known to be due to the transmission of different genes in different eggs and sperm of the same parents, whereas no such differences could occur within the single egg which gave rise to identical twins. Other traits can be arranged on a quantitative scale according to the relative degrees of concordance which they exhibit in one-egg as compared with two-egg twins, and this scale serves to arrange the traits in the order of their sensitiveness to environmental influence. Physical traits in general show high concordance in one-egg twins; in reaction to mental measurements one-egg twins also show greater resemblance than two-egg twins, though the effects of education are clearly in evidence. In reactions to emotional tests there is less difference in the amount of concordance and apparently a greater effect of environmental influences.

One of the chief lessons learned from studying twins, as well as by other methods, is that each individual inherits many potentialities. Some of these, like our blood-types, are realized in all the environments which a human being encounters. These we call hereditary. Others, such as the resistance which we exhibit to certain diseases, and particular mental and emotional reactions, are realized only in certain environments. Variations in these we call environmental. But variation in all of these characters depends on the same biological principle: what human beings are is determined by the way in which the hereditary nature responds to its environment.

THE ORIGIN OF BIOLOGICAL DIFFERENCES

Since all men do not respond in like ways to a similar environment, there must be differences in heredity between persons and groups similar to those between two-egg twins and brothers and sisters. This indicates that there must be some biological mechanism which preserves the general resemblance between parents and offspring, while permitting at the same time particular differences between related persons. Heredity in common parlance is the name usually applied to the transmission of resemblances, but since a lack of resemblance, a variation, may be transmitted—once it has appeared—with equal fidelity, the mechanism of heredity is best described simply as the transmission of genes.

As indicated under 'What is Race', if the material particles, the genes, remained always the same, all human beings who are descended through hundreds of thousands of generations from the same ancestors would have remained alike in all hereditary characters. In general of course they have remained alike in the hereditary characters by which we recognize them as human beings, and this means that every one of thousands of genes nearly always makes an exact duplicate of itself each time a new cell, a new egg or sperm, is formed. Thus in general the offspring get descendants of the same genes that the parents had, and hence resemble them.

But once in a while when a gene makes a replica of itself, the copy is not quite exact, and the new gene produces a different effect. The new form then acts as an allele of the old and this is the usual source of the variety of alleles, such as the change from *A* to *a* in the case of albinism. That is what happened when the first person with woolly hair appeared in Norway. Suddenly woolly hair appeared in one child of two straight-haired parents, both from families which had never contained a woolly-haired individual. This child transmitted woolly hair to some of his children, and now a number of Norwegians, all related by descent to the original woolly-haired individual, have this quite un-Norwegian type of hair. This kind of sudden change in a gene is called a *mutation*. Perhaps the first man from whom the Negroes inherited woolly hair got it in this way, by mutation, although the story is probably more complex than that; or perhaps human hair was first woolly and a gene mutated from woolly to straight and thus Indians and Europeans got their straight hair. How it happened in history is not known; nor is it known exactly how mutations occur today, in spite of the extensive biological research on this question during the last 30 years. What is important for an understanding of race differences is the fact that *mutations do happen*. It has been shown that genes can change suddenly from one state to another, in somewhat the same way as a light can be switched from bright to dim and back again.

The effects of such changes may be observed as hereditary variations in the structure or functioning of the several systems of the human body—white spots on head or body, various diseases, skin colour, eye-defects, dwarfism and many other variations have arisen in this way. In fact this is probably the chief or only source of new hereditary variations in man, as it is in animals and plants generally.

In general mutations arise suddenly, appear not to be adaptive responses to environmental conditions, and are generally less useful or desirable than the condition from which they arose. It is known from experiments with animals and plants how to make mutations happen more often. Treatment with X-rays, radium, and certain chemicals will make it more likely that an old gene may change into a new one, usually in a less useful form than the old. The effect seems to be directly on the gene rather than by way of a change in the body of the parent. In this way the origin of new genes by mutation, even when brought about artificially, is quite different from the method by which some of our grandparents thought that new characters arose. It used to be supposed that changes in the body or mind, such as greater muscular development, came about in response to the needs of the body, and could be passed on as such to the children. It is in one way unfortunate that this does not occur, for all of us have to begin to learn where our parents began and not where they left off. On the other hand, we are glad to escape the mutilations and deleterious changes caused by accident or disease in our ancestors. There is no evidence that new hereditary characters arise by direct effects of the environment on the body or in response to need. Such acquired characters are not the source of the inherited differences we see in members of the same family or tribe.

Nor is it possible that inherited effects of past environments can account for the differences between the great racial divisions of man. Many people of course still think that the African is black because of inherited effects of hot sun, but it is much more likely that genes for skin colour, like others, change once in a while by mutation and that persons with genes for darker skin colour have been more successful in Africa than persons with fairer skin.

We should remember that the present opinion of most biologists on this question does not rest on absolute disproof of the inheritance of acquired characters. Such disproof would obviously be impossible, because many of the alleged instances of this kind happened so long ago that they cannot be studied now, and it is in any case impossible to prove a universal negative. I think biologists believe rather that positive proof has been provided of the origin by random mutation of most of the hereditary differences which have been studied in plants, animals and man. This view rests chiefly on the proof of the gene theory of heredity, for once heredity was shown to occur by means of genes which change by mutation, then the older views about the origin of variations became unnecessary.

The discovery of the gene mechanism, which began with the work of Mendel, and the confirmation of the idea and its extension to all plants, animals and man are matters that underlie the development of the modern biological views about race which are described under 'Heredity and Environment'. Those who are interested in the details of the gene theory will find it described in the books listed in the bibliography.

Another parallel stream of development in biology which had a strong influence on thinking about race was initiated by the great work of Darwin, published in 1859. He showed that the varieties of living organisms had reached their present condition by a process of descent with modification, guided by the principle of natural selection. In his theory, hereditary variations, of unknown origins, provided the raw material from which the environment selected the better fitted or adapted characters and combinations for survival. Once it was shown that variations arose by random mutation, the way to differentiation of races and species as particular collections of genes, fitted to particular environments, was open. Discussion of the details of this theory would take us too far afield, but some applications of it will be found below.

HOW RACES FORM

If all men living today are descended from common ancestors, and there is good evidence that this is the case, how has mankind become divided up into different races? History alone cannot answer this question, since the great groups of man had already become different before written history began. We must find out about it as we find out about other scientific questions, by studying the processes responsible for it.

We can ask ourselves: why should not all men have remained biologically alike? We studied that question in the last chapter and found that the elements of heredity, the genes, sometimes change by a process called mutation, and this gives rise to a great variety of genes. These, by coming into new combinations during reproduction (the baby has father's nose, mother's hair, and Uncle John's bad eye-sight) produce an almost endless array of kinds of people, so that literally no two persons are the same.

Now the process of heredity is such that we should expect this great variety to continue within any population in which genes have assumed different allelic forms by mutation. This is implicit in Mendel's original theory that genes enter into all possible combinations with each other and are not changed by this process. If we find persons of three genotypes such as *AA, Aa* and *aa* in certain proportions in a population at one time we should expect, other things being equal, to find them in the same proportions many generations later. The main reason for this is the constancy of gene reproduction. Whenever, in the process of growth and in the production of the sex cells (egg or sperm) one cell gives rise to a new one, each gene produces a replica of itself for the new cell; that is *A* produces a new *A, a* another *a, B* a new *B* and so on through the thousands of genes in each cell. They pass on unchanged from generation to generation except in the rare event that one changes by mutation to a new form in which case it reproduces in the new form and augments the variety. The proportions of *A* to *a, B* to *b,* etc., are not expected to change in the population if matings among all different genotypes occur at random, that is if *AA* persons are equally likely to marry *AA, Aa* or *aa* persons and similarly for all other genotypes. Then *AA* persons will always transmit *A* in all sex cells, *Aa* will transmit *A* in one half and *a* in the other half of the sex cells, and *aa* will transmit *a* in all sex cells. With persons choosing their marriage partners usually for reasons unconnected with genotype (which will usually be unknown to the prospective mate) all the genes in the population can be thought of as constituting one pool out of which two are drawn at each new birth. If 90 per cent of the alleles of one gene in the population are *A* and 10 per cent are *a,* then the following combinations will be found:

Eggs		Sperm		Children
0.9 *A*	×	0.9 *A*	=	0.81 *AA*
0.9 *A*	×	0.1 *a*	=	0.09 *Aa*
0.1 *a*	×	0.9 *A*	=	0.09 *Aa*
0.1 *a*	×	0.1 *a*	=	0.01 *aa*

In the population of children the proportion of *A* to *a* is also 9 to 1; it has not changed, and other things being equal, will not change. This extension of Mendel's rule is known as the Hardy-Weinberg rule from the English mathematician and the German physician who independently called attention to it in 1908. It tells us that in large populations in which mating takes place at random with respect to genotype, the relative frequencies of the different alleles of each kind of gene will tend to remain the same, provided also that mutation does not alter the frequency of one allele more than the other, that all of the genotypes have equal chances of marrying and leaving offspring, and that the gene proportions in the population are not altered by emigration or immigration.

If these conditions hold, a population will not change but will retain the genetic variety with which it began. In order to find out how populations become different and diverge from each other to produce the mosaic of different populations in the world today, we must ask whether the conditions responsible for constancy actually do hold. The most important clue comes from the observation that the populations in different parts of the world seem to be fitted for or adapted to the conditions under which they live. Certain hereditary characters such as black skins appear to have been more successful in Africa, others more successful elsewhere. Studies of animal and plant populations have shown that the proportion of a population having those combinations of characters which are advantageous in certain places. as for example in a desert, tend to increase there generation after generation until they constitute the bulk of the population. They gradually supplant the other combinations, although the latter may survive better in the forest or in the mountains. The chief means by which such changes occur is by differential reproduction, certain genotypes leaving more offspring than others. This is the process which Darwin called natural selection. It tends to produce local races and eventually species which are fitted or adapted for life in that locality. This means that all genotypes do not have equal chances of leaving offspring in all environments.

A specific example of the effect of natural selection on human populations is the recent discovery that normal persons who transmit a gene for sickle cell anaemia (which is usually fatal in children who receive such a gene from both parents) have more children than persons without such a gene. This advantage of the carriers of this gene occurs only in areas where malicious (falciparum) malaria has been prevalent. In such areas as in the low coastal regions of British Honduras or in low areas in West Africa, natural selection tends to increase in this way the frequency of the gene. This is sufficient to counterbalance the adverse selection against those who get the gene from both parents for these usually die before they can transmit the gene. Consequently this gene is commoner in certain African peoples and their descendants elsewhere than in peoples whose ancestors have not been exposed to malaria. This produces great regional differences in the frequency of this gene. It is largely a peculiarity of Africans, whose ancestors it may have enabled to survive in malarial regions. Other traits common in Africans such as dark skins and certain of the blood group genes (cf. 'A Biologist's View of Race' below) may also have been favoured by natural selection in certain environments.

Natural selection, favouring some genes in certain places and others in other environments has probably been the most potent factor in causing changes in gene frequency and thus in producing racial differences.

A second factor is sometimes involved in shaping the particular collection of genes which becomes a biological race. It may happen that the frequency of a gene may increase or decrease in a locality, not because it confers some advantage or the reverse, but simply because of accidental or chance fluctuations, which are much more serious in a small population than in a large one. The extinction or spread of family names which occur in small communities may be due simply to a run of luck in a family in the proportion of sons and daughters. In societies in which the name is transmitted through males only, a family with many sons would have its name spread in a small community, while one with no sons would have its name disappear, so that in neighbouring villages a name would be common in one and absent in the other. In large cities such fluctuation would not be noticeable, but small populations may diverge from each other by such accidents. Differences among races in the proportions of persons with different blood group genes may have come about in this way. Such accidents must have been of great importance in earlier stages of human history when the human reproductive communities must have been very small. This risk which new variants or combinations run in small populations has been called random drift.

Finally, after these factors have acted, it is obvious that migration and mixing of different groups may lead to changes in old races or the formation of new ones. This can be seen going on today. New races are forming in the Hawaiian Islands, for example, by the mingling of Chinese and European immigrants with the native people; and in the United States and in South Africa by intermarriage among the descendants of marriages between Negroes and Europeans.

Since biologically races are populations differing in the relative frequencies of some of their genes, the four factors noted above as those which upset the equilibrium and change the frequencies of genes are the chief biological processes responsible for race formation. They are: (a) mutation or change in the elements of heredity, the genes; (b) selection, being differential rates of reproduction, fertility or survival of the possessors of different genes; (c) drift, or the accidents of gene sampling in small populations; (d) differential migration and mixing of populations.

None of these processes would result in hereditary differences among groups of people unless something interfered with the complete freedom of intermarriage among all persons which has been referred to as random mating, for otherwise all would be members of the same biological or reproductive group. Thus we must add a fifth factor of a different kind. This is isolation, geographical or social. Once the other factors are present, isolation is the great race-maker. If the whole population of the world constitued one marriage circle, in which any individual had an equal chance of marrying any other, then the great variety of people which is kept up by mutation and combination of genes would be distributed more or less evenly over the world. Obviously neither condition actually obtains.

The variety of the world's population is distributed in clusters. For example, most of the dark peoples are in one cluster in Africa, although another group occurs in Melanesia, most people with yellow skins are in north-east Asia, most light-skinned people in Europe or countries settled by Europeans, and so on.

Between these separated groups there is relatively little intermarriage. Choice of marriage partners is limited to those who live near, speak the same language, profess the same religion, and belong to the same class or caste.

These divisions of the world's populations did not always exist as at present. Once there was no human being in the American continents, nor in the islands of the South Seas, nor in Australia. There may even have been a time when the human race was actually one marriage community, because even today all races have many of their genes in common, as though they had all obtained them from a common source.

If it were not for the geographical and cultural barriers which separate people today, we could think of all of the genes in the human race as constituting one great pool.

But the world's population is obviously divided up into many different gene pools *within* which combinations occur more or less at random, but *between* which genes are less frequently exchanged because of the rarity of marriage between different groups. These different gene pools or marriage circles are likely to differ in the genes they contain, that is, different mutations may occur in different separated populations; selection may change the proportions of genes in different populations; the changes may occur by accident or by different rates of migration or intermixture. But however the original difference between two populations may have arisen, the difference will persist only if something makes intermarriage between them infrequent, and this is why isolation is so potent an influence in forming different groups of people. Isolation is often partial; it is anything which tends to cut down exchange of genes between groups. We all know the ways in which our choice of marriage partners is limited. They are not only geographical, but religious, social, economic, linguistic, that is to say, the isolating factors are largely cultural. Thus a common biological community tends to be broken up by non-biological factors into sub-communities, which may then tend to become biologically different.

Races form because of the operation of biological processes. These are determined by the nature of heredity, which provides for a variety of stable hereditary elements, genes, transmitted according to regular laws or principles; and by the nature of the environment, which is broken up into a variety of partially isolated habitats. Particular genes or groups of genes are more successful in (i.e., adapted to) certain environments, others in other environments. These views have been tested experimentally with a variety of plant and animal populations. They have only begun to be tested by observations on human populations, but the basic conceptions derived from experimental biology appear to be generally applicable to all bi-sexual animals including man.

A BIOLOGIST'S VIEW OF RACE

The groups that become partially separated and different go by many names; races, hordes, tribes. All of them have this in common, that they differ from other groups by maintaining a different proportion of the same kinds of hereditary elements—genes.

This is nowhere more clearly shown than in the distribution of the genes which determine certain properties of the blood. There are four kinds of people, called A, B, AB, and O. These four kinds of persons differ in the substances they contain in their red blood cells.

It is well known that the red colour of human blood is due to red particles which float in the transparent straw-coloured fluid which forms the liquid part of the blood. As soon as blood is taken from the body and allowed to stand, it tends to congeal in a red mass which is called a clot. If the clot is allowed to stand for an hour or so, it contracts and a pale transparent yellowish fluid oozes out. This is called blood serum.

Blood has always played an important part in beliefs, not only about relationship but about the qualities of different persons. If turns out that some of these qualities of blood are quite specific. For example, it is possible to transfer blood from a strong healthy person to one who is ill or has lost a great deal of blood, but only if the transfer (transfusion) is made in specified ways. The rules governing blood transfusion were discovered 60 years ago, when it was shown that the presence or absence of certain substances in the red blood cells are responsible for the success or failure of blood transfusion. These substances in the red cells are called A and B substances, or A and B antigens.

In the serum are other substances which react with the antigens in the blood cells. These are called antibodies. For example, if serum is taken from a person in the A group, it will cause clumping of the cells of a B group person when these are placed in it. Consequently we say that the B persons have anti-A substances or antibodies in their blood. Therefore if cells from an A person are transferred into the circulation of a B person, the cells of the A person will form clots which clog up some of the small blood vessels and this is likely to cause the death of the person who was to have benefited by blood transfusion. When all these combinations of cells and serum are carefully studied it is found that persons can give and receive blood according to the diagram below:

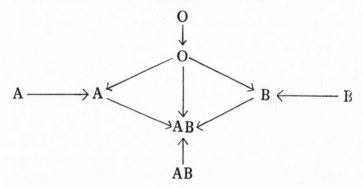

The blood group of each person is determined by his genes. The alleles of this blood group gene are called A, B, and O. Every person can be easily placed in one of the four groups, O, A, B, or AB (Table I), and we find that the genes responsible for these groups are present throughout the world, although the proportions of these different genes differ somewhat from place to place and from race to race.

TABLE I.

Person of blood group	Has this substance in his red blood cells	Has these antibodies in his blood serum	Has these alleles
A	A	anti-B	AA or AO
B	B	anti-A	BB or BO
AB	A and B	none	AB
O	none	anti-A and anti-B	OO

These different groups of people have the same kinds of antigens in the blood, and the variety in the antigens is due to variation in the gene, which probably arose by mutation.

Related people who probably got their genes from the same source have similar proportions of the A and B alleles. This produces the great cluster of blood group O in the American Indians, in whom B is rare or absent, while A is generally also uncommon. There is a group of Indians in Peru in which all persons tested were found to be of group O. Their nearest neighbours are a tribe with 90 per cent group O. Probably A

TABLE II. The proportions of persons belonging to each of the four blood groups in different populations (per cent).

	O	A	B	AB
North American Indian (Chippewa)	87.6	12.4	0	0
South American Indian (Matto Grosso)	100.0	0	0	0
Australian:				
Aborigines West	48.1	51.9	0	0
East	58.6	37.8	3.6	0
Europeans:				
English	47.9	42.4	8.3	1.4
Swedes	37.9	46.1	9.5	6.5
Greeks	42.0	39.6	14.2	3.7
Russians	31.9	34.4	24.9	8.8
Asiatic:				
Japanese	30.1	38.4	21.9	9.7
Chinese	34.2	30.8	27.7	7.3

and B were lost from the first tribe, either by accident when its ancestors migrated to a new home, or by some selective factor operating in the new environment.

Notice too the rise in the proportion of blood group B as we go east across Europe from England to Russia (Moscow).

There are some interesting situations in groups known to have split up by migration within historic time. The Icelanders are descended from Vikings from Scandinavia and 'Westmen' from Ireland who settled on the island in the ninth century A.D. Although the majority are supposed to have come from Scandinavia, and Iceland was politically united to Denmark until 1944, the blood types of the Icelanders are much closer to those of the Irish than of the Danes.

TABLE III. Percentage of population in each blood group.

	O	A	B	AB
Icelanders	55.7	32.1	9.6	2.6
Irish	55.2	31.1	12.1	1.7
Danes	40.7	45.3	10.5	3.5

The Basques, living near the Spanish-French frontier, are unlike both their Spanish and French neighbours, who resemble each other more closely than either resembles the Basques.

TABLE IV.

	0	A	B	AB
Basques	57.2	41.7	1.1	0
French	39.8	42.3	11.8	6.1
Spanish	41.5	46.5	9.2	2.2

As a final example, two groups of people living near each other in Hungary are very unlike each other in blood group distribution. One group is composed of gypsies with a large proportion of blood group B like some peoples of western India, whence the gypsies migrated long ago. The other is composed of 'natives', long settled in Hungary with less than half the proportion of group B. Similar evidence exists for other groups who live near each other. The reason, of course, is found in the rarity of intermarriage between the different groups. This shows that a common environment does not by itself cause convergence, and that there are barriers other than geographical ones which cause peoples to remain distinct. Of course this would happen only if the genes retained their integrity and were passed on uninfluenced by the combinations in which they had taken part.

All these facts could be illustrated just as well by other human genes which can be classified objectively and accurately. The so-called M and N blood types, the varieties of the recently discovered Rh blood gene, genes for taste-blindness, colour-blindness, and others all appear in their several varieties in nearly all human populations but in *different characteristic proportions*. It is important to emphasize that it is varieties or alleles of the *same* genes that are found in all races.

What has caused the separated populations of the world to diverge in this way in the proportions of different forms of the same genes is not known, but we may suspect that natural selection, favouring different alleles in different environments has been an important factor. It is now known, for example, that in European populations persons who get ulcers of the intestine are much more likely to be of blood group O, than A or B or AB; those with a cancer of the stomach are more likely to be of blood group A than of O, or B. There may be other diseases to which persons of blood group B are more susceptible in certain environments. Research on connexions between blood group genes and disease and other agencies which may act selectively is proceeding in many countries and may be expected to elucidate the part that natural selection plays in changing the frequencies of such genes.

Blood typing has certain obvious advantages over measuring or photographing in attempting to study the nature and origin of group differences. Blood typing immediately reveals the genetic constitution of the person tested, so that the distribution of these genes in a population is known from the blood group distribution. Description of a population by the genes found in it prevents the loss of the individual in the group because in general there is no 'average' blood type. There are only characteristic proportions in which the same elements are mixed.

These differences in proportions are racial differences, that is, they indicate partial separation of the population in which the different proportions are maintained. The differences may be just as great between populations living in the same city as between populations living half a world away from each other. In Table V are shown the blood group varieties in two caste communities in Bombay, as determined by two Indian investigators.

The blood types of these groups are quite different, and differences like this were also found in six other gene-determined characters. They are in fact at least as different in these traits as American whites and American Negroes, who are separated by the low frequency of intermarriage. These Indian communities are separated by customs which cause marriages to be contracted only between members of certain specified sections within the caste.

TABLE V.

	O	A	B	AB
Indians (Bombay C.K.P.)[1]	34.5	28.5	28.5	8.5
Indians (Bombay K.B.)[2]	51.0	24	20	5.0

1. Members of the caste community Chandraseniya Kayasth Prabhu.
2. Members of the caste community Koknasth Brahman.

These conditions permit the maintenance of gene differences between the groups. No one hesitates to call such differences 'racial' as between Europeans and Negroes, everyone being aware that the ancestors of the Negroes now living in other parts of the world came from Africa a few hundred years ago where they had been practically isolated from the populations of other continents. But there would be a good deal of hesitation in referring to the two Indian caste communities as belonging to different races; the members of these two caste communities have lived together in peace and mutual respect for 2,000 years or more. This is good evidence that biological racial differences are not themselves the cause of race friction or prejudice. Probably the members of these castes do not recognize the biological differences which the scientists found, and after getting on well together for so long their behaviour will probably not be influenced by this new knowledge.

The important thing is not to have an easy and certain answer for every question about racial classification, but rather to understand, from such instances, the nature of racial differences. Once these are seen to consist of collections of individual hereditary elements which do not blend even within the same population, then we can see in a different light the external differences from which we had earlier formed ideas about the fixity of 'racial types'. When we look around us from this second point of view, we find a good many facts which fit together into a consistent picture.

In the first place, no very radical changes in classification of the great branches of mankind are suggested when they are compared by the gene method.

Geographical isolation aided by natural selection has undoubtedly been the great race-maker, and this is clearly reflected in the differences in the frequencies of several genes as between European, African, Asiatic, American Indian and Australian racial stocks. Even these great branches are not discontinuously different, having most of their genes in common. European and Asiatic 'intergrade' in eastern Russia and Siberia, Australian and Asiatic in the southern Pacific, and the other Pacific peoples show resemblances with, and no sharp differences from, Asiatics and Americans. Even the Australians and Europeans, separated so widely (except for the recent migration of Europeans) show clear evidence of common origin.

A racial classification of mankind based on the gene frequency method was that of Boyd (1950) who recognized five major races as follows: (a) European or Caucasoid, (b) African or Negroid, (c) Asiatic or Mongoloid, (d) American Indian, (e) Australoid. These can be characterized as groups by the relative frequencies of some eight genes, most of them concerned with blood antigens. It is obvious that they represent groups isolated geographically. The American Indians separated from their Asiatic ancestors only some 10,000 to 15,000 years ago, so they retain many mongoloid traits but still can be distinguished as a group. In addition to these, transitional groups are recognized, such as the peoples in the Pacific Islands, and in North Africa, and a hypothetical race not now in existence except as a small relic population, the Basques of Spain and France.

On the other hand, another study also published in 1950 by three American anthropologists, Coon, Garn and Birdsell, recognized 30 races, based largely on the classical criteria of physical type. Some of the 30 such as Neo-Hawaiian, American coloured and South African coloured are interesting as examples of races in the making. The authors thereby recognize that race is not something fixed and unchangeable, but a stage in the process by which human populations adapt themselves to special conditions. All of the 30 races above can be grouped into the same five categories recognized by Boyd and by anthropologists generally, since they are clearly based on geographical isolation.

It cannot be said at present that one classification is more correct than the other. The classification is in part a convenience and thus may be somewhat arbitrary, and should be determined by the purpose for which it is to be used. But it must be also a 'natural' classification and express the evolutionary processes which have brought about the racial diversification of mankind.

The classification into a few large races is perhaps the one best justified. Races which have lived in one place for long ages seem to be fitted to live in just such a region. Biologists say they are 'adapted' to the physical conditions, just as those plants which are best able to get along with infrequent rainfall or in extreme cold have survived in desert or mountain conditions.

Not much is known about the adaptive value of most physical characters in human races. Skin pigment appears to be advantageous where people are exposed to strong sunlight; great chest capacity and a large volume of the red blood cells which carry oxygen may be adaptations to high altitudes. Resistance to specific local infectious diseases must be an extremely important adaptative quality.

In man, ability to succeed in a great variety of environments is connected with the most important way in which he differs from lower animals, that is, his ability to learn and to profit by experience and especially to live in organized societies and to develop culture. The religious, moral and ethical traditions which all societies develop in some form, language which permits oral and written communication between generations and between different societies, the evolution of political and economic institutions and of literature, art, science, technology and industry—all of these reflect the peculiar mental adaptability and plasticity of man. All civilizations increase the selective advantage of genes for mental capacity ana educability and these are found in all races.

No race is uniform with respect to mental traits any more than with respect to physical traits, or blood group or other genes. It is in fact this variety which permitted each race to adapt itself to a variety of environments. In the past, as today, persons must have been found to accomplish successfully all the varied tasks which are required in every human society. We may suspect that when the genes influencing the normal operations of the brain and nervous system are subjected to as extensive study as has been devoted to properties of the blood, a great variety of genotypes will be revealed. If there are, as reliably estimated, millions of different combinations of genes as expressed in the blood, not less should be expected in respect to genes influencing behaviour and mental capacity and special abilities. It would be surprising if these were to be distributed uniformly in all environments in which natural selection has probably fitted different groups to cope with different conditions. We know relatively little now about the distribution of such genes; they are much more difficult to identify and to study objectively than genes which can be classified by physical or chemical means. Perhaps such methods must be used before the knowledge we need can be obtained.

But much past experience should make us prepared to find that the biological capacities to absorb new cultural acquisitions are very widely distributed, however many local differences in the proportions of genes are found.

Peoples of ancient cultural traditions have been able quickly to adapt, as whole societies, to new technical and industrial methods; this has happened in Europe and in Asia and is now happening in Africa. Some of the peoples included in the Soviet State have in two generations changed from a hunting and gathering or a nomadic and pastoral way of life to operating an industrial economy based on machines.

In the light of the recent rapid development of similar technologies in all parts of the world the question may well be asked whether this growing uniformity in productive methods, with the greater ease of communication and consequent increase in the movements and migrations of peoples, and especially in the speed of urbanization, will tend to make all people alike. The best answer to this question comes from recalling the reasons for the existence of the enormous biological variety in all human populations. These reasons trace to the origination of gene differences by random mutation and the maintenance of these differences by the integrity of individual genes and the tendency to maintenance of variety as expressed in the Hardy-Weinberg rule. Other factors operating through migrations and changes in mating patterns will be discussed below under 'Race Separation and Race Fusion'.

RACE SEPARATION AND RACE FUSION

Two processes are clearly in evidence in our human species. One of these is race formation, by which distinctive collections of genes are gathered together; the other is race fusion, by which these collections are disposed. The essential condition for race divergence is always separation, partial or complete isolation, which reduces the frequency of marriage between two groups. We can call the group within which marriages are contracted the *marriage circle*. We can think of the population of the world as living within marriage circles of differing sizes. These circles overlap and permit some intermarriage between circles but less than within a circle.

Now anything which affects the size of the circle, that is, the number of people within the marriage circle, and the degree of separation between circles, will affect the distribution of genes. Every marriage circle is a potential race. I have already pointed out that members of two different caste communities in the city of Bombay are as unlike in the frequency of certain genes as are members of African and European marriage circles. Even if we did not know of the customs preventing marriage between members of these different castes, we should have to infer that they existed. Some of these caste communities are very large (several million) and others quite small (20,000 to 30,000).

The population of a large and geographically diversified area like that of Europe must perforce become broken up into smaller marriage circles. One such was based on caste, the royal families who married within their own circle. More circles were based on geographic isolation, for much of the population lived in villages and marriages were usually contracted between members of the same or nearby villages. If long continued this would lead to some biological divergence and the development of local peculiarities. City people too were partly isolated into different marriage circles, the barriers often being religious or social or linguistic. But such divergences never proceeded very far, for the history of Europe, in numbers of human generations, is a short one, and peoples in other parts of the world, although they could recognize Europeans, could seldom distinguish the different varieties. Whether one recognizes few or many races in Europe is a matter of taste about which anthropologists do not agree.

The important fact for us in the present connexion is that the marriage circles tended to change as economic, social, and political conditions changed. The movements from country to city which the development of industry greatly accelerated, resulted in a very great enlargement of the marriage circles. Now boys met girls from different parts of the country and wherever other barriers were absent the expected took place. The incipient peculiarities of separated communities were merged in the larger group. The development of cheap transportation had an important effect, especially as between different countries. Most important for Europe, connexion with America became very close, and in the American cities members of different European marriage circles met and became members of the same circle. Moreover, the social and economic class barriers tended to get lower as political democracy spread.

These considerations show only that the conditions tending to change gene distribution may be responsive to external factors of many kinds. They do not explain why one group should spread and another contract. Sometimes this is due to pure luck, just as whether we are exposed to a fatal disease may be a matter of chance. Sometimes factors which are only secondarily biological will be decisive, such as customs of early or late marriage, decreed for religious or economic reasons, which determine the rate of natural increase of the group. Sometimes the conjunction of great military or religious leaders will cause one group to expand or migrate at a fortunate time while another disappears for no apparent biological reason.

These are cultural changes, and yet they have greatly affected the distribution of genes. The net effect of industrialization in Europe and the Americas has been to increase the size of marriage circles, and thereby to reverse the tendency to isolation by which races tended to diverge. Genes in the European world now have a much greater mobility and will tend to spread themselves more evenly. One effect is to make it less likely that members of this large community will marry relatives and thus bring to expression those hidden recessives, many of them deleterious, which nearly everyone conceals. In this sense enlargement of the marriage circle is beneficial.

Such effects are of course not peculiar to Europe. They accompany urbanization wherever it occurs and the history of the world is replete with other movements of peoples and minglings of races. We often hear it said that intermarriage between races has had biological consequences. There is no good or extensive evidence of this and much to be said on the other side. It is true that the immediate offspring of mixed marriages often have a hard time, falling between two racial communities without belonging to either of them. But the effects in such cases are usually of a social and economic and psychological nature rather than biological. That populations with new biological combinations of traits may arise in this way may be seen in the American Negroes, in the Cape Coloured of South Africa, in some of the populations of Central and South America and the Caribbean in which genes from European, American Indian and sometimes from African ancestors are mingled. Race fusions of this sort have been going on ever since bands of people acquired the means of mobility and migration. Its effects are reflected in the variety found within all human races. Whether the mixture was remote or recent, the result is that all human beings are hybrids or mongrels containing genes from a wide variety of different ancestors.

At times the mingling of races may tend to break up adaptive combinations of genes assembled under the influence of natural selection over long generations of living in one set of environments. This becomes of less importance as man learns to control his environments. He now begins to adapt his environment to his needs rather than the reverse which is the only way open to other creatures. Today he gets rid of malaria by inventing and using DDT to destroy the mosquitoes which transmit it and consequently need not depend upon the slow process by which natural selection builds up inherited resistance to the disease.

One result of recent studies of plant and animal populations suggests a possible biological reason why the genotypes of most human individuals contain unlike alleles in most of their genes. Such hybrids (heterozygotes is the technical phrase) frequently have greater vigour and biological efficiency. The great success of hybrid corn is due to this, and in many animal populations natural selection appears to favour unlike combinations of alleles in preference to the pure or homozygous state. Perhaps man too may owe his position as the most successful and adaptable of animals to his mixed genetic nature.

However this may be, it is in any case clear that the evolutionary processes by which man adapted himself to the varied environments of this planet did not include the formation of pure or uniform races since these do not exist anywhere. Rather the process by which he was able to colonize all the habitable parts of the world was first by the assembly of varied combinations of genes formed under the influence of natural selection and other natural forces. These differed in proportions as different natural conditions required. Race is a stage in this process, always as a flexible means rather than as a fixed or determined final stage. Second, he developed culture and a great variety of techniques by which he bent his physical environments to his human needs and purposes. Cultural acquisitions are transmitted by language and written records, a form of inheritance separate from and independent of biological heredity. This second mode of adaptation is now the most important one by which he conquers new environments such as Antarctica yesterday, and outer space tomorrow. Race is not a stage in this process and its biological function is now a secondary one.

The persistence of race prejudice where it exists is a cultural acquisition which as we have seen finds no justification in biology. It serves no biological function in a world which is now progressing beyond the need of race formation as a means of adaptation. The conditions of modern life, deplorable as they are for the many peoples over whom hangs the threat of insecurity and war are nevertheless those which will tend further to reduce the importance of the conditions which formed biological race differences. This does not mean that biological race differences will disappear; the effects of thousands of generations of human evolution will not be more quickly altered. But they may now be viewed in proper perspective and based on knowledge rather than prejudice. The knowledge of the operation of heredity which we now have should lead also to better understanding of the nature of the biological diversity of individuals which lies at the basis of group diversity. The emphasis on the uniqueness of individuals which this new knowledge promotes should thus improve relations within as well as between human groups.

Men are social beings and religious beings as well as biological ones, and they must depend upon their immediate fellows however close they may be drawn to others in the world community. Attachments to place, to neighbours, to members of the same community of thought and spirit have values which all men need and this is true in spite of all the abuses perpetrated in the name of communities based on race. These need not be given up when the tolerance and sympathy with which we regard members of our own group are extended to all others.

BIBLIOGRAPHY

BOYD, W. C. *Genetics and the races of man*. Boston, Mass., Little, Brown & Co., 1950.

COON, C. S.; JARN, S. M.; BIRDSELL, J. B. *Races—a study of the problems of race formation in man*. Springfield, Ill., C. C. Thomas, 1950.

DAHLBERG, G. *Race, reason and rubbish*. London and New York, Columbia University Press, 1946.

DOBZHANSKY, T. *Evolution, genetics and man*. New York and London, J. Wiley & Sons, 1955.

DUNN, L. C., *Heredity and evolution in human populations*. Cambridge, Mass., Harvard University Press, 1959.

DUNN, L. C.; DOBZHANSKY, T. *Heredity, race and society*. New York, Mentor Books, 1959.

HUXLEY, J. S.; HADDON, A. C. *We Europeans*. London and New York, Harper, 1936.

LAWLER, S. D.; LAWLER, L. J. *Human blood groups and inheritance*. 2nd edition. London, Heinemann, 1957.

PENROSE, L. S. *Outline of human genetics*. London and New York, J. Wiley & Sons, 1959.

THE SIGNIFICANCE
OF RACIAL DIFFERENCES

by
G. M. MORANT

Doctor of Science (London)

INTRODUCTION

Mankind must always have been divided into groups of one kind or another. The groups at one time may have been single families or communities made up by a small number of families, and at the other extreme there are the large nations of modern times. The feelings that people have regarding their relations to members of their own groups and to members of other groups must always have had profound social and biological effects. It has been argued that such feelings are rooted in human nature, which has so often displayed its dual facets of greater amity in dealings with familiar kindred and neighbours and greater hostility in dealings with unfamiliar aliens. Whether such attitudes are 'natural' or not, relations between communities must have been of fundamental importance in moulding the history of mankind.

The literary discussion of differences between groups of people can be traced back to early records and it is still a vital topic. It has taken various forms which are all concerned in one way or another with the description of differences between groups of people and theories regarding the causes of such differences. How far are the observed distinctions due to essential differences in quality, and how far can they be attributed to modifying conditions of life? There has been much scientific discussion of this problem in the past 100 years —involving new kinds of evidence collected for the purpose and new methods of treatment—but no decisive solution has yet been reached.

Popular views of the matter are still nebulous enough to be swayed by anyone who chooses, for his own ends, to spread 'racial' dogmas which cannot readily be proved true or false. There is still a good chance that a doctrine will be widely accepted if it accords with what people want to believe. As these matters concern everyone, it cannot be expected that discussion of them will be free from bias—either on the platform or in the study. It would be idle to suppose that all inquiries purporting to be scientific regarding group differences are disciplined and dispassionate. In generalizing from a mass of evidence of various kinds and of varying degrees of precision there is bound to be some scope for the expression of personal preferences. Nevertheless, there is a core of agreement between all inquirers who have investigated the particular problem on scientific lines. They suppose that it should be treated in a certain way: suitable methods have been devised accordingly and some results obtained by applying these methods are unquestioned. There is, however, little appreciation of the scientific treatment beyond the circle of those who have been concerned with it directly.

In his book *Race and Psychology* in this series Professor Klineberg has discussed the methods, and summarized the evidence and conclusions, of psychologists who have investigated 'racial' differences in mentality. The topic treated is really the same as that which has been discussed in a literary way for more than 2,000 years. In the following section of the present essay this kind of literature is referred to with the object of showing why it failed to reach conclusive results, so that the need was felt for a treatment of an entirely different kind.

A broad, but somewhat artificial, division is commonly made between mind and body. The scientific investigation of group differences in body qualities is the concern of physical anthropologists, and their ultimate aim is to interpret such evidence in terms of racial histories or pedigrees. There have been parallel investigations dealing on the one hand with group differences in body characters, and on the other with group differences in mental characters. The former line of inquiry is more advanced than the latter, chiefly perhaps because it is the easier to treat in a systematic way. In these circumstances it may be profitable to summarize what has been achieved in dealing with group comparisons regarding the physical constitution of human beings, with the hope that the methods and general conclusions of this study may suggest ways of facilitating group comparisons regarding mental constitution. Discussion of relationships between these two sides of the same problem is the principal theme of this article.

In considering these matters no sharp distinction can be made between certain questions which are of purely academic interest, and others which might be of practical importance because views regarding them could influence the attitudes adopted by peoples towards one another. Looked at from one point of view racial differences in body characters cannot be considered to be of much practical importance; in a rational world the fact that peoples differ in appearance would not by itself be a factor influencing their attitudes and intercourse. As things are, the real practical importance of group diversity in body characters is due to the fact that some of them make obvious distinctions between peoples. This is so, however, on account of only a few of the characters which are used by physical anthropologists for purposes of racial classification. Among those responsible for conveying an immediate impression of distinction, skin colour is outstanding, but the colours of the hair and eyes, the form of the hair and the shape of the face are also important. The history of humanity might have been very different if there had been no differences in colouring between peoples.

Skin colour is believed to make more marked distinctions between populations than any other attribute of the body. Most of the other physical characters of racial significance distinguish groups far less effectively, and few make any absolute distinctions in the sense of separating all members of one community from all members of any other. The situation for skin colour gives a false impression of the nature of racial diversity in general, but appreciation of that situation must have predisposed people to believe that there are marked distinctions between populations on account of mental characteristics. Actual or supposititious group differences in such ways are of primary practical importance, but examination of them is an intricate matter, and relevant scientific investigations are still in their infancy.

THE LITERARY DISCUSSION OF DIFFERENCES
BETWEEN GROUPS OF PEOPLE

An essay by David Hume, the Scottish philosopher, published in 1741 opens with the sentence: 'The vulgar are apt to carry all *national characters* to extremes; and having once established it as a principle that any people are knavish, or cowardly, or ignorant, they will admit of no exception, but comprehend every individual under the same censure'. The writer proceeds to discuss the question whether national character is determined by moral—meaning educational and social—causes, or by physical causes such as climate and natural surroundings. It is concluded that the influence of the former, through the medium of man's imitative nature, is paramount, and that the latter are of little account. 'If we run over the globe, or revolve the annals of history, we shall discover everywhere signs of a sympathy or contagion of manners, none of the influence of air or climate.'

Arguments of various kinds are advanced in support of this conclusion. A typical one, for example, is the observation that numerous instances may be found of the same people appearing to have different characters in different historical ages. Comment of a different kind is made in a footnote, where the writer remarks: 'I am apt to suspect the Negroes to be naturally inferior to the whites. There scarcely ever was a civilized nation of that complexion, nor even any individual, eminent either in action or speculation.' Cases may be cited today to counter this argument.

Hume's essay is a typical contribution to a kind of discussion which has been carried on for more than 2,000 years. The ancient Greeks may be said to have started it and Unesco would not be concerned with the matter if it had been settled to the satisfaction of everyone, or even, perhaps, to the satisfaction of all informed people of good will. The form of the discussion and the kinds of evidence referred to have varied according to the knowledge and opinions current in the ages in which the participants lived. And there have always been two sides to the question.

Human nature is exceedingly complex and human affairs are exceedingly complex also. The problem of assessing the significance of differences between peoples is concerned, on the one hand, with the roots of human nature and, on the other, with the complexities of behaviour in individuals and in societies. It is not to be expected that discussion of the topic could be a simple matter. There are various classes of evidence which are more or less relevant to it. A broad, but rather artificial, distinction may be made between one part of the evidence which is 'literary' in character and another part which may be labelled scientific.

The earlier discussions of the problem are predominantly of the literary variety. In assembling their testimony those taking part could range over knowledge accessible to them regarding all peoples in the world and all periods of history. A particular writer would have to select classes of evidence relevant to his arguments, and for each class it would be necessary to propound a generalization supposed to be substantiated by a multitude of facts. Another writer might arrange his thesis under different heads and select different classes of evidence. Two writers considering the same point might generalize from the same class of facts—some of which might be unsubstantiated or misleading—in different ways. There was ample scope differences in both interpretation and emphasis. The evidence could be marshalled in different ways and plausible arguments might be advanced to support opposite conclusions. Nobody could say the last word and the door was always left open for further discussion. There were no crucial arguments which could settle the matter for good but, rather, an abundance of subsidiary arguments which could be made to suit one side or the other according to the inclinations of the disputants. A salient feature of the debate has been its inconclusiveness. The fact that it has been so long continued and that it is still vital is proof of the major importance of the theme.

In recent times the terms used in the dispute have been modified owing to widened knowledge of man's nature and history. Comparisons between the characteristics of different populations are still made on the traditional literary lines: the evidence referred to by some writers is confined to the kinds of observations and generalizations found in works published 200 years ago. More often discussions of the topic today are on the same general lines, but reference is made to scientific observations, methods and hypotheses accumulated in the past 100 years, and these are still being added to and changed. At the other extreme there are discussions carried on primarily, if not entirely, in terms of the newer system of knowledge.

Scientific contributions to the topic are of several kinds. In the first place, the scope of knowledge of human societies has been enlarged by discoveries made by archaeologists, and by systematic observation of primitive and other peoples in all parts of the world made by anthropologists and others. (In earlier times generalizations regarding mankind as a whole—such as those of Aristotle or Rousseau—were questionable because information relating to primitive peoples was scanty and untrustworthy.) In the second place, another class of relevant scientific evidence concerns what man is in himself—the genesis and development in geological time, and in the individual, of his physical and mental constitution. Revolutionary discoveries regarding the mechanism of heredity—justifying the new name of 'genetics' for that study—are particularly relevant. The scientific contributions of both kinds may be said to come within the scope of 'man biologically considered', supposing that this discipline embraces both body and mind, and man considered both individually and collectively.

It might be suggested that the problem of group differences should be considered as a purely scientific one and that literary discussion of it is obsolescent. This would be to take a narrow view of the situation, however. The literary discussion of the matter was concerned with vital questions which still need to be interpreted, and many of the kinds of arguments used were valid and cogent. But they failed to provide a conclusive solution of the problem. If a scientific treatment can provide one, then this should be able to resolve in satisfactory ways the questions considered earlier. The argument of this pamphlet is that a solution on scientific lines has not been reached yet, but that such an approach has gone far already towards clarifying the nature of the problem and indicating the way in which it may ultimately be solved. As an introduction to an explanation of this point of view, it is appropriate to consider why the literary treatment failed to reach a solution.

In brief, the literary discussion of differences between populations proved to be inconclusive because (a) in general the problem was not clearly defined; (b) there was no systematic method of assessing the relative influence of factors determining observed differences between groups; (c) these differences, expressed in terms of qualities of individuals, were not defined in ways suited for precise comparison, and (d) there was no systematic way of comparing groups of people. This is drastic censure of a type of discussion to which some of the world's greatest writers have contributed, and it cannot be anticipated that improvements which might offer more promise of attaining a conclusive result could be made easily. The hope must be that use of scientific methods will show how the problem may be treated with system and precision.

Some points of weakness in the literary discussion of it need to be considered more fully. It is a commonplace observation that differences in mental disposition and behaviour are to be expected if groups of people representing markedly different cultures are compared, though it may be difficult to say, except in vague terms, what the distinctions are in such extreme cases. A hundred native Australians, and 100 Chinese and 100 Englishmen, say, would not be expected to react in the same ways in response to the same situation. It would be difficult, indeed, to imagine any situation to which the three groups would respond uniformly. The problem is to decide why the groups of people are distinguished by their behaviour, or, in other words, why they have different 'characters'. It may be that there are 'natural' differences between them, or their difference in mentality might be due to the circumstances of their lives, or the interaction of distinctions of both these kinds might account for the situation observed. If it is decided that living conditions are significant, then part of the problem will be to assess the relative influences of different kinds of such conditions, whether social or material.

The first issue is to decide between, or to assess the relative influences of, 'natural' or 'inborn' constitution, on the one hand—avoiding for the moment the question of how these and other terms involved should be defined—and the sum total of social and material surroundings, on the other. In the literacy discussion of differences between peoples this primary issue has often been ignored or disposed of in a cursory or dogmatic way. The essay by Hume referred to, for example, is concerned with the question whether 'national characters' are determined by 'moral' or physical causes, and the possibility of there being 'natural' distinctions between the peoples compared is only mentioned in the unfortunate footnote. The author *suspects* that Negroes are naturally inferior to whites, and the argument he advances in support of this belief is that cases are lacking of Negroes being highly civilized as a nation or distinguished as individuals. If the criterion is achievement, how can proper allowance be made for inequalities in opportunity when estimating whether one people is naturally superior to another? In fact the first issue was evaded by Hume, as it was by most of the other contributors to the discussion until recent times.

307

An extreme dogma regarding it was a characteristic, however, of the modern literature of racialism. The arguments of this school were mainly of the literary variety, but free use was made of scientific jargon. Natural, or racial, differences were supposed to be paramount and immutable. The counterblast to this doctrine was partly in the form of writings of the literary type, with a leavening of scientific facts and theories. The contestants on both sides were inclined to take up extreme positions and the counter to the complete affirmative was often the complete denial. It was difficult to be impartial when so much was at stake. Some of the better members of the opposition sought to restrain their supporters. Friedrich Hertz wrote in the preface to the English edition of his book *Race and Civilization,* published in 1928: 'Several critics of this book believe that I deny any correlation between race and mentality. I wish, therefore, to state once more that I do not assert definitely the absolute mental equality of all races; nor can the opposite be demonstrated convincingly. What history and ethnology seem to teach is that the fundamental traits are the same in all races, and that the adaptability of individuals of one race to social and cultural conditions created by other races is not limited by inherited qualities. But probably there is at least a diversity of temperament between certain races and even small differences may sometimes have great consequences. However, those theories, which try to explain almost everything by temperament, seem completely superseded today.'

Literary, or any other, comparisons of different populations have to be made in terms of qualities of people. Qualities which are the same for all people in the world are clearly irrelevant, and any considered must show some degree of variation so that grades of the qualities distinguish different individuals. The terms commonly used in the discussion are those of everyday speech and writing—intelligent or stupid, energetic or slothful, cheerful or melancholy, courageous or cowardly, and so on. These are personal qualities and the problem is concerned with comparisons of them between *groups* of people.

In ordinary speech comparisons are frequently made between groups of people, whether these are major divisions of mankind, or national populations, or smaller communities such as professional or other social classes. It is customary to speak of a group of any one of these kinds as if the collection were a single individual. Examples of this usage may be found in almost any copy of a newspaper and in many political speeches and discussions. It is a generally accepted way of economizing words which passes unnoticed in ordinary conversation, but it is a menace to clarity of thought. Almost invariably the practice conveys the impression that the distinction between two groups compared is greater than it can be supposed to be if the case is examined in detail. This was Hume's point when he remarked that the vulgar are apt to carry all national characters to extremes.

What is the meaning of a statement that white people are more energetic, say, than Negroes? Is it to be understood that all white people are equally energetic and that all Negroes are equal to one another in showing a lesser degree of energy? This interpretation is manifestly absurd. If pressed for an explanation the author of the statement might say that his meaning was that display of energy is more common among white people than among Negroes, or that on the average the former are more energetic than the latter. The question would have to be considered as a group one requiring use of terms which can properly be used in comparing groups. It clearly concerns the relative frequencies with which different grades of the quality are found in the two populations compared, which is a statistical matter. But, if this is admitted, then the lack of precise definition of the qualities treated, and of grades of these qualities, become evident. The literary treatment is halted at this stage. Its devices seem to be quite incapable of dealing with the intricacies of the situation.

Its evidence, too, is not of a kind permitting precise analysis. The literary inquirer is essentially concerned with records relating to the past: man's nature is judged from his history. Until recent years there was no systematic collection of records giving descriptions of the qualities of groups of people. Such qualities in earlier times have to be inferred from knowledge of a miscellaneous kind relating to the lives and actions of communities, and to their thoughts in so far as they are known from records that have survived. But all this information is indirect when the aim is to assess the qualities of the actors. Suppose that the object is to decide whether one population was superior or inferior to another in courage. Can military achievements alone be accepted as the criterion, or must allowances be made for the manifold circumstances which determined enterprise and success in war? The evidence might be interpreted by different investigators in different ways, and the discussion is more likely to be an interminable debate than a demonstration offering any hope of final conclusions.

However, the literary discussion of group differences is examined, it appears to show limitations which deny the hope of reaching any final solution of the fundamental issues. The equipment is inadequate for the complicated task. The question today is whether a scientific treatment of the problem can promise to give more profitable results.

DEFINITION OF THE PROBLEM

Human populations differ in mentality and behaviour: the problem is to discover why this is so. There are also obvious differences between populations in body qualities and there is the parallel problem of interpreting these distinctions. The latter problem has been investigated intensively in recent years, and for various reasons its methods and results are further advanced than those of the problem of group differences in mentality. In considering group differences in mentality it may help to review in some detail what has already been achieved in dealing with group differences regarding man's physical constitution. An argument of this article is that doing so clarifies the situation and indicates how treatment of the more difficult inquiry can best proceed.

To start with, the two problems can be defined in precisely the same way. In both cases there are two main issues, the first being to determine whether, or how far, group differences are 'natural', and the second being to determine the extent to which various conditions of life are responsible for them. The problem as a whole can thus be divided into two parts, but the concise definitions of these given above are too abstract to have any precise meaning. The two main questions can only be considered with reference to qualities of people, and initially, at any rate, it is necessary to consider the matter in the case of such qualities considered singly. The situation may be different for different qualities. It is known, in fact, that the situations may be very different for different physical qualities and it would not be surprising if the same was found for mental qualities. Hence there can be no general solution of the problem, but only one which has reference to a particular quality or set of qualities. Some may distinguish populations in one way and some in another. This is an important point and one which can easily be overlooked in grand generalizations regarding differences between populations in mentality or physique. Conclusions of that kind can have little meaning unless the qualities to which they refer are specified.

The term 'quality' has been used hitherto because it appears to be the word used in ordinary speech which can best convey the meaning intended. In scientific literature it is now customary to use the term 'character' for the purpose. A character in this sense is a quality or attribute possessed by all human beings, and the only ones of interest in this discussion are those which are variable, so that different grades of them distinguish different people. Hair colour is a character and red hair is a grade of it; intelligence is a character of which different grades are exhibited in different individuals; stature is a character and grades of it can be defined by ranges of the measurement of height.

Characters are of various kinds, and a broad distinction can be made between two classes of them. Those of the first class show differences in degree in different people, and in many, but not all, cases it may be possible to measure such variation on some kind of scale. If such measurement is possible the character is called a quantitative one. It can also be said to exhibit continuous variation, but this term may also be applicable to other characters showing differences in degree (such as skin or hair colour) which cannot be assessed on any simple scale. Any particular character of the second class divides a community of people into two or more distinct categories (as a system of blood groups does), so these characters exhibit discontinuous variation. Under this head there is the special case of a character which may be said to be either present or absent in a particular person.

The classification of characters is a complicated matter, but there must be some reference to its complexities in any summarized account of the biological comparison of human populations. One difficulty concerns the distinction between what may be called normal and abnormal variation. The characters of the vast majority of people are determined by factors which operate in ways which can be called normal because they are usual. Small numbers of people, however, may be affected by unusual conditions which will result in one or other of their characters being abnormal. Such people are often recognized because they fall beyond the customary extremes for the populations to which they belong.

Regarding stature, for example, people called dwarfs and giants occur occasionally in all large populations: dwarfism is due to diseased conditions, of which some can be attributed to bad nutrition during the period of growth, and giantism is also due to disease. Two comparisons of the statures of groups of people representing different populations may be made for (a) those whose heights fall within the bounds of normal variation, and (b) those whose heights are judged to be abnormal. Usually, however, the question of biological distinctions between populations is considered for normal ranges of characters, and these embrace the vast majority of people.

The problem as a whole—referring to both mind and body—can now be enunciated in other words. The first stage in treating it is the classification of variable characters so that it will be known for each character: (a) whether the grades it exhibits in individuals are due to 'nature' alone, or (b) whether they are due to conditions to which the individuals are subjected during life alone, or (c) whether both 'nature' and conditions of life determine grades of the character.

Having obtained conclusions of this kind for a number of variable characters, the next stage will be to collect records of them for several series of individuals representing a number of suitable populations. Comparisons of these sets of data can then be made, with the object of disclosing the extent and significance of differences between the populations. Terms are used here which need to be defined or replaced by better ones, but before considering this point it may be noted that rewording the problem has modified it considerably. In the earlier version differences between groups were referred to in a vague way, and emphasis is now placed on characters considered singly. If a solution can be obtained for a number of characters considered singly it may be possible, of course, to give a more general conclusion referring to them conjointly. Something will be achieved, however, if the problem is solved for a single character, and there should be a good hope of reaching this limited objective.

To clarify definition of the problem, it is necessary to state more precisely what is meant when a character is said to be determined by 'nature'. Non-technical synonyms for 'natural' are *inborn, innate* and *hereditary*. The matter concerns potentiality rather than outward expression, although inner being has to be judged from outward manifestations. Technical synonyms for 'natural' are *genetical* and *racial*. Genetics is the science of heredity and any explanation of the concept required by geneticists would involve technical terms which are not widely understood. Questions regarding race in man are the concern of anthropologists and their way of regarding the matter can be expressed in more familiar terms.

Race is essentially a concept which relates to groups rather than to individuals, and the groups in question are distinguished on account of the ancestry of the peoples comprising them. The task of the anthropologist concerned with problems of racial classification would be far easier if humanity had been organized in such a way that regional populations usually remained as isolated units for considerable periods of time—embracing 50 or 100 or 1,000 generations, say. Such a group of intermarrying people can be called a 'racial' population. In the world as it is there are few ideal groups of that kind, but communities having practised intermarriage for a considerable number of generations can be counted as racial populations. The aim in classifying them is to reveal the ways in which they are interrelated owing to descent, so that pedigrees may be constructed in which the units are not individuals but populations. In doing this the investigator chiefly uses evidence that the people hold in themselves, manifested by personal characters of such a kind that they persist during the course of generations while conditions of life may be changed. These may be called racial characters and guidance from geneticists is needed in distinguishing them.

The primary problem regarding distinctions between populations can now be reworded again. In the first place it is to determine what characters make racial distinctions between populations; this concerns what people are in themselves owing to descent, apart from what they become owing to the modifying influences of the environments to which they are subjected. The further aim is to determine the extent and significance of racial differences.

RACIAL DIFFERENCES IN BODY CHARACTERS

Differences between the body characters of groups of human beings must have been a topic of interest long before men acquired the means of recording their impressions. In ancient literature there are numerous accounts of peoples and early pictoral art provides representations of them. The descriptions of both kinds are alike in giving pictures of typical members of populations. In general the verbal accounts list the features of a particular group of people as if they were those of a single person. Members of the community must have differed in appearance among themselves, but usually no attempt whatever was made to describe such variation. Delineation of 'types' was the conventional way of treating the matter and differences between the characteristics of types were usually exaggerated. This was so in the case of the peoples known to the early writers who described them. Accounts purporting to be authentic were also given of peoples believed to be living on the fringes of the known world, and these communities were usually credited with more or less extraordinary characters—somewhere between human and sub-human beings.

The general position regarding description of the varieties of man was little changed until the eighteenth century had nearly ended. Most parts of the inhabited world were known by then, but belief in the existence of kinds of humanity radically different from, and inferior to, that of civilized people died hard. It was finally discredited by inquirers who surveyed the evidence critically and sought to systematize man's knowledge of man. Their works—notably those of Professor Blumenbach of Göttingen—were widely discussed in the first decades of the nineteenth century. At that time the best accounts of many peoples in remote lands were still merely travellers' tales. Like the ancient Greek writings they usually described a population as a type without giving any account of differences between its members. Anyone can appreciate easily differences in appearance between individuals of the community to which he belongs. When he encounters a remote community with some characteristics markedly different from those of his own group his attention is focused on these, and all the strangers may appear to be alike. The ways in which the groups differ will be described—and exaggerated, perhaps —but not the distinctions between members of the unfamiliar group. Verbal description of such distinctions in a form likely to give a proper impression of them would be a lengthy and tedious undertaking.

The literary records relating to differences between human groups in physical characters were responsible for an erroneous view of the matter which prevailed generally before the age of systematic inquiry and which still persists in popular belief. According to this view there were clear-cut differences between ancient peoples, and all the individuals belonging to any particular group were very similar in appearance, as the historical records implied. The position was supposed to be much the same for existing peoples living in lands remote from those of the observers, as the accounts of travellers implied. It had to be admitted that the populations of the native countries of the observers were each made up of people who showed very considerable diversity in their body characters: otherwise the extent of variation within groups was underestimated. As relevant information of a new and more cogent kind accumulated it became evident that variation within populations was of the same order for nearly all groups described by good records. Those of the late pre-historic and historic past, and those of the present in remote parts of the world were (or are), in fact, little less variable than those of the present in more civilized lands. The new estimates make all people approximate to one another in this respect, and they show that the differences between types are less than had previously been supposed. Supposititious group distinctions diminished as adequate descriptions accumulated.

This change of view was due to the collection of evidence of a new kind. New schools of anthropology began to amass descriptions of peoples by applying techniques which were designed to be as direct and precise as possible. The aim of the investigators was to compare populations in such a way that their racial relationships and histories would be revealed. The series of 'subjects' were of two kinds, one being of living people and the other of skeletons excavated by archaeologists, and usually the sizes of the series were ridiculously small compared with those of the populations represented.

It was clear that not all body characters would be able to serve the purpose in view. A choice had to be made of a number believed to be of racial significance, that is to say of those which people inherit from their parents and which are affected little, or not at all, by environment. Such characters could indicate group relationship while others could not do so. In considering this question it is easier to recognize unsuitable characters than to select those which can best be used for the purpose. In innumerable respects all men are alike; taking a broad view they can all be said to be built to the same pattern and endowed with the same faculties. This is believed to be so for men in all parts of the world and for a period extending back long before the beginning of recorded history. The ways in which men differ are of small account compared with the ways in which they are alike, but the former make up the class defining individual and group distinctions. Differences of either kind are expressed in terms of variable characters. Some of these show discontinuous variation in dividing mankind into two or more distinct groups, while others—including all that can be expressed as measurements—show continuous variation.

Some variable characters are suitable for the purpose of making racial comparisons and others are unsuitable. Every variable character must be determined by a constitutional, or genetical, factor or factors, and with few exceptions all variable characters must be affected to a greater or lesser extent by conditions to which people are subjected during life. There are a few variable characters which are believed to be determined solely by heredity. Some of these (such as blood groups) are constant in individuals throughout life, while others (such as hair and eye colours) may show changes with age but are normally almost constant for the greater part of adult life.

At the other extreme there are variable body characters which are obviously to a considerable extent affected by environmental conditions. In this class there are some (such as many physiological measurements) which show rapid and considerable fluctuations in individuals, and others (such as those dependent on the bulk of soft tissues in the body, which can be assessed by weight and girths of the trunk and limbs) which fluctuate at a slow rate. There are some characters (such as sensory acuities, which are subject to age changes throughout the span of life) which show still slower changes in individuals, though it may not be possible to demonstrate that a change is influenced by any living conditions.

Variable characters behave, as it were, in so many different ways that the question of selecting those which can best be used to reveal constitutional, or racial, differences between populations is very involved. It is not unlikely that all of them have some racial significance, since all are dependent to a greater or lesser extent on genetical factors, but in particular cases this can only be assessed if there is some means of allowing for the effects of both environmental conditions and age changes. Characters which are more affected by these disturbing factors are less suitable for the purpose of disclosing racial distinctions because treatment of them would be difficult or intractable; characters less affected by the disturbing factors are more suitable for the purpose; characters entirely unaffected by them are ideal.

These considerations were implied, rather than clearly stated, by the anthropologists who began, about 100 years ago, to collect records of body characters of groups of people in a systematic way. The investigators were in general agreement in supposing that most characters of the adult skeleton are suitable for the purpose of revealing racial differences, and measurements were taken to describe them. The use of metrical methods gave a precision in treatment which had previously been lacking. The scope of the inquiry was extended in time and space as excavated series of skeletons from various parts of the world became available. Certain body measurements of living people were also accepted as being suitable for purposes of racial classification. These are really indirect measurements of the skeleton, taken by locating on the skin points on underlying bones. It was recognized that other body measurements—such as weight and girths, which are largely dependent on living conditions—were unsuitable for the purpose.

Other characters generally accepted by the earlier systematizers are the colour of skin, hair and eyes and the form and texture of the hair. Precision in recording these was encouraged by the use of the colour and other scales. The frequencies of certain skeletal and other physical abnormalities in different populations were also considered to be of racial significance.

The earlier anthropologists of the modern school supposed that differences between suitably chosen groups of people in the characters selected could be taken to indicate diversity in origin, and that by taking grades of the differences into account a racial classification could be inferred. Choice of the accepted list was necessarily somewhat arbitrary. The assumption made was that the characters used are determined primarily, if not entirely, by heredity. The fact that environment influences some of them to some extent was not, however, denied. It is patent that this is so, for example, in the case of skin colour, since light skins are darkened by exposure to sunlight, but allowance can be made for this and after such adjustment the character appears to be one which makes marked racial distinctions. Some of the characters are more useful than others because populations can be differentiated to different extents.

This zoological classification of man was well established by the end of the nineteenth century, and a considerable bulk of records had been collected. It was to be expected that the methods of the inquiry would be modified as knowledge increased. The most important new ideas having a bearing on the issue are those built up by the science of heredity, the methods and conclusions of which have been consolidated in the present century. Geneticists are now the authorities who can best decide what characters can best be used for the purpose of racial classification. They have made important contributions to the list by adding new characters of the theoretically ideal kind. Among these are the human blood groups, some systems of which have been recorded for large numbers of people in all parts of the world. In general, genetical examination of the characters accepted earlier as being suitable to reveal racial distinctions has not modified to any great extent the beliefs held regarding their suitability.

The first stage in making racial comparisons between populations is to distinguish characters of racial significance. Before any of these can be accepted for the purpose it has to be shown that their grades in individuals are determined primarily, if not entirely, by hereditary factors. This question must be considered for each character considered singly, and each presents a separate problem because relevant considerations are peculiar to each. Having decided on a suitable set of characters, and having discovered any special circumstances regarding them—such as the need to restrict records to adults in the case of stature and other skeletal characters—the next stage is the collection of series of data describing the characters in a number of suitably chosen populations. The comparisons are between groups not individuals, and the question is how can the records best be treated for the particular purpose in view. It may be remembered that one of the weakest features of the literary discussion of group differences is that it has no systematic method of making comparisons between groups of people. The modern scientific treatment of the same problem uses techniques which make it possible to deal with group data in a systematic way.

These methods were first used in treating records for body characters and they have been extensively applied in that field. They have also been used to some extent in treating records for mental characters. It will be convenient to summarize experience gained from treatment of physical characters, which concerns not only the ways in which the records can best be reduced—i.e. arranged in a convenient form—but also comparisons between the sets of reduced data representing different populations. It will be seen that in the latter process new conceptions are gained which clarify the nature of group differences. If these conceptions, due to experience in dealing with body characters, are applicable in dealing with mental characters, then treatment and interpretation of the latter may be assisted.

318

The first question concerns ways in which records of body characters for different populations are treated to give comparisons between these groups of people. In all cases statistical methods of one kind or another are used. This is because statistics is the science which deals with the systematic treatment of group data. Its methods may be very simple—as in merely counting the numbers of people with different grades of eye colour among a series representing a particular population—or they may be very elaborate, involving complicated mathematical formulae and lengthy calculations. In all cases they aim at giving a concise and precise abstract of the information. It has been pointed out that body characters used in making racial comparisons can be divided into classes, such as measurements of the size and form of the skeleton, colours of skin, hair and eyes, blood groups, and so on. Different statistical devices have to be used in dealing with different classes. Only one class will be discussed, viz. that of measurements. All these refer to what are called quantitative characters, to distinguish them from qualitative characters which cannot be assessed on a continuous scale. The general considerations involved are, however, very similar for quantitative and qualitative characters. As a preamble, it is convenient to refer to a few more terms, most of which are commonly used in discussing any statistical situation. A *population* is defined as any assemblage of individuals considered, and treated, as a single group. A *racial population* is a community which is believed, in the light of any evidence available, to be made up of individuals whose ancestors—or at least the majority of them—had intermarried for a considerable number of generations. Large rather than small groups are referred to, and owing to the nature of human societies it is necessary to admit that the limits of racial populations are often nebulous. Mankind is organized as a hierarchy of groups within groups. A *sample* is a set, or series, of individuals belonging to the same population for whom records of one or more characters are available. Sampling is necessary because it is seldom if ever possible to obtain records for all members of a population at a particular time, and populations have extension in time. A sample is said to be *drawn at random* if it gives a fair representation of the total population without bias favouring any special section of it. In most cases a sample does not refer to all the members of a population but to one of its natural subdivisions, such as the men, or women, or boys or girls of a specified age range.

The simplest case is that of records of a single character for a single sample of a particular population. An example of this kind is provided by the heights of 91,161 British men aged 20 who were measured in 1939 when they were called for medical examination under a military training act. To

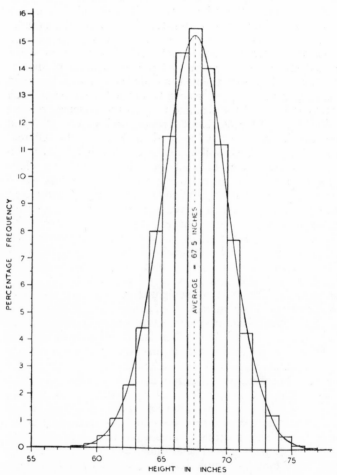

FIG. I   THE   DISTRIBUTION   OF   HEIGHTS,   FITTED   WITH   A
NORMAL   CURVE, OF   91,161   BRITISH   MEN   AGED   20

THE   DISTRIBUTION   IS   GIVEN   BY   DR. W. J. MARTIN   IN   'MEDICAL   RESEARCH   COUNCIL
MEMORANDUM'   No 20 , 1949.   ITS   RANGE   IS   FROM   48   TO   81   INCHES   AND   THE
EXTREME   FREQUENCIES   ARE   TOO   SMALL   TO   BE   SHOWN   ON   THE   SCALE   OF   THIS
DIAGRAM.

reduce the long series to order, the total range of heights can be divided into a number of equal parts and it is convenient to choose inches (1 inch = 2.54 cm.) for this purpose. The number of men falling in each inch group can be counted, and these frequencies can be represented by the heights of rectangles, as in Fig. 1. The set of blocks represents the total series of men and it is said to be the *distribution* of their heights.

The reduction is very simple so far, and it provides an abstract of the information which is more precise than any verbal description could be. It is also entirely free from any preconceived ideas regarding the heights of British men which might be held by the person manipulating the records. The diagram shows at a glance that most of the men had heights close to the average value, and that on passing from this value towards either extreme the frequencies decline in a regular fashion. The process of arranging the data—either as a table or in the form of a diagram—goes far towards exhibiting their meaning and indicating the ways in which information for groups can best be treated.

The importance of this preliminary treatment in dealing with records of human characters was first stressed by Adolphe Quetelet—the Belgian astronomer, who was also eminent as a meteorologist, statistician and anthropologist. He showed that distributions of the kind can be adequately represented by a class of mathematical curves. The type of these which is most generally applicable is known as the Normal Curve and it is shown fitted to the distribution of heights of British men in Fig. 1. The grades of heights defined by the breadths of the blocks in that diagram were chosen arbitrarily. If narrower blocks had been used the form might still have been regular, since the sample is a large one. If its size could be progressively increased, narrower and narrower blocks could be used and the outline would be expected to show a closer and closer approach to the continuous curve. The Normal Curve can be supposed to represent the distribution of heights in the population sampled.

This way of manipulating sets of measurements and inferring characteristics of populations from them is the basis of systematic treatment of records for body characters. Experience has shown that the Normal Curve is the typical form of distribution in the case of all metrical characters of racial significance for all racial populations. The measurements may be lengths or arcs of living bodies or skeletons, or they may refer to shape instead of size, as in the case of indices (e.g. the cephalic index which assesses the shape of the skull by expressing the maximum breadth as a percentage of the maximum length), or angles (e.g. one assessing the extent to which the jaws project).

A close approach to the form of the theoretical curve cannot, of course, be expected in the case of small samples representing a few hundred individuals, and no importance should be attached to minor peculiarities of such distributions. For most cases encountered in practice the approximation to the form of a Normal Curve becomes closer as the size of the sample is increased. Other forms occasionally found may differ from the typical form to some extent, and the explanation usually is that the series does not represent a single racial population but a mixture of two or more, or that a single population is represented but that the sample was not selected from it in a random way. When measurements of racial significance are treated the Normal Curve is the rule.

This experience indicates the way in which the next stage in the treatment—viz. the comparison of different groups— must proceed. Populations will be compared by comparing the distributions provided by samples, and all those acceptable for the purpose can be represented by Normal Curves. In what ways can Normal Curves differ? The most important distinctions between them are on account of two of their features. Still considering the case of a single character, the averages for two distributions may be different, and they may differ in spread or scatter. The average of a set of measurements is a familiar concept. The scatter of a distribution is concerned with the magnitude of differences between readings for individuals. The significance of one criterion assessing it is also commonly understood: this is the range, which in the case of the character considered is the difference between the heights of the tallest and shortest men in the sample. The range is not an efficient measure of variation, however.

A much better criterion commonly used for the purpose is derived from all the measurements of the sample. It is called the *standard deviation* and a larger value means that a distribution has a greater spread. A Normal Curve is defined completely by its average value and by this measure of variation. Standard deviations are available for numerous series of living people representing racial populations in all parts of the world, and for numerous series of skeletons (or in most cases of skulls only) representing racial populations in past times. This evidence is for a considerable number of measurements which are accepted as racial characters. It is extensive enough to justify generalizations regarding the extent to which different populations differ in variability.

In general, distinctions between the groups in this respect are much less than is commonly supposed. Modern European populations tend to be rather more variable than those in other parts of the world, but this is no more than a tendency to which exceptions may be found. Least variation is found for isolated island communities, but there is no sharp distinction between them and mainland peoples. The series of skulls for which standard deviations of metrical characters are available give an appreciation of relative variability within racial populations during the past 7,000 years. The earlier series are usually found to be rather less variable than modern ones, but the change throughout the period was far less than is commonly supposed. This question can only be discussed precisely by referring to evidence of a statistical kind and giving conclusions in statistical terms, but a fair impression is conveyed by the statement that all racial populations for which there are adequate records exhibit variation of the same order. The belief derived from literary accounts that modern racial populations in remote parts of the world, and all racial populations of earlier times, are (or were) decidedly less variable than those of Europe today can only be called a popular fallacy.

It must be concluded that the form of the distributions of metrical and racial characters in racial populations is not a criterion which makes distinctions of importance between such groups, because it is almost uniform. The degree of variation exhibited by the distributions is less uniform but diversity in it is not very significant. The most important way in which the groups differ is in showing different average values of any particular character. The essential question is: to what extent do racial populations differ in average values of racial measurements, and how does diversity between them in this respect compare with diversity between individuals belonging to any particular population? An answer to these questions will give a proper appreciation of the significance of racial differences.

There can be no general and simple answer to them because it is known that different characters may give markedly different answers. Two situations are illustrated in Figs. 2 and 3. The former refers to stature and it shows (at the top) the

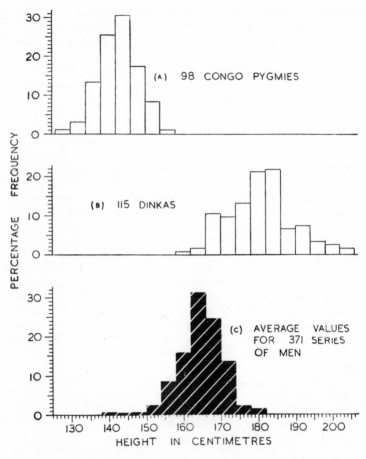

FIG. 2.   DISTRIBUTIONS OF HEIGHTS FOR :

(A) THE ONE AMONG 371 SERIES HAVING THE
SMALLEST AVERAGE (143 CM. FOR 98 CONGO
PYGMIES)

(B) THE ONE HAVING THE LARGEST AVERAGE
(180 CM. FOR 115 DINKAS OF THE NILOTIC
SUDAN)

(C) THE AVERAGE VALUES FOR THE 371 SERIES
OF MEN

distribution of heights for a sample of Congo pygmies, who are believed to be the shortest, or one of the shortest, people in the world. In the middle of the diagram the distribution is shown for a sample of men representing a Sudanese tribe which is one of the tallest communities in the world. The ranges of these two distributions meet—so that the tallest pygmy and the shortest Dinka had heights which were very close—and it is probable that they would be found to overlap to some extent if the heights were available for larger samples representing the two populations. This is a comparison of extreme groups. At the bottom of Fig. 2 the distribution is shown of *average* heights for 371 series of men representing racial populations in all parts of the world, and like the other two it shows a close resemblance to the form of the Normal Curve. It is clear that in the case of comparisons between most pairs of racial series the distributions of heights must overlap to a considerable extent, and for many pairs the difference

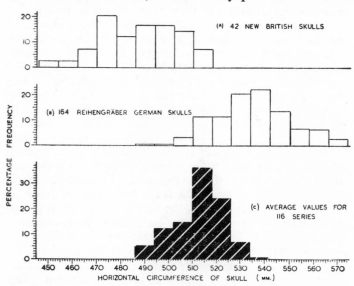

FIG. 3 DISTRIBUTIONS OF HORIZONTAL CIRCUMFERENCES OF SKULLS FOR :

(A) THE ONE AMONG 116 MALE ADULT SERIES HAVING THE SMALLEST AVERAGE (489 MM FOR 42 NATIVES OF NEW BRITAIN)

(B) THE ONE HAVING THE LARGEST AVERAGE (535 MM FOR 164 REIHENGRÄBER GERMANS)

(C) THE AVERAGE VALUES FOR THE 116 SERIES

between the averages must be very small compared with the range covered by either distribution. This is the situation for stature, and for that character it can be said that variation between groups (i.e. between average measurements for them) is of the same order as variation within groups (i.e. between different individuals belonging to the same group).

Fig. 3 illustrates the situation for another character, viz. the horizontal circumference of the skull. As in the case of stature, the distributions are shown for the series (among 116) which has the smallest average and for the series which has the greatest average. The ranges for these extreme distributions overlap to a considerable extent, and they are decidedly closer together than the extreme groups in the case of heights. The distribution of the *average* horizontal circumferences for the 116 series is also shown, and it is clear that most pairs of the series must have distributions which overlap to a marked extent. For this character it can be said that variation between groups is appreciably less than variation within groups.

The situations are thus different for different characters, and these can be graded, by analysis of the kind considered, according to the extent to which they are capable of distinguishing racial populations. At one end there is stature, which may make the greatest distinctions, and the situation is very similar for the cephalic index (i.e. the maximum breadth of the skull expressed as a percentage of its maximum length). Of those suitable for the purpose, these are the two measurements which, as far as is known, can be used most effectively to detect racial differences. The situations for most of the other characters are not far removed from that for the horizontal circumference of the skull. Near the other end of the gradation there are a few characters for which variation between groups is decidedly smaller than variation within groups, and all pairs of distributions for racial populations overlap to a marked extent. These are the measurements which are of least use when the aim is to reveal racial distinctions.

It is important to appreciate that in the case of all characters hitherto examined some degree of variation between groups has been found. All body measurements make distinctions between different people belonging to any particular population, and no measurement is known to have identical averages for all populations. Different characters are capable of distinguishing racial populations to different degrees and all do so to some extent. If there is diversity within the groups then the existence of some real racial differences can be presumed.

An outline has been given of the way in which the problem of racial differences in body characters can be treated systematically. The first stage involves selection of a number of characters suitable for the purpose, and collection of records of them for samples representing a number of suitable populations. The next stage in the case of metrical characters is examination of the typical form of distribution of the measurements. This indicates the way in which comparisons between the groups—based on data for samples from them—must be made and these comparisons elucidate the nature of racial differences.

It should be pointed out that one way in which distributions differ may be of more importance in dealing with mental than with physical characters. For the latter class the Normal Curve is the typical form of distribution and an example given is for this form in the case of stature. The distribution of average heights given by 371 racial series is shown in Fig. 2. It can be calculated from this that if pairs of the series were selected at random, then about one pair in three would be expected to differ in average height by less than 4 cm. This indicates a degree of separation of distributions which is not very rare. Such a grade of distinction would occur with approximately

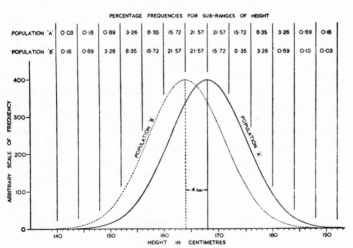

FIG. 4. IMAGINARY DISTRIBUTIONS OF HEIGHTS, IDEALISED AS NORMAL CURVES, FOR TWO POPULATIONS HAVING AVERAGE VALUES DIFFERING BY 4 cm AND THE SAME SCATTER (GIVEN BY A STANDARD DEVIATION OF 7 cm)

the same frequency in the case of the cephalic index, and with much greater frequency in the case of some other measurements of the skeleton which are less able to differentiate racial populations.

Fig. 4 shows imaginary distributions of heights for two series of individuals, the distributions being idealized as Normal Curves and superposed. The difference between their averages is 4 cm. and they have the same scatter—defined by a standard deviation of 7 cm.—which is of the order found in practice. The curves overlap to a marked extent and they indicate that there are very tall and very short men in both populations. Many members of the taller population ('A') are shorter than many members of the shorter population ('B').

The percentage frequencies for equal (4 cm.) sub-ranges of height are given for both communities in the diagram. They are exactly the same for heights 164-168 cm., owing to the fact that the Normal Curve is symmetrical. For all sub-ranges above 168 cm. population. 'A' has the greater frequency, and on passing towards the upper extreme its relative preponderance increases continuously. For the sub-range 172-176 cm. the relative frequency is nearly twice as great for population 'A' as for population 'B': for the sub-range 188-192 cm. the ratio is 6 to 1. The position is precisely the same on passing from the central sub-range towards the lower extreme, but with frequencies for population 'B' predominating over those for population 'A'.

This example shows that when, for a particular character, the difference between the averages for two populations is small compared with differences that may be found between pairs of individuals belonging to either group, then is should be expected that considerable differences will be found between the relative frequencies in the populations of individuals having extreme values of the measurement. This is not a consideration of much importance in the case of group comparisons for stature or any other body measurement, but it may be of greater significance in the case of mental characters.

RACIAL DIFFERENCES IN MENTAL CHARACTERS

Scientific treatment of the problem of group differences in body characters has been developed in the past 100 years. It is now taken for granted that the inquiry must proceed in a particular way: evidence of a certain kind must be collected, and the methods used in dealing with the records are established. Progress must depend on the accumulation of more evidence needed to enlarge the scope of the investigation and to consolidate its provisional conclusions. It is clear that the problems of racial differences in physical and mental characters are very similar in several respects, but some circumstances are different in the two cases because the classes of evidence to which they refer are different in nature.

The situation in pre-scientific times may be considered first. Whenever groups of people gained knowledge of one another the members of each must have been quick to appreciate distinctions between themselves and the strangers in physical and mental characters. Mentality could only be judged by customs and behaviour, and when the peoples brought into contact were at markedly different levels of civilization the comparison encouraged the more advanced to believe that the 'savages' were beings of a different kind. As in the case of descriptions of body characters, both the early literary accounts of primitive peoples and those of travellers in recent times tended to exaggerate distinctions, while as knowledge increased particulars generally accepted became less extraordinary. The fact that there is social order even in the most backward communities was increasingly recognized.

The two kinds of literary evidence were also alike in describing groups as 'types', so that a community was treated, with reference to both body and mind, as if it was a single person. Individual differences within groups were either ignored or were referred to in an anecdotal, or in some other inadequate, way. It is only in recent times that there has been any proper appreciation of the fact that fundamental differences between groups cannot be assessed at all precisely except on the basis of adequate knowledge of *variation within groups*. With regard to this matter an important difference must be recognized between the situations for physical and mental qualities.

The variable body characters used for purposes of racial classification are essentially of a personal kind and their grades in individuals are physically determined and durable. Ideal characters are absolutely stable throughout life (as in the case of blood groups) although records for many used are confined to the adult stage of development, and some of the characters may be influenced to a certain extent by physical environment. Social environment has no direct influence on this class of body attributes. The situation is very different in the case of mental characters. Their outward manifestations provide the evidence to be interpreted, and these are obviously determined to a large extent by experience and fortuitous circumstances of life. Man has an imitative and sympathetic nature and to a large extent his behaviour must conform with that of the community to which he belongs. In many respects social environment dominates his conduct.

Beneath, as it were, the tendency towards uniformity within groups imposed by such conditions there is individual diversity due to differences in natural propensities and gifts. The aim is to evaluate these personal characteristics, and this can only be done by making proper allowances for the modifying effects of social environment and—if it should prove to be necessary —for the modifying effects of physical environment as well. On this account the position is more involved for mind than for body, and it must be anticipated that satisfactory conclusions will be more difficult to reach in the former case. On account of other circumstances, too, treatment of the 'mental' problem is more difficult than treatment of the 'physical' problem. A contrast must be made between the confused world of behaviour, which is always difficult to interpret, and the physical world, of which some aspects can be described in precise terms.

There seems, however, to be general agreement today among psychologists who have considered the matter that treatment of the problem of racial differences in mentality must proceed on the same lines as those established in dealing with the parallel problem regarding body characters. This point of view is taken for granted in Professor Klineberg's book, *Race and Psychology;* the implication is that such is the scientific way of treating the problem, which should lead to conclusions of greater worth than any which can be reached by literary discussion alone. It is significant that Quetelet, who was chiefly responsible for establishing the method of treatment for physical characters, was unable to apply it to mental characters. In his last discussion of the 'moral and intellectual' faculties of man, given in *Anthropométrie* in 1871, he only considered social statistics, such as those relating to marriages, mental deficiency and criminality. The imperfections and limitations of evidence of this kind were fully acknowledged. It is of little value when the aim is to reveal fundamental differences between peoples because the records only have an indirect bearing on that topic, because they are affected by adventitious circumstances, and because they are not collected in a uniform way in all countries.

Many of the characters used by anthropologists for purposes of racial classification relate to the form of the body, and many of these so-called morphological characters can be assessed as measurements of size or shape. This class is distinct from that which is made up by characters relating to ways in which the body works. Considering function in the widest sense, characters assessing it can be sub-divided into two broad classes labelled physiological and psychological, but these two merge into one another and some characters can be supposed to belong to both of the arbitrary sub-divisions. If a function is more clearly physical in nature it is called physiological, and if more clearly mental it is called psychological, but particular characters may have essential aspects of both kinds. The three classes of characters can be arranged in the order: morphological—physiological—psychological. The physical aspect of man's entity is predominant at one end of the scale and absent, or unappreciated, at the other.

The systematic collection of physiological records for groups of people began in the first half of the nineteenth century. Tests of strength were among the earliest, and methods of testing reaction times, the acuity of senses and the functioning of the respiratory and other systems were standardized later. The method in all cases was essentially the same. A test of one kind or another was applied and the result could be given in terms of some kind of physical scale. The faculties assessed in such ways are more complex in nature than morphological characters, and measurement of many of them depends on the subject's appreciation of what he is required to do and on his willingness to co-operate. This is a complication of particular importance when primitive peoples are tested.

Other disadvantages of the physiological tests—as regards their suitability as racial criteria—are the inadequacy of information regarding the relative influences of hereditary factors and conditions of life in determining scores, short-term fluctuations in individuals apart from motivation, and changes with age throughout the span of life. For these reasons interpretation of group records of physiological characters is particularly difficult. Anthropologists are not yet able to use such evidence for purposes of racial classification, and records of the characters collected in standardized ways are scanty for peoples at lower levels of culture. Those available for such communities have corrected erroneous beliefs previously held

331

regarding group differences in sensory acuities. At one time it was commonly believed that hunting peoples were decidedly superior to more civilized peoples in vision and hearing, and this was supposed to account for their skill in the chase. Tests of the senses of American Indian and other hunting peoples have shown, however, that they are not clearly distinguished from urbanized communities in that respect, and the conclusion must be that skill in tracking is not due to outstanding sensory qualities, but to experience which enables them to be used efficiently. With regard to such questions, the general impressions of observers are not to be trusted; the need is for evidence which is as direct and precise as possible.

The records of physiological characters have shown that very considerable variation is normally found within communities, and group distinctions depend on differences between average values which are very small compared with those frequently found between individuals belonging to the same group. This situation is the same as that found for the morphological and other characters used in racial classification. Knowledge of peoples in all parts of the world is comprehensive enough to show, too that all men living today, apart from a small proportion suffering from diseased conditions, are alike in all essential ways concerning both form and function on lower planes. We are all of the same kind, and qualities which distinguish our sub-groups are of minor importance compared with the innumerable qualities which we all possess. This generalization applies to the form of human beings, to the more physical of their physiological functions, and to the more mental of their physiological functions (such as senses, reflex actions and 'instincts').

It is commonly supposed that the same generalization also applies to higher mental qualities, and that there may be group differences in these in degree but not in kind. Professor Klineberg takes it for granted that intelligence in a Negro is comparable in every way with intelligence in a European. The only outstanding anthropologist who has questioned this point of view is Lévy-Bruhl. His thesis was that primitive thought is essentially different in kind from that of civilized man in having a different conception of individuality, and in being unable to reason in a logical way. Discussion of this matter may be confused unless terms are clearly defined and used in the same ways by both parties. The ultimate issue concerns inborn aptitude and disposition, and not mental traits imposed by tradition and social environment.

It is not disputed that habitual modes of thought are different in people living in primitive societies and in those reared in civilized communities, though evidence of logical thought is not absent among the former and the latter are not free from irrational beliefs. Evidence relevant to potential differences between such groups is provided by cases of peoples recently at a primitive level of culture who have become attached to civilized communities, such as Negroes in North America. There can be no doubt that in such circumstances they tend to adopt rational modes of thought. Evidence provided by tests of mental characters also appears to give strong support to the hypothesis that all men have basic mental qualities of the same kind. Many of these are variable in the sense that different individuals may exhibit them in different degrees.

This point of view has to be accepted or rejected before it can be decided whether or not the investigation of racial differences in mentality can be carried out on the same lines as those followed in investigating racial differences in other characters. If it is accepted, then the inquiries can proceed in ways which are almost identical. Characters will be considered singly and tests must be devised to assess their grades in individuals. There is the same need to select characters suitable for the particular purpose in view, and proper allowances must be made for special circumstances in making and interpreting group comparisons. With such safeguards it can be supposed that the method can be used to assess racial differences in mentality, and this implies that it is applicable universally—to all peoples and to all aspects of man's being.

Difficulties encountered in applying the method are greatest in the case of mental characters owing to the nature of these. In the first place there is the difficulty—not encountered at lower levels—of distinguishing discrete mental characters. This is bound up in practice with the formulation of tests which can be applied to distinguish grades of the characters in individuals. The branch of experimental psychology concerned with this matter was not established until the first decade of the present century, when the earliest intelligence tests were devised, and it is still developing its methods. The relevant tests in use today are of two kinds, relating to intelligence and special skills and abilities on the one hand, and to character and temperamental traits on the other. It is often difficult to decide what faculty (or faculties) is (or are) being assessed by particular tests. They all require that subjects shall comprehend a task and do their best in performing it. There is good evidence that, in the case of intelligence and some special abilities, hereditary factors must play a considerable part in determining grades in individuals, but the extents to which they may be modified by nurture and environment are uncertain. The suitability of the characters for use as racial criteria is hence difficult to assess. Little seems to be known about the role of heredity in determining traits concerning temperament and personality.

In his book Professor Klineberg gives an account of the application of intelligence tests to various racial communities, represented chiefly by series of children. Difficulties encountered in obtaining and interpreting the records are discussed. It is admitted that the test scores are determined by the interaction of hereditary and environmental factors which cannot be disentangled. Another point relevant to the assessment of such evidence in terms of racial differences is that there are many populations to which the tests have not yet been applied in any uniform way. The scope of the records is far less extensive than that for records of physical characters, and hence generalizations regarding mankind as a whole should be more restrained.

If a broad view is taken, the tests have revealed a situation for group differences in mental characters which is very similar to that for body measurements. Every racial community shows great individual variation: members of any one are expected to show a range for intelligence from exceptional stupidity to exceptional ability. Verbal accounts which purported to describe the type of a community without indicating the extent of difference between the people composing it are thus seen to be very misleading for mental, as for physical, characters. The distributions for the former, as for the latter, show that most people stand close to the average for their group, and frequencies decline progressively on passing from that central mass towards either extreme. The typical form of distribution given by scores for intelligence tests appears to be that of the Normal Curve, as for stature and other body measurements.

While remembering that the tests of mental characters are not ideal for the purpose, it can safely be concluded that they demonstrate the essential nature of racial differences in mentality. These are now seen to be of far less significance than had commonly been supposed. As in the case of body measurements, group distinctions are revealed by comparisons between pairs of distributions which exhibit considerable scatter.

For the vast majority of comparisons, if not for all of them, the paired distributions must overlap to a marked degree. As far as can be judged, individual variation in mental characters is of the same order for all racial communities, and typical forms of distributions are probably uniform. Group distinctions of significance may still be found between their positions, i.e. between average values of the characters.

The general situation for mental characters that can be assessed on some kind of continuous scale appears to be precisely the same as that for body measurements of racial significance. It may be recalled that for the latter the extent to which suitably chosen populations are differentiated is not the same for all characters. At one end there is the situation for stature (illustrated in Fig. 2), in which case the range for any population is about half the range for all normally formed men in the world. For practical purposes it can be supposed that the extreme distributions touch but do not overlap. The only other body measurement known to differentiate racial populations as effectively as stature does is the cephalic index.

It seems unlikely that there are any inborn mental qualities which distinguish racial populations to the extent that stature does. In the case of mental characters which differentiate racial populations most clearly the situation may be comparable with that illustrated in Fig. 3. To appreciate this it must be remembered that the extent of distinctions between groups is indicated by distributions which are presumed to be *extreme* for all racial populations. There is considerable overlapping of the extreme groups. In the case of most comparisons between pairs of population the distributions would overlap to a far greater extent. It may be that for some other inborn mental qualities the situation would be better represented by a diagram showing extreme distributions as close together as those in Fig. 4.

This vague summing up of the situation regarding racial differences in mental characters accords with that given at the end of Professor Klineberg's book, where he writes; 'As far as we can judge, the range of capacities and the frequency of occurrence of various levels of inherited ability are about the same in all racial groups.'

It has been pointed out that all the body measurements accepted as racial characters make distinctions between racial populations. Some of the characters differentiate the groups to a lesser, and some to a greater, degree. The situation is the same in the case of body characters of racial significance which do not show continuous variation (such as blood groups), and it is also the same in the case of variable body characters which are not suitable for use in distinguishing racial populations (such as body weight and physiological measurements). Characters are said to be variable if they exhibit different grades in individuals belonging to any particular population. The general rule is that all variable body characters make some distinctions between racial populations.

In other words, variation within groups is always associated with variation between groups. This is a rule which applies not only to man but also to all other forms of life. In the case of those which have been most fully investigated, such as some birds, regional groups within a species show geographical gradations in colouring, say, which are comparable with those found for human populations. Absolute uniformity in group characteristics is never found for variable characters. Group diversity must be supposed to be due to the interaction of a considerable number of factors, some of these being purely, or predominantly, of a biological nature while others relate to external circumstances. In the case of man, social institutions, which have not been uniform, and 'historical accidents' must have played a considerable part in determining the formation of the racial populations existing today. Some diversity between these groups, expressed in terms of variable characters, must be expected and it is actually found.

There seems to be no reason why the general rule regarding variation within and between groups should not apply to mental, as well as to physical, characters. If variable characters of the former kind showed identical distributions for all racial populations that would be a situation unparalleled, as far as is known, as regards any physical character in man or in any other animal. It seems to be impossible to evade the conclusion that some racial differences in mental characters must be expected. Existing evidence may not be extensive and cogent enough to reveal them, but it must be inferred that some exist. A reasonable surmise at present is that group diversity tends to be less in degree for mental tests than for body measurements, and greater refinement in the technique of observation may be needed to detect racial differences in mental characters.

The only assumption made in reaching the inference in question is that similar conditions must be expected to produce similar results. It does not depend on any presupposition that there is any association in individuals between the body characters used in classifying racial populations and the mental traits hitherto used in comparing the groups. Professor Klineberg discusses this matter. He comments on the fact that extensive inquiries have failed to reveal any relationships, within normal ranges, between head size and shape and body size and colouring, on the one hand, and intelligence or personality traits, on the other. The conclusion is that 'anatomical or structural differences between racial groups are *not* necessarily accompanied by corresponding psychological differences'. It is still possible, or even probable, that there is association between some physical characters of racial significance and some mental characters of racial significance—the former perhaps being physiological or biochemical rather than morphological. Even if characters of mind and body were entirely independent, it would still be legitimate to infer that the conditions responsible for variation within and between groups for the one class must be expected to have effects of like kind for the other class.

If the conclusion that the existence of some racial differences in mental characters must be presumed is accepted, then it is appropriate to recall a point regarding the nature of group differences commented on above in the discussion regarding body measurements. For a particular character showing continuous variation, the distributions representing two populations are most likely to overlap to a marked extent. The differences between the averages may be very small compared with the range for either distribution. Even when this is so, there may be a marked difference between the relative frequencies in the populations of individuals having extreme values of the measurement (as illustrated in Fig. 4). This may be a distinction of importance in the case of some mental characters. There may be almost equal proportions of stupid, mediocre and able people in two populations; even so, exceptional ability may be found with a frequency of 1 in 1,000 in the one group and with a frequency of 1 in 10,000 in the other. Having a larger proportion of exceptionally able members may be a factor which tells decisively in favour of a population in the course of centuries or millenniums.

THE SIGNIFICANCE OF RACIAL DIFFERENCES

The problem is to discover natural, or racial, distinctions between human populations, apart from distinctions which are due to diversity in conditions of life. An outline has been given of the scientific method of treating the problem which has been applied for rather more than 100 years. The literary discussion of earlier times had failed to reach any adequate solution. In considering the scientific investigation it is convenient to make a broad distinction between body and mind. The general methods used are the same in both these spheres, but application of them started earlier, and it is more straightforward and better established, on the physical than on the psychological level.

The first stage is distinguishing separate personal qualities or attributes—called characters—which are suitable for the particular purpose in view. This is a complicated matter which involves consideration of evidence of various kinds. The case of any character which might be suitable has to be examined separately because relevant conditions are peculiar to each one. Few physical, and no mental, characters are believed to be ideal criteria in making racial comparisons, but a certain number of both kinds can be selected which may be supposed more or less suitable, while other characters are recognized as being definitely unsuitable. Some characters can only be used if certain conditions are respected, such as restriction to a particular age range. A requirement in every case is that there should be fairly precise definition of grades distinguishing different people, such as those given by metrical or other scales in the case of body attributes, or by specially devised tests in the case of mental qualities.

These are essentials of the scientific treatment of the problem, and some people to whom it is a matter of interest dislike the conditions imposed. It may be pointed out that men cannot be understood by summing up any list of their qualities: the essence of their being eludes description in any precise terms which can be catalogued. As far as can be seen at present, the only alternative to following the disciplined method, which necessitates consideration of characters singly, seems to be discussion of the problem in general terms with little, if any, hope of reaching any decisive conclusions.

The second stage is collection of records of the selected characters for series of people representing suitably chosen populations. When they are available the sets of data have to be compared, and this is essentially a statistical process. The counting of heads is another step in the scientific treatment which is disliked by some people who are interested in the general problem. It is an essential part of that treatment, however, for which there is no verbal substitute. The purpose in view must be remembered, and clearly some kinds of comparisons between populations can only be made adequately in purely verbal terms.

To anyone who follows the systematic treatment referred to, the descriptions provided by distributions for separate characters indicate the nature of differences between the groups of people. The problem is reduced to comparisons between pairs of distributions, and when these have been made for a number of characters recorded for a considerable number of populations then some generalization regarding racial differences may be permitted. At present the situation can be summed up with much greater confidence for physical than for mental characters. In the case of all those of the former kind which are used in making racial comparisons, it can be stated that significant racial distinctions are usually found whenever data for two groups are compared.

The conclusions so far are definitely established. There are racial differences in physical characters, but whether the situation is the same or not for mental characters is a question which cannot be answered definitely at present—mental characters being more difficult to define and assess, and none hitherto used being very satisfactory for the purpose of making racial comparisons. The following summing up of the situation for mental characters appears to the writer to be as definite as any which can be justified at present.

It is unlikely that there are any racial differences in mentality which make an absolute distinction between all members of one population and all members of any other. It is probable that there are some mental characters showing continuous variation which make significant racial differences between *some* pairs of populations. The comparisons of this kind can be illustrated by overlapping distributions, and it is probable that the extreme groups tend to be separated to a lesser degree for mental than for physical characters. The hypothesis that for any particular variable mental character distributions in all racial populations are precisely the same is probably incorrect, because for physical characters in man, and for characters generally in other animals, variation within groups is always associated with some degree of distinction between groups. It is probable that different mental characters suitable for the purpose of making racial comparisons differentiate racial populations to different degrees, as is the case with physical characters.

The general inference is that there are racial differences in mentality, although clear demonstration of them—regarding particular characters and particular pairs of populations—is not available yet. Anyone who enunciates this conclusion is liable to be misunderstood; discussion of the problem has always tended to run to extremes. On the one hand there have been writers who asserted that there are racial differences of profound significance, and opposed to them have been others who have vehemently denied the existence of any inborn inequalities between groups of people. Few have argued that both these parties are in error. Any admission of racial differences is suspected by the 'levellers' to have a sinister implication, and the proponent of it is likely to be suspected of claiming superiority for the group to which he belongs.

As literate peoples became better acquainted with others beyond their frontiers the prevailing beliefs regarding racial distinctions in body and mind were slowly modified. In general the significance of racial differences appeared to be progressively reduced as knowledge increased. The modern scientific investigation of the question tended at first to modify the earlier beliefs in the same direction, and it almost looked as though the ultimate solution of the problem might be a denial of the existence of any racial differences. But this conclusion is manifestly untrue in the case of physical characters, and in the writer's opinion is very unlikely to be proved true in the case of mental qualities.

No dogmatic statements regarding particular group distinctions in innate mental characters can be justified at present. The matter has often been discussed in the case of comparisons between Negroes in general on the one hand, and people of European descent in general on the other. The earlier view that mental processes in the former are different in kind from those in the latter is now abandoned. The application of intelligence tests has suggested that differences between the two groups in inborn factors relating to abilities must be very small. Interpretation of the differences in terms of true racial distinctions is uncertain, and it may be presumptuous to conclude that there probably are none. Negroes might well be found to be superior in some abilities.

In another way the position for mental characters is not unlikely to be the same as that for physical characters. For the latter no racial population is found to be near the higher or lower extreme in many ways. One group may be outstanding for one character and one for another, and all groups are unexceptional in most respects. Group diversity of such a kind tends to equalize all peoples when a final summing up is made for all characters. Variety among populations would be a boon to humanity if all had good opportunities to develop their potentialities.

RACE MIXTURE

by
Harry L. Shapiro

*Chairman, Department of Anthropology,
American Museum of Natural History,
New York*

INTRODUCTION

Nowhere in the world today have differences in race been completely effective as barriers to the production of hybrid offspring. Since there is no reason to believe that this situation was any different in earlier stages of human history, we may conclude, even in the absence of other evidence, that the intermixture of populations and races must be a very ancient phenomenon, occuring wherever the opportunity for it arose. This conclusion, however, is borne out by more than a syllogism. Historic and archaeological data support it. And the present distributions of racial variations and intergrades can be explained most reasonably only by a widespread and very old process of hybridization.

Leaving aside for the moment the thorny question of what a race is, one might go so far as to generalize and say that race mixture must be coeval with race differentiation. Certainly these two processes of fusion and differentiation have gone along together in human history as they have in other forms of life and evolution.

Although race mixture may, therefore, be as old as mankind itself, this does not mean that antiquity clothes it with the dignity of a natural and widespread process or confers upon it an easy acceptance. Indeed, the fact that this is not the case is one of the reasons for this essay and it will therefore be one of my purposes to discuss why this is so nowadays while, in the past, the situation seems, as far as we can reconstruct it, to have been quite different. Before, however, proceeding further, I think it would clarify things if I define more exactly the biological limits of my subject.

Race mixture, as a phrase, is employed very loosely in common language. It may refer to an intermarriage between Negro and white, to the mingling of various closely related European stocks as, for example, in the United States, and even to an international marriage between, say, an Englishman and a Frenchwoman. Yet these kinds of mixture are racially quite different and socially have distinctive consequences. The reason for this latitude of usage is that the word race is applied with an equal looseness to all kinds of population groups whose mingling consequently has been indiscriminately described as race mixture. Race, at least in English, antedates any attempt to give it scientific speciality. Webster's definition illustrates how widely it is used and how various are the nuances it may suggest:

> The descendants of a common ancestor; a family, tribe, people, or nation, believed or presumed to belong to the same stock; a lineage; a breed; also more broadly, a class or kind of individuals with common characteristics, interests, appearance, habits, or the like, as if derived from a common ancestor; as the *race* of doctors, the *race* of birds. 'The whole race of mankind.' Shakespeare. 'Whence the long race of Alban fathers came.' Dryden.

In a literary way, race, therefore, may be applied to any group with a common characteristic, genetic or not, physical or otherwise, innate or acquired. It is, of course, as in so many other words, the context which defines significance. Since it fills a literary need and has established itself firmly in the language, it has proven difficult if not impossible to alter its meaning or at least to restrict it within a scientific definition. Consequently, the simultaneous use of the word in literary and in scientific writing, each with its own meaning, has served to create misunderstanding, as one class of users reads into the word overtones not intended by the other.

This confusion is enhanced further by the subtle changes the word race undergoes from one language to another, and by the emphasis it has received in recent decades, when it was employed pseudo-scientifically for political and nationalistic purposes.

I have touched on these semantic problems not to preface a discussion of the scientific concept of race but to indicate why some definition of the subjet I propose to discuss is necessary. It has long been evident that physical differences between groups of mankind vary from those that are barely perceptible and can be expressed only in statistical terms to those that are easily recognized and about which there is a common agreement. Thus, although the English, the Germans, the Swedes, the French and other European national groups may sometimes insist on distinguishing themselves from one another as races, they do in fact share many physical characteristics; they overlap very considerably in their ranges of variation; and in the proportions or frequencies of their known genes they resemble one another closely. Such physical differences as they do exhibit are, compared to the full range of human variation, relatively minor and are frequently exaggerated by differences in custom, dress, language, and other non-racial attributes. From a biological point of view, random intermarriage between such closely related populations may involve, in a very large proportion of cases, no greater diversity than may occur in marriages within national limits. And the offspring of such international unions are usually indistinguishable from the natives of the parental country in which they are bred and raised. The difficulties, and they are often real, that may arise from such crossings of national borders are likely to grow out of cultural differences rather than biological ones. But on the whole, these, when they do occur, are personal problems of adjustment, and even where large social groups display a distinct and even hostile attitude toward such intermarriages, they do not lead to the creation of a permanent minority group or a distinct and physically recognizable entity within the society of which they are a part. From the point of view which I propose to take here, this is an important distinction. It is also in the nature of things that contiguous groups are not only genetically closely related but that intermixture between them has been going on for a very long time; in fact, the former often being the consequence of the latter. The history of Europe for 2,500 years and for a much longer prehistory is full of explicit evidence of much population movement, of settlement and resettlement, of invasion and conquest. All this has meant a constant reshuffling and mingling of genetic elements and thus the weaving of a biological interrelationship far too complex for complete unravelling by any known method of analysis.

This pattern of interrelationship and intermingling characterizes all areas of the world, so that any classifier of mankind is likely to have a very difficult time indeed drawing arbitrary racial lines between neighbouring peoples. The situation, however, is vastly different when geographically remote or physically isolated groups are compared with each other. Then it is easy to discern notable and distinctive physical variations of a racial order. Thus, it is possible to see in the continuities of mankind a pattern of racial differentiation distributed geographically. Without digressing into the dynamics of genetic differentiation and the effects of mutation, selection, drift and other possible mechanisms on this process, it is generally recognized that isolation is the way these differences are preserved once they are established, and the longer and more complete this isolation, the greater are the differences likely to become.

In this day of world-wide communication and complete geographical exploration, it is often difficult to realize how recent these phenomena really are and, on the contrary, how isolated from each other geographically remote groups were throughout most of man's past. Even at the height of Roman expansion, only a small fraction of the world and its inhabitants were known. Other expanding empires in the past, like China, India or Arabia, were similarly familiar with only a small part of the world and had extensive physical contact with even more limited areas. Although intermarriage, migrations, conquests, the rise and fall of empires, trade and other distributive forces were constantly breaking down population assemblages, shuffling people and spreading genes, these movements were limited and never world-wide. Thus racial differences, blurred and obscured *within* large areas, were preserved between remote groups. And if it is frequently difficult, if not impossible, to distinguish between the members of populations inhabiting the same general area, we find that the inhabitants of widely separated regions offer no such difficulty. No one, on physical grounds, would confuse a Central African Negro with a Mongoloid from China, or either of them with a Scandinavian. These distinctions and others of the same order require no special skill to discern or scientific procedures to demonstrate. They are the product of mankind's history and for the first time became known in their full range only recently.

Five hundred years ago, at the dawn of the age of expansion, Europeans knew of African Negroes principally from classical references to them, from mercantile contact with the Near East where some were to be seen, and from their knowledge of the people of North Africa. Few had ever laid eyes on any of them until after the end of the fifteenth century. As far as the inhabitants of central and southern Africa were concerned, their acquaintance with the white man was equally vague. In addition, Europeans had some information derived from Marco Polo and other rare travellers of some of the peoples of the Middle and Far East and the islands of Indonesia. They knew nothing of the American Indians inhabiting two continents. They had never heard of the Australian aborigines. Not till much later did they discover the existence of the Bushmen of South Africa, the Polynesians, the Melanesians, the Eskimo, the Paleo-Asiatic tribes of north-east Asia, and many other groups that had pursued their development through countless centuries without any contact whatsoever with Europeans. Although some of these people knew of each other, most of them in turn had equally little or no contact or knowledge of one another's existence.

But, with the explorations of the past 500 years, all this came to an end. The long period of relative isolation ceased. Not only were European contacts with these varied populations established with varying degrees of intimacy, but new relationships of far greater complexity were made possible between those groups themselves, as world trade, labour demands, commercial exploitation and population pressures began to exert their multifarious influences in a world freshly opened to the increasing efficiency of transportation systems.

In this fashion, and through many more routes than I have indicated, a new era of racial intermingling began, similar and yet different from the process of mixture that has always characterized human history. The genetic process of population mixture such as occurs between different Negro stocks, between the Chinese and the people on their borders, between various European nationalities, leads to an interchange of genes or hereditary factors and brings about a diffusion of traits and a mingling of inherited characteristics. Since the differences between the parental group in these, and numerous similar instances, are usually relatively slight, the offspring of the process differ from either parental group to an even slighter degree and the process of assimilation, except when complicated by cultural factors, is an easy one. Intermixture between fully developed and distinctive racial groups is genetically speaking the same process, but it begins with parental groups that are markedly different, both in physical appearance and in genetic make-up, and consequently the offspring, even if intermediate between the parental groups, remains physically distinct. Where they resemble one parent group more than the other, then the initial physical difference is virtually maintained. In the past, most population mixtures, with a few exceptions, were of the first kind. Since 1500 an increasing amount have been of the second variety. It is this second type of race mixture with which I am concerned here.

In the subsequent pages, therefore, race mixture, unless otherwise defined, will refer to those mixtures occurring for the most part since *circa* A.D. 1500 between the more fully developed racial groups. This is not meant to imply that race mixture in a strict sense can be confined to these only. Students of race are well aware of a number of populations whose origins arise from mixtures between major racial groups that took place well before 1500. But, for the most part, these old mixed groups have achieved quite a different position from the more recent hybrid groups. Their racial origins have lost cultural or social meaning or they have become completely integrated within the population of which they form a part. Moreover, the very antiquity of such established hybrid populations renders their origins and their development more inaccessible to analysis. Although I recognize the danger of setting up an arbitrary distinction in a *continuum* of human hybridization, recent or ancient, I have selected this particular segment because it is the kind of mixture which is so singularly characteristic of our own time; because it illustrates most explicitly the nature of the process of hybridization; because the process has created a vast population, new in the world; and because it has created a series of profound problems demanding our best understanding.

NUMBERS AND DISTRIBUTION

One of the keys to understanding the present distribution of hybridization is a knowledge of the population movements of modern times. For after all it is the contact between people previously isolated from each other that has resulted in present-day race mixture. And what makes this so striking a feature of the recent biological history of mankind is the unprecedented movements of population in the past 500 years. Although migration is nothing new in man's history, never before have human groups moved in such numbers, over such vast distances, in so brief a time.

The Mongol streams of the thirteenth century, although comparable in the distance traversed, were confined to a relatively small number of conquerors. Similarly, the historically significant *Völkerwanderung* of the Early Christian era shrinks to the level of a local upheaval when set against the vast eruption of peoples that has occurred throughout the world from 1492 to the present day.

Not only were the post-Columbian readjustments of population on a scale hitherto unknown, but the character of the movement and its origins were much more complex and varied than those of previous migrations. It is impossible, in a limited space, to do justice to the history of this migration, but some idea of its magnitude and ramification emerges when we recall that the period began in the Renaissance and reached its apogee in the modern industrial age. During much of this time, revolutions in political, religious, social and economic affairs in Europe and elsewhere were creating stresses and providing motivations for wholesale migrations. Moreover, the complexity of the phenomenon was greatly increased by the untold number of African natives added to this stream of humanity and by the numerous Chinese, Hindus, Japanese, and other Asiatics also drawn into these currents of population adjustment that followed the increasing integration of the world.

So varied a movement cannot be broken up into mutually exclusive categories or phases, but it is possible to discern in this vast population adjustment two contrasting, although frequently overlapping, forces. The first, and older, was the conquering and exploiting aspect of European expansion. It involved, at most, relatively few men and it began from southwestern Europe. The second factor was largely a colonizing and settling activity which began later and finally affected an enormous number of people from all parts of the world, but especially Europe. The first of these aspects created the great empires and extended the political and economic control of Europe. It engulfed practically all Africa, it managed to exert control over a large part of Asia and for a time, at least, held sovereignty over all the Americas. The colonizing impulse was more restricted, finding its major resolution in the New World and in the sparsely inhabited areas of the Old World that were suitable for settlement.

Although 1492 conventionally recalls the discovery of the

New World, it also represents an era rich in the discovery of hitherto unknown parts of the Old World. Contemporary with the exploration of American shores, European navigators were rounding Africa, sailing into the Indian Ocean, opening up trade with the East Indies and China, and traversing the wide reaches of the Pacific.

If the New World captured the imperial energy of western Europe first, it was not to remain the only theatre of that activity. The same nations spread their hegemony over the newly discovered regions of the Old World as well. Spain gained control of the Philippines; Portugal acquired scattered footholds in China, India, and the islands to the south; the Dutch won the East Indies; while England and France fought for India. But colonization in these already densely settled and flourishing areas never amounted to much. The European expansion here was simply one of exploitation, and has remained political and economic to the present day. Africa, which was partitioned later, fell largely to the same powers—with the addition of Italy, Germany, and Belgium as imperial factors consistent with their increased importance in this later epoch. As in the case of southern and eastern Asia, the European control of Africa was merely for economic and political advantages except in South Africa, which proved to be suitable for European settlements on a large scale. The islands of the Pacific and Australasia also came under the same imperial influences, with Australia, New Zealand, and Hawaii alone becoming significant areas of colonization and settlement.

Only in the northern tier of Asia were the imperial powers of western Europe shut out. The vast expanse from the Urals to the Pacific, inaccessible from the south and blocked by China on the east, remained an easy conquest for Russia, which possessed a natural entry into the region. The sparse and loosely organized settlements of Siberia not only yielded readily to Russian control but also provided little opposition to a vast Russian colonization that has recently been taking place hardly known to the outside world.

Thus, although the European *imperium* has spread over the major portion of the world during the 450 years since Columbus, the actual movement of European populations within this period has been limited to only a fraction of the area at any one time within the control of European powers.

The first colonizers to leave Europe came from Spain, often as adventurers who remained to settle in the New World as land-owning overlords. Having established their primary base in the West Indies, they soon invaded the mainland, until their hegemony stretched from California and the southern United States to the tip of South America. All this vast region, except for Portuguese Brazil, was Spanish. It has been estimated by Rosseeuw St. Hilaire that about three million Spaniards all told emigrated to Latin America during the first 150 years after the discovery. Kuczynski, a leading authority on population, feels however that this is an excessive figure, since not enough shipping was known to have been available during this period to transport such a number.

The settlement of the northern parts of the New World began slowly in the latter part of the sixteenth century, gathering momentum in the following century as the Atlantic coast settlements came into being. The colonists were largely English, with some representation from various other northwest European countries. It is doubtful if the volume of colonists who settled in North America had, by the time of the Revolution, overtaken the Spanish migration in numbers.

During the sixteenth and seventeenth centuries, the tide of European migration set firmly toward the New World. In the eighteenth century the flow continued to move in the same direction but with minor diversions toward South Africa and Australia. In the nineteenth century the tide became a flood. Not only was the number of migrants increasing amazingly, but new sources of supply were opening up all over Europe. For the first three centuries Spain, Portugal, the British Isles, Holland and France were the principal suppliers of colonists. In the nineteenth century Germany, Ireland, and later Italy, Austria-Hungary, Poland, and Russia, not to mention the smaller countries of Europe, poured forth thousands upon thousands of their natives to join the greatest *hegira* in the history of man.

Most of this movement followed the lines already established. From 1820 to 1935 Kuczynski estimates that 55 millions entered the Western Hemisphere from Europe alone. By far the greater portion of this number settled in the United States. Many, of course, returned after a temporary residence, but the net number of permanent settlers in this period was probably well over 35 millions. During the same century about four millions migrated to Australia and over a million to South Africa.

On a smaller scale than this movement to the New World has been the Russian expansion into the vast Asiatic hinterland. Millions of peasants have been moved to the forests, mines, and fertile plains of Asiatic Russia in tempo immeasurably increased since the Russian Revolution.

This spilling over the bounds of Europe did not, however, continue without its profound effect upon movements of people on other continents. It set up movements of native population within the areas of immigration and in some cases resulted in the extermination of the aborigines. But, in addition to these local consequences, the expansion of Europe also drew into itself a series of subsidiary non-European migrations. One of the most significant of these was the resettlement in the New World of approximately 15 million Negroes from Africa. The Spaniards, almost immediately after establishing their settlements, began to ship Negroes to their plantations as slaves, to replace the unsatisfactory Indians. After 1600 the Dutch and the French also engaged in this traffic, and by 1650 the English were also actively involved. The shipments continued as late as 1830 to Cuba and 1860 to Brazil. The total numbers thus transported can only be estimated. Between 1655 and 1787, 676,276 were known to have been legally imported into Jamaica, and, in the year 1771 alone, 47,146 Negroes were carried in British vessels. From these figures it is obvious that the movement was on a large scale. DuBois has calculated the following numbers of Negroes imported into the New World: 900,000 in the sixteenth century, 2,750,000 in the seventeenth century, 7,000,000 in the eighteenth century and 4,000,000 in the nineteenth century. Total, 14,650,000.

This total represents those who actually arrived in America. If the enormous loss of life that took place aboard slavers were added, the total number of Negroes leaving Africa would be much greater.

Historically, the Caribbean area was the centre of the slave traffic, and it is here that the Negroes in the New World have most completely replaced other elements. As one moves north or south from the tropical belt the proportion of Negroes decreases. Similarly the concentration of Negroes relative to the population declines from east to west. This is very evident, not only in the United States, but especially in South America. It is tempting to attribute this form of distribution in part to ecological factors of climate and environment which might have conditioned the manner of Negro dispersal in the New World, but historic factors must also have been effective.

In this connexion it is worthy of comment that the distribution of Europeans in Central and South America also reveals a distinct pattern. The relative frequency of population of such origins is least along the Andean and Cordilleran system, precisely where the native populations were heavily concentrated in highly organized civilizations. It would repay investigation to determine whether or not the well-organized masses of aborigines were able, in these regions, to hold their own more effectively against European encroachment than in other regions occupied by loosely associated hunting tribes. Moreover, the survival of native population in these regions offers another explanation for the relative absence of Negro settlement.

In the Old World, too, migrations of non-European populations have been stimulated by European expansion. Although the Chinese, Arabs, and Hindus had been expanding long before the advent of the white man in their worlds, the rate and extent of their migrations were enormously increased during the nineteenth and twentieth centuries as a result of conditions made possible by European hegemony. The Chinese, for example, increased their flow of emigrants to the East Indies, the Philippines, South-East Asia, Hawaii, the United States and various other parts of the world. The Hindus were moved to Africa, Fiji, and South-East Asia as labour requirements demanded. More recently the Japanese, who previously had been closely confined to their own islands, began a movement of emigration in various directions. These migrations of Asiatic people, although on a smaller scale and with a different history from the European expansion, nevertheless form part of the same picture of a world in population readjustment.

From this complex reshuffling of population has issued a varied array of hybrids, their number and nature depending on a variety of factors. No one knows, however, precisely how many racially mixed people exist today. One reason for this is the sheer difficulty, if not impossibility, of counting them. In many areas where they are most numerous, accurate enumeration is out of the question because neither the enumerators nor the enumerated can always supply sufficiently accurate information on racial status. And in other instances, even if a census were possible, it is regarded as undesirable or impolitic to make one. Since some of the difficulties encountered illustrate certain characteristic phases of the hybridization process, it may be profitable to consider a few of them.

It may at first glance seem paradoxical that anyone of mixed racial origin be unaware of it, but let us see how it actually comes to be so. Negroes, for example, were first introduced into the present limits of the United States as slaves, now well over 300 years ago and even earlier into the Spanish and Portuguese colonies of Central and South America. The evidence is abundant enough, as Gilberto Freyre has shown for Brazil, to demonstrate that almost immediately and everywhere sexual relations between the white masters and their slave women were established and frequently regularized as a system of concubinage. The half-caste children produced by such miscegenation formed a distinctive class designated by such terms as Mulatto, or they might revert to their maternal status or be elevated by their fathers to a higher one. In time, those who had become identified culturally and socially with either parental group would tend to become assimilated to one or the other racial strain. Thus after the passage of centuries, some mixtures dating back many generations might be forgotten, particularly where genealogies were not preserved, or even suppressed where damaging to social pretentions. It is, of course, a fine question how much should be made genetically of a Negro strain that no longer is recognizable in a man who can pass as white or of a white strain in one who appears to be pure Negro. But in the United States, where any recognizable appearance of Negro ancestry serves to label a man as Negro, many people of considerable white admixture are classed as Negro and in the frequent absence of family records of mixture would regard themselves as such. In fact, for census purposes, all individuals of pure or mixed Negro ancestry are listed as Negro. Attempts to determine the number of mixed Negro-whites in the United States, therefore, can only be estimates; and these vary enormously.

It must also be remembered that the so-called phenotype or physical appearance of an individual is not always a safe guide in determining racial mixture, since many individuals of mixed ancestry may actually not give evidence of it in their general physical aspect. And where such individuals have been brought up in ignorance of their genealogical or family history and in close cultural or social relationship with the racial strain they resemble, they may not be aware of their mixed heredity.

How important the cultural factor can be in determining racial status is illustrated by the situation common among Mestizos. In many Latin American countries where Indian and white mixtures are well established, the generally accepted criterion of racial status is largely cultural. Thus

Mestizos who have adopted Spanish customs, speak Spanish and wear European dress are often considered Spanish even though anthropologically they may reveal mixed origins. Conversely, mixed bloods who speak native languages and wear native clothing are classed as Indian. Consequently the official size of the Mestizo population is likely to be smaller than the actual one. Such losses vary, of course, in different countries according to local cultural attitudes, and this emphasizes the necessity of considering the mutual interrelationship of culture and biology when considering race mixture as a whole.

If the exact number of racial hybrids is unknown, there is, however, no doubt that the overwhelming number of them are to be found in the New World. If we consider first the Indian-white crosses, something like 16 millions have been estimated as living in South America. This is twice as many as those listed as pure Indian and is almost 20 per cent of the total population of all South America. These round figures do not, of course, suggest the pattern of their distribution, which is far from uniform. In certain countries, like Argentina, they constitute only 2 per cent of the population. They represent a similarly negligible number in Uruguay and Brazil, although in the latter country it is probable that much of the early crossing with Indian populations has been absorbed into other racial crosses and is no longer identifiable. On the other hand, Paraguay is virtually a Mestizo country with an estimated 97 per cent of the people of this category. Venezuela is also predominantly Mestizo, with 70 to 90 per cent so classified. Such countries as Peru, Bolivia and Ecuador fall between these two extremes.

In Mexico and Central America, the number of Mestizos listed in the census counts is also high. Something in the order of 12 to 13 million Mestizos are to be found here, exceeding even the Indian contingent. In many areas of this region the Mestizos form more than 50 per cent of the population.

Mestizos in the United States and Canada are relatively few. According to the 1930 census there were about 141,101 who were recognized as Indian-white crosses in the United States, while in Canada for the same year they were about 65,000 in number.

Thus for the New World we obtain the astonishing figure of 28 to 29 million Indian-white crosses.[1] This for reasons

---

1. Rosenblatt estimates the number of Mestizos as 30,933,000 and Indians as 15,619,358.

mentioned above is a minimal estimate and even at that is probably twice the number of pure Indians. On the whole, the Mestizos are to be found in greatest numbers where the aboriginal population of Indians was most concentrated in settled agricultural communities and least where they were thinly distributed in nomadic, hunting societies.

The Negro-white crosses, or Mulattoes, represent the other large group of mixtures in the New World. Their number is particularly difficult to estimate because perhaps even more than among Mestizos, the line between mixed and pure Negro is hard to establish. Thus, in the United States, social attitudes and genealogical obscurities tend to place many in the category of Negro, and in Brazil, where another large section is to be found, racial distinctions are officially avoided. Rosenblatt, however, gives the following figures for the Western Hemisphere: 8,113,180 Mulattoes and 23,201,000 Negroes. Other crosses such as Negro-Indian, white-Negro-Indian, and varying kinds of mixtures that include Chinese and East Indians are also to be found, but their number is relatively small.

Summarizing the total situation, Rosenblatt gives the following figures: white, 152,000,000; Negroes, 23,201,696; Indians, 15,619,358; Mestizos, 30,933,335; Mulattoes, 8,113,180. Total, 247,245,099. From this array, it appears that the mixed populations comprise one-sixth of the total population of the Western Hemisphere. That hybridization (as defined for the present discussion) represents in the New World a far greater phenomenon in absolute numbers and in relative proportions than anywhere else, may be seen by contrasting the situation here with other parts of the world where hybridization has been proceeding in recent centuries. The most significant of these areas are South Africa, Malaya, Indonesia, Oceania (particularly Hawaii) and India. In South Africa there are close to one million coloured people who represent the offspring of Negro-white crosses with some additional elements, and, although they form a considerable part of the population, they number less than half the total of the whites and a small fraction of the total Negro. In South-East Asia the principal mixtures are between Chinese, mainly migrants from southern China, and the native populations. Their total number is difficult to assess. An indirect estimate by Lasker suggest hardly more than four million. Everywhere they are a minority and often a small one, although their heavy concentration in urban centres and their control of mercantile and financial activities often give them a prominence out of proportion to their actual number. Fewer in number are the crosses between Europeans and native populations, generally referred to as Eurasians. Their total in 1940 was in the vicinity of 200,000, most of them originating from Dutch-Indonesian mixtures. In India the number of Eurasians, the principal group of mixtures, is small; 140,000 according to the Thorners. Finally, in Oceania, race mixture—including white-Polynesian and Chinese-Polynesian crosses—is very widespread, and in some islands a predominant part of the population; their total numbers, however, hardly exceed 100,000.

Although these figures are admittedly very approximate, their total—something less than six million—falls so far short of the estimates for the mixed populations of the New World that we can have little hesitation in recognizing that the latter is the main centre of race mixture in modern times.

One of the questions that arises from this survey of the extent, numerical and geographic, of race mixture, is why the Western Hemisphere should be the area of its greatest concentration. The answer lies, it seems to me, in the fact brought out earlier that most of the colonization that characterized recent European expansion was directed toward the New World. Compared with the vast flood that flowed to America, the movement to Asia, Africa and other parts of the Old World was a mere trickle. Perhaps the relative propinquity of the eastern coast of America to the Atlantic countries of Europe, perhaps the more favourable climate and possibly the early engagement by America of European energy and activity may all have played a part. But certainly among the principal factors must have been the easy and rapid conquest of the native populations combined with the fact that, over much of the areas first encountered by Europeans, the thinness of the settlements gave an impression of a vast region practically empty and open to European settlement. Asia, on the other hand, was a continent occupied by large and populous kingdoms and empires that could at first easily repulse the feeble bands of Europeans. The first landfalls of the Portuguese, Spaniards, Dutch, French and English in the Far East were precarious and hardly conducive to extensive settlement. Moreover, the teeming populations left little if any room for large-scale migrations from Europe. There were areas attractive for trade, for empire building; but not for colonization. Africa, on the other hand, was unattractive to European settlers on the score of climate. In South Africa, where the

environment was more congenial, the first European settlements were established. Australia and New Zealand, although seats of active colonization, never rivalled America in the numbers they attracted, the former because of the limited area suitable for European settlements, and the latter because it is a small country.

Thus the overwhelming migration from Europe, carrying in its wake a massive population from Africa, both meeting the native American Indians, brought together three distinct racial strains and set the stage for the extensive intermixtures already described.

This survey of the number and distribution or racially-mixed populations leaves little room to question the world-wide nature of the racial hybridization set into being in modern times. On this score alone, its universality would call for serious study. But in addition we have seen that the numbers involved are far greater than is ordinarily conceived. Even these estimates are unquestionably far over on the side of under-estimation. As a minimum, 2.5 per cent of the world's population falls into this category, and, if the information were more adequate, the percentage might prove to be considerably higher.

RACE MIXTURE—A MODERN PROBLEM

If race mixture enjoyed complete acceptance in the modern world, its offsprings would ultimately be absorbed by the society into which they were born and consequently no problem would exist. The various countries where races had mingled would have achieved, or would actively be in the process of doing so, populations thoroughly mixed as to race and varying from each other according to the components of their respective mixtures. In such societies, segregation or stratification on a strictly racial basis would not occur. The fact is, however, that mixed bloods do frequently occupy a distinctive position, form a special class in the social structure and have continued over a long period of time to represent an unabsorbed and sometimes an increasing element in the populations where they exist. To the extent that this situation has developed, it is a measure of the lack of acceptance of the process of miscegenation and an index of the degree of the rejection that mixed bloods suffer.

Now the phenomenon is too manifold and diverse in its origins and expressions to be summarized readily in a simple paradigm. And it would, moreover, be a mistake to suppose that race mixture in our day always leads to a rigid social stratification. There are instances where it has not. It has not in Paraguay, where hybridization between Indians and Spaniards has embraced virtually the entire population. It has not in such countries as Mexico, where some Indian blood is no hindrance to an individual's mobility in the social structure. It often did not, in the earlier phases of miscegenation, even in areas where the mixed bloods later became insulated in the social body. For example, the early Dutch in Indonesia looked upon mixture with the native population with a benevolent eye. Official policy even encouraged it as a way of consolidating the position of the Dutch in the islands and of providing a class of native-born subjects loyal to the interests of the Netherlands and attached to it by bonds of blood relationship. A similar attitude characterized the British in India, where miscegenation was also at first tacitly fostered. Despite these and other exceptions, the fact remains, however, that to a large extent miscegenation has produced caste-like groups in the societies where it has occurred.

It is a legitimate inquiry, under the circumstances, to ask why this is so. Especially is it pertinent when it is recalled that miscegenation in the more remote past did not generally lead to the creation of such permanent social classes based on race such as we frequently see today. In part, of course, that former readiness to accept miscegenation can be explained on the grounds that the participants were closely related biologically in most cases and that such mixed individuals as resulted were physically indistinguishable from the rest of the population. But this is not the whole answer, because the anthropological evidence is abundant that, in the past, even hybridization between racially distinct groups followed the same pattern. It would be an oversimplification, however, to suggest that race mixture in earlier periods was always an easy process of absorption, or to imply that the intermingling of diverse strains was universally free and unaffected by social restrictions. It has been proposed, although not generally admitted by all competent students, that the caste system of India, for example, owes part of its origin to initial race differences, but even here the racial significance, if there were any originally, has been obscured by other developments. In other regions—Ethiopia may be taken as an example—racial differences between the ruling class and the general population might perhaps suggest racial segregation. But in such cases the survival of initial racial differences is attributable to an aristocratic class tradition rather than to social segregation based primarily on race.

The racially mixed group as a distinct and more or less permanent entity within a population is, then, generally speaking, a modern phenomenon and lies at the root of the whole problem of race mixture. Its explanation is not simple and much more investigation is necessary before we can speak with finality about the factors responsible for its development. I shall mention below some of those I consider important, but this list is not by any means meant to be exhaustive, nor are all these items applicable to all situations.

RACE CONSCIOUSNESS

It seems to me impossible to consider race mixture without reference to race consciousness. Awareness of racial distinctions is universal. All people recognize the physical differences they see between themselves and members of other races, and when the differences are great they become increasingly aware of them. The first Europeans to be seen by such isolated people as the Polynesians were recognized at once as a different race of men and became the objects of great curiosity. The strange visitors, to their own great embarrassment, were often amusingly subjected to thorough handling. Similarly, literary records of Western as well as Asiatic origin reveal an ancient knowledge of racial differences. But this universal ability to see obvious physical differences in skin colour, hair form and other well defined racial features did not lead in earlier ages to an elaborate orientation of human relations within a rigid racial frame of reference. Such a development is recent. Modern man is race conscious in a way and to a degree certainly not characteristic previously. It would lead to too great a digression to examine all the reasons for this development.

Thus, where racial consciousness is strongly developed, the hybrid's physical deviation from the parental group labels him as, at least partially, of different racial origin. From the point of view of either parent race, his genetic connexion with the other tends either to distinguish him racially from their own or to associate him racially with the other. Indeed, race attitudes are so axiomatically interwoven with the position of racial hybrids that, in some situations and from certain points of view, no significant distinction is made between the mixed group and the socially inferior parental group. In the United States, for example, although the existence of admixture is fully recognized and is reflected by the usage of such terms as 'mulatto' and the now slightly old-fashioned 'quadroon' and 'octoroon', these mixed Negro-whites are generally classed with Negroes. Similarly the Cape Coloured of South Africa are to some extent linked with Negroes and are subject to the same general, if ameliorated, racial attitudes.

When exclusive racial attitudes are characteristic of both parental groups, the hybrid may be an object of exclusion by both. This is the fate of many Eurasians, both in China and India, where they find themselves not fully accepted by whites or the native populations.

NUMBERS

The number of hybrids within a society undoubtedly plays a part in the role they come to occupy. Where there are few, they tend to become absorbed into either parental group. This process is all the more rapid where one of the parental groups is also negligible in numbers. But even where the number is relatively large, but is thinly distributed, the forces of disintegration continue to operate effectively.

On the other hand, large numbers relative to the total population or occurring in heavy concentration, seem to offer a more favourable environment for the building up of a group identity.

COMPETITION

The effect of economic competition is difficult to assess accurately, although the feeling engendered by it often looms large in the subjective aspects of racial segregation. Like many other influences on the whole situation, its influence is interwoven with other aspects of the problem. Frequently one finds that 'mixed bloods' are excluded from occupations reserved for the dominant race and any pretension to such favoured positions is resented and discouraged. On the other hand, they are sometimes encouraged or permitted to fill jobs not generally open to the 'native' group. Eurasians in Java and India frequently monopolized the minor clerical positions in government offices. So, too, the Cape Coloured are often favoured in types of employment not generally open to Negroes. In *ante-bellum* days in the southern United States, Mulattoes and other mixed Negroes were frequently trained for jobs demanding manual skills, but were never employed in any administrative or directive capacity regardless of their condition or capacity.

Economic restrictions of this sort give a kind of caste aspect to the hybrid group and eventually become a matter of deep resentment on its part. At the same time, the pressures of the half-castes to rise in the economic scale as their education improves seem to constitute a threat to the dominant group, who react against what seems to them to be aggression that must be confined.

Competition can take even more direct form as, for example, when the mixed-bloods compete directly with the lower economic levels of the dominant group. Such conflicts arising in a racially conditioned class system serve to aggravate the fear and antagonism based on race. Thus it has frequently been observed that the secure upper classes in the Southern States were able to entertain a more tolerant and benign feeling toward Negroes and Mulattoes than the 'poor whites' were able to do in more immediate competition with them.

CULTURE

In some respects cultural differences must be taken into account. In the kinds of race mixture that we are considering here, the parental groups are sharply differentiated in their ways of life, their values and even in the apparently unimportant *minutiae* of daily living. Although these have obviously not prevented the production of mixed offspring, no matter how diverse they may be they are far from negligible as determinants of attitude. They affect the way the parental groups think about each other and the way the eventually distinctive mixed group is looked upon by both.

Usually where a highly civilized group is mixing with a race on a simpler cultural level, the cultural resistance is apt to be on the side of the more complex culture. This is true not only of whites intermingling with simpler native people, but also applies with equal significance to other civilized

362

people such as the Chinese. Thus Chinese men mixed freely with Hawaiian women before women of their own country were available. As Chinese brides became increasingly accessible, traditional Chinese values and feelings of cultural superiority tended to discourage further out-marriage. The difference between the Chinese way of life and that of the local population is often felt very strongly by many Chinese families in Hawaii and any tendency to marry outside the group, even with part-Chinese, is strongly resisted by them.

When two groups of people with backgrounds of high cultural achievement mingle, the mutual intolerance for each other's values can often render the mixed blood unacceptable to either camp, as has already been pointed out for Eurasians.

IMPERIALISM

The importance of the development of imperialism in framing the characteristic attitudes toward race mixture cannot be neglected. This system is based upon the conquest of native people, either peacefully or by force of arms, and it is maintained by a ruling and governing class of aliens—in our day mostly Europeans. Whatever the economic or political necessity for it may be, the fact remains that it universally results in an inevitable class distinction between the rulers (Europeans) and governed (natives). Since the ruling class is generally a relatively small one compared to the mass of the native population, it can sustain its prerogatives of power and privilege only by inducing the native population to recognize them. This, of course, can be achieved by military coercion or by various other less costly devices. Sometimes, once submission is achieved, the superior or more complex civilization of such a ruling class provides it with enough prestige for this purpose; or the benefits it confers on the conquered may be sufficient to win support. Sometimes the Europeans, by preempting the position of a previous ruling class, may fit readily into an existing traditional pattern. Sometimes it is the ascendancy of a strong, efficient government that enables the conquerors to enjoy their hegemony, or conversely the absence of a determined and organized resistance.

But in virtually all colonial situations where Europeans have imposed themselves as a conquering class on a native people, this very act creates a chasm between the two. As members of a different culture, the rulers as a class rarely, if ever, understand the natives. They look down on them from a sense of their own superiority, developed in part from a conviction that their own civilization reflects an innately greater ability and in part from the very position of authority they hold. Even when they recognize a picturesque or quaint aspect in native life, it remains something foreign, perhaps even illogical, and never quite right. As rulers, they also are concerned with the security of their position, which must be protected from encroachment. Exclusiveness becomes a feeling of necessity. And symbols of membership in the ruling class take on enhanced significance.

Under these circumstances, any breaking down of the solid front of the ruling class is resisted firmly. The native must be kept in his place. And by extension this applies to the half-caste, too. For if the mixed-bloods were fully accepted, all the laboriously created prestige would be threatened and probably destroyed. Thus purity of blood is highly prized in most colonial situations, although it must be admitted that exceptions occur. But so strong is this feeling that even when there is good reason for believing that some remote ancestor may have had native origins, it is likely to be denied or suppressed.

BIOLOGICAL CONSIDERATIONS

While many people are deeply influenced in their racial attitudes by cultural considerations, they are not likely to assign their feelings directly to them. Thus when the European encounters a bare-footed native wearing bizarre clothing, or watches one eating in an apparently unmannerly fashion, or observes some, to him, superstitious and meaningless ritual, he sees these departures from his own standards of behaviour not simply as cultural differences, but as indications of inferiority. It is a subtle thing which the traveller rarely escapes. Even where the conventions and trappings of a foreign culture are impressive in their complexity, this strangeness often lends them an air of unreality, of *opéra bouffe,* that in the end renders them somewhat childlike if not ridiculous. Although we are accustomed to use the European as the examplar of such reactions, they are far from being exclusively his. Chinese and other literature of travel is full of similar examples in which cultural differences are equated with inferiority. Even in the instances, and they are not few, where a native people on a simple level of culture first come into contact with Westerners, they have been known to attribute superiority and even a god-like quality to them because of their superior equipment. Thus the big ships, the cannon and the metal tools of Captain Cook so deeply impressed the Tahitians that they transferred to him and his fellow-Englishmen the superiority they recognized in his material possessions.

But whatever the source of these feelings concerning a racial hierarchy, they are widespread and few people escape their effects altogether. When hardened into a confirmed article of belief, they become a significant factor in shaping attitudes towards race mixture, since, if races can be arranged in a linear order from inferior to superior, then miscegenation of a superior race with an inferior one will lead to the production at best of something less good than the superior race. The varied guises that this conviction assumes are legion, but basically it seems to rest on two general ideas, both fundamentally genetic. One is that biologically the races of man in some manner or other fall into a kind of *échelle des êtres* somewhat like Cuvier's evolutionary concept. According to this, certain races are more primitive than others, closer to the primate ancestors from whom mankind evolved, and others more advanced, more 'evolved' and consequently in the forefront of human evolution. Such differences are assumed, of course, to be innate, and not the passing effects of a particular situation or environment.

The other conviction is that the races of man differ in their psychological attributes, including intellect and personality. In these, too, the races are considered to be susceptible of an hierarchical arrangement. To some extent such an ordering may reflect a belief in the evolutionary sequence implied in the *échelle des êtres* concept, with the most 'evolved' race necessarily endowed with the greatest abilities.

The arrangement of mankind into successive and ascending categories, biologically and psychologically, obviously offers a reason, if not a justification, for a variety of social and economic inequities that are taken to reflect their inevitability. But a closer examination of the evolutionary process in general and of what is actually known about human evolution in particular provides us with little or no support for this conception. For it would imply that human evolution, or rather racial differentiation in man, was a kind of evolutionary relay race with one group of mankind starting off from where the previous one had stopped and ceased to evolve or differentiate farther. To some extent, perhaps, this view has been encouraged by the relatively 'primitive' characteristics of such races as the Australian aborigines who, in some of their cranial structures, are closer to the simians than other races. But even the Australian aborigines, in other features, are as remote from our primate ancestors as any other group.

The evidence we do have suggests, on the contrary, that races have been differentiating more or less independently and at the same time. This differentiation has apparently proceeded by the accumulation of gene differences probably most, if not all, adaptive to the environment where a particular race developed. Anatomically, this differentiation has advanced sufficiently in a number of instances so that phenotypic distinctions have become well defined with little or no overlap in the diagnostic traits. Intergrades and transitions between the extreme degrees of physical differentiation also occur, but do not invalidate the tendencies here described. Thus we cannot assert that the existing races represent a sequential series of evolutionary stages with each advancing from the level of its predecessor to the next step. And even if it were possible to claim that one race branched off from another, we still cannot assert that the parent race ceased to evolve once the branching occurred. Actually, the genetic mechanisms known to us suggest quite the opposite, as I have already indicated.

If races were, indeed, to be graded according to their supposed possession of anthropoid-like features, it would no doubt surprise some members of reputedly superior races to discover how many of their characteristics might have to be given a low rating on such a morphological scale. For example, the frizzy hair, the thicks lips and the hairlessness of the Negro are more 'evolved' from a simian level than the corresponding features of Europeans. This kind of comparison in the long run proves of little significance.

Similarly, the comparison of races for biological fitness have thus far not revealed any striking or valid differences that might suggest ideas of superiority of one over the other. Some evidence does exist that environmental adaptations develop in races, making them perhaps better suited for the conditions under which they live than invading and differently adapted groups. For example, recent research on the dispersion of body heat indicates that Negroes have a more efficient physiological mechanism for this purpose than whites have. This in itself of course would not necessarily mean a biological superiority of the Negro except under the conditions where his special adaptation might provide him with an advantage. This same kind of specialization gives the Eskimo a distinct superiority in his own environment over other races, but the advantage disappears and may become a detriment when the Eskimo moves into another area. It is sometimes claimed that those races that live in less extreme types of environments, and are consequently less committed to a high degree of specialized adaptation, can fit into a wider range of environmental niches. But even if this were true, such races would be difficult to place in a biological scale of value, since such judgements end up by being relative and tentative at best.

In the last analysis, however, it is the psychological differences that are considered the most significant by the adherents to a belief in racial hierarchy. For even if a protagonist of this conception be forced to admit the shifting sands of the biological argument, he retreats to the apparently obvious strength of the psychological evidence. And to many people, unfamiliar with the specialized literature on the subject, the natural and innate superiority of their own race over all others seems too self-evident to require scientific demonstration before acceptance. Thus there are two kinds of evidence adduced on this question: the common one employed by the so-called 'man in the street' and the one based on quantitative data collected to support or test its validity.

Let us consider the common argument first. It often runs something like this. Europeans (any other highly civilized group with appropriate modifications would serve as well) have motor-cars, radios, ocean-going liners, large cities with major architectural monuments, efficient public services, centralized and elaborate governments, and a whole host of complicated things and institutions. Negroes or Melanesians or any other native group living in a simple society have none of these things or institutions, or only obviously inferior versions of them. Since it takes ability and skill to make these superior things or to run these complicated institutions, the Europeans are obviously superior. Similarly the music, the art, the literature and science of Europe provide a measure of the greater ability of Europeans.

Moreover, the Westerner when he visits or settles among these simpler people, finds them occupying inferior social and economic positions to his own, and, for the most part, behaving in a fashion or subject to customs which he does not understand and therefore regards as unreasonable or illogical.

These, of course, are cultural arguments, although they are taken to reflect psychological differences. It would, of course, be unwarranted by any critical evidence now available to deny dogmatically any psychological factor in these cultural differences, but it is abundantly clear from the great mass of anthropological investigations that such psychological deductions drawn from purely cultural comparisons can be grossly misleading or even completely erroneous. There are too many temporal and non-genetic elements that play a part in the development of any culture to overlook in evaluating its status. Indeed, it is a rather tired *cliché* to recall the former cultural inferiority of many people who now pride themselves on their superiority.

Of a quite different character is the evidence derived from psychological testing or morphological comparisons of the brain. The latter type of investigation, in part quantitative and in part qualitative, attempted to demonstrate physical differences between races in the mass of brain tissue and in its organization. Although certain statistical differences have been discovered, not all of them conform to preconceived notions of racial ranking. But the major difficulty with this line of thinking is the lack of proof that ability is directly correlated with size of brain or with any of the morphological features thus far studied.

Psychological testing, on the other hand, has seemed to offer a far more reliable method of appraising ability, and a very considerable corpus of quantitative data bearing on this has been accumulated. If these results are taken on their face value, certain racial differences emerge, although not always consistently. Experts, however, are now fairly generally agreed that such tests are rather better indexes of achievement, or may we say phenotypic intelligence, than they are of the innate and genetic abilities. The effect of educational, social, economic and even emotional factors can be considerable, and test scores have been shown to fluctuate with changes in them. For these and other reasons, many psychologists are extremely averse to drawing conclusions on racial differences in ability from the test data, although in all fairness it should be noted that some of them do consider these sufficient evidence of such distinctions.

But in no case am I aware that professional psychologists have made any claim that the psychological differences are of the same order as diagnostic morphological differences in race. In this respect it is clear that the differences in psychological scores are a matter of statistical mean differences. In other words, according to the test data, races where they differ do so in their averages which reflect variation in the ranges of the scores and the frequencies in the various categories within the ranges. No two races are discontinuous or non-overlapping. Actually, in most instances, the overlap is very considerable and sometimes even the ranges are very close. All that can be claimed is that one race may have a larger percentage of higher scores than another. Moreover, it is worth restating that the higher scores of the supposedly lower race are above the lower scores of the reputedly superior one. In all cases, the observed difference between races is far less than the variation within any one. Thus it would be impossible to assign anyone to a particular race on the basis of his test score, as one might do for many people on the basis of their morphological characters. In view, therefore, of the kind of difference the tests can show and the uncertainty that exists in their proper interpretation, any far-reaching conclusion as to racial differences based on them would at present be unjustified.

I have gone into these problems at some length because current convictions of the kind I have been analysing have most profoundly influenced attitudes towards the mixture of races. But even beyond the belief that where inequality between races exists mixture can lead only to a product inferior to the superior race, there is the dogma that mixture in itself is a process that allows incompatible traits to be combined in the hybrid, thus making the process of miscegenation a dysgenic or unfavourable one. This view may even conceivably be held while admitting each race to be equally adapted to its own milieu and of equal psychological value. The evidence for this hypothesis, however, is not very convincing. I shall deal with some of it in a later section.

DOWN TO CASES

PITCAIRN

Previously I had mentioned the manifold variety of the origins and the diverse expressions of race mixture. I can, I think, best illustrate this by a series of case histories which may also help to clarify some of the issues that surround this subject.

These examples are drawn from various parts of the earth, represent a number of different crosses and have developed under widely contrasting circumstances.

Perhaps the best known of them all is the small group of Polynesian-English mixed bloods that live on Pitcairn Island in the South Pacific. Here, on a tiny volcanic island only about two miles long and about half as wide, were resolved the train of events that the famous mutiny of the *Bounty* set in action. This episode, famous in British naval annals, occurred in the year 1789 shortly after H.M.S. *Bounty* had departed from Tahiti where she had been dispatched under the command of Lieutenant William Bligh to collect breadfruit plants. Reports brought back to Europe by Cook and Bougainville described the breadfruit as a remarkable tree capable of supplying a staple article of food with a minimum of effort. British planters in the West Indies, eager to obtain so easy a source of foodstuff for their slaves, had petitioned for the expedition with which Bligh had been entrusted. Now after six successful months in Tahiti, with the ship's hold full of potted trees, the return trip was interrupted by the mutiny of 25 of the men out of the crew of 44. The mutineers were led by Fletcher Christian, one of Bligh's officers, and a native of the Isle of Man where his family had long been prominent.

The mutineers, seizing the ship, put Bligh and those faithful to him adrift in a small open boat and reset the *Bounty's* course for Tubuai, an island 300 miles south of Tahiti. Here, an abortive attempt was made to establish a settlement, which failed because of the hostility aroused in the natives by the behaviour of the mutineers. Returning after this to Tahiti, the mutineers split into two groups: one, consisting of 16 men, preferred to remain in Tahiti, where a number of them had already established liaisons with native women and had been welcomed into the island homes; the other contained nine men headed by Christian. These men, apparently anticipating a possible punitive expedition once the news of the mutiny reached England, were eager to leave Tahiti, where they could not hope to escape capture, and to find a more remote and perhaps inaccessible island where they might remain undetected. Accordingly they, together with 12 Tahitian women and six Tahitian men, set sail from Tahiti in September 1789, and until 1808 were virtually lost to the world. In the latter year their retreat on Pitcairn, some 2,500 miles south-east of Tahiti, was discovered by Captain Mayhew Folger. During this interval much had happened on the island. All the Tahitian men and all but one of the Englishmen had died—most of them violently, and after only a short sojourn in their new home. In addition, Folger found eight or nine surviving Tahitian women and 25 children, offspring of six of the Englishmen and their native wives. None of the Tahitian men had left issue, perhaps because they were murdered too soon after the settlement on the island.

From this handful of children—half-Polynesian, half-English—the little colony increased by leaps and bounds, until 50 years later there were almost 200 inhabitants on the island. By this time, fear of overpopulation and the recurrence of water shortages induced them to request of the British Government the use of Norfolk Island, some 4,000 miles to the west, as a new home. This considerably larger island had recently been abandoned as a penal colony and was temporarily unoccupied. In 1856 the entire colony moved there and set up a new establishment, but subsequently several families returned to their beloved Pitcairn. In 1864 there were 45 descendants of the mutineers living on Pitcairn, the remainder having gone on to Norfolk. At present there are on both islands about 1,000 descendants of the original colony, not counting those who have married out of the community or settled in New Zealand, Australia and elsewhere.

As an example of race mixture the Pitcairn Islanders are far from typical. But it is the very singularity of the colony that is full of meaning in interpreting race mixture as we commonly see it. Simply as a cross between Polynesians and English they can be matched in many parts of Polynesia where the same kind of mingling has occurred, often with notable results, as in New Zealand. But unlike all other mixtures of this kind in Oceania, and indeed unlike virtually all race mixture wherever it occurs,[1] the Pitcairn Islanders have lived and developed their common life completely separated from the societies from which they were originally derived. Now it is an almost universal consequence of race mixture that the mixed bloods live in contact with the parental groups and in one or the other of the parental societies. This can, as we have seen, have profound consequences on the status and position of the mixed group. And since social status works both ways, affecting those within it by their own attitude as members of a special class and by the attitude of

---

1. The only parallel to Pitcairn known to me is Tristan da Cunha where a community of mixed Negro-Europeans have lived in isolation for well over 100 years.

others toward them, the association of a mixed group with one of its parental societies can be a decisive influence on its development. Where mixed bloods form a class suffering legal disability, economic injustice or social prejudice, they are victims of the attitudes, well or ill-founded, of the dominant element in their society. The extent to which these circumstances affect the behaviour and psychological traits of the members of such a class is difficult to appraise. And it is equally difficult to assess the degree to which these socially conditioned characteristics in turn reinforce the attitudes that encourage them. Many competent students are convinced that they are significant.

It is because of all this that the Pitcairn Islanders' complete separation from and independence of all other societies assume added importance, for here the entire community was of the same mixed origin, was free from any social structuring imposed upon it by a larger society and escaped the influences that prejudice subtly works upon its object. This, then, is a community where social prejudice, at least, is not a factor to be considered and where we can study the consequences of race mixture divorced from the concomitant effects that being a part of a larger group might impose.

On the other hand, in any consideration of the colony, its very isolation must be kept in mind, as it must be in appraising any small community remote from the world and cut off from the intellectual and material stimuli of a larger society. For the first 18 years of its existence, the Pitcairn colony remained unvisited by any ship. The children growing up in the first generation of the community had never seen anyone not a member of their little family, for the early colony lived as one extended family with John Adams, the surviving mutineer, as their *pater familias*. Even after 1808, when their existence became known, callers were rare and their visits very brief. Not until the 1820's did ships begin to call at Pitcairn to obtain water and fresh foods. As American whaling became increasingly active in the Pacific, these visits increased in number, reaching their highest frequency in the 1840's. With the decline of whaling, Pitcairn once more reverted to its former loneliness. These contacts, although important in bringing to the islanders the goods of the outside world for which they had acquired a taste, were brief and had little or no influence on the social structure of the colony.

It would, of course, be futile to attempt to rate Pitcairn against other communities, mixed or otherwise. There are too many variables impossible to standardize that would have to be taken into account. But it is evident to anyone visiting the island that here is a well-organized settlement, conducting its own affairs successfully under a system devised by the islanders themselves. Like people anywhere, of course, they vary, but the visitor is invariably impressed by the pleasant, friendly manners of the islanders, their charm, their hospitality and self-confidence. There is no trace here of a people conscious of inferiority. They are all literate and have from the earliest days maintained a school system by their own efforts. Equally notable is the vigour of their Church. Previously adherents of the Church of England, they were converted to Seventh Day Adventism at the end of the last century. The way in which they made this shift in adherence is typical of their wisdom in managing their own affairs. In making the change, the community was faced with a situation that might have been serious in its consequences. The population was divided on the issue of conversion, and, recognizing the danger of a tiny community being split between two rival Churches, decided to put the matter to a vote, with the minority pledged to go along with the expressed wish of the majority. Thus the whole community unanimously adopted Seventh Day Adventism and preserved the religious unity of the colony.

Remarkable in so small a community, especially one cut off from the developments of the outside world, are some of the social institutions which were established on Pitcairn and maintained there ever since. A democratic rule developed early, with all men and women enjoying equal political rights, long before political rights were granted to women in the Western world and indeed before they were even very seriously discussed there. Education was, from the first, recognized as a necessity and, as the local institutions took form, all children were required to attend school until their sixteenth year. The various families on the island were taxed for the maintenance of the school. Teachers were selected from the students and supported by the revenue levied on the people. Here, too, the Pitcairn islanders were in advance of educational developments in greater centres of civilization.

The culture that emerged on Pitcairn also reflected the mixed origin of the colony and in a rather striking way illustrates the decisive roles that sex and environment may play in creating a new society. The cultural resources available to the new colony were, of course, English and Tahitian. But it is obvious on reflection that not all the content of either of these cultures could or would be drawn upon, since one culture, the English, was accessible only through men who were sailors by occupation, and the other, the Tahitian, was represented by women, who were familiar with the crafts and skills traditionally exercised in Tahiti by their sex. In addition to this, the colony on Pitcairn faced an unfamiliar environment and, in transplanting their traditional ways, both the Tahitian women and the English sailors found themselves without the usual technical equipment needed to practise whatever skills and arts they knew. Even such a basic and necessary object as a nail was not available, not to mention a variety of common tools that could not be fashioned on Pitcairn. Thus we find tapa cloth universally used by the colony in its early days. The making of this bark cloth is traditionally a woman's job in Tahiti and could be carried to Pitcairn intact. Similarly, cooking being a woman's concern, the Tahitian technique of an underground oven was standard on Pitcairn. House building, on the contrary, was the result of a complex of influences. The Tahitian style of house would have been unsuitable in the colder climate of Pitcairn, but in any event it probably could not have been built by the women, who in Tahiti leave the framing of a house to the men. The Englishmen, probably only as adept in carpentry as sailors of those days might be expected to be, were handicapped by the lack of essential building materials and of tools. We find them, as a consequence, building houses ingeniously put together, the frame mortised, the walls constructed of roughly hewn planks fitted into slotted uprights, the interiors provided with bunks as in a ship's cabin. The roof, however, was thatched in the Tahitian manner, since roof thatching is prepared in Tahiti by the women, and this was a contribution the Tahitian women on Pitcairn could make to this novel house.

The following is a brief tabular history of the origin of some of the elements in the culture of Pitcairn before it was affected by the introduction of foreign goods. (See page 356.)

One of the common allegations made about race mixture is that it produces inferior human beings. This belief is stated in various ways that all come to the same thing: mixed bloods combine the worst features of both parental groups, they are inferior to both stocks, or, at best, they are intermediate and therefore a debasement of the superior group. This kind of statement is put forth with respect to the psychological (intellectual), moral and biological characteristics of the hybrids.

For the most part, the evidence for this belief is strained through a subjective sieve and rarely takes account of the effect upon the hybrid of his social psychological and economic position in the society whose more favoured strains are compared with him. But more fundamental is the lack of reliable measures for many of the qualities in which the mixed blood is supposed to be deficient.

Origin of elements of culture on Pitcairn

	Tahitian	English	Original
The household arts:			
Underground oven	+		
Food preparation	+		
Tapa-making	+		
Use of calabash	+		
Dress style	+		
Hats	+		
Houses:			
Building materials		+	
Structure		+	+
Roof thatch	+		
Arrangement			+
Household equipment:			
Furniture		+	
'Linens'	+		
Lighting	+		
Fishing:			
Gear		+	
Methods	+	+	
Boats	+		+
Agriculture:			
Tools		+	
Methods	+	+	
Family life			+
Social life:			
Social organization			+
Separation of sexes at meals	+		
Position of women			+
Dance	+		
Music	+	+	
Surf-riding	+		
Kite-flying	+	+	
Private ownership of land		+	
Common fund			+
Education		+	
Religion		+	+

As far as the Pitcairn Islanders are concerned, I can offer no objective data on their psychological or moral qualities. None, to my knowledge, is available. Certainly there have been many published impressions of these traits of the islanders and most of them are enthusiastic. How far the romantic aura that surrounds these people has seduced their visitors is beyond calculation. In the mid-nineteenth century the typical reaction was delight in finding so moral, upright and virtuous a colony sprung from mutineers, from violence and from murder. Nowadays, being less concerned with religious matters and having on the whole rather different values, the visitor is less impressed by these qualities and is likely to prize other aspects of their character. For my part, I can only report that, allowing for their isolation and for a consequent lack of sophistication, I found the Pitcairn Islanders an intelligent and attractive people. And I was struck by the number of men and women of impressive character possessed of the qualities that make for leadership.

Although biologically rather more of what might be called objective information is accessible, still it can only be used for comparative purposes with caution. Even such standard criteria as physical vigour, longevity or health cannot be properly used for such purposes without reference to diet, climate and various other environmental conditions. Both on Norfolk and Pitcairn Islands the physical condition of the islanders was excellent. In spite of the inbreeding, which has especially characterized Pitcairn, I found no physical deformities or obvious signs of degeneration. On Pitcairn, with a population of 200 (1936), there were no individuals incapable of taking care of themselves, nor any cases of serious mental deficiency. This is an excellent record compared with the frequency of such cases in Europe and the United States, especially in remote, inbred villages. In view of the fact that neither on Pitcairn nor Norfolk is there any resident medical service or even trained nursing aid, the longevity of the population is impressive. In 1924, out of a population of about 600 on Norfolk, there were 24 who were over 65 years of age, with the oldest reaching 95 years. On Pitcairn there were 12 between the ages of 65 and 86 in a population of 200.

There have been some claims that hybrids are smaller and weaker than their parents. Davenport and Steggerda on the basis of their study of race mixture in Jamaica believe their data demonstrated this conclusion. The Pitcairn and Norfolk evidence is quite the contrary. Indeed, there is evidence here of hybrid vigour comparable to the vigour that can be demonstrated experimentally in a large number of animal and plant crosses. For example, if we take size as a measure of heightened physiological vigour, as is done for maize or crossbred domestic animals, we find that the average stature of the parental groups is 171.4 cm. for Tahitian males and 170.6 cm. for the mutineers (based on British Admiralty records but possibly a little low since some of the sailors were not fully mature men). The modern Englishman averages around 172 cm. The F_1, or first generation descendants, averaged 177.8 cm. (minimum 5 ft. 9½ in., maximum 6 ft. ¼ in.). This represents an average increase of over two inches, with the shortest male exceeding the average of his parental groups by a considerable margin. Although this striking increase has not been fully maintained in the present generation, it is still almost an inch above the parental average.

As another index of this vigour, the reproductive rate of the islanders is equally notable. I have already referred to the prodigiously rapid growth of the colony which has produced in 160-odd years well over 1,000 descendants. This may be appreciated from the birth rate by generations. The first generation averaged 7.44 children per mating, the second 9.10, the third 5.39. Since then there has been a further decline. The rate in the second generation is one of the highest on record for any community and reflects an unusual reproductive vigour.

As far as the evidence goes, then, the Pitcairn experiment lends no support for the thesis that race mixture merely leads to degeneration or at best produces a breed inferior to the superior parental race. In fact, we see in this colony some support for heightened vigour, for an extended variation and for a successful issue of the mingling of two diverse strains.

RACE CROSSING IN JAMAICA

Jamaica is one of the Greater Antilles in the West Indies. It is a rugged, even mountainous island, with an area of 11,000 sq. km. Discovered by Columbus in 1494, it became a part of the Spanish Empire and a seat of Spanish settlement. It remained in Spanish hands until 1655 when the British seized possession and expelled the Spaniards. The first Spanish settlers, mostly men, found an aboriginal population, the Arawak Indians, with whom they mixed freely. But the

Indians as a people did not long survive this contact. Enslavement and newly introduced diseases rapidly reduced their number until they finally became extinct. How much of these people has survived in their successors is not known. Negroes were introduced soon after white occupation began, since they were considered more adaptable to slavery. The Negro population grew rapidly and by the middle of the seventeenth century exceeded the number of whites on the island. The importation of fresh slaves, mostly from West Africa, continued up to 1847. Some Indian coolies were introduced in 1845 and 1868. In the 1920's the population was distributed as follows: Negroes, 660,420 (76.9 per cent); coloured, 157,223 (18.3); East Indian, 18,610 (2.2); whites, 14,476 (1.2); Chinese, 3,696 (0.4); not stated, 3,393 (0.4).

In 1929, Davenport and Steggerda published a study of race mixture in Jamaica, concerned mainly with the genetics of a cross between whites and Negroes and with an appraisal of the consequences of such hybridization. Since miscegenation between these two racial groups is numerically one of the major areas of race mixture and also happens to be a focus for much of the discussion on race mixture generally, this publication has a special interest. It also is one of the very few available investigations purporting to deal with the biology of Negro-white crosses.

Davenport set up his survey as an anthropometric and psychological examination of three groups of subjects: Negroes, descendants of the West African slaves introduced into Jamaica during the course of over three centuries, beginning shortly after the settlement of the island by the Spaniards; whites now resident on the island; and browns, the offspring of a mingling of these two racial stocks. Most of the browns apparently represent a long established class of half-castes and are not the produce of recent miscegenation. Davenport's general conclusions may be reduced to two areas of interest. One involves the existence of racial differences between the two parental stocks, particularly as they relate to physical and psychological characters. The other is more concerned with the quality of the hybrids (browns) compared with Negroes and whites. His opinion of the browns in this context is not high. He considers them inferior to both parental groups both biologically and intellectually. Moreover this inferiority is, in his interpretation, still further deepened by what he regards as evidence of the disharmony that occurs when incompatible traits from different races are combined in hybrid individuals.

Within its own field of research, *Race Crossing in Jamaica* is one of the most outspoken attacks on miscegenation, particularly between Negroes and whites. And, since it has been widely quoted, it demands careful examination.

A comparison of the physical traits of the browns reveals them much closer to the averages of the Negroes than to the whites. Indeed, in some instances the browns fall statistically below the means of both parental groups as, for example, in stature and weight. This prepotency of the Negro characteristics in the browns is considered as possible evidence of the genetic dominance of Negro traits over those of whites in such a cross, but Davenport correctly points out that it is more likely the consequence of repeated backcrossing with Negroes over a long period of time—that is, a much greater proportion of genes derived from its Negro than its white ancestry.

Aside from the inferiority of the browns in stature and weight, Davenport stresses their physical disharmony. The evidence of this seems to be primarily the relativity short arms of some of the browns, particularly in three women. Davenport can only be said to be making a mountain of a molehill here, since the relative proportions he finds so unusual are equalled in a number of whites and indeed some of the latter show an even more marked tendency in the same direction. In any event, it is difficult to see how any cogent theory of disharmony can be based on such flimsy evidence. The ridiculousness of the effort is made apparent when Davenport suggests that, because of their relatively short arms, the browns so endowed would have difficulty in picking things off the ground. By the same token the whites, who characteristically have shorter arms than Negroes, would be afflicted by the same disharmony and thus inferior to the Negroes.

A much more serious fault lies in the comparability of the data derived from the three groups under examination. Unless we can feel confident that each sample adequately represents its group and that they are drawn from approximately the same stations in life, the results of the comparison are, of course, suspect to the extent that they depart from such minimal standards. The description of the data given by the authors provides enough room for serious doubt on that score. For example, the age composition of the three groups is far from equivalent, but—what is more disturbing—the browns contain a relatively high proportion of males who are aged between 16 and 20. Males of 16, or slightly over, are still far from having reached their mature physical development. Any comparison, therefore, with groups that are considerably older would be biased by this fact. The inferiority, therefore, of the browns in stature, weight and several other traits can easily be attributed to age alone. Parenthetically, however. I can see little reason for assigning inferiority or superiority to such differences in bodily dimensions or weight. Such thinking would lead us into a hierarchy of physical virtue based on stature or avoirdupois, whose obvious *reductio ad absurdum* needs no underlining. Another indication of non-comparability lies in the differences of socio-economic status between the three groups.

But perhaps as significant as any factor of non-comparability is the genetic relationship of the three groups to each other. This is a fundamental necessity for such an investigation that is never even discussed by the authors. There is, of course, no reason to suspect that the Negro population of the island is not the one to which the browns owe part of their ancestry. But there is much reason to doubt that the white group in the comparisons fully represents the population of whites that also contributed to the cross. This study sample is made up of individuals from Kingston whose families have long been settled in Jamaica. Another contingent consists of 20 farmers of German origin whose families have been settled in the interior of the island since the 1830's. The third and last comprises 19 Cayman Islanders who are of British stock but not residents of Jamaica and who are, in certain respects, quite distinct from the others in the sample. Now it is known that the Spaniards occupied Jamaica for about 150 years before the British took the island. The records make it clear that the Spanish population, at least in the beginning, was predominantly male and that they mixed extensively with the aboriginal Indians at first and, after their extinction as a group, with Negroes. How much the present day browns owe to these Spanish settlers, no one knows. None, at any rate, are included in Davenport's white sample. On the other hand, he does include a group of Germans who are said to have remained isolated throughout their residence in Jamaica. It is a very small settlement and could have contributed but very little to the brown mixture. Finally, the Cayman Islanders, although British and presumably similar in origin to the British who were settled on Jamaica, were actually not themselves involved in producing the browns. The differences between these various national groups of whites in their physical characteristics are considerable and consequently a failure to compare the browns with the kind of whites from whom they are actually descended might lead to erroneous conclusions.

Thus far I have analysed the results of the comparisons of the physical traits. The psychological examinations, however, form an equally important part of the study. Twenty-six different tests were employed. Six of them formed a group designed by Seashore to test musical ability and another eight comprised the Army Alpha Test used in testing the United States Army during World War I. Davenport's general conclusions from these tests is that there are racial differences in psychological characters, that the Negroes surpass the whites in musical ability but are inferior in planning and judgement. The browns he considers to be inferior in their performance to both parental groups. In part, this low rating of the browns is the result of a crude comparison of the actual scores of the three groups and does not take into account the validity of the differences in score. When this is done, however, much of the inferiority of the browns disappears and they emerge roughly similar to the Negroes. This is more consonant with other investigations.

The racial difference, however, between Negroes and whites remains. It is a matter of controversy whether or not psychological differences between various races exist. It is, however, a subject fraught with difficulty because the methods of measuring innate intelligence or other psychological traits, apart from any influence by environment and conditioning, is far from solved. Professional psychologists have become increasingly aware that the test technique does not eliminate altogether the effects of such factors as education, language, culture, motivation and *rapport* with the tester, and that the validity of the sample must always be critically scrutinized. Premature conclusions, therefore, are not warranted, not only because the criteria of science demand careful and responsible investigation, but also because this subject happens to carry overtones of social and political implication that are of the utmost seriousness. Davenport, unfortunately, as I have already indicated, did not ensure the reliability of sampling demanded for such deductions. Nor did he consider the effect of any of the non-genetic variables that might have affected the scores. Furthermore, some of the tests he used are now regarded as peculiarly susceptible to such variables.

Although it would be rash indeed to deny altogether the possibility that psychological differences between races exist, it is surely clear from the nature of the information we have that such differences would be of quite another order from those associated with physical race. In the latter sense we can distinguish well-defined races by their phenotypes or physical appearance. As I pointed out earlier, no one has any difficulty in recognizing the physical distinction between a north-west European and a west coast African. There is no overlap in the diagnostic differences between them. No west coast African of unmixed origin or of normal development has a skin colour anywhere approaching the pigmentation of the European. Conversely no north-west European except possibly for a few mutant individuals has hair like that characteristically encountered in Africa. These characters are technically phenotypic, but there is no doubt that their expression is largely if not wholly controlled by genetic factors. Thus far, all the psychological evidence, if we accept it as valid, presents a quite different picture. In this category of characters, the races are distinguished from each other not by discontinuous or non-overlapping traits but by different ranges or distributions which actually overlap each other to a very considerable extent. Thus, although Davenport can write that the Negroes do better than whites in the Seashore musical tests, this refers only to average scores. In fact, the figures themselves show that many of the whites did better than some Negroes. Conversely, in the tests in which the whites were on the average superior, some Negroes surpassed some whites. Thus if I described a man as having dark brown skin, short frizzy hair, thick lips, facial prognathism and a low broad nose, he could be identified correctly only as a Negro. But a similar list of psychological traits would give no certain clues to his origin whatever. It would become possible only if a large group were described in statistical terms and even then only by an expert in such matters. It is obvious from this that the broad, sweeping generalizations implicit in Davenport's study, associating as it does psychological and physical differences in race, tend to give the former the character of the latter and thus a quite erroneous impression.

HAWAII

Race mixture has had a field day in Hawaii. Polynesians, all kinds and degrees of Europeans and Americans, Puerto Ricans, Chinese, Japanese, Koreans, Filipinos, not to mention smaller contingents of other populations, have met here and produced a bewildering array of hybrids. The extraordinary fact about all this—extraordinary in the light of conditions in many other areas of race mixture—is the relative absence here of friction, prejudice or social rejection. There is no colour bar in Hawaii and no legal disability based on race, although contact between the same races elsewhere has given rise to them. Why, one might ask, has Hawaii become the seat of such an amicable arrangement? The answer, it seems to me, lies in the history of the Hawaiian islands and in their relation to the imperialism of the Western World.

When Captain Cook discovered the islands in 1778, he found them populous and administered by a strong feudal-like system. He made no attempt to claim them for Britain: in fact he was murdered by the natives and his expedition withdrew. By the time Vancouver and subsequent expeditions reached Hawaii, the islands had become consolidated or were rapidly becoming so under the rule of Kamehameha I. Thus in the early nineteenth century, when European powers were seizing every scrap of unclaimed territory to which they had access, the Hawaiian islands were able to resist these man-œuvres, since they were governed by a strong monarchical government capable of maintaining its hegemony over the islands. There was no political vacuum inviting imperial expansion. Of course, the balance of power in the Pacific played a part in preserving Hawaiian independence, but where a strong centralized native government was lacking, as in the Society Islands, the Marquesas and in many other island archipelagos, these succumbed to French or British control.

When, therefore, Americans and Europeans began settling in the Hawaiian islands in the early years of the nineteenth century, drawn there by commerce, adventure or missionary enterprise, they were legally foreigners whose advancement and prosperity depended on the good will of the Hawaiians. To own and hold land in that feudal society required permission and special dispensation or possibly marriage with a daughter of a chief. To pursue missionary work with any hope of success, the Hawaiian chiefs and royal family had to be won over tactfully and their acquiescence sued for with the respect exacted by a ruling class. From the very beginning of this contact with the Western world, therefore, the Hawaiians were in the position of authority. Never having been conquered, they remained the masters. Their chiefs and kings continued to be persons endowed with power and entitled to the respect and evidence of homage that their traditions demanded. Such a situation created a pattern of relationship to which the Americans and Europeans had to conform. And racial tolerance towards the Hawaiian had necessarily to become an accepted social and official pattern.

Since the potential and actual wealth of the islands—the land—remained in the hands of the native families, intermarriage was frequently an economic advantage that brought a social position to the white man which he might not otherwise easily achieve. His children, therefore, would acquire status and prestige in the beginning not so much from their white ancestry as from the status and land they inherited from their native mothers. Enough of such marriages took place to entrench half-castes firmly in the upper social and economic levels of Hawaiian society. With the native race enjoying social and economic dominance, miscegenation with it could not lead to the social rejection of the half-caste, since to do so would also imply an intolerable rejection of the Hawaiian. Moreover, the half-caste had family connexions with a rising class of whites. Thus race mixture in Hawaii very early acquired an official acceptance and, publicly at least, led to no social segregation. This pattern was extremely important for the far more numerous offspring of mixed marriages on lower levels of Hawaiian society, as it fixed the terms of social tolerance under which they existed.

Later, when Chinese and Japanese labourers for the plantations began to be imported in large numbers, they entered a situation where, racially at least, official tolerance was the accepted mode. Social prejudice and economic resentment against these newcomers did develop and at times became quite acute, but it could not degenerate into a crude, open, racial form since that would have involved the Hawaiians and the part-Hawaiians. The pattern of racial tolerance had to be extended to include all the various races that were joining and mingling with the Hawaiian population.

When, in 1900, the Hawaiian Kingdom came to an end and the islands were annexed by mutual agreement to the United States, the tradition of racial tolerance, established for over a century, was firmly enough implanted in the Hawaiian way of life to withstand continental influences stemming from different attitudes. This, at any rate, was true up to World War II, before the large-scale migration of mainland population in connexion with wartime activities took place. Some hints have come through that the sudden increase of settlers conditioned to another tradition has to some extent affected the situation described above, but these may merely be reflexions of difficulties of readjustment rather than indications of a fundamental change.

While the picture drawn here of conditions in Hawaii represents an unusually benign resolution of a complex racial situation, it should not be taken to imply that race or race mixture does not exist as a factor at all in Hawaiian life. That they do is obvious from any careful consideration of that life. It must be remembered, first of all, that the various racial groups that entered the islands as labour recruitments, came mainly in fairly considerable numbers. As such, they were settled on plantations where they naturally tended to form cultural isolates, separated from Hawaiian life by its unfamiliarity and by barriers of language. Moreover, their own tendency was to reproduce in this alien land the familiar elements of their own culture with all its values. Later, as the members of these labour groups were able to free themselves from plantation work and to establish themselves in such urban centres as Honolulu, they generally settled in tight residential sections where they could continue to enjoy the cultural security that close association with one's fellows gives. Thus some continuity of racial and cultural identity was maintained. For the most part it is a voluntary type of segregation which has, however, tended to break down to a large degree as acculturation and economic prosperity permitted. These racial and cultural entities serve, as long as they persist, to act as nuclei for their respective groups and to keep alive some of the traditions brought to the islands. While they continue to exist, they also keep alive a social centre that affects the contacts of their group and their marital patterns.

That some cohesion still exists along these lines is evident from the in-and-out marriage rates of these racial groups. It is a fairly general pattern that the immigrants tend to marry within their own group when partners are available. But, with continued residence in Hawaii, they all show an increasing inclination to marry outside the group. The rate with which this occurs varies from group to group and depends, apparently, on a number of factors too complicated to go into here. The out-marriages, however, are not random, but follow patterns distinct for each group. To some extent these out-marriages are reflexions of opportunity but also of a variety of cultural and possibly racial attitudes. The striking thing, however, is that each group reveals a stronger inclination to marry half-caste Hawaiians than any others when they do marry outside their own circle. Thus the Chinese are more likely to marry mixed Chinese-Hawaiian, while the whites show an equally persistent trend towards Caucasian-Hawaiian mixed bloods in preference to any other group.

The mixed Hawaiians, thus, by a steady growth through primary crosses, by intermarriage with 'pure' racial groups and by their own high natural increase, are expanding at a more rapid rate than any other major contingent of the population. And although it is unlikely that all the groups will be dissolved into one racially mixed population in the very near future, the present trends suggest that the mixed bloods are destined to become one of, if not the, major element in Hawaii's population.

FINAL REMARKS

Although the ubiquity and growth of hybridization have suggested to some prophets a future world inhabited only by various degrees and kinds of racially mixed populations, this is an extreme interpretation that need not be endorsed to emphasize the significance of the process we have been considering. For the fact of the matter is that, right now, race mixture is an important phenomenon in certain portions of the earth and of great indirect significance even to countries where its physical results are in a sense of academic interest only. We can, for example, scarcely hope to understand the populations, of such countries as Mexico or Brazil, to name only two, without a knowledge of the history of the miscegenation that has produced them. Nor can we, even though seated in Europe, escape altogether the effects of race contacts and race mingling as they occur in such distant places as South Africa.

But to recognize the importance of race mixture in the modern world does not unfortunately provide us with the solutions to problems which it raises. These, though sharing certain genetic similarities, are infinitely varied and must be studied each in its specific context if we are to acquire the necessary background with which to deal with them. Thus the history of race mixture in Peru, for example, with its emphasis on cultural considerations, presents a vastly different situation and calls for a different treatment from the problems created by miscegenation in East or South Africa, where the resulting tensions are tied up with race consciousness and a struggle for power.

Although we may acknowledge the subtly differing and multifarious forms that race mixture assumes in different parts of the world, we can still draw from them some generalizations of wide pertinence. One of the most commonly held beliefs, where race mixture is regarded with disapproval, is that it leads to an eventual deterioration of the population affected by it. Whether or not this represents a rationalization to justify established patterns of social, economic and political custom which race mixture might threaten is difficult to say. The strength of this conviction is, however, far from commensurate with the evidence of it. Studies of racially mixed groups have in some instances demonstrated quite the reverse, as we have already seen in the Pitcairn Islanders. Fisher's investigation of the Rehobother Bastards, a cross between South African Boers and Hottentots, found them to be a similarly healthy and exceptionally vigorous people. Even Davenport's claims to have discovered evidence of deterioration and disharmony among the Negro-white hybrids of Jamaica do not, on close inspection, carry conviction. There is, therefore, no reliable documentation that race mixture as a biological process is inevitably a deleterious one.

On the psychological side, the consequences of race mixture are rather more controversial. Although many broad and sweeping distinctions have been drawn between races, distinctions which are considered to have a profound bearing on the quality of mixed populations, the difficulties in measuring objectively the innate psychological characteristics of races are still far from solved, and many competent authorities consequently reject as unjustified the conclusion that races differ psychologically in a significant way. In any event, the differences, such as they are, with their burden of cultural conditioning, reflect not discontinuous racial distinctions but variations in distribution and range. Under these circumstances we find, even where such differences exist, that many individuals of the supposedly inferior race are equal if not superior to a large proportion of the summations. To take an average of a large and varied population and apply it indiscriminately to all its members is to falsify its meaning and to misrepresent the actual situation. In our tendency to generalize people into groups, populations or race, we run the risk of losing the individual in the statistical mean or average. The

387

range of intelligence in various races as expressed by the I.Q. is such that if the I.Q. is to be established as a criterion of suitable mating then one might argue that some race mixtures are eminently more defensible than numerous marriages within a race. In other words, it all depends who is crossing with whom.

Indeed, on theoretical grounds, one might maintain that hybridization, by producing a wider range of types, does in fact have certain very real biological merits. Although the available investigations on racially mixed groups are not unequivocal on this point, nevertheless experimental data on a wider variety of animals and plants lead us to anticipate that the same genetic phenomena found among them might be expected in the human species as well. If this be true, then recombinations of parental racial characters would yield new forms, some of which might prove exceptionally viable and vigorous. As Dobzhansky has pointed out, variety can be a distinct advantage to a population undergoing changes in its environment. For the larger the number of variants the greater the chances are that one among them will be better fitted to survive, and, thus, the population as well.

Although the emotions and impulses that lead to race mixture are no respecters of social status, the fact remains that the continued and more intimate contacts that are likely to provide the opportunities occur more frequently among the lower levels of both groups. This does not necessarily mean that biologically inferior representations of their respective races furnish most of the parents of mixed bloods, for it is not entirely clear to what extent biological selection follows on social stratification. But the economic and social inferiority of the parental groups can and often do place an especially heavy burden on their mixed progeny, which, added to the disabilities they suffer anyway as half-castes, tends to reinforce their marginal position. The importance of this factor in establishing the status of the half-caste is often overlooked by the casual observer. Its significance can be readily appreciated by comparison with mixed groups who have fortunately inherited economic and social dignity by virtue of their parents' position.

The great injustice, after all, that has been placed on the mixed-blood is that he is judged, not as an individual, an elementary right to which he is entitled, but as a member of a group about which there is much prejudice and little understanding.

BIBLIOGRAPHY

ADAMS, Romanzo. *Interracial marriage in Hawaii.* Macmillan Co., New York, 1937.

DAVENPORT, C. B. and STEGGERDA, Morris. *Race crossing in Jamaica.* Carnegie Institution of Washington, Publication No. 395. Washington, 1929.

FISHER, Eugen. *Die Rehobother Bastards und das Bastardierungsproblem beim Menschen.* Jena, 1913.

LIND, Andrew W. *An island community: ecologial succession in Hawaii.* University of Chicago Press, Chicago, 1938.

SHAPIRO, Harry L. *The heritage of the Bounty. The story of Pitcairn through six generations.* Simon and Schuster, New York, 1936.

WAGLEY, Charles. *Race and class in rural Brazil.* United Nations Educational, Scientific and Cultural Organization publication, New York, 1952.

PART THREE

THE ROOTS OF PREJUDICE

by
ARNOLD ROSE

*Professor of Sociology at the
University of Minnesota, U.S.A.*

INTRODUCTION

Prejudice of one group of people against another group has existed in most parts of the world and at all periods of history. It has not been universal, in the sense that all cultures or all people have displayed it; but it has been prevalent enough to serve as a basis for conflict between nations and between groups within a nation. It practically always involves discrimination, which means mistreatment of people without their having done anything to merit such mistreatment.[1] It has thus been a source of human unhappiness and misunderstanding wherever and whenever it has arisen. Although certain individuals have exploited prejudice to gain political power or economic advantage for themselves, there is no example of a whole people advancing themselves or their civilization for a long period of time on the basis of it. It has been, rather, a blight from almost every standpoint.

Yet there is still relatively little understanding of the causes or even of the effects of prejudice, except on the superficial, obvious level. On later pages we shall see that it has not even been studied by scientists sufficiently to make them certain of

---

1. We use the term prejudice to refer to a set of attitudes which causes, supports, or justifies discrimination. Since discrimination itself consists of observable behaviour, it is a more useful subject for study. But since in this article, we are searching for *causes* of behaviour, we must direct our attention to the mind of the person who practises discrimination. Prejudice is taken as the mental state corresponding to the practice of discrimination.

its causes, although there have been some startling discoveries and stimulating suggestions. Outside the ranks of social science, most people hold quite erroneous ideas about it— ideas which themselves are sometimes born of prejudice and which are sometimes even detrimental to those holding them. We shall now proceed to consider the varied sources of prejudice, moving from the more obvious and rational causes to the less apparent and unconscious ones.

PERSONAL ADVANTAGE AS A CAUSE OF PREJUDICE

Perhaps the most obvious cause of prejudice is that it creates advantages and material benefits for those who are prejudiced. Prejudice can provide an excuse or rationalization for economic exploitation or political domination. It can enable a man to justify to himself acts that he would ordinarily be unwilling to engage in. It can be exploited by shrewd, self-seeking manipulators when it occurs in other people. It can offer opportunities for taking sexual advantage of minority group women, and it may give people at the bottom of the social ladder an apparent superiority over the minority group. The fact that individuals and groups can and do gain advantages for themselves out of prejudice becomes a cause of prejudice.

Imperialism, especially when practised by persons of European origin on non-Europeans, has frequently been attended by prejudice. Even when there has been no noteworthy development of prejudice in the home country, those who go forth as colonial administrators, traders, or extractors of the natural resources of undeveloped lands, learn that callousness toward subject peoples, and an attitude of racial superiority, will aid them in their venture. Within limits, a harsh manner and exacting demands will gain a large output from workers who have no means of defence or retaliation. Payment of low wages and provision of only a minimum of life needs to these workers will mean larger profits.

Racial, national, or religious antagonisms can be built up to deflect class antagonisms. A relatively small number of exploiters can maintain their dominant position by dividing their subordinates and encouraging them to be hostile to one another. One group may be given the sergeant's role of keeping all other groups in line by force. In return for this they have the satisfaction of being regarded as belonging to the superior group, even though they are themselves exploited. This procedure may be used in a perfectly 'natural' way, so that it is obvious to no one.

Techniques akin to those of imperialism may be employed *within* an independent nation. Prices or rents of houses can be kept at a high level by obliging people to live within certain small, segregated areas. Wages can be kept low for people who are not allowed to work in any but certain exploited jobs. Public facilities and benefits may be kept at a minimum for people who are segregated to the greatest extent.

It is difficult to tell how much of this use of prejudice and discrimination for purposes of exploitation is conscious and how much unconscious. Some that appears unplanned and unconscious is occasionally revealed to be quite deliberate. One young man who had just answered a questionnaire designed to test for anti-Semitism made a revealing remark in this connexion. He said, 'I have no strong feeling about Jews either way' (the test did not show him to be anti-Semitic). 'But I am studying to be a banker, and if my employers are anti-Semitic, I'm going to be anti-Semitic too, as I want to get ahead.' Perhaps we shall never discover for certain how much of prejudice is deliberate and how much unconscious. But that is of little consequence, as the effects and the underlying causes are always the same. Deliberate use of prejudice to exploit a group of people is hardly different from the unplanned and non-directed utilization of group differences to gain every possible advantage from the situation. Both can be considered together as a cause of prejudice.

The gains to be secured may be political as well as economic. Group differences can be fostered to keep a certain party in political power. Modern dictators have been experts in the technique of 'divide and conquer' both to retain power in their own country and to extend their conquests abroad. Studies have been conducted in several countries which show how Hitler secured supporters—now called fifth columnists— by offering them the positions and property then held by Jews and by appealing to a latent feeling of racial superiority. In democratic countries where prejudice is prevalent, some politicians successfully base their campaign for office on theories of racial supremacy. Most of the organizations formed for the apparent purpose of fostering race hatred have been shown to have political domination as their ultimate aim.

Economic or political exploitation as a cause of prejudice has definite limitations. In the first place, it must be balanced against the costs of prejudice to be mentioned in a later section. It is probable that in the long run imperialistic countries could have gained even greater economic advantages if they had not employed prejudice, discrimination and violence. Individuals who exploit prejudice become extreme victims of the psychological costs of prejudice. Another burden they lay upon themselves is the realization that they are exploiting and cheating. Most people dislike thinking of themselves as unfair and dishonest, or without ideals. Even the building up of a psychological defence to rationalize unfairness and dishonesty may be only partially successful; it certainly creates rigidities in the personality. Thus, the advantages of prejudice do not seem great when balanced against its cost. Moreover, there are progressively fewer opportunities for exploitation through prejudice as hitherto subordinated peoples have now organized themselves to stop it. Throughout the world, imperialism is retreating. Exploited minority groups within nations have also made great strides towards improving their position and reducing victimization. They have had active support from many members of the majority group who have realized the costs and dangers of prejudice. Thus, exploitation and domination are decreasing, at least in so far as they stem from prejudice, and they are thus less effective as causes of prejudice.

There are other apparent advantages of prejudices. We can only refer briefly to the difficult subject of men of the dominant group taking sexual advantage of minority group women. 'Gains' of this sort are obviously balanced by social losses for the dominant group as a whole. A society in which there are frequent demands for casual and loveless sexual intercourse is not a well-organized or satisfying society, either to its men or to its women.

Finally, as John Dollard has pointed out, there are some prestige gains in a society based on prejudice. If people have no other basis of prestige, they get a certain satisfaction simply out of being members of the dominant group. Although they are at the bottom of their own racial, national, or religious groups, they can feel superior to the minority groups. The weakness of this kind of gain is surely obvious: the prejudiced person who gains a prestige satisfaction out of feeling superior to a minority group is diverted from other, more important, kinds of prestige satisfaction. He loses ambition, and allows himself to be manipulated by those higher on the prestige scale in his own dominant group. People who live under such unfavourable circumstances that they might be expected to join reform or revolutionary movements are sometimes kept from doing so by reluctance to lose the trivial prestige that raises them above the minority group.

IGNORANCE OF OTHER GROUPS OF PEOPLE AS A CAUSE OF PREJUDICE

Prejudice is nearly always accompanied by incorrect or ill-informed opinions regarding the people against whom it is felt. Many of the false beliefs take the form of what social scientists call 'stereotypes'. These are exaggerations of certain physical traits or cultural characteristics which are found among members of the minority group and are then attributed to all members of the group. When stereotypes exist, an individual is judged, not on the basis of his own characteristics, but on the basis of exaggerated and distorted beliefs regarding what are thought to be the characteristics of his group. All members of the group are falsely assumed to be alike, exceptions being ignored or their existence denied.

Stereotypes take strange forms. They are usually unfavourable to the subordinated group, but not always. Stereotypes about Negroes in South Africa and the United States, for example, depict them as brutal, stupid, and immoral, but also as happy, generous and faithful. This pattern makes sense in terms of the effort to use Negroes as servants and unskilled workers, because the 'good' traits seem to justify their treatment as childlike subordinates and to indicate their satisfaction with this treatment.

A stereotype applied to one group of people at one time may be applied to another group at a later time. In England during the seventeenth century the Scottish Lowlanders were stereotyped as coarse, cruel, and animal-like people. By the nineteenth century, this stereotype was applied no longer to the Scots, but to the Irish. Stereotypes can change very rapidly: in Western countries before 1940, the Japanese were thought of as sly but weak, rigid and unimaginative. After the outbreak of war with Japan in 1941 the stereotype of the Japanese still included slyness, but shifted to include toughness and resourcefulness as well. After the victory over Japan in 1945, and the beginning of a successful occupation, the stereotype dropped slyness and substituted gullibility.

A stereotype applied to a group of people in one country may not be applied to that group in another country, but rather to another minority group. The stereotype about Jews in Central Europe includes a belief in their strong sexuality and tendency towards sexual perversion. This is not the case in the United States, where, although there are other stereotypes regarding Jews, the sexual stereotype is applied rather to Negroes, especially in the Southern states.

The ignorance which supports prejudice has a great range. It may take the form of false information about people's physical characteristics, cultural practices, or beliefs. It may take the form of myths about superhuman powers or child-like weaknesses. The prejudice of Germans about other peoples included stereotypes about the French as immoral degenerates, about the British as bumbling fools, about the Americans as narrow-minded wastrels, about the Russians as stolid and stupid ignoramuses, about the Jews as scheming perverts. This is just an illustration of the astounding range of ignorance that can occur in one modern country.

Stereotypes and other incorrect beliefs about groups of people are not necessarily least frequent when there are many members of the minority group about, who, through their appearance and behaviour, disprove the false beliefs. The strongest prejudice and the largest number of false beliefs about Negroes are to be found among the whites of South Africa, who live among a black population which outnumbers them by four or five to one. There are many more stereotypes about Negroes in the Southern states of the United States than in the Northern states, although Negroes form a much higher proportion of the population in the former than in the latter area. But no generalization can be made in the opposite sense either: areas with a small minority group are not necessarily freer of stereotypes about their members than are areas where they exist in large numbers. In Germany after World War I there were proportionately few Jews living in Bavaria. Yet there were apparently many more false beliefs about Jews in Bavaria than in cosmopolitan Berlin, where there were more Jews. Until a few decades ago there were more false beliefs about American Indians in North America, where they were few in number, than in South America, where they are much more numerous. These and similar facts disprove the widely held opinion that prejudice is strongest where minority races are largest.

One of the requirements for ignorance about a group of people is social isolation, which can occur even where there is considerable contact. People can live next door to each other as neighbours, one person can even work in another's home or shop, but still they will not necessarily get to know each other as human beings. Both physical and social segregation usually accompany prejudice: they are among its effects, but also among its causes, as they promote ignorance and ignorance bolsters prejudice.

Ignorance among the mass of people enables the propagandist for economic exploitation or political domination to gain his ends more easily. If one group of people knows nothing about another group or has false beliefs about it, it is susceptible to the camouflaged demands of the exploiters. People can even be misled as to whom their real enemy is by a propagandist who plays on their ignorance.

It is apparent from this brief discussion (a) that ignorance takes the form either of absence of knowledge or of false belief; (b) that ignorance itself is not so much a direct cause of prejudice as it is a pre-condition or bolster of prejudice. In the latter capacity, ignorance is a more important factor in prejudice against some groups than it is against other groups. Where it is a significant factor, information which fills gaps in knowledge or contradicts false beliefs can be a valuable weapon against prejudice. Not only does such information weaken directly one of the supports of prejudice, but it partially nullifies the propagandist's attempts at exploitation.

RACISM, OR THE 'SUPERIORITY COMPLEX', AS A CAUSE OF PREJUDICE

The problems of intergroup relations may be classified according to three types. One kind is political in motive. This intergroup tension is based on a struggle for power. Such rivalries have been frequent in international relations, and a modern example of them may be found in the long-standing hatred between France and Germany. Sometimes one country may contain two groups struggling against each other for political power. Much of the violence, discrimination, and prejudice that has divided the Serbs and Croats in Yugoslavia was of this nature.

A second class of intergroup tensions arises from differences of religious belief. The history of the West was marked for many centuries by violence between Christians and Muslims and later between Catholics and Protestants. Part of the modern conflict between Fascism, Communism, and democracy is caused by a difference in belief, although most of it is based on a struggle for political power. Belief differences between groups frequently involve the notion that non-believers are agents or advocates of sin, heresy, corruption, or some other form of evil. To persecute them is to do justice or perform a service for the Lord. Belief differences are especially associated with prejudice when one group has a strongly developed conviction that its own beliefs are superior to all others. Such an ideology has been more strongly developed in connexion with the Jewish, Christian, Muslim, and Shintoist religions than with the Hindu, Buddhist, Confucianist, and most forms of pagan religion. It is perhaps for this reason that prejudice is more frequently found where followers of one of the former religions are dominant. This is true even though some of these religions consider unfairness and violence to be abhorrent.

Whereas intergroup tensions based on the struggle for power or on differences of belief have existed since the beginning of recorded history, the third type—racism—seems to be largely a modern phenomenon. It was at least rare until its modern development less than two centuries ago as a perversion of early biological science, and it still has not spread much into cultures other than those of the West. That there were physical differences among people had always been obvious, of course. Some individuals of ancient and medieval times regarded individuals with different physical features as obnoxious (although others considered such physical differences to be especially interesting or desirable). Yet all men, whatever their physical traits, were regarded as human beings (or at worst fallen angels), quite different from the creatures called animals. When the natural historians of the eighteenth and early nineteenth centuries were classifying and describing species, they introduced the notion that men were to be classified into five races, which could be graded like species of animals, into higher and lower. Scientific biologists soon corrected this early error by showing that mankind was of one origin and that racial differences were later developments, so that no one race could be ranked higher than any other. Nevertheless, the concept of races was seized upon and elaborated into a whole new basis for intergroup antagonism which is now called racism.

Racism is a set of popular beliefs which includes the following elements:

1. The differences between groups—differences in body and in mind—are all due to hereditary biology, and nothing can change them. According to this theory, for example, if Negroes are, on the average, not as intelligent as whites, this is due to their heredity and can no more be changed than their skin colour.

2. A second part of this theory is that habits, attitudes, beliefs, behaviour and all the things we *learn* are determined for us before we are born. For example according to this popular theory, Jews are born to be sharp businessmen and Japanese are born to act in an insincere manner.

3. All differences between a minority group and the majority group are thought to be signs of inferiority. For example, according to this popular theory, Jewish religion, Catholic religion, and the Negro's expression of religion are all inferior to the white Protestant's religion.

4. If there should be biological crossing of the groups, the children will be more degenerate than either of the parent groups. Civilization—including family life, religion and morals—will disappear and men will become savage animals. The details of what would happen if there were 'intermarriage' are usually left to the imagination, and just the ugly word 'mongrelization' is used to suggest the results. Because of this, everything must be done to prevent the two groups from having easy social relations with each other. For example, if parents allowed a Jewish boy to 'date' a Gentile girl, the two might want to get married, and the children of such a marriage would be 'lost'—according to this theory. Another example: if Negroes were allowed to eat in the same restaurants as whites, they might become so bold as to ask whites for their daughters' hands in marriage—according to the racist theory.

These racist beliefs have become so widespread, so unconscious, and so traditional among many peoples of the West that racism may be regarded as an independent cause of prejudice today. Some social scientists consider it to be the only really important kind of prejudice between peoples, and they use the term 'race prejudice' to refer to all the things we are considering in this article. Where racist beliefs occur they apply as much to religious groups, national groups, or groups of other types as to the strictly racial groups defined by anthropologists.

To understand better how racism has become a root of modern prejudice, it is important to examine its history in several countries. One of the first countries in which it developed was the United States. At the beginning of the nineteenth century Negro slavery was well established in the United States. Little attempt was made to justify it, however, except on the grounds of economic convenience and the fact that it had existed for a long time. Many people, including large slaveholders, were in favour of abolishing it as incompatible with the growth of democracy. Prejudice was not particularly associated with slavery, since white people accepted freed slaves on their own merits and since many wealthy white people allowed their slaves to go free. Certainly there was no prejudice against Negroes on any of the racial grounds we have just examined.

About that time a great new profit was discovered in slaves: the invention of the cotton gin and of a process for extracting sugar from cane, coupled with new facilities for international trade, made the Southern states a region of great potential wealth. This required cheap labour that could be held to the unpleasant task of growing and picking cotton and sugar cane. Not enough free people would do this work; not even immigrants from Europe, brought over especially for the task. So, many more Negro slaves were brought in (although this was now illegal); the area of cotton growing was greatly extended; many people grew wealthy rapidly; and the South maintained a precarious dominance of power in the nation as a whole because of its wealth. During this period pressures were exerted to abolish slavery: other countries were abolishing slavery, it was now considered to be immoral and barbarous; and some of the poor whites of the South did not like a system which gave all power to the wealthy slave owners. In this setting, the concepts of racism served perfectly as a justification. The Negroes were declared to be a childlike race, which must be directed in work for its own good and which must be kept inferior to the poor whites for the good of civilization. Prejudice of the racist variety took hold of the South and has remained there to the present day.

In Western Europe during the first half of the nineteenth century, racism was a doctrine elaborated only by a few writers. This does not mean that there was no prejudice, but simply that prejudice was then religious and cultural in character rather than racial. At first, racism had little popular appeal, as democratic and humanitarian ideology was generally dominant over the older aristocratic ideology. By 1870, however, the aristocrats, in a desperate search for tools and allies to support their waning power, seized upon racism as a useful propaganda device. In Germany two groups of politicians discovered that by building up anti-Semitism, at that time a weak remnant of an ancient religious antagonism, they could also build their own political strength. One of these groups was led by court chaplain Stoecker and other 'romantics', who wanted to create a new kind of reactionary social order much like modern Fascism. The other group was led by Chancellor Bismarck who was trying to maintain himself in office against the opposition of the growing Liberal and Socialist parties. The latter had Jewish leaders, and anti-Semitism seemed a useful policy even though Bismarck was not personally anti-Semitic. His successors in the German Government continued to use anti-Semitism until it became part of the popular tradition.

In Russia, the corrupt and inefficient Tsarist government also sought to gain political support by adopting racism. In 1880 the Tsarist police began a programme of propaganda against Jews which was racist in tone, and instigated the first of a series of pogroms against them. The device did help to divert the peasants and some city workers from their real troubles for a number of years, but nevertheless the Tsarist government ultimately fell.

In France there was the famous Dreyfus case, in which anti-Semitism was used as a political weapon.

Racism was thus a body of traditions—some general, some specific—that became part of the popular culture of some Western countries but not of others. Where it was accepted, it influenced people to think in terms of biological race superiority and to act in a violent and prejudiced manner towards certain minority groups. Wherever it has existed it has superseded, or at least become interwoven with, all other bases of group antagonism.

IGNORANCE OF THE COSTS OF PREJUDICE AS A SOURCE OF PREJUDICE

Many people believe that the harmful effects of prejudice are felt only by those against whom it is indulged. There can be no doubt that restriction of employment opportunities, lack of access to facilities (both publicly and privately owned) that are meant to serve the population in general, the presence of bias and antagonism in law enforcement officials, and many other manifestations of prejudice, are directly harmful to those people whom they affect. But it is not so obvious that those who feel the prejudice, and who enforce the discriminations which are its visible manifestations, are themselves victims of their own attitude and behaviour. This misunderstanding might itself be regarded as one contributory root of prejudice, since few people would so strongly maintain a kind of behaviour which they considered to be harmful to themselves. It is therefore necessary for us first to examine the ways in which prejudice is harmful to the prejudiced.

1. In the first place, there is the direct economic waste entailed by failure to use the full productivity of manpower and the fullest demands of the market. In so far as people are kept unemployed because of prejudice, or are employed at lower tasks than they are capable of handling, there is waste. Every employer loses by not hiring the most efficient workers available, and every consumer loses by having to pay higher prices for his purchases. The loss is most serious and most obvious during periods of manpower shortage, but it can be demonstrated to exist at other times also. It usually takes an indirect form, and thus is not readily apparent to most persons. Also, as we have seen, some people benefit directly from prejudice, and so are especially unlikely to notice the indirect loss. While prejudice is just one among many sources of loss, it is seen to be a significant one when we note its connexion with low standards of living in several parts of the world. In such regions, even if natural resources are abundant and there is no overpopulation, prejudice keeps productivity per person low. The Southern states of the U.S.A. provide an obvious illustration of this.

2. A second type of economic cost of prejudice is that which arises out of social problems which are aggravated. Much of this cost is borne by a government budget. Where pre-

judice creates social problems, the government must control or alleviate them. Even a government run by the most prejudiced people finds it imperative to control communicable diseases and epidemics, maintain a police and jail system, offer some protection against accidents, and provide a minimum of direct relief so that starvation will not be too obvious. The costs are frequently more direct. The bad health of a group of people kept down by prejudice creates an unhealthy environment for the prejudiced. The costs of crime are met not only by the government but also by the criminals' victims.

3. A third group of costs is to be measured in terms of time wasted before being translated into terms of money. A casual inspection of the front pages of the world's newspapers would indicate that the people of countries where prejudice prevails spend much time in discussions on how to treat minority groups. Only in prejudiced countries are congresses and parliaments frequently engaged in debate and legislation concerning minority groups. Many of the private organizations ranging from businessmen's groups and unions to sports groups and social clubs in these countries find it necessary to take time to consider how and in what degree to apply their prejudiced policies in specific cases. In terms of the primary aims of these congresses and organizations, such activity is a waste of time. The group could turn its attention to matters more directly connected with its own well-being, or it could release its members sooner to pursue their own interests.

Then, too, the existence of more laws and rules creates more opportunities for litigation and for contesting the rules. Give people a grievance and an enormous amount of time will be spent in indulging it. The prejudiced peoples of the world impose on themselves a huge burden simply by obliging themselves to decide how and to what extent in specific cases they shall hold down the people against whom they are prejudiced. This burden has to be measured in terms of time and mental energy.

4. A fourth cost of prejudice is seen most clearly in the relation between nations today. Each nation is anxious to gain the goodwill or respect of other nations, whether its ultimate aim be peaceful accommodation or domination. Diplomacy, international economic assistance, participation in world organizations, and all other governmental activities directed towards other nations, are aimed at

acquiring prestige and influence. These efforts on the part of some nations are partially nullified by acts of prejudice within those nations. Few people will regard with complacency acts of violence and discrimination against members of their own race or nationality in another country. And many other people wonder whether an ally is to be trusted if it engages in acts of prejudice against minority groups. While prejudice is only one factor among many, a survey of international attitudes today would show that there is no complete trust or respect for nations in which prejudice prevails.

The diplomatic efforts and goodwill activities of these nations cannot have their full influence. This is especially true when the diplomats themselves manifest prejudice against their allies.

Fully two-thirds of the people of the world today are members of races towards whom much prejudice has been shown. Some of these people have now formed important nations, and others show signs of developing in that direction. It is these peoples especially which regard prejudice in other nations as part of the foreign policy of those nations. Much of the rational and expensive efforts in the diplomacy of the latter nations is thus wasted by prejudice.

5. Thus far we have been counting the measurable economic waste caused by prejudice. There are also psychological forms of waste that cannot be easily translated into money, time or effort, although their effects may be more devastating in the long run. Our fifth damaging effect of prejudice on the prejudiced arises from the fact that it creates barriers to communication. A great deal of knowledge and culture is lost to prejudiced people, because they will not meet and talk with those who have this knowledge and culture. There is little realization on the part of the prejudiced of how much they miss in this way, but the lack of recognition does not alter the fact. As the hitherto subordinated peoples have secured independence, they have turned particular attention to learning and science. Though they have a great deal of lag to make up, some of their developments in this field are already approaching those of the hitherto dominant peoples. Thus the barrier to communication created by prejudice is having an ever-increasing damaging effect on the prejudiced.

6. Prejudice serves as an outlet for frustration, as we shall

have occasion to emphasize on later pages. A number of studies have shown that the presentation of a frustrating situation will, in most circumstances, increase prejudice towards any group that happens to provide a convenient outlet. Since the prejudices we are concerned with are manifested by whole groups of people, the frustrations which give rise to them must be extensive and serious ones. Such frustrations arise from external circumstances such as economic depressions, lack of satisfaction in family relations, and so on. These are admittedly difficult problems. But prejudice does not solve them. At best it can temporarily relieve the feeling of frustration. This temporary relief is harmful, since it prevents the search for, and action towards, the real solution of the frustration. This point will be given fuller attention in a later section.

7. Recent researches have shown the correlation between prejudice and other kinds of rigidity and narrowness, at least in Western culture. While the cause is not yet clear, the connexion is so strong that it may fairly be inferred that the maintenance of prejudice will be accompanied by a closed mind towards anything new and an inability to accept and reciprocate fully any human relationship. Clearly, anyone who has these personality defects is missing much of what life has to offer.

8. Prejudice is partially characterized by fear and anxiety in relation to the groups against which it is directed. In Europe during the Middle Ages, many people terrified themselves and their neighbours with beliefs that Jews were agents of the Devil and that they engaged in ritual sacrifices of Gentile children. Many of the minor Nazis of modern Germany were convinced that Jews were engaged in an international plot to enslave their country. Prejudiced people everywhere exaggerate the numbers and power of the minority groups in their home areas. These and other facts indicate that a feeling of terror is a motive for an act of terrorism. The fears and anxieties are based on false beliefs, but the psychological pain they cause to those who feel them is real enough. Prejudice thus contributes to unhappiness.

9. When prejudice is part of the culture of a people, it can shift its direction from one group to another. The history of countries where prejudice has existed shows that different minorities have been the objects of prejudice at different times. The objects of prejudice are not as stable

as is commonly thought. The immigration of a new nationality group to a country where prejudice is entrenched—as of Indians to South Africa or of Chinese to the United States—can be the basis of a new focusing of prejudice which had previously been directed to another group. The devolopment of tensions between governments—as between France and Germany in 1914 and 1938 or as between the Vatican and Germany in the late 1930s—can become the basis of popular false beliefs and discrimination against peoples or religious groups. No group of people is safe from prejudice when any other group is already its object.

10. Closely associated with prejudice is disrespect for law and unwillingness to settle disputes peacefully. When one group of people is prejudiced against another group, it is generally unwilling to apply the usual laws and standards of behaviour to the persons who are the objects of prejudice. Violation of the law when it is to be applied to such persons is one of the most typical forms of discrimination. In many countries of the world it has been found that unchecked violence and deprivation of civil rights directed against one group can easily spread to all other groups. When laws are misused or ignored, they become weakened, and illegality becomes part of the entire culture. Where a dangerous cultural practice exists, any person or group may become its victim.

Yet there can be little doubt that prejudiced people believe that prejudice cannot be directed against them or that it has no harmful effects on them. If they understood the consequences of their own attitudes and behaviour, they could at least question their own prejudices. This has not only been demonstrated logically, but also empirically, by direct questioning of prejudiced people. Even when aware of the action of prejudice on minority groups, they are not aware of the *reaction* of prejudice on themselves. Ignorance of the full consequences and repercussions of prejudice is thus a pre-condition or necessary cause—although not a sufficient explanation—of prejudice.

THE TRANSMISSION OF PREJUDICE TO CHILDREN

We may digress from our discussion of the specific causes of prejudice to consider how it is passed along from generation to generation. It is customary in countries where racism prevails to assume that it is natural and inevitable that one group should disdain or look up to another. We have already seen that prejudice is frequently a result of deliberate propaganda: yet the fact that it is often found in fairly young children gives rise to the incorrect assumption that it is inborn. Actually, prejudice is learned. Studies show that it can be learned by children as young as four years old.

The teaching of prejudice takes place in the same informal manner in which other aspects of non-material culture are taught. Children may be taught prejudice by their parents, their teachers, their friends, their Sunday school teachers. Parents are the most important influence. While some parents do not want their children to be prejudiced, others teach prejudice to their children because they themselves grew up to believe that it was proper and natural. Parents teach prejudice to their children by their own behaviour, by their expressions of disgust, by forbidding certain associations, by their choice of observations, by their indications as to what is humorous or degrading, and so on. Sometimes older people will even make fun of children to get them to be prejudiced. But much of the time older people do not realize that they are teaching prejudice to children. At the dinner table, while the children are listening, a mother will tell her husband about her troubles with the Negro or Polish maid. Not only do the children absorb this, but they also come to imitate her behaviour towards the maid, which unconsciously expresses her prejudice in almost every act.

At church or Sunday school, Christian children may learn from the Bible story that 'the Jews' killed Christ. Biblical scholars point out that only a few Jews were against Jesus, and that most of them thought he was a good religious teacher. It was the Romans who punished people at that time and they believed he was dangerous to their government. But Sunday school teachers do not always point out these facts. To make matters much worse, they sometimes identify the people of ancient Palestine with the Jews living in present-day Europe and America, and transfer the blame for a crime that happened two thousand years ago on to people who are living today. Other religious and folk teaching has similar myths which promote prejudice in children.

Some school text-books help to create prejudice. Surveys in several countries have revealed that text-books, especially history books, give derogatory descriptions of people of other nations and disparage minority groups within the nation itself. An immigrant group, for instance, is not usually described in terms of what its members hold dear and consider proper. Rather, the immigrant group is judged by the standards of the majority group. People may be loyal, hard-working, kindly and ambitious, but if they are poor and ignorant and have not yet learned the customs of their adopted nation, they are looked down on in some text-books as well as by most of the native-born people.

Older children teach prejudice to younger ones. Children quickly develop rules about all sorts of things, and each member of the neighbourhood gang is expected to follow the rules. If prejudice is one of the 'rules' in the community, older children are sometimes even more forceful than parents in teaching prejudice to younger children. Sometimes they make up stories about how dangerous or stupid members of minority groups are. These stories are imaginative child's play, but their effect can be very powerful in determining future attitudes. One study of prejudice among adults showed that quite a number of people claimed that their prejudice arose from bad childhood experiences. But when the stories were examined more closely, it was found that the incidents were not known to have actually happened, but where mostly scare stories circulating among the local children. The number of crimes committed by Negroes, Mexicans, and other minorities is actually much smaller than many people think.

Thus we see *how* children, and adults, learn prejudice. Like most other things, they learn it from each other, and especially is it true that the old teach the young. As it passes on from generation to generation, it changes a little. It comes to be applied to new minority groups, and once in a while it ceases to be directed at what were formerly minority groups. Sometimes it grows stronger and sometimes it gets weaker. But it is always taught in the same way as games, good manners, swear words, or anything else in the non-material culture.

The teaching of prejudice is, of course, not inevitable. Some parents, even those who live in dominantly prejudiced cultures, bring up their children to be broadminded and free from prejudice. Also, children and adults who have been taught prejudice can un-learn it. Wise parents, teachers, friends, and books can explain the errors and dangers of prejudice. General education or a religious or humanitarian impulse can lead to a self-examination which sometimes dissolves prejudice.

THE PSYCHOLOGY OF PREJUDICE

Thus far we have been considering prejudice in its rational aspects—as serving a certain purpose, or as a result of ignorance or as a kind of tradition which is learned. There is also an irrational function which it fulfils, for it apparently satisfies a psychological need. This is a very important factor, for without it prejudice might die a natural death after a few generations, if people realized that they were dupes of a few persons who exploited prejudice or that they were blind followers of a harmful tradition.

People have different theories as to what constitutes the psychological basis of prejudice. Some of the theories have been disproved by scientific studies by psychologists and sociologists, yet are still believed by many people.

One such idea is that prejudice always arises instinctively against people who are different. This may be called the 'dislike of differences' theory. When some people are asked why they dislike Negroes, they will say it is because Negroes are so black and dirty, or because Negroes are dangerous. Others will say they do not dislike Negroes, but that you cannot treat a Negro as you can a white man, because a Negro is like a child or an animal and cannot act like a man. All these statements are expressions of prejudice. They assume that there is something about the minority group which naturally causes the majority group to regard it as inferior.

There are several things wrong with the 'dislike of differences' theory:
1. It does not explain the stereotyping that goes with prejudice. Many Negroes are no more dangerous or dirty than many white men. Most Negroes are not even black, and a few are so light-skinned that they can pass as whites. If Negroes do not always behave like fully responsible people,

that in itself is partly due to prejudice. Even if the prejudiced person maintains that most Negroes have these undesirable traits, he will admit that there are exceptions. Yet he is prejudiced against the exceptions too.

2. There are a lot of differences among people against which there is no prejudice. And there are many places in the world where people of different races and religions live together without prejudice. Red hair is just as striking a characteristic as dark skin, and yet few people have prejudice against people with red hair.

3. The 'dislike of differences' theory does not explain the fact that prejudiced people make contradictory statements about those against whom they are prejudiced. Prejudiced people say they dislike Jews because the latter are 'always trying to push themselves into places where they are not wanted', and also because 'Jews are clannish; they keep to themselves'. Prejudiced people observe that 'Negroes are lazy, and have no ambition' and yet they are the first to strike down a Negro who tries to secure education or a better job or home.

Another largely fallacious theory of prejudice is that people become prejudiced because of unpleasant experiences with members of minority groups. It is true that a bad experience with a person can make one dislike that person ever afterwards. But why should the dislike be turned to all people with the same colour of skin or the same accent? If a fat person does one some harm, one does not forever thereafter hate all fat people. If one has a quarrel with a member of the Baptist church, one does not feel the need to fight all Baptists. Obviously, a lot more is needed to explain prejudice.

One of the most important steps in understanding prejudice was taken when the psychologists developed the 'frustration-aggression' theory. In simpler language this is called the 'scapegoat' theory. It is based on a great deal of sound scientific knowledge. Studies of human behaviour have shown that some people are steadily prevented from doing the things they want to do and are consequently not happy. This is called 'frustration'. Then they are likely to strike at something or try to make somebody else unhappy. That is, they become 'aggressive'. When, as often happens, a person cannot hit back at the specific thing that makes him unhappy, he finds a substitute. Among the ancient Hebrews, there was a periodical ceremony of driving into the desert a goat 'burdened with the sins of Israel' to perish there. We still use the term 'scapegoat' to refer to an innocent substitute who gets punished for someone's troubles or anger.

Everyone uses a scapegoat. An occasional action, when we are stopped from doing something we want to do or become angry for some reason, is to kick a chair or other convenient object or throw something on the floor. Small children do this frequently. Little harm is done if the scapegoat is not a living creature, but sometimes a man will beat a dog or a child, not so much because of what the dog or child did as because the man is angry about something else. One who is reprimanded by his employer will sometimes come home and pick a fight with his wife. He cannot talk back to his employer so he vents his anger upon his wife. The dog, the child, and the wife are scapegoats, and they suffer because they are scapegoats.

Occasionally a whole group of people, perhaps a whole country, feels frustrated. Perhaps such people do not know what the trouble is, or perhaps they do know but there is nothing that can be done about it. They may feel frustrated by bad economic conditions, unemployment, low pay, as many Americans in the Southern states have been for a long time. Or they may feel frustrated by failure to become the leading nation of the world, as the Germans were after losing World War I. Nothing they do seems to bring prosperity or glory to their land, and so they take it out on a scapegoat. It is frequently a low grade politician who says 'Here is your scapegoat. It's the cause of your trouble. Kick it and you'll feel better'. According to the theory we are considering, this is why there has been so much prejudice and violence against Negroes in the American South, and against Jews in Nazi Germany.

In any country, some people feel more frustrated than others. Some people are unable to earn even the basic necessities of life. Others get these, but fail to achieve higher ambitions. Some children are frustrated by not doing well at games, or by not getting enough affection or support from their parents. Some children feel that they are unfairly treated by teachers. There are various ways of meeting frustrations:
1. By trying to eliminate the frustrations.
2. By keeping away from the things that are frustrating.
3. By understanding the inevitable character of the frustration and deciding that it is necessary to put up with it, at least for a while.
4. By refusing to realize the cause of the frustration, and taking it out on some scapegoat.

Certain politicians benefit by leading people to scapegoats. One thing that helped Hitler to secure power in Germany was his persuading the German people that the Jews were the cause of all their troubles. In South Africa politicians are sometimes elected to office after a campaign devoted merely to raising white people's fears about Negroes. Some writers and radio speakers become popular and wealthy by telling people to hate the bankers, or the English, or the Jews. This may sound odd to anyone who looks at the situation objectively; but it does not sound odd to people who have troubles and do not know what to do about them. They feel a little better by having a scapegoat, just as each one of us feels better by kicking or pounding something when we are angry. Thus, people often follow the politicians who make them feel better. But having a scapegoat does not really solve any problems. In fact, people are steered away from the solution of their real problems when they have a scapegoat. The only one who benefits is the politician or the writer, as he gains power over the whole people by being the leader in kicking the helpless scapegoat.

During times of business depression, when many people are unhappy and frustrated, there is an increase in violence against Negroes in the Southern states of the United States. The big depression of the 1930s saw the birth, in the United States, of 114 organizations which spent their time and money in spreading hate against Jews. Similar organizations were started by pro-Germans in all the free countries of Europe—some of them by agents of Nazi Germany, and others by people who hoped to benefit by German domination of the world. The leaders of these organizations hoped to get control of the governments of their countries by following the anti-Semitic propaganda that had been so successful in Germany. They did not achieve all their aims—Hitler was finally defeated—but they did succeed in creating hatred and fear of Jews. It is known that many of these same people are now waiting for the next depression or the next war to come along so that they can finish their work. They know how to use frustrating conditions for their own advantage.

Frustration explains the force behind prejudice. But it does not explain why certain minority groups are chosen as scapegoats. To explain this, psychologists help us out with another theory—the 'symbolic' theory. This theory is based on the important fact that one thing can stand for something else in the unconscious mind. People often find themselves liking something, certain foods or some scenery, for example, without knowing why. If such feelings could be traced back to their origin, it would be found that these new foods or new scenery 'remind' people of some pleasant experience in their past. There need not be any real connexion at all. The unconscious mind is always making connexions so that one thing will substitute for another.

There can also be substitutes, or 'symbols' as the psychologists call them, for things disliked. Probably everyone has had the experience of disliking something at first sight, without any reason for doing so. The unconscious mind had made a symbolic connexion there, too.

Now, the question is: Why are certain minority groups disliked by so many people? Obviously, they must be symbolically connected with something very important to many people. Such things would include an interesting life with new opportunities, money, a belief in being kind and just to others, family life and sexual satisfaction, good health, and so on. Toward all these things most people have mixed attitudes: we like them, but we also dislike them. We may be a little afraid of some of these things, or we may wish to rebel against them. But we cannot say so: it is not proper to dislike these important things. So the dislike becomes unconscious, and can be expressed only through a substitute. Minority groups become substitutes for important things in the culture with which they have deep psychological and historical connexions. We cannot publicly admit dislike, or fear, or the wish to revolt against these things. So we apply these attitudes to their substitutes, which are frequently minority groups.

Let us take an example of how this would work out for one type of case. All of us have had the experience once in a while, of disliking a thing that is good for us. Most of us have kicked up our heels at our parents, at our church, at practices that are said to be healthy and so on. That seems to be a natural human way of behaving, if it happens only once in a while. But some people will not admit that they would like to rebel, and these are usually the ones who would most like to do so. They pretend that they adore their parents at all times, that they always have 'pure' feelings about sex and religion and so on. Since this is not *really* the case, they have to give vent to their rebel feelings in some way. And they do so by having prejudices against minority groups.

It is not only a matter of disliking the objects of prejudice; it is also a matter of fear. When people hate something strongly, they are usually also afraid of it. It is of course sensible to hate and fear certain things, but when the danger is imaginary there is something wrong with the person who hates and fears. That is the situation when there is prejudice against minority groups. Most of the fears connected with prejudice are imaginary, even though they seem real enough to those who have them.

1. Take, for example, the fear of large numbers. Many people who are prejudiced against Negroes, or any other minority group, say that there are *so many* Negroes. They are afraid they are going to be 'overwhelmed' or 'dominated' by Negroes. If these people are asked: 'What percentage of the people in this town are Negroes?' they usually give a falsely high number. The real facts are available to them if they wished to know them. But prejudiced people seem to wish to hold on to fears about the large numbers of Negroes.

2. Another fear is that minority groups have too much power. Prejudiced people say that Jews own the big banks and run the government. Even a little investigation will indicate that this is not so. As a matter of fact, in some countries Jews are kept out of the banking business and out of many government posts because of prejudice. There are no Jews in many of the biggest and most powerful industries.

3. There is the fear that members of the minority may be spying for foreign governments. For years before World War II many Americans were afraid of Japanese spies. When the war came, hundreds of Japanese-Americans were arrested because they were suspected of spying. There were many rumours of various kinds of secret work for the Japanese Government. But when it was all investigated, *not a single* Japanese-American was discovered to have been helping the enemy. The Japanese Government knew about Americans' prejudice and hired only white Americans as spies.

It is wise to be afraid of some things. But the fear that goes with prejudice is always harmful, because it is a fear of something imaginary.

We can now bring together the ideas dealt with in this section: Why do people learn prejudice and hold it so strongly that they do not wish to give it up?

1. It is *not* because people naturally dislike any person who looks different, behaves differently, or speaks in a different manner from themselves. In fact, people pay attention to

differences only when they have prejudices first. Then they hold themselves apart and despise or hate the differences of the other people.

2. It is *not* because prejudiced people have had unpleasant experiences with minority groups. Some have, and some have not. Those who have had unpleasant experiences with minority groups have also had unpleasant experiences with other people. They remember some unpleasant experiences because they are *already* prejudiced.

3. In part, people have prejudice because they are frustrated and unhappy in a general way. Depression, unemployment, and low wages are among the main causes of frustration for a country as a whole, but there may be other causes. There are many things which cause fear and anxiety among large numbers of the people. When people do not understand the cause of their frustration, or feel that there is nothing they can do to stop it, they look for a scapegoat. Certain kinds of politicians gain popularity by naming the Negroes, the Jews or some other group as the scapegoat.

4. People are willing to use these groups as *scapegoats* because the groups have become *symbols* of other things they dislike. They cannot openly show their dislike of these other important things, since they would regard that as improper or foolish. Also, they like or admire the other thing at the same time as they dislike it. So they switch all the dislike over to the symbol—the minority group.

5. Fear of imaginary dangers is an important part of prejudice. One of the reasons why prejudiced people dislike or hate minority groups is that they imagine all kinds of fearful things about them.

PREJUDICE AS A WARPING OF THE PERSONALITY

A number of students have sought to explain prejudice as a type of mental disease. Some mental disorders can be traced to inadequacies in personality development, and prejudice is regarded under this theory as resulting from a particular kind of mis-development. Prejudice arising from this source is quite non-deliberate and cannot be eliminated by rational appeal or the application of laws. Most studies of this aspect of prejudice take the form of a comparison between groups of prejudiced and unprejudiced persons, based on a number of questions about personality characteristics and personality development. The items where significant differences appear are then integrated into a clinical picture of the 'prejudiced personality'. One study, by Frenkel-Brunswik, Sanford, and others, at the University of California, is based on a detailed comparison between the personality traits of known anti-Semites and the personality traits of known non-anti-Semites. By comparison, the typical anti-Semite was found to be a compulsive conformist, exhibiting anxiety at the appearance of any social deviation. He appears to be a person with little insight into himself, who projects his own undesired traits on to other people, so that he blames people against whom he is prejudiced for traits which are characteristic of himself. He has a tendency toward stereotyped thinking and is unimaginative. He tends to have unconscious inferiority feelings centring mainly in a feeling of sexual inadequacy. He expresses strong filial and religious devotion, but unconsciously manifests hatred of parents and indifference to moral values. He exhibits an aversion for emotionality but unconsciously has a feeling of inferiority toward it. He is prone to aggressive fantasies.

Another study was conducted in New York City by Jahoda and Ackerman. They secured detailed reports on 50 patients who had expressed anti-Semitism while undergoing psychoanalytic treatment, and tried to determine what role, if any, anti-Semitism played in their unstable mental make-up. It appeared that anti-Semitism resulted from some distortion in personality structure and fulfilled certain needs. Anxiety and lack of security in group membership are among the principal traits of anti-Semites. Fearing attacks on their integrity as individuals, these persons counter-attack against Jews, the handiest object. The anti-Semitic personality type in this study, too, has an overwhelming desire to conform, to appear 'respectable' and to attach itself to dominant organizations, and is characterized by outward submissiveness and inward aggressiveness.

Hartley also made a study of the personality traits of the prejudiced person. Since he found that intolerance toward one minority group is usually accompanied by intolerance toward other minority groups, his description applies to all prejudiced people and not only to anti-Semites. The method of study employed by Hartley was to use a social distance test of the type invented by Bogardus, a test requiring respondents to state whether they thought ethnic groups were similar or dissimilar, a freely written essay on the respondent's 'personality' and a salience test, in which pictures of individuals of different minority groups were shown to the respondents, who were asked to guess their personality and attitudes. Hartley's subjects were students at several colleges. His summary of the characteristics of the intolerant personality follows: 'unwillingness to accept responsibility; acceptance of conventional *mores;* a rejection of serious groups; rejection of political interests; a desire for groups formed for purely social purposes and absorption with pleasure activities; a conscious conflict between play and work; emotionality rather than rationality; extreme egotism; compulsive interest in physical activity, the body and health. He was likely to dislike agitators, radicals, and pessimists. He was relatively uncreative, apparently unable to deal with anxieties except by fleeing from them'.

These studies of prejudice as the expression of a warped personality have certain weaknesses when considered by themselves. But when taken in connexion with other factors underlying prejudice, they add much to our understanding. They probably are most useful in explaining extreme cases of prejudice.

CONCLUSION

On preceding pages we have seen that prejudice is indeed a complex thing. There are background factors and immediate factors which account for its presence in any individual or group of people. This complexity makes it difficult to eliminate prejudice, as action taken against one root does not necessarily affect the other roots. Perhaps we can best summarize our findings by suggesting what kinds of action will contribute toward a reduction of prejudice. These are *not* listed in the order of their importance but simply according to convenience of presentation.

1. One thing would be an intellectual appreciation by prejudiced people of the fact that prejudice harms them, financially and psychologically. Involved in this is a recognition that the gains that seem to come from prejudice are to some extent temporary and illusory. These gains, which can be classified as economic, political, sexual and prestige, sometimes divert the prejudiced person from more

satisfactory and more permanent gains. Prejudiced people need to be shown how they are exploited because of their prejudice.

2. A second activity helpful in diminishing prejudice would be the provision of accurate information about the minority groups against which there is prejudice. This should include facts which break stereotypes, and explanations of the causes that give rise to differences between minority and dominant groups. Facts of this type are learned not only through books, newspapers and speeches, but through personal contact on a friendly and equal basis.

3. One of the most important traditions to combat is that of racism. This can be attacked not only when it is applied to minority groups, but also whenever biological explanations are applied to *any* social phenomenon.

4. Legislation which penalizes discrimination reduces the occasions on which prejudice is made to seem proper and respectable, as well as eliminating some of the worst effects of prejudice. Legislation against discrimination is thus one of the most important means of breaking traditions of prejudice.

5. A tradition on which prejudice is based can be maintained only by being transmitted to children. If the transmission of prejudice through the home and play group can be counteracted by the school and church while the child's mind is still flexible, prejudice cannot long survive. Also, if the public can be led to consider that manifestations of prejudice are shameful, many parents will refrain from displaying their prejudice in front of their children. Where this happens, children are less likely to acquire prejudice.

6. Direct efforts to solve major social problems will not only divert people from prejudice, but will remove some of the frustrations that create a psychological tendency towards prejudice. The most important single step of this type is the provision of economic security.

7. Demonstration that many of the fears about minority groups are imaginary might help to dispel those fears. There is probably a need to inculcate a more thorough understanding of the fact that fear or hatred of a minority group is a mere substitute for real fear or hatred of some other object, towards which people are unwilling to express their true attitude. A general programme of mental hygiene needs to be developed to get people to be honest with themselves.

8. Any effort to develop healthier and saner personalities will diminish prejudice. Such efforts usually require the guidance of psychiatrists.

A concerted programme which included all these activities would, in a generation or two, at least greatly reduce prejudice. But many of these activities are difficult to put into practice. Further scientific research is needed to indicate just how important each of these factors is, and how they can be manipulated most easily. Both research and action aimed at diminishing prejudice are under way in several countries. The future is hopeful if even a small group of people in each country is organized to eradicate this most serious blight on all civilization.

RACE AND PSYCHOLOGY

by
OTTO KLINEBERG

Professor of Psychology
Columbia University, New York, U.S.A.

INTRODUCTION

There is an Article in the Universal Declaration of Human
Rights which reads as follows:

> Everyone is entitled to all the rights and freedoms set forth
> in this Declaration, without distinction of any kind, such
> as race, colour, language, religion, political or other opinion,
> national or social origin, property, birth or other status.

One of the obstacles to the realization of this part of the
Declaration is the belief, widely and stubbornly held, that
some races and peoples are inferior, and that they therefore
do not have the same 'rights' as others. In Nazi Germany this
belief formed part of the official government policy, with the
result that some groups—the Poles, for example—were regarded as fit only to be slave labourers, and others—such as
the Jews—were largely exterminated. The Nazis represent an
extreme, but by no means the only, example of those who
hold the belief that some ethnic groups are superior and
others inferior.

Even scientists have in some cases attempted to support
the argument in favour of a racial hierarchy. It is a curious,
although perhaps understandable fact, however, that those
scientists who have expressed themselves in this manner, have
usually arrived at the conclusion that their own people are
superior to all others. Some of the German scholars, for
example, were convinced that the people of Northern Europe

excelled the rest of mankind in intellectual endowment as well as in character and morality. An Italian anthropologist was equally certain that the peoples of the Mediterranean were responsible for most of the great contributions to our civilization.

These rival claims are historically interesting, but they do not help us to arrive at the truth concerning the relation of race to psychology. We need a more objective method, a more certain technique; one that is not so dependent on purely subjective judgements as to who has superior intellectual endowment, or what is a greater contribution to civilization. We need proof that is scientifically sound; evidence that is scientifically acceptable.

Psychologists have developed a method which, with all its faults, appears to have certain advantages for this purpose —the psychological test. Instead of having to decide whether a German scientific discovery represents a higher intellectual achievement than an Italian painting, the test permits us to present to a group of Germans and Italians a series of problems to solve, and we can then determine who solves them more quickly and more effectively. If some one else doubts our results he may repeat the study, using the same or other subjects, and the same or other tests. If his results agree with ours, our confidence in them is increased; if not, we must suspend judgement until other investigations help to determine who is right.

This is all that would be necessary to settle the question of superior and inferior races if psychological tests were perfect instruments for the measurement of native or innate differences in ability. It is true that they were accepted as such for a long time, at least by some psychologists and educators, as well as by many laymen. We now know, however, that they are far from perfect. The successful solution of the problems presented by the tests depends on many factors—the previous experience and education of the person tested, his degree of familiarity with the subject matter of the test, his motivation or desire to obtain a good score, his emotional state, his *rapport* with the experimenter, his knowledge of the language in which the test is administered, and so forth in addition to the native capacity of the person tested. It is only when such factors are 'held constant' that is to say, when they are in essential respects similar for all subjects tested, that we have the right to conclude that those who obtain higher scores on the test are *innately* superior to those whose scores are lower.

This makes it immediately obvious that we must use great caution in interpreting the results when a psychological test is administered to two different racial or national groups. Living under different conditions, dissimilar in culture, education and point of view, such groups may differ widely in the test results not because they have an unequal heredity but because they have an unequal social environment. The great French psychologist Alfred Binet, who was responsible for developing the first scale of intelligence tests in 1905, was aware of this limitation in the application of his method. He pointed out that his tests could safely be used in order to arrive at inborn differences only if the various individuals or groups tested had had substantially the same opportunities. Many psychologists neglected or forgot Binet's wise counsel, and drew unjustified conclusions from their data.

SOCIAL AND CULTURAL FACTORS

The social and cultural background and experience of the individual may affect his test performance in many ways. His very attitude toward the test itself may play an important role, altogether apart from the specific abilities or information required to solve a specific problem. An extreme example of this phenomenon is to be found in a situation described by the American psychologist S. L. Pressey in his book *Psychology and the Newer Education* (1933). An investigator was testing children in a mountainous region in Kentucky where educational opportunities were at that time rare and inferior. He was using an American revision of the Binet scale, which included the following question: 'If you went to the store and bought six cents worth of candy and gave the clerk 10 cents, what change would you receive?' One boy replied, 'I never had 10 cents and if I had I wouldn't spend it for candy, and anyway candy is what your mother makes'. The examiner tried again. 'If you had taken 10 cows to pasture for your father and six of them strayed away, how many would you have left to drive home?' The boy answered, 'We don't have 10 cows, but if we did and I lost six, I wouldn't dare go home'. The examiner made a final attempt. 'If there were 10 children in a school and six of them were out with measles, how many would there be in school?' The answer came promptly. 'None, because the rest would be afraid of catching it too.' The test situation frequently requires the subject to react to an imaginary situation as if it were real; if he has had no previous experience or training in doing this, he may find it difficult if not impossible to give the examiner the correct answer to the question. This does not necessarily prove that he is incapable of subtracting 6 from 10 in a situation which is meaningful to him in terms of his own interests and needs.

The very act of competing against others in a test situation is itself influenced by the values and attitudes developed in a particular society. Professor S. D. Porteus in *The Psychology of a Primitive People* (1931) tells of an interesting experience in the course of administering psychological tests to a group of Australian aborigines. The tests that he used were made up of a series of mazes, the problem consisting of tracing a pathway through the maze until the exit was successfully reached. Each subject was, of course, expected to perform the task by himself, without any assistance from others. This situation turned out to be a strange one for these Australian natives. They are accustomed to solving their problems together, in groups. 'Not only is every problem in tribal life debated and settled by the council of elders but it is always discussed until a unanimous decision is reached.' The subjects were frequently puzzled by the fact that the examiner would give them no assistance when they experienced some difficulty in solving the problem of the maze. This was particularly true in the case of one group of natives who had recently made the psychologist a 'blood brother' of their own tribe, and they could not understand why he refused to help them. Such an attitude naturally resulted in a great deal of delay, as the subject would pause again and again for approval or assistance from the examiner. It goes without saying that the test scores suffered correspondingly.

A similar indifference to the kind of competition taken for granted in our own society was noted by the present writer in an investigation undertaken among the Yakima, a tribe of American Indians living in the state of Washington on the west coast of the United States. The tests used were a group of performance tests, in which no knowledge of language is necessary, and the task consists of placing pieces of wood of various shape into the appropriate areas of a wooden frame. The scores obtained depend on the speed with which the task is completed and the number of errors made in the process. The subjects are told to put the pieces in their correct places 'as quickly as possible'. These Indian children, however, never hurried. They saw no reason to work quickly. Our culture places a premium on speed, on getting things done in as short a time as possible; the Indian children had not acquired this attitude. They went at their task slowly and deliberately, with none of that scrambling impatience that is so often found among American children. The Indians, as a consequence, took much longer to finish the tests, though they made somewhat fewer errors than the white Americans with whom they were compared.

The writer made an analogous observation among the Dakota (Sioux) Indians in the state of South Dakota. There it is regarded as incorrect to answer a question in the presence of others who do not know the answer: this might be interpreted as showing off, or as bringing shame to others, and is consequently condemned by the whole group. These Indian children also have developed the conviction that it is wrong to reply to a question unless one is absolutely certain of the answer. Psychologists who have given the Binet test to these children have observed that they never guess at the answer: if they are not sure, they keep quiet indefinitely. This, too, reduces their scores to a certain extent, since a guess may succeed, and since credit is given for an answer that is even partly correct.

Another psychologist, Professor S. E. Asch, has noted that the Hopi Indian children of Arizona refuse to compete against one another. One school teacher tried to get them to do so by an ingenious method. She wrote a number of arithmetic problems on the black-board, lined up the children, each one facing one problem, and instructed them to turn around as soon as they had finished. She observed that as each child completed his problem he looked along the line to see how the others were progressing; only when they were all through did they turn around, together. This attitude would also reduce test scores, particularly in the application of group tests, which are administered to a number of persons at the same time.

As a final example in this context may be noted the experience of the anthropologist Margaret Mead with Samoan children, and reported in her *Coming-of-Age in Samoa*. She was administering the Binet test, which has as one of its items the Ball-and-Field problem. A ball is lost in a circular field, and the task of the subject is to trace a pathway along which he would walk in order to find the ball. These Samoan children, instead of tracing the most efficient pathway, used the occasion to make a pretty design. Their aesthetic interest was evidently stronger than their desire to solve the problem presented to them.

These examples all indicate the possibility that the cultural background of the individual may determine his general approach to the test situation in such a manner as markedly to influence his test score. In addition to this general effect, what an individual learns—or does not learn—as the result of his membership in a particular society may also affect his performance in a number of very specific ways. A few concrete examples may help to make this point clearer.

In one portion of a psychological test in wide use in the United States, the National Intelligence Test, the subject is presented with one word followed by five other words; out of these five, he is to underline the two words which represent what the first word in the line must necessarily have. Thus, one line reads: Crowd (closeness, danger, dust, excitement, number). The correct answers are *closeness* and *number,* since only these two are invariable, characteristics of a crowd. Two American psychologists, Fitzgerald and Ludeman, conducted a study of Indians in South Dakota by means of this National Intelligence Test. On this particular item, many of the Indian children made the 'error' of underlining the words *danger* and *dust,* and frequently also *excitement.* For these Indians, a crowd usually does mean danger, dust and excitement. The authors point out that 'there is some indication that the Indian considers answers to be logical and correct due to his environment and because of his experience'.

Another portion of the National Intelligence Test consists in a series of incomplete sentences in which the task of the subject is to supply the missing word. One such sentence reads '. . . should prevail in churches and libraries': the correct answer is of course *silence.* Anyone who has visited an American Negro church in the south of the United States knows, however, that *silence* is neither the rule nor the ideal. The worshippers are expected to respond, to participate actively and audibly; in many of these churches a religious service would be regarded as a failure if silence prevailed. On the basis of their experience, southern Negro children would be less likely than others to answer this question 'correctly'.

One of the clearest and most obvious ways in which social and educational background may influence test results is through its effect on language. Most of the psychological tests in general use, including those devised by Binet, are verbal in character. For the successful solution of the problems presented, not only must the subject have an adequate comprehension of the questions asked; not only must he be able to answer intelligibly once the solution has been reached; he must also be able to manipulate words successfully in order to reach a solution. So important is language facility in many of these tests that psychologists can often reach quite an accurate estimate of a subject's mental level merely by knowing the extent of his vocabulary. This fact early led to the conclusion that these intelligence tests were unfair to the foreign-born, or to others (like the American Indians in the United States, for example) who had inadequate knowledge of the language in which the test was administered. Even if they spoke and used that language with relative ease, they were still handicapped if that were not their native language, or if they were bilingual.

This was demonstrated years ago. Welsh children speaking only English obtained better scores on the Binet scale than those who spoke both Welsh and English. In Belgium, the Walloon children, who spoke only French, were superior to Flemish children who spoke both French and Flemish. In the United States, children of Italian parentage who still spoke Italian in their homes were inferior to those who spoke only English. In Canada, Ontario Indians who spoke nothing but English were superior to those who were bilingual. This result has been found in the case of other groups as well. It is not to be interpreted to mean that bilingualism causes a definite or permanent intellectual inferiority; it more probably is due to the simple fact that the vocabulary of a young child is so limited that if he learns words in two languages, he will not know so many in either one. With the passage of time, the handicap due to bilingualism will be more than compensated by its undoubted advantages.

Another way of approaching the problem of the effect of language is to compare two ethnic groups both with linguistic tests and with performance tests; in the case of the latter, no language whatsoever is used. The task may consist in solving simple geometric problems, or finding a pathway through a maze, or drawing a man, or filling in what is missing in an incomplete picture, etc. When such tests are used on groups of bilingual children they almost invariably do much better than on the usual type of linguistic tests; this has been demonstrated in a number of cases, including many immigrant groups and American Indians in the United States and Canada.

This does not mean that language is the only educational and social factor which enters into test comparisons; the examples cited above indicate the many different ways in which test results may be affected. In the early days of testing, many psychologists believed that the elimination of the handicap due to language was equivalent to eliminating the influence of culture in general. One psychologist, for example, Professor Florence L. Goodenough of the University of Minnesota, devised a performance test consisting in 'Drawing a Man'; scores were determined not by the aesthetic quality of the drawing, but by the inclusion of the largest possible number of essential aspects, by proper attention to bodily proportions, etc. She regarded this test as 'culture-free' that is, independent of the previous background and experience of the subjects, and therefore capable of measuring native differences in intelligence. In 1926, she conducted a study by means of this test, and reported definite differences in the 'intelligence' of various immigrant groups in the United States, as well as between whites and Negroes. In the years that have passed since then, many investigators have made use of this test, and they have been able to demonstrate that, contrary to the earlier view, the results are indeed affected by many aspects of previous experience. Professor Goodenough herself has now recognized this fact, and very honestly and courageously points out her former error. Writing with Dale B. Harris on 'Studies in the psychology of children's drawings' in the *Psychological Bulletin* for September 1950, she expresses the opinion that:

> the search for a culture-free test, whether of intelligence, artistic ability, personal-social characteristics, or any other measurable trait is illusory, and . . . the naïve assumption that the mere freedom from verbal requirements renders a test equally suitable for all groups is no longer tenable.

She goes on to state that her own earlier study reporting differences among the children of immigrants to the United States 'is certainly no exception to the rule' and adds, 'the writer hereby apologizes for it'.

If every test is 'culture-bound' that is to say, affected by the whole complex of previous education, training and experience, can the use of tests give us any information at all about racial differences, or similarities, in intelligence? If we cannot disentangle hereditary from environmental influences in the results, has the testing method any relevance at all to our problem? We can of course legitimately say that racial differences in intelligence cannot be demonstrated by means of the tests, for the reasons given; we can at least say: 'Not proven!' Is that all we can say? Or is there some more positive manner in which the tests may be used to answer the questions we are raising?

Let us look at the problem a little differently. It is true that the test scores obtained by two different groups are due to the interaction of hereditary and environmental factors which cannot be disentangled. The inferiority of one of these groups to the other may then be due to an inferior heredity, or to a poorer environment, or both. Suppose now we make the two environments more similar; equalize them as far as possible. If as the environments become more alike, the difference in test scores tends to disappear; if when the environments are to all practical purposes equalized, the difference in test scores disappears completely; we then have a strong argument in favour of the environmental rather than the hereditary explanation of the observed differences. What do the results show?

EFFECTS OF CHANGES IN THE ENVIRONMENT

If a test which has been found to be useful in establishing differences among children in Paris or New York is administered to children in Mozambique or New Guinea, we could hardly expect the latter groups to do as the former. That should be obvious, though unfortunately it has not always been recognized. The examples given above indicate some, though not all, of the ways in which the different backgrounds of these groups would affect the scores obtained. There are, however, a number of countries in which groups of different ethnic or racial origin live side by side, and it would seem at first sight a simple matter to use such groups as a basis for comparison. If in the United States, for example, we find Americans of Scandinavian, Italian, Chinese, Negro and American Indian origin, all living in an 'American' environment, can we not assume that they all have the same cultural background, the same educational and economic opportunities, so that any differences in test results could with scientific safety be attributed to differences in hereditary capacity?

Unfortunately, this is not the case. The American Indian, for example, usually lives on reservations separate from the surrounding community; he usually goes to different schools; he lives a different life; he speaks English, but frequently not too well; his economic status is on the average inferior. The Negro, although his position in American life has improved markedly in recent years, is still in most cases subject to very definite handicaps; his economic status is also on the average very much below that of the whites; the schools which he attends have certainly been inferior in the past, and to a certain extent are still inferior today; he finds it more difficult to obtain certain types of employment, or to participate fully in American life.

Once that is understood, it should not be surprising to find that American Indians and Negroes, adults as well as children, do on the average obtain test scores inferior to those of whites. But, it must be noted, this is a difference *on the average*. There are many *individual* Negroes who obtain scores higher than those of a great many individual whites. What is more important, there are sometimes whole groups of Negroes who do better on the tests than groups of whites with whom they have been compared.

This important fact first aroused widespread interest at the time of World War I, when over a million recruits in the American Army, including many Negroes, were given psychological tests. The results showed in the first place that Negroes from the south (where educational and economic handicaps were greater) obtained scores which on the average were definitely inferior to those of Negroes from the north (where such handicaps, though they existed, were much less severe). Even more strikingly, the *Negroes* from some of the *northern* states turned out to be superior to the *whites* from some of the *southern* states! This was true in the case of both types of intelligence tests used, one depending on language, the other a performance or non-language test. It began to appear, at least to some psychologists, as if the colour of the skin were less important in determining success with the tests, than the opportunities given to the individual to acquire the needed abilities.

Further evidence began to accumulate. Two American psychologists, Joseph Peterson and Lyle H. Lanier, became aware of the importance of comparing Negroes and whites not only in situations in which their respective environments were very different, but also in situations where their environments were approximately the same. In a study published in *Mental Measurement Monographs,* 1929, they pointed out

that : 'a useful check on the reliability of a given race difference obtained in any locality and under any specific set of
circumstances is to take what seem to be fairly representative
samplings from widely different environments and to compare
the various results as checks upon one another with a view
to determining just which factors persistently yield differences
in favour of one or the other race.'

In line with this reasoning, they administered a number of
psychological tests to white and Negro boys in several cities,
including Nashville (which is in the southern state of Tennessee, and where Negro and white children go to separate
schools), and New York (where there is a unified public school
system for all children). Results showed that in Nashville there
was a marked superiority of the white over the Negro children,
whereas in New York there was no significant difference
between the two racial groups. Here again we have evidence
in favour of the view that, when the environments are similar,
the test results appear to be similar as well.

As an indication of the wide differences in test scores,
within the same racial group, which accompany differences in
the environment, one finds, at one extreme, a group of Negro
children in rural Tennessee obtaining an average Intelligence
Quotient of 58, and, at the other extreme, Negro children in
Los Angeles, California, with an average Intelligence Quotient
of 105. For the white population as a whole, an I.Q. of 100
is to be expected; that is by definition the standard or norm
with which these results are to be compared. In the inferior
environment of rural Tennessee, the Negro score goes far
below this standard; in the more favourable environment of a
big city like Los Angeles, the Negro score reaches and even
exceeds by a small amount the 'normal' Intelligence Quotient.
This is an important result and its implications for so-called
racial differences in innate capacity appear to be obvious.

There is, however, another possible explanation of these
results which must be considered. The Negroes living in New
York, Los Angeles, and other places not in the south of the
United States, have for the most part come from the south.
That is to say, either they themselves or their families
formerly lived in one of the southern states, where there has
always been the greatest concentration of Negroes, and to
which the African slaves were usually brought; for one reason
or another they left their homes and migrated northwards. It
has frequently been suggested that in any such migration there
would be a tendency for people with greater energy and

initiative, with greater potentiality for adaptation to a new environment, and therefore presumably with superior intelligence, to leave; whereas those with inferior intelligence remain behind. This is usually referred to as the hypothesis of *selective migration*. In terms of this hypothesis, Negroes in the north would obtain better scores on intelligence tests, not because they had profited from the opportunities presented by a superior environment, but because they were naturally brighter to start with. They proved it, so the argument runs, by migrating. If selective migration really operates in this way, then the superiority of Negroes in New York over those in Tennessee would prove nothing about the effect of environment.

The argument in favour of selective migration is not very convincing. Why should superior people migrate? Is it not just as reasonable to assume that those who are successful, who have position and status in their own community, who have acquired property, who are leaders, would be more likely to stay where they are? Is it not likely that those who have failed, who have not succeeded in establishing any roots, who cannot find a job, would be most eager to search for greener pastures? Since one can defend with equal logic either side of the argument, it becomes important to obtain objective and definite facts regarding the nature of migration in relation to intelligence.

This was attempted in a series of investigations carried out in 1934 and 1935. The first question studied was: Why do people migrate? A series of personal interviews, either with the migrants themselves or with their families, indicated that a number of factors were responsible. Some of the migrants left for the north in the hope of improving their economic position or obtaining a better education; these were possibly the more intelligent ones. Others, however, migrated because they could not find jobs in the south, or because they were in trouble with the law and were about to be arrested, or because they were invited north by a friend or relative who was already established there; in none of these cases is there any indication that migration was determined by superior intelligence. Apparently migration occurs for a variety of reasons, and no one factor—such as intelligence—can be regarded as exclusively responsible.

A second approach to this problem was more direct. Those who migrated had previously gone to school in the south; they had been in competition, therefore, with others who had not migrated. If the theory of selective migration is sound, then the migrants should reveal in their school marks a definite superiority over the remainder of the population. A careful search through the school records in several southern cities, and a detailed statistical comparison of the school marks obtained by the migrants and non-migrants, respectively, showed no differences between the two groups. Some of the migrants were superior, others inferior, still others about average. Thus, there was no evidence that those who migrated were 'selected' for their superior intellectual ability. Some sort of 'selection' undoubtedly does occur, since not everyone migrates, but it is a 'selection' in which many different factors enter. It may be added that studies of migration of whites from rural communities in the United States to large cities, and of a similar type of migration in Germany, showed the same results. Selective migration cannot be used as a principle of explanation. In the context of our present discussion, that means that the superior results obtained by Negro children in Los Angeles or New York are not to be explained by the exodus of the best genes in southern Negroes, but by the better environmental opportunities provided by the northern cities.

This last conclusion is strengthened by the results of a third approach which was made to this problem. In New York City there are many Negro children who have come from the south; some have arrived only recently, others have lived there for several years. If the environment of New York, which is certainly superior to that from which they have come, exerts a favourable influence on the test scores, such an influence should increase with the number of years the children have lived in New York. This is exactly what the investigation showed. Several different tests were applied to a large number of Negro school children, both boys and girls, and it was found that there was a close relationship between test scores and length of residence in New York. There were many exceptions, of course; this result did not hold for every individual, but the general trend was clear and undeniable. In general, those who had lived there the longest obtained on the average the best scores; those who had arrived only recently from the south, the poorest scores. This result has been obtained also in the case of two other cities, Washington and Philadelphia, where similar investigations were conducted. The conclusion is justified that, as the environments of two different racial groups become more and more alike, the differences in test scores are reduced and tend to disappear completely. There is no indication that a racial factor enters into these results; on the contrary, the evidence points clearly *away* from an explanation in terms of inherited racial differences in intellectual capacity.

In view of the demonstration that there are no culture-free tests, that is to say, that there are no tests which do not to some extent reflect the influence of previous experience, the direct comparison of two racial groups *with previous experience eliminated* would appear to be impossible. One American psychologist, Miss Myrtle B. McGraw, believed that there was a way in which this could be done, namely, by comparing children *before* they had been influenced by the social environment in which they were living. With this in mind she studied white and Negro infants, living in Florida, aged 2 to 11 months, administering to them the 'Baby Tests' developed at Vienna by Hetzer and Wolf under the direction of Professor Charlotte Buehler. Her results, which are reported in *Genetic Psychology Monographs,* 1931, showed the white babies to be on the average definitely superior to the Negro. The author regards this as an indication of the innate inferiority of the Negro children.

For many reasons this conclusion cannot be accepted. Even at this early age the effect of the environment is by no means negligible. The performance of an infant on the Baby Tests is clearly influenced by general physical development, which in turn depends on adequate nourishment. In this respect the Negro children were definitely at a disadvantage. They came from homes that were economically inferior, and they were relatively deficient in weight, which in itself is an indication that they were not as well nourished or as healthy as the white infants with whom they were compared. These facts are not unimportant simply because the children were so young; on the contrary, the relation between physical and mental development would if anything be closer at the beginning of life than later. The very nature of the Baby Tests themselves contributes to this result, since the abilities measured by the tests are as much 'motor' as they are 'social' or 'intellectual'.

This interpretation is supported by a more recent study of Negro and white infants at New Haven, Connecticut, made by a physician, Dr. B. Pasamanick, under the direction of Professor Arnold Gesell, the famous child psychologist of Yale University. The results appeared in the *Journal of Gene-*

tic Psychology in 1946. In this study, the Negro babies showed both a physical and mental development equal to that of the whites; the tests revealed no significant differences between the two groups. The investigator points out that as the result of the careful dietary controls introduced in the United States during the war, the Negro mothers in this group received adequate nourishment both during pregnancy and after the birth of the children, and were able to take much better care of the children. They were in fact not markedly different from the white mothers in this respect. The general economic level of the Negro group had also improved markedly as the result of the opportunities created by the development of defence industries. As a consequence, the Negro infants in this study started out, physically, on essentially equal terms with the whites. As a further consequence, they showed no inferiority or retardation in early psychological development. With equalization of the environment, we see once again, this time in babies in the first year of life, an equalization in test results.

Another ethnic group which has been studied in considerable detail, and with a large variety of tests, is the American Indian. In general, their test scores are the lowest of all groups examined in the United States; their average Intelligence Quotient is in the neighbourhood of 81, instead of the 'normal' 100. This result is not at all surprising, in the light of the 'cultural' factors discussed above. Not only do most American Indians occupy an inferior economic position in comparison with the rest of the American population; in addition, their whole background and previous experience are so different from those of white Americans that it can hardly be expected that they should do equally well on tests that have been designed for use with the latter. Their relative unfamiliarity with the English language frequently constitutes an additional handicap. In one study conducted among the Indians of Ontario, Canada, it was demonstrated that they obtained considerably better results when examined by means of non-language or performance tests than when the usual language tests were used. This result has been duplicated in the case of other American Indian groups as well.

On the more positive side, the late Professor T. R. Garth of the University of Denver, Colorado, tried to discover what would happen if American Indian children were given the opportunity to live in a social environment similar to that of other American children. He therefore made a study of Indian children who had been placed in white foster homes, cared for by white foster parents. His results are reported in the *Psychological Bulletin,* 1935. These Indian foster children obtained an average Intelligence Quotient of 102, which is a striking improvement on the usual American Indian average of 81. This result would show conclusively that when the social environments of the two ethnic groups are similar the test scores are similar also, were it not for the possibility that those Indian children who had been taken into white homes were unusually bright. It may very well be that when white families take Indian children into their homes they attempt to choose as far as possible children of superior intelligence. This is the problem of 'selection' once more, referring in this context not to migration, but to choice of children who will receive exceptional educational opportunities.

Unfortunately we do not know in this case exactly what factors entered into the selection of these Indian children. Professor Garth did his best to eliminate the possibility of explaining the superiority of these foster children on a hereditary basis by testing also the siblings (brothers and sisters) of these children. The siblings had not been taken into white homes; they remained on the 'reservation' in the customary Indian social environment. They obtained a much lower average Intelligence Quotient, namely 87.5. This suggests that it is the environment, and not heredity, which is responsible for the result, since children from the same families reacted so differently under the two sets of environmental conditions. The proof is not complete, however, since even in the same family the inherited capacity of two different children cannot be assumed to be similar in every instance.

More convincing evidence does come, however, from a later study conducted by Professor J. H. Rohrer of the University of Oklahoma, and published in the *Journal of Social Psychology* in 1942. He administered intelligence tests to the Osage Indians, who are exceptional in that they live under social and economic conditions which are similar to those of the whites with whom they were compared. This is mainly due to the fortunate accident that on the land which was given to them by the American Government as a 'reservation' oil was later discovered. As a consequence, the economic position of these Indians improved substantially, and they were able to create for themselves and their families living conditions, and a social and educational environment, far superior to those of most American Indian communities. With these facts in mind, it is illuminating to look at their performance on the intelligence tests; on two different tests, one a non-language test, the second depending on language, they obtained average Intelligence Quotients of 104 and 100 respectively. The apparent inferiority of American Indian children disappeared completely; if anything, they were slightly superior to the white children going to the same schools. There can be no doubt in this case that when American Indian children are given educational opportunities comparable to those of whites, their test results improve correspondingly.

This result can definitely *not* be explained by selection. It was *after* the Osage Indians had been given their land that oil was discovered; they did not choose this particular region. They were merely lucky, and their good fortune gave them opportunities denied to others. This is reflected not only in their superior economic status, but also in their greater success in solving the problems presented by the intelligence tests. The conclusion is justified that, given equal opportunities, American Indian children reveal capacities equal to any others.

The net result of all the research that has been conducted in this field is to the effect that innate racial differences in intelligence have not been demonstrated; that the obtained differences in test results are best explained in terms of the social and educational environment; that as the environmental opportunities of different racial or ethnic groups become more alike, the observed differences in test results also tend to disappear. The evidence is overwhelmingly against the view that race is a factor which determines level of intelligence. As formulated in the Unesco 'Statement on Race': 'It is now generally recognized that the intelligence tests do not in themselves enable us to differentiate safely between what is due to innate capacity and what is the result of environmental influences, training and education. Wherever it has been possible to make allowances for differences in environmental opportunities, the tests have shown essential similarity in mental characteristics among human groups.'

SOME RELATED PROBLEMS

In addition to the question as to the relation of race to the average innate intelligence of the different groups, there are several problems which require further discussion. These problems, too, have been approached from many different viewpoints, and with a frequent disregard for the line of demarcation between fact and fiction. They are the concern not only of the psychologist but often also of the biologist, the anthropologist, the sociologist and the historian. In what follows, they will be examined in the light of the contribution which can be made to their solution through the application of psychological techniques. Reference will be made to other aspects only when this is necessary to understand the purpose and the results of the psychological investigations.

PHYSIQUE AND MENTALITY

There is a widespread popular belief that the physical appearance of an individual gives us a substantial amount of information regarding his psychological characteristics. The assumption is often made, for example, that a high forehead indicates superior intelligence, a receding chin means weakness and lack of determination, thick lips denote sensuality, and so on. Books of fiction are particularly rich in such allusions. Perhaps the most famous literary expression of this is to be found in Shakespeare's *Julius Caesar*:

> Let me have men about me that are fat;
> Sleek-headed men and such as sleep o' nights;
> Yond' Cassius has a lean and hungry look;
> He thinks too much: such men are dangerous.

Races, after all, consist of groups of men who differ from other groups in their inherited physical characteristics. If these are in some manner related to mentality we would have a basis for believing in inherited psychological differences between races. Some anthropologists have expressed themselves to this effect. Professor A. L. Kroeber of the University of California, for example, wrote in 1934: 'There is . . . no sound reason to expect anything else but that races which differ anatomically also differ in some degree physiologically and psychologically.' Professor Franz Boas of Columbia University wrote in the first edition of his famous book *The Mind of Primitive Man* in 1911: 'It does not seem probable that the minds of races which show variations in their anatomical structure should act in exactly the same way. Differences of structure must be accompanied by differences of function, physiological as well as psychological; and, as we found clear evidence of differences in structure between the races, so we must anticipate that differences, in mental characteristics will be found.'

It is significant that this passage does not appear in the later edition (1938) of this book, and it seems highly probable that Boas changed his mind on this point. In any case, neither Kroeber nor Boas thought that this relation between 'structure' and 'function' indicated that some races were psychologically *superior* to others but merely that they were different. Both these anthropologists, and Boas in particular, have been leaders in the attack upon the notion of a racial hierarchy.

Even in the more restricted meaning, however, the view expressed above cannot be regarded as acceptable; the inference from physical to psychological characteristics is very doubtful indeed. There has so far been no scientifically acceptable demonstration of a relationship between anatomical features and traits of personality. To mention one example, an investigation was made into the degree of correspondence or the correlation between the height of the forehead on the one hand, and scores in an intelligence test on the other. The popular view was not substantiated. The students with high foreheads did not turn out to be more intelligent than those whose foreheads were low. A similar result was obtained in the case of many other physical characteristics. There appears to be no difference, either in intelligence or personality, between blondes and brunettes, between people who are tall or short, round-headed or long-headed, who have round or narrow eyes, or thin or thick lips. Even the size of the head appears to have no significant relation to psychological characteristics, except in extreme or abnormal cases. We are safe in concluding that none of the specific anatomical features which have been used in racial classification have any meaning as clues to mentality. Research is continuing in this field, but the emphasis is being placed on the total constitution rather than on single physical traits; there is still no certainty, however, as to whether such a constitutional approach will turn out to be a sound one. In any case, it will have little or no relevance to the problem of race, since all racial groups include a number of different constitutional types. We are justified in concluding that the anatomical or structural differences between racial groups are *not* necessarily accompanied by corresponding psychological differences.

441

THE UPPER LIMITS OF ABILITY

Another way of approaching the problem of racial or ethnic differences in intelligence is to look at the superior rather than at the average members of the group. It has been suggested that the contributions of such a group will depend not so much upon the ability of the majority, as upon its outstanding or exceptional individuals, those who are at the upper end of the distribution scale. Ethnic groups have therefore been compared in terms of the frequency of occurrence of men of 'genius'. This is obviously a difficult and complicated task. There is no simple criterion by which we can recognize the man of genius, and history is filled with examples of men who were accepted as such only long after their death, or conversely, of men who were highly regarded at one time and later passed into oblivion. In addition, the creations of genius build upon the achievements of an earlier day; one cannot expect a Beethoven to emerge suddenly in the Fiji Islands without the background of European music which serves as his heritage, or an Einstein to develop a theory of relativity in Nigeria without a knowledge of what his predecessors in physics have discovered. In terms of their own cultural background, there have undoubtedly been inventors, innovators, 'men of genius' in all societies.

To turn once again to the contributions of psychologists to this problem, it becomes immediately apparent that the upper limits of ability, as measured by intelligence tests, are reached by members of many different ethnic groups. One striking example is furnished by the case of an American Negro girl who at the age of nine years obtained an Intelligence Quotient of 200. This is a very remarkable performance. It means that this nine-year-old girl did as well on the test as the average 18-year-old. There are very few children indeed, out of the many thousands who have been tested all over the world, who have matched this achievement. This particular child is apparently of pure Negro ancestry— there is no record of white admixture on either side of the family. Her background is superior; her mother was formerly a schoolteacher, and her father is a university graduate. The psychologists who described her case in the *Journal of Social Psychology* in 1935, Professors Witty and Jenkins, believe that in her case there was the optimum combination of excellent biological inheritance and a favourable opportunity for development. In any case, it is clear that Negro ancestry is not accompanied by any special limitations on an individual's capacity for achievement. This child was of course exceptional, but there are a great many Negroes to be found at the upper end of the distribution curve. The results of the tests lend no support to the view that Negroes differ from whites in their ability to produce outstanding individuals.

THE EFFECTS OF RACE MIXTURE

The problem of race mixture has important points of contact with the whole problem of the relation between race and psychology. In the minds of most people, the decision as to the relative superiority and inferiority of different racial or ethnic groups would necessarily determine their attitude toward the mixing of races. Those who regard another racial group as inferior usually object to intermixture on the ground that this would reduce the quality of their own, presumably superior, race. In that case, acceptance of the position developed here, namely that there is no indication that some races are biologically inferior to others, would presumably eliminate all serious objections to race mixture.

The problem is, however, somewhat more complicated. The attitude toward ethnic mixture is so bound up with emotional and even religious considerations, that it is not an easy matter to look upon it as a purely scientific issue. In addition, even from the scientific point of view, it has sometimes been argued that race mixture is biologically harmful in itself, and that the question of original superiority or inferiority of the racial groups which enter into the mixture is irrelevant. This is the position taken, for example, by the American geneticist C. B. Davenport, who in a series of publications has described what he regards as the unfortunate consequences of race mixture. A hybrid people, in his view, is disharmonious, badly put together. The mixed population may inherit some characteristics from one parent race, others from the other, and the two sets may not combine properly. The arms and legs of the Negro, for example, are long in proportion to his trunk, whereas those of the whites are relatively short. A racial mixture might result in an individual with the long legs of the Negro and the short arms of the white; he would be at a disadvantage, says Davenport, because he would have to stoop more to pick up a thing on the ground! This does not appear to be such a very great disadvantage. Besides, if the hybrid inherited the short legs of the white and the long arms of the Negro, he could pick things off the ground more easily than either the Negro or white parents. Davenport's views have been challenged by other geneticists, who have pointed out that size is not inherited separately for different organs of the body, and whose careful investigations do not show any greater disharmony among hybrids than among either of the parent races.

This is a matter for the biologists to settle; but it is of concern to the psychologist as well, and the hybrid has been studied by means of psychological tests in the hope of throwing some light on the effects of race mixture. Davenport himself, with his colleague Morris Steggerda, applied psychological tests in Jamaica to groups of whites, blacks (pure Negroes), and browns (white-Negro mixtures). The results showed that the blacks were only slightly inferior to the whites, and that both whites and blacks were definitely superior to the browns. This is interpreted as supporting the view that race mixture has harmful consequences, and that the disharmonies which it produces are to be found in the mental as well as the physical sphere.

Other studies do not, however, support this conclusion. They show either that the hybrids are intermediate in score between whites and Negroes, or—when careful anthropometric measurements are used on a population which is relatively homogeneous from the economic and educational viewpoints—that there is no relationship whatsoever between degree of intermixture and test scores. Taking all the results together, they indicate neither a definite superiority nor an inferiority of the hybrids as compared with parent groups. The effects of race mixture are neither good nor bad in themselves; they depend on the quality of the individuals who have entered into the mixture, and on the manner in which the hybrid is accepted or treated by the community as a whole. This last point becomes clear if we contrast the descriptions given of Chinese-white crosses in Shanghai and Hawaii. The former are described as maladjusted unfortunate individuals who are found mainly in the less savoury occupations of the city; the latter are spoken of as achieving a healthy integration with every aspect of life in Hawaii. It is clearly the attitude towards the hybrids, not any special hybrid biology, which determines their place in the community.

The Unesco Statement on Race summarizes clearly the conclusions which the available information justifies: '. . . no convincing evidence has been adduced that race-mixture of itself produces biologically bad effects. Statements that human hybrids frequently show undesirable traits, both physically and mentally, physical disharmonies and mental degeneracies, are not supported by the facts.'

And further: 'There is no evidence that race mixture as such produces bad results from the biological point of view. The social results of race mixture, whether for good or ill, are to be traced to social factors.'

THE PROBLEM OF RATE OF GROWTH

Another problem in this field to which psychological tests can make a contribution relates to the rate of mental development in individuals of different racial or ethnic origin. It has occasionally been suggested that whereas Negro and white children, for example, might show no differences in intelligence at an early age, the superiority of the whites would be revealed later, owing to the fact that they continue their mental growth for a longer time. Some observers have insisted that 'savage' children develop more quickly and are far more precocious than Europeans; they complete their development at an earlier age and have less capacity for further modification and progress. It has even been suggested that this may be related to certain anatomical and physiological differences, which result in an earlier closure of the sutures of the skull in the so-called inferior races. This would mean that the brain no longer has room to grow, and as a consequence further mental development would be impossible.

This whole notion must now be regarded as one of the many myths which have developed in connexion with the problem of race. Mental growth is certainly not determined by anything so mechanical as the presence or absence of open sutures in the skull. Cases could be cited almost *ad infinitum* of individuals who continue their mental growth throughout life, without being hampered by the fact that their skulls no longer increase in size. In any case, as far as racial groups are concerned, such anatomical and physiological differences have never been demonstrated; on the contrary, careful studies of Negro and white children show no difference in the average age at which the sutures of the skull finally close.

When intelligence tests are administered to children of different ages, there is some slight indication that the difference in test scores between Negro and white children becomes more marked with increasing age. The evidence is conflicting, however; not all the relevant investigations show this phenomenon. When it does occur, it can be explained by factors that have nothing to do with hereditary differences in rate of mental development. It has already been indicated that many groups of Negroes live in an inferior educational and social environment; a number of investigations have revealed that, as children—white as well as Negro—grow up in such an inferior environment, their *relative* mental level (as compared with other children of the same age) tends very definitely to drop. One such study was conducted among canal-boat children in England. These children went to school only occasionally, and their homes were intellectually at a very low level. It was revealed that the average Intelligence Quotient of the very young children, six years old and younger, was fairly high, in the neighbourhood of 90, but that it declined sharply with age; the oldest group, 12 years of age and over, had an Intelligence Quotient of only 60. Similar results were obtained in the case of American children living in the mountains of Kentucky and Virginia. These were *white* children, and no one has as yet suggested that this might be due to a racial factor affecting rate of mental growth. What appears to happen is that an inferior environment exerts a cumulative negative influence as the years go by, and this affects both white and Negro children in the same manner. There is no scientific basis for the belief that races differ in this respect.

DIFFERENCES IN SPECIFIC ABILITIES

Another possibility which must be considered in connexion with racial differences is that even if racial groups obtain similar scores in an over-all test of intelligence, they may perhaps differ in specific capacities, for example, verbal ability, memory, numerical ability, musical skill, and so forth. The results of research in this field do not support such a view. Tests of specific capacities are subject to the same cultural influences as tests of intelligence; they do occasionally suggest differences between ethnic groups, but there is no indication that these are hereditary in character. There is some evidence, for example, that Jewish children are superior to others in tests involving language, and inferior in tests which involve motor or spatial manipulation. Negro children appear to do a little better than whites in tests involving memory. In tests of musical ability, no consistent difference emerges between Negro and white groups.

For specific as well as for 'general' capacity, however, the same conclusion appears to emerge. As the cultural and educational environments become more alike, the observed differences tend to disappear.

DIFFERENCES IN PERSONALITY AND TEMPERAMENT

When we turn from alleged racial differences in intelligence or capacity to a consideration of differences in what might be called non-intellectual traits, we find very much the same situation, and justification for very much the same conclusions. Here, too, we find differences, but they are inconsistent, and they appear to be related very definitely to factors in the social environment rather than to biology.

Some aspects of personality and temperament seem to be related to the physiological activities of the organism, and there is a considerable literature which is concerned with this relationship. It has been pointed out, for example, that the blood pressure of the Chinese is somewhat lower than that of Europeans, and that their basal metabolic rate, which is a measure of the tempo of physiological change in the body, is also lower. Some investigators have seen in this fact an explanation for the apparently more relaxed tempo of activity in China as contrasted with the Western world. A much more probable explanation would be the reverse of this, namely, that when life is busy and hectic, this causes a rise both in blood pressure and basal metabolism. Many other factors may enter—for example, diet, climate, occupation, etc.—which contribute to the final result. The best indication of the correctness of this explanation is to be found in the fact that Chinese living in the United States or Europe show a rise in blood pressure and basal metabolism, and Europeans living in China show a corresponding decrease.

There have been many attempts to study more directly the differences in personality and temperament among racial or ethnic groups. The tests used vary considerably in nature. They include the measurement of such relatively simple phenomena as speed of performance; questionnaires or interviews designed to measure degree of neuroticism; the creation of test situations in which particular forms of behaviour, such as

447

cheating in an examination, for example, may be observed; the presentation of pictures or even ink-blots which the subject interprets, the theory being that in such interpretations he 'projects' certain aspects of his own personality; and so forth. In what follows, a few examples will be given of the methods employed, and the results to which they have led.

As far as speed is concerned, one investigation (mentioned above) indicated that American Indian children living on a reservation reacted more slowly than the white children with whom they were compared. Another group of Indian children, attending a modern school where many of the teachers were white and where the general atmosphere was quite similar to that of a comparable white school, reacted much more quickly. The new environment caused a change in behaviour so as to eliminate what might otherwise appear to be an Indian 'racial' characteristic.

One test, known as the Pressey Cross-Out Test, represents an attempt to measure emotional responses. It consists of a series of words presented to the subject, who crosses out all those words which he regards as *unpleasant* or *wrong,* or as referring to matters about which he *worries,* etc. In one study, this test was given by the authors of the test, Professors S. L. and L. C. Pressey, to a number of different American Indian tribes; the results are reported in the *Journal of Applied Psychology,* 1933. There were marked differences in the results obtained from the various tribes; what is more important for our purposes, the scores appear to reflect the degree to which these various Indian groups had been exposed to the ideals, manners, customs, and attitudes of the whites. The more the Indians had retained their own traditional culture, the less did their 'emotional' responses resemble those given by white subjects, and conversely. The authors conclude that the tests really measure the 'degree of contact with the white man's culture'. This conclusion is clearly in harmony with the point of view being presented here.

The questionnaires that have been designed for the study and recognition of *neurotic tendencies* in individuals may be useful if applied within one cultural group, but they may be very misleading when used for group comparisons. In one investigation, two Chinese psychologists made use of a Chinese translation of one such questionnaire, the Thurstone Neurotic Inventory. When they applied it in China, they found that Chinese students were very much more 'neurotic' than Americans. The investigators accepted this result at its face value, and in some alarm suggested that this was due to the lack of adequate mental hygiene services in Chinese universities! The fact is, however, as other psychologists, both Chinese and American, hastened to point out, that one cannot interpret the results in the same manner in two different national communities. The questions simply do not have the same significance in the two contexts; the mere fact of translation itself alters the meaning of the questions to some extent. The factor of cultural background enters into personality tests just as it does in the case of tests of intelligence; perhaps even more so.

As a final example may be mentioned the application of the Rorschach technique to Chinese living in America. This technique was devised by the late Swiss psychiatrist, Hermann Rorschach, as a means of personality diagnosis. It consists in a series of symmetrical ink-blots which are shown to the subject, who states what he 'sees' in them. It is in wide use in many parts of the world at the present time, and appears to be a useful method. In the particular study to which reference has just been made, it was possible to compare Chinese born in China with those who had lived their whole life in the United States. There were some important differences, but the most striking conclusion that can be drawn from the study is that the American-born Chinese showed marked alterations in personality pattern as compared with those born in China. In the words of the authors, T. M. Abel and F. L. K. Hsu, they were in the process of 'merging into the American way of life'. Once again we see how two groups of different racial origin become more alike as they are exposed to a similar social and cultural environment.

RACE AND ABNORMAL BEHAVIOUR

Still another approach to the problem of race and psychology is represented by a consideration, not of the average, nor even of the superior individuals in a group, but rather of those who exhibit abnormal or deviant behaviour. It has been suggested that the characteristics of races may be discovered through their exaggerations and distortions as well as through their more usual manifestations. In 1921, the British psychologist William McDougall published a book (*Is America Safe for Democracy?*) in which he defended the view that suicide, for example, was an index to racial differences in psychology. One would find, he said, much more suicide among Nordics than among Mediterraneans, because the former are *introvert,* that is to say, they turn their energies and emotions inward, upon themselves. If a situation arose in which a Nordic discovered that his wife was in love with another man, says McDougall, he would be more likely to kill himself, whereas someone of Mediterranean origin, being an *extrovert,* would be more likely to kill his wife or his rival. Some statistics are presented in support of this notion, but they are fragmentary and incomplete, and are not to be taken too seriously. As a matter of fact, a fuller examination of all the available statistics indicates that, among the countries whose populations are regarded as predominantly Nordic or North European in physical type, Sweden and Denmark have suicide rates which are high, whereas Holland and Norway have relatively low rates. Besides, we know that suicide rates vary with religious background (lower for Catholics than Protestants), with residence (higher in the city than in the country), with occupation, socio-economic level, cultural attitudes, etc. —none of which have anything to do directly with racial origin.

As far as crime in general is concerned, studies in the United States have revealed a very striking tendency for immigrants to take over rather quickly the patterns of behaviour characteristic of the native population. Figures show that first-generation Italians and Irish, at least in certain parts of the country, commit homicide somewhat more frequently than the American population as a whole; after one generation in the United States, however, the statistics for this crime become quite similar. Conversely, Irish immigrants are arrested for gambling less frequently than native Americans; after one generation, the figure for gambling rises to approximately the American level. Of course, neither the Irish nor the Italians are 'races' in the strictly anthropological sense; they are national groups which are far from homogeneous in inherited physical type. At the same time it is important to note that we encounter here the same phenomenon to which reference has frequently been made above, namely, that when the social environments of two groups become more alike, their psychological reactions—abnormal as well as normal— also turn out to be similar. It may be added that the situation is substantially the same for the incidence of mental disease as for crime. No racial factor has been discovered to be responsible.

CULTURAL DIFFERENCES

In what has been said here, there is no implication that all ethnic groups are alike in their behaviour. Of course they are not alike; or rather, they are alike in some respects but not in others. A Chinese and a Frenchman, simply as human beings, will have a great deal in common; they will also differ because one has been brought up in one society, the other in another. They will also differ in their physical appearance, their inherited physical type or 'race' but as has been indicated above the differences in 'race' that is to say, the physical and anatomical differences, appear to have nothing to do with the differences in behaviour.

Why, then, are there differences in behaviour or in 'culture' between such groups, if race plays no part? How did such differences arise? This is not an easy question to answer. The causes may lie deep in history; they may be related to the physical environment, to contacts with surrounding peoples, to the inventions and discoveries of individuals, to the problems which had to be solved, and to the ways hit upon, sometimes by accident, for their solution. In most cases, we simply do not know how or why they arose in the first place. For our purposes, the important thing is that they are there. Far from denying them, we must recognize their existence and understand their nature. In understanding them, however, we must beware of two important errors. The first error is to ascribe them to race. The second is to look upon other cultures as inferior to our own, simply because they are different.

The first of these errors has already been discussed at length. The second is also important, however, and leads to attitudes of condescension and feelings of superiority which are not conducive to good human relations. It is an error which has manifested itself all through history, and to which many different peoples have contributed. Perhaps it has been reflected most frequently in the writings of Western man, but it is by no means exclusive to them. There is an account of a Chinese emperor who wrote to the King of England in 1793, stating: 'We possess all things. I set no value on objects strange or ingenious.' But there is no people which possesses 'all things'. The world is richer for the variety of ways of life which have been developed in different nations. No one nation has a monopoly on what is good and true and valuable in human civilization.

At this particular moment it may be of value to look

once more at the contents of a letter written by an Eskimo who could not understand why men hunt one another like seals and steal from people they have never seen or known. He apostrophizes his own country: 'How well it is that you are covered with ice and snow! How well it is that, if in your rocks there is gold and silver, for which others are so greedy, it is covered with so much snow that they cannot get at it. Your unfruitfulness makes us happy and saves us from molestation.' He expresses his surprise that Europeans have not learned better manners from the Eskimo, and—the crowning touch—proposes to send medicine men as missionaries to teach them the advantages of peace. Yes indeed, we can learn something from the ways of life of others.

People differ of course, but not because of their race. As John Stuart Mill, the great English philosopher and economist, expressed it: 'Of all the vulgar modes of escaping from the consideration of the effect of social and moral influences upon the human mind, the most vulgar is that of attributing the diversities of conduct and character to inherent natural differences.'

THE ROLE OF HEREDITY

A final word of caution. Psychologists and other scientists do not hold the view that heredity plays no part whatsoever in the explanation of psychological differences. *Individuals* and *families* are not equally endowed; some are superior in their inheritance of mental capacity, others inferior. No one can safely deny this fact. There is overwhelming evidence in its support. That is quite a different matter, however, from saying that *races* or *ethnic groups* differ in their psychological inheritance. For that there is no evidence. On the contrary, every racial group contains individuals who are well endowed, others who are inferior, and still others in between. As far as we can judge, the range of capacities and the frequency of occurrence of various levels of inherited ability are about the same in all racial groups.

The scientist knows of no relation between race and psychology.

RACE RELATIONS AND MENTAL HEALTH

by
MARIE JAHODA

INTRODUCTION

Modern biological and psychological studies of the differences between races do not support the idea that one is superior to another as far as innate potentialities are concerned. Within each race abilities and achievements cover a range which is much wider than that between the averages of various races. The conscience of the world as it is expressed in religious and other ethical systems recognizes the value of an individual without making this recognition dependent on an individual's intelligence or achievement. Yet, notwithstanding science and ethics, the idea of the fundamental inferiority of some races is slow to die in the minds of many.

Because of this persistent, though unsupported, idea of innate superiority or inferiority, race relations present one of the most critical problems in today's world; they engage the passions of men now, as they have done in the past, to an extraordinary extent. These passions often smoulder under the surface. But periodically they erupt into open violence of a peculiar kind, differing from the violence unleashed in wars between nations and from the violence which an individual may commit against another of his own race. Modern wars are fought by persons who do not know those whom they kill. When they come face to face with a member of the enemy nation it is, as a rule, for one of them the last moment; modern weapons spread anonymous death. Racial violence, on the other hand, is often carried out from man to man with the intention to do bodily harm to a particular individual. But, in contrast to other forms of violence between individuals, the ultimate justification of the act is given in terms of who the victim is rather than what he has done. Physical violence against an individual because of his race often meets with a curious condonement and silent approval from other members of the aggressor's race, even though they themselves do not engage in it. And even where racial violence is officially frowned upon, there are many who admit to a sympathetic understanding of acts designed to humiliate a member of another race, of discrimination against him, or of the expression of wholesale dislike for the members of another race.

Our problem here is to understand both the crude violence and the polite antagonism against groups of different origin, or against an individual, solely for the reason that he is a member of such a group; in other words, to understand the problem of racial prejudice.

It should be clear from the outset that race relations need not inevitably be based on mutual prejudices. In Brazil, Jamaica, Cuba and Hawaii, for example, several races live without signs of overt conflict. Yet it is a comment on the general state of affairs that these few examples should be so well known as exceptions to the rule. In any case, the following discussion deliberately concentrates on race relations where they present a problem; and even more narrowly on one specific aspect of the problem, the meaning of racial antagonism for those who feel it.

This is, of course, by no means the only aspect of the problem. Race relations are a complex matter; they can be studied from many possible points of view. But no biological, political, historical, social or economic explanation can in the long run dispense with some at least tacit assumptions concerning the motives of those who engage in racial hostilities. The development of a comprehensive theory of personality, the foundation of which was laid by Freud, makes it possible to replace these common-sense assumptions by a systematic view of man's motives as they affect the relations between races. The following discussion is largely based on the theoretical statements and empirical findings of psychoanalysis.

The fact is sometimes overlooked that psychoanalysis is not only a therapy for persons suffering from mental and emotional disturbances. It is also a comprehensive general theory of personality which applies to the sick and the healthy mind alike. Using psychoanalysis is, therefore, not tantamount to asserting from the outset that racial antagonism is a symptom of mental disease. As will become clear further on, the question of the relation between racial antagonism and mental health is fairly complex. Psychoanalysis, in its scope unparalleled by any other psychological theory, will here first be used to enlarge our understanding of the motives for racial antagonism; in the light of this it will then become possible to inquire into its relation to mental health.

Psychoanalysis as a theory has, of course, many flaws and presents difficulties for empirical study which occasionally appear insurmountable. What Churchill said about democracy, can well be applied to psychoanalysis too: it is the worst theory ever proposed, except for all the others that have so far been tried. In the face of this handicap it will be necessary to bring to bear on the problem confronting us not only psychoanalytic interpretations but also empirical findings and concepts from other studies in the human sciences, even though much of this work is based on different theoretical premises.

Before embarking on the psychological analysis of the meaning of racial antagonism, a specification of the term 'racial' is necessary. Current biological thought uses the concept race in a statistical sense, meaning that the frequency distribution of genes differs among groups of people who do not freely intermarry [10].[1] Colloquially the term race is broader and purely descriptive; it connotes any group of the population with such common characteristics, interests, appearance, habits, or the like as are physically visible or visible by virtue of their assigned social position.

Since we are here dealing with the antagonism of people against what they perceive to be a race, it must be the colloquial meaning of the term which will be used in the discussion.

THE PSYCHOLOGICAL FUNCTION OF PREJUDICE

There exists a large body of research on the reasons people give for their dislike of various racial groups. If one asks people in the United States of America, for example, to explain their antagonism to Negroes, the odds are that they will use one or more of the following phrases: they are inferior, they are lower class, they are low in intelligence, they force out the whites, they are lazy, sloppy, dirty, immoral, oversexed, troublesome, childish,

---

1. Figures in brackets refer to the bibliography at the end of this chapter.

they have a bad smell and carry diseases. If one inquires why Jews are disliked, one learns that they have all the money, control business, are capitalists but also communists, are clannish but also intrude on other people's affairs, are smart, intellectuals, think themselves better than others, work too hard but never do manual labour, and are noisy, bad-mannered and emotional.

Before one takes this array of statements as data for an interpretation of the state of mind of the person who makes them a question must be faced: are these perhaps realistic descriptions of what the majority of Negroes and Jews are like? The question is crucial. For if these descriptions are broadly speaking accurate, racial antagonism must obviously be interpreted differently than if they are figments of the imagination.

There is every reason to believe that groups which do not intermingle freely with members of other groups, which have traditions of long standing, their own way of bringing up children and special social institutions, norms and values will develop common characteristics. The fact of belonging to a group which is the target of strong racial antagonism must be assumed to be a particularly weighty influence on the behaviour and character of members of that group. It is conceivable that many Negroes are lazy because the assertion of white supremacy denies them the fruit of industriousness; that some crave for sex relations with white women because the white community has established a taboo against such relations, a symbol of their alleged inferiority against which they rebel. Equally, it is possible that centuries of persecution have made some Jews clannish while others try to intrude into the Gentile world in an effort to escape their fate. R. Loewenstein[17] has examined the particular psychological conflict in which Jews find themselves in the western world in his book *Christians and Jews*, and has concluded that while the 'so-called Jewish psychological traits are common to all human beings . . . they may take on a special tinge due to the special situation in which Jews live'.

There is general consensus that such psychological differences between races as may exist express themselves not in each single individual but in different frequencies of qualities in any one race; the variation within each group is assumed to be greater than the variation between groups. The actual frequencies of psychological attributes within any one group are not known. Nothing but a colossal statistical investigation could discover whether Jews and Negroes actually are in their majority what so many members of other groups firmly believe them to be. Even if such a study were made, it would not be possible to infer from it whether such racial characteristics as might emerge are the result of racial inheritance or of the environment in which the majority of these groups find themselves. The most plausible assumption in the light of modern genetic thought is that heredity and environment continuously interact in the most intricate fashion.

In view of this situation it could be argued that it is a small and pardonable mistake if, in the absence of scientific knowledge, those who allege certain psychological characteristics of racial groups do not base their judgement on a view of the entire race but are content to infer it from the qualities of those whom they have personally met. The question, then, of whether racial antagonism is based on fact or fancy, becomes a question of the adequacy of inference. In psychoanalytic terminology, the adequacy of 'reality-testing' by persons with racial antagonism is at stake.

There is a steadily growing body of empirical evidence to show that inadequate reality-testing is characteristic of many who feel hostile to racial out-groups. A drastic demonstration of this was given by Professor Hartley [11] who included in a study of racial antagonism three *non-existent* groups whom he called the Danireans, the Piraneans, and the Wallorians. A large proportion of those who disliked Negroes and Jews also expressed a dislike for these fictitious groups and advocated restrictive measures against them.

The idea that racial antagonism is determined from within rather than by adequate reality-testing is supported by Merton's [20] argument that the very same qualities which are given as reasons for disliking another racial group—the 'out-group' as the sociological jargon terms it—are often highly appreciated when found in a member of the 'in-group'. In comparing current beliefs about Jews and Japanese in the United States with those about Abraham Lincoln he says: 'Did Lincoln work far into the night? This testifies that he was industrious, resolute, perseverant and eager to realize his capacities to the full. Do the out-group Jews or Japanese keep these same hours? This only bears witness to their sweatshop mentality, their ruthless undercutting of American standards, their unfair competitive practices. Is the in-group hero frugal, thrifty and sparing? Then the out-group villain is stingy, miserly and penny-grinding', and so on.

Several psychoanalytically oriented studies have taken the problem a step further by actually investigating the nature of the experience with members of the disliked group. In some cases it was found that the antagonism persisted without any personal contact whatsoever. In others, the antagonistic person maintains that his judgement is based on direct experience with members of the disliked group; yet his descriptions of such contact are bare of all individual characteristics; it is as if he had met not an individual human being but the incorporation of his idea manifesting only the allegedly typical qualities. But perhaps more interesting are those who were able to evaluate the individuals whom they met correctly without letting such an experience interfere with their general judgement of the group. In a study of army veterans by Bettelheim and Janowitz [4] one man was quite explicit on his general dislike for Jews, and then continued: 'There was one Jewish fellow in our outfit whom I liked especially, he wasn't like the ordinary run of Jews, that's why I remember him.' This is a typical case of the notorious remark 'Some of my best friends are Jews, but ...'. Even more remarkable is the case of a man included in another study [1] who when not quite in control of himself would call an opponent 'dirty Jew' and generally complain that Jews take advantage of others. His first contact with Jews occurred in childhood when he established a friendship with a Jewish boy and his family which lasted for years. As an adult he had several Jewish friends. His anti-Semitism existed notwithstanding such friendly contacts. In these cases reality is assigned the place of exception; the rule is established by untested preconceptions. Such ways of thinking in persons of normal intelligence require explanation.

Psychoanalytic theory assumes that inadequacy in reality-testing fulfils a psychological function. The attitude in question meets a need of the individual which he is unable or unwilling to satisfy more rationally. If adequate reality-testing threatens to undermine the functionally significant attitude, it is avoided at all cost. The dislike of out-groups is in such cases based on rationalization, that is to say on socially acceptable pseudo-reasons which serve to disguise the function which the antagonism has for the individual.

This is not to say that every expression of racial hostility based on inadequate reality-testing is necessarily a rationalization of hidden motives. After all, the occasion for reality-testing is not always available. Prejudgements in the light of insufficient evidence are continuously made by everyone, not only with regard to out-groups but also about many other categories of human experience. By and large, the inclination to make generalizations often results in some economy of mental effort. Such prejudgements can, however, harden into rigidly stereotyped thinking which eschews reality-testing even when facts are available. Only where this is the case is it reasonable to search for the psychological function fulfilled by the rigidity of the prejudgement. Racial prejudice, in its narrowest sense, is an attitude towards out-groups which refrains from reality-testing not just because the mental effort is too much but because the attitude itself fulfils a specific irrational function for its bearer.

It follows that racial antagonism based on inadequate reality-testing can be of two kinds: first, there is antagonism based on the assumption that others whose example one follows know what they are talking about. A child will believe that coloured persons are lazy without ever having seen one just as readily as he will believe that the earth rotates round the sun without asking for the evidence, or understanding it when given. Where racial antagonism appears among young children it is, as a rule, of this kind. They take over parental attitudes or those of other adults without giving the matter another thought. This may also occur in adults; it is undesirable, but easily understood.

Second, there is prejudice in the narrower sense of the term. The distinction between rational though misinformed antagonism and irrational prejudice is not easily made. The crucial test for determining the type of antagonism in an individual lies in the reversibility of his views when exposed to facts which are incompatible with them. It is the frequency of irreversible racial antagonism which raises the question of the prejudiced person's mental health.

Yet, it may be objected, there surely is a third type of racial antagonism; it is claimed by most who defend their prejudices. Adequate reality-testing, they argue, has led them to assert the inferiority of certain races. This may be a logical possibility. It is, after all, conceivable that a man may meet a whole series of exploiting Jews or unintelligent Negroes. These qualities exist in all races sufficiently often to make such a chance occurrence possible. Granted this logical possibility, the arguments used in the defence of prejudice give little support to the idea that it is often based on such statistical misfortune in encounters with people belonging to another race. Let us examine some of them.

In the stupendous dilemma in which the Union of South Africa finds itself with regard to its racial problems one might expect the apartheid policy to be based on the assertion of adequate reality-testing. But this is not the case. Gwendolen Carter [6] says in summarizing her sober and extensive studies: 'They [the Nationalists] admit, somewhat reluctantly, that there are more highly developed Africans: ... Beyond this, there is

459

something irrational, but none the less compelling, in the Nationalist attitude toward non-Europeans, an instinctive distaste, even horror at the thought of being associated with them on equal terms.... The most extreme example of this sentiment is bound up with the phrase: "Do you want your daughter to marry a Native?" ... One of the most surprising features of Nationalist arguments is the frequency with which they justify apartheid measures on the ground that they are necessary for preserving an acute colour sense. In other words, it almost seems as if Nationalists fear that close proximity, rather than intensify distaste, may blur the differences felt between Europeans and non-Europeans.... But the fear of a white minority lest it lose its distinctive identity is a sentiment which may override more mellow considerations based on personal experience. European South Africans, and Afrikaners in particular, are often devoted to individual Africans with whom they have an easy and mutually satisfactory relationship, but this is very different from the attitude they hold towards Africans in the mass, who somehow tend to take on the worst features of savagery and unreliability of the most drastic stories about Africans they have ever heard.'

This account of the irrational elements in the idea of white supremacy captures the way and even the language in which some white Southerners in the United States express their antagonism against Negroes.

Since the value of a psychoanalytic interpretation of prejudice is predicated on the assumption of inadequate reality-testing for irrational motives, it becomes important to recognize how such irrationality can be detected. The South African example has illustrated a general characteristic of rationalizations: they betray themselves through leading to logically untenable positions. Why this should happen with such regularity is explained in psychoanalytic theory.

In Freud's view two basic processes govern the working of the mind, the primary and the secondary process. The primary process occurs in the unconscious where drives, wishes and instincts strive for gratification; it follows its own laws and is not bound by logic and reason. The secondary process, however, used in adaptation to reality, is based on logic and reason. Ordinarily, both processes occur in normal persons together or alternately, but in the adult person this happens under conscious control. By and large we know whether we are day-dreaming, that is whether we are engaged in the primary process, or dealing with reality, that is, engaged in the secondary process. Sometimes, however, the two processes play into each other without the individual being aware of the fact. The contamination of the secondary by the primary process leads to logical inconsistencies. When prejudicial attitudes are strongly anchored in the unconscious, where primary processes prevail, efforts to deal with the matter rationally are often not successful. There is method not only in madness, but also in logical flaws.

Examples of such contaminated thought by those who defend or explain their prejudices abound; they come from the most diverse sources and are, of course, as a rule produced in complete ignorance of Freudian theory.

In 1827, Macaulay writing in the *Edinburgh Review*[1] brilliantly attacked an example of such thought, needless to say without psychological explanation. In an essay entitled 'Social and industrial capacities of Negroes', he takes to task a Major Moody who had produced a report to the Colonial Office about the conditions of some Colonial Negroes who had recently been freed from slavery. The Major does not say that he is prejudiced. But Macaulay infers it from the confrontation of excerpts from different parts of the report. Major Moody claims to have discovered 'that there exists between the White and Black races an instinctive and inconquerable aversion, which must forever frustrate all hopes of seeing them unite in one society on equal terms'. He also shows, however, that the main and not infrequent form of union between black women and white men is based on physical desire. As Macaulay points out the fact contradicts the opinion: 'Because the Whites form with the Blacks those illicit unions to which the motive is physical, but do not form those legitimate unions to which the motive is moral, he actually infers that the cause which separates the races is not moral, but physical!'

Scientific thought represents one major effort to avoid the contamination of secondary by primary thought processes. That this goal is not always achieved in research on race questions is illustrated by the following quotation from a comparison of the mental abilities of Jamaican Negroes and white persons: 'The Blacks seem to do better in simple mental arithmetic and with numerical series than the Whites. They also follow better complicated directions for doing things. It seems a plausible hypothesis, for which there is considerable support, that the more complicated a brain, the more numerous its "association fibres", the less satisfactorily it performs the simple numerical problems

---

1. Reprinted in *Critical, historical and miscellaneous essays and poems* [18].

which a calculating machine does so quickly and accurately [1]. These examples demonstrate how irrational motives in prejudice can be discovered by examining the logic of an argument.

To discover the nature of these motives it is useful to examine the content of the beliefs about out-groups. Between the two lists of stereotyped beliefs about Negroes and Jews given before there is a significant difference. While the Negroes are called lazy, dirty and oversexed, that is without control over their instincts, the accusation against the Jews—that they control industry, have all the money, are ambitious and push ahead—go in the opposite direction: they have too much control.

These two types of accusation correspond to two types of neurotic conflict: the conflict which arises when man cannot master his instinctive drives to fit into rationally and socially approved patterns of behaviour; and the conflict which arises when man cannot live up to the aspirations and standards set by his conscience. In psychoanalytic terminology the accusations against the Negro imply that his Id, that is the instinctive part of the human equipment, dominates his Ego, that is the reality-oriented function of man; the accusations against the Jew imply that the Super-ego, that is man's conscience, dominates. In such conflicts, shame over one's untamed nature or guilt over one's unachieved standards impede the functioning of the ego and, in severe cases, the conflict becomes paralysing.

That this parallel between the content of racial stereotypes and the basic conflicts of man is not fortuitous will be demonstrated below. Here, it is worth noting that under the National-Socialist regime in Germany, where the Jews were the major target for out-group hostility, the stereotyped beliefs about them combined what the existence of two target groups on the American scene permits to be separated. In Germany, the Jews symbolized both the conflicts with the id and the conflicts with the super-ego. [2]

Individuals vary, of course, in their selection of what they believe to be attributes of an out-group. There are some whose hostility is unspecific: they experience a diffuse emotional hatred without feeling a need for rationalization. Others accept the entire gamut of concrete accusations levelled against the out-group which is current in their own social group. In between these extreme positions there are persons whose rationalizations appear to fulfil a specific function for their personalities.

---

1. Davenport and Steggerda, quoted in M. F. Ashley Montague, *Man's most dangerous myth: the fallacy of race* [22].
2. For a discussion of this point see Bettelheim and Janowitz [4].

Ample evidence for this latter type was found in a study using detailed case histories of persons under psychoanalytic treatment who also happened to be anti-Semitic [1]. One of these patients, for example, disliked the Jews because they were 'emotional and untamed' but also 'shrewd, capable and industrious'. The life history of this man demonstrated that he, too, was shrewd, capable and industrious, but unable to experience any warm emotion. This inability was actually one of the reasons which made him look for help in psychoanalytic treatment. There it emerged that very early in life this man had found himself in a conflict of loyalty to an overstrict, rigidly joyless mother and a happy-go-lucky father who spent little time at home, perhaps not surprisingly considering the atmosphere of gloomy righteousness which pervaded it. For the little boy the conflict between the parents presented itself as an irreconcilable dichotomy between being happy and being good. Under the dominant influence of his mother he chose the path of goodness and success, trying valiantly to suppress, as she did, all tender and warm feelings. Yet the suppression did not wholly succeed, and as a result he suffered from loneliness and emotional emptiness in an outwardly successful life. The culturally prevalent stereotype to the effect that Jews manage to combine emotions with success was a fearful reminder to that man that he had built his life on a false premiss. By despising the Jews for the combination of qualities that he had denied himself, he tried to defend his own unsatisfactory device of a way of life. Since he could not satisfy his own longing for emotional warmth, the burden was easier to carry if he found emotionality in others despicable. He acted like a thief who joins the crowd shouting 'Stop thief' in an effort to divert attention from himself. For him, it would have made little psychological sense to rationalize his anti-Semitism by accusing the Jews of being capitalists, communists, or bad-mannered. Neither would it have made sense to hate Negroes or Catholics, for the very combination of qualities which he needed to hate in order to make bearable their absence in himself, are not easily attributed to either of these groups.

The psychological mechanisms employed in this case in order to support a precarious equilibrium are what psychoanalytic theory and practice have identified as defence mechanisms; in this case a person's projection of what is wrong in himself on an outsider and denial of inner conflict. It is of great importance to realize that defence mechanisms are exactly what the name implies: an effort to safeguard the ego from inner conflict. It is reasonable to assume that everyone, prejudiced and unprejudiced, healthy or sick, uses defence mechanisms in the effort to establish a workable psychic equilibrium. Their existence is a sign of striving for health rather than a symptom of disease. Many authors [1] have pointed to the positive function which defence of this kind fulfils. It is well known that the function of an external enemy in producing group cohesion is so important that if one does not exist he is often invented. The point is documented in much recent history.

Sofer [24], discussing the racial situation in Uganda, points out that: 'irrational, incorrect, and distorted views ... serve positive functions for the individual and his group. In this situation, for instance, there is no doubt that they help to assuage for the Europeans' uneasiness about the fact that while the rationale of their presence in the country is their contribution to African advancement, great disparities exist between the advantages which they and Africans presently enjoy.'

Defence mechanisms must thus be judged in relation to the degree to which they succeed in banishing disabling inner conflict. In the case of race prejudice, this goal is not often achieved. Particularly where different racial groups live and work within one society, as is the case in Africa and in the United States, the conflicts which defence mechanisms are meant to eliminate are often, in fact, intensified by contact with the rejected group. The man whose life history was given above tried—unconsciously, to be sure—to save himself by hating the Jews. But once he had fixed his defensive needs on the Jews, the very sight of them became a reminder of what was wrong in himself, thus aggravating the problem that he tried to deny. Prejudice often becomes an obsession with those who use it in a futile effort to restore their crippled self. Even though it is meant to achieve emotional, and often also material gain, it hurts the prejudiced person himself as well as the victim whose very existence keeps the conflict alive.

The hatred of the out-group serves the function of supporting the person who entertains it. However spurious the relief that comes from this type of defence, it is a vitally important function in the psychic economy of the insecure person. It is easier to reject others than it is to reject oneself. Yet, what one rejects in others often reveals and intensifies what is wrong in oneself.

Since it is often reality which threatens to destroy the defensive bulwark of the prejudiced person, it is reality which he tries to

1. See, for example, Ernst Kris [15].

manipulate so that it will better fit his psychological needs. Thus, prejudiced persons use whatever social power they have at their disposal to create conditions which compel the target group to become as the stereotype prescribes. A vicious circle is set in motion, an example of what Merton [20] has called the 'self-fulfilling prophecy'. In some southern parts of the United States, for example, the Negroes are rejected because they are lower class and uneducated. Because they are so regarded, opportunities for advancement and better education are denied to them; as a consequence many Southern Negroes do indeed suffer from low status and low educational level, thus apparently justifying the original act of discrimination. Much the same could be said about the apartheid policies in South Africa: while the native populations are rejected because of their different culture, the means of reducing the difference are nevertheless eschewed. Instead, all policies are designed to intensify the difference. It may well be, however, that South Africa is about to demonstrate that such manipulation of reality does not constitute an effective support for the psychological defence mechanisms at play. For the inexorable fact of the South African economy is that it depends largely on African labour, thus requiring contact between the races which apartheid aims to destroy.

Let us recapitulate the argument presented so far. A psycho-analytic interpretation of prejudice is legitimate only if there is reason to believe that the antagonism against another race is not based on rational judgement of this group's actual qualities. Since scientific knowledge about the distribution of psychological attributes in various races does not exist, the question arises whether the attributes concerned are rationally inferred by persons who feel racial antagonism. There is evidence from several sources to support the idea that many prejudiced persons employ inadequate reality-testing. This evidence derives in particular from examination of the contact they have had with members of the group they are judging. Granted that inadequate reality-testing need not imply hidden motives for children or naïve adults, prejudice can be defined as an attitude toward an out-group which is irreversible by evidence to the contrary and which fulfils a psychological function for the bearer of the attitude. The discovery of the irrational component in prejudice is made possible because prejudiced persons use rationalizations; or, in other words, the irrational element in their thinking about race which follows primary process lines is so strong that it interferes with thinking which aims at relying on the secondary process. An examination of the content of beliefs about other groups demonstrates the nature of the unconscious motivation; it is a defence against inner weakness. The use of such defence mechanisms is universal; the demonstration of their role in the thinking of prejudiced persons does not stamp them as psychologically sick. What is more, the social position of many groups who are the target of prejudice often provides a kernel of reality in the otherwise unrealistic perception of the group by the prejudiced person.

THE PSYCHO-GENETIC ORIGIN OF PREJUDICE

Now the question arises: Why are these people so vulnerable? What is it that requires such intense though spurious defence effort? The fact that racial prejudice is historically and geographically so widespread suggests that it represents an effort to deal with a basic and probably universal human conflict.

A first clue to the nature of this conflict stems from studies concerned with the relation between prejudice and social status. Contrary to popular belief, there is no clear-cut relationship between racial antagonism and a person's current status in life. Prejudiced persons are found among the rich and the poor as well as in the middle of the social hierarchy. The relationship becomes strong, however, when a person's social mobility is considered; that is when his feelings of tolerance or intolerance for other groups are related to his movements up or down the social ladder. In the study of army veterans mentioned before [4] it was found that the highest frequency of intolerance against racial out-groups occurred among those who were socially in a worse position at the time of the study than they had been before the war. What further strengthens the clue to the nature of the conflict is the fact that among a small group of veterans who had undergone a rapid *upward* social mobility, intolerance was also very high, higher than among the stable group or among those who had only gradually improved their lot. Obviously, a certain amount of frustration helps to bring to the fore the conflict, whatever it is, to which racial antagonism is an attempted solution. But the frustration is not solely the consequence of economic deprivation, otherwise the frequency of the phenomenon when status radically improves would remain unexplained.

What is, then, the psychological experience common to upward and downward social mobility? There is much evidence to suggest that any sudden change in external conditions of life brings the individual face to face with the question of his own identity. In the life-long effort of every human being to define himself to himself, to acquire, maintain and develop an identity as a person, the external circumstances of his existence are used as props. His name, home, occupation, habits and established relations with others serve to define who he is. Any sudden change in these conditions requiring changes in his habitual responses to the world and producing changes in the way other people respond to him brings to the fore anxieties about himself. The psychological experience of refugees—surprisingly enough an apparently untouched field of research—or even the experience of a casual traveller who finds himself an unknown person alone in an unknown culture may bear out this general statement. Some people, to be sure, can discover new aspects of their own identity through some such experience without feeling deeply threatened by it. But most of us would rather not do without the props which our social existence offers us in maintaining and developing our identity and inner security.

The idea that uncertainty about oneself is at the root of racial antagonism is strengthened by evidence from studies contained in the book *The authoritarian personality* [2]. These studies set out to discover the type of personality which is most often given to intense feelings of racial prejudice. The style of life of the authoritarian personality was found to be one which needed particularly strong external props in order to maintain a semblance of inner security. Conformity to conventional values is an essential aspect of the authoritarian person who 'seems to need external support—whether this be offered by authorities or by public opinion—in order to find some assurance concerning what is right and what is wrong. . . . External criteria, especially social status, are the yardsticks by which he [the authoritarian person] tends to appraise people in general and the ground on which he either admires and accepts, or rejects them. Such values form the basis of a hierarchical order in which the powerful are seen at the top and the weak at the bottom. This may well be an over-all tendency in modern culture which, however, he [the authoritarian person] displays to an exaggerated degree' [2].

The basic personality features found to exist in those given to strong racial antagonism are: a rigid adherence to conventional values; a submissive, uncritical attitude toward idealized authorities of the in-group; a tendency to condemn, reject and punish people who violate conventional values; an opposition to the imaginative and tender approach to life; a disposition to

467

think in rigid categories, a preoccupation with the theme of dominance and submission, a generalized cynicism about human nature; a tendency to project outwards unconscious emotional impulses; and an exaggerated concern with the sexual behaviour of others.

The manner in which this personality profile of the prejudiced person was discovered is fully described in *The authoritarian personality*. This is not the place to enter into a discussion of the techniques employed in the studies. But it is of some interest to note that Jean-Paul Sartre [23] in his *Portrait of the anti-Semite*, arrived intuitively at much the same picture as these empirical studies.

To be able to achieve some sense of their own identity authoritarian persons need a black-and-white perception of the world. (The metaphorical expression 'black-and-white' fits in all too well with the fact that those groups which are most frequently the target of prejudice have a black skin.) And with this need for clear-cut and sharp categories goes, inevitably, a disinclination to look closely at their own or other people's motives. There must be in them a dim fear that a full understanding of people would blur the sharp divisions which serve to tell them where they belong and who they are.

Psychoanalytic theory and practice support the idea of the universality of this conflict. It manifests itself first and forcefully in early childhood when the infant's initial complete dependence on parental love and care is gradually replaced by the development of a super-ego. This is achieved through a process of identification with one or both parents. It is inherent in the social function of parenthood that this identification should be fraught with difficulties, at least in the western industrialized civilization. It is not only rejecting or emotionally-exploiting parents who make the process hard to achieve. Every parent has to control, reject and punish in order to make a child fit to meet the standards of the society into which he was born. As the child's personality develops, these inevitable constraints and controls compel him to appraise himself. And when impulsive behaviour meets with adult restrictions doubts arise in the child's mind about his own worth or that of his parents or about both. Before self-control, internal standards and the ability to understand the need for rules and regulations is acquired, punishment and disapproval can make the child feel that he is unwanted and unloved.

The lack of clarity of the self-image, inevitable for all at one stage of development, may remain a basic feature of a personality. Case histories of persons who feel strong racial antagonism show that their identity conflict was particularly severe. In many cases this is a consequence of a fundamental disunity between the parents or of disturbed relations between the child and one or both of his parents. Even where no obvious failure in human relations occurs, the psychological hazards of early life are great on account of the child's inability to interpret events at that stage rationally.

In any case, to the extent that the child retains his early insecurity—and, to some extent, probably everybody does—he experiences the apparently clear-cut identity of someone else as evidence of his personal failure which is deeply resented. If he can make himself believe that the other's seemingly clear identity connotes inferiority then the personal confusion is easier to bear. At least he is not a Negro, or not a Jew, however uncertain he is about the more positive aspects of his identity. Being visibly different is, then, an out-group attribute which on one level threatens the insecure personality because it confers apparently a clear identity on the out-group; on another level it is a help because it permits the in-group member to find at least one aspect of his own identity, albeit a negative one. What this amounts to is that for a person without a stable sense of identity a person who is different is the object of both attraction and repulsion. The weaker an individual, the stronger is the threat he experiences when confronted with difference and the stronger is the emotional response. Fundamentally, then, the antagonism against the out-group is the concomitant of self-rejection.

Bronowski [5] in his essay on violence, recognizes the ubiquity of the identity conflict when he interprets individual violence as a result of the wish to demonstrate that one is a man 'in a world in which the sense of being unneeded walks with us like a shadow'.

Members of socially under-privileged out-groups can, of course, also experience this same conflict of identity. The way in which they use the existence of the dominant group in dealing with this conflict is, however, somewhat different, though equally irrational. Considering the frequency and degree of humiliation to which target-groups of prejudice are often exposed, retaliation would appear to be a rational response. But unless the brutality against the out-group approaches that of the Hitler regime and makes psychological adjustment impossible, many Jews and many coloured people seem to try to placate their enemies. The reason for this is that, within a given power structure of society, their self-rejection cannot be alleviated by rejecting the dominant white or gentile group. No safety can be derived from hating the all too obviously powerful group. Consequently, and with the peculiar logic of psychological events, there exists colour prejudice among Negroes, anti-Semitism among Jews. What those who experience this cannot accept in their own individual personalities is attributed to the group into which they were born. In order to acquire some self-respect they adopt the language of their enemies whose standards and values they imitate by rejecting the group to which they belong. Needless to say their defensive effort is even less successful than that of people belonging to the dominant group.

In this unending effort to come to terms with oneself, the establishment of one's sexual identity plays a crucial part. Unresolved conflicts in that area may well be the most frequent source of anxiety and insecurity in adulthood. When things go well, the child emerges at the age of five or six years from a turbulent period more or less unscathed, having developed a strong identification with the parent of his own sex and the confidence to love, in full recognition of the difference, the parent of the other sex. The domination of either parent and the submission of the other—a very frequent pattern in family life—may be one source of difficulties in forming a solid identification and thus the nucleus for a stable sense of identity. The domination of the father may terrify a small boy or so impress a small girl that each identifies with the person of the other sex. In this manner the psychological basis for later homosexuality may be established. But even where this complete confusion of the sexual roles is avoided or overcome, the vicissitudes of the process of acquiring one's sexual identity are so complex that many adults bear the mark of their early struggle in that area as an anxiety over their male or female adequacy.

It is thus not surprising that racial antagonism, an outcome of an unstable sense of identity, has generally a pronounced sexual component. In South Africa the taboo against inter-racial sex relations has been incorporated into the Immorality Act which makes even a casual sexual relation between persons of different races a crime. The agonies that follow from breaking this law are the theme of Paton's sensitive and beautiful novel *Too late the phalarope*. Intermarriage is against the law of the land not only in South Africa but also in some parts of the United States. The very fact that such laws need to be established testifies to the existence of strong tendencies to break them; the fact that in the United States only about 20 per cent of the

Negro population, according to anthropological estimates, are of unmixed African origin, testifies to the frequency with which the taboo is broken.

Indeed, wherever the taboo against inter-racial sex relations is established, its breaking can be taken for granted—which demonstrates that the inner conflict of the powerful white group is only intensified by it.

Philip Mason [19] in his history of Rhodesia describes with much psychological insight the probable cause of events that followed the arrival of the first Europeans: 'The invaders brought at first few women of their own and they were not all saints or monks; what sometimes took place between those first Europeans and the women of the hunting tribes they made servants, or of the slaves they imported, must usually have been a matter of physical gratification and no more, with no element at all of shared life or common endeavour; the experience was so far from satisfying to a people of conscience, whose only book was often the Bible, that they came to look on it with horror and repulsion and as soon as women of their own kind were in the country the community began a determined effort to keep themselves pure in race and in their way of life. 'And somewhat later: 'It may be stated crudely, heavily over-simplified, using old-fashioned words. There was no love but only lust between that first official of the Netherlands East Indies Company and that first Hottentot servant-girl. Therefore he regarded what had taken place with remorse and repulsion and tried to forget it . . . to make sure that there were no marriages, there must be no danger of the common interests, the shared misfortunes, that make love instead of lust. The gap between his mind and the woman's had bred his horror; because of his horror the gap must be widened and fortified, so that he should not cross it again, so that he should never be reminded of *what he disliked in himself* [italics supplied]. The horror had grown from lust instead of love; because of his horror, love, which might be lasting, had grown more horrible than lust. So marriage between black and white became more shocking than a casual encounter, provided, that is, that the casual encounter was between white man and black woman.'

In psychoanalytic terminology, the gratification of the id was intolerable to the super-ego. These early settlers found themselves in a conflict between their Protestant consciences and their desires. Their sense of identity was based on standards of morality which they could not follow in the extraordinary circumstances in which they found themselves. In an effort to assuage the conflict they felt impelled to regard their experiences with coloured women as alien to their egos, and did what they could to eradicate opportunities which might allow their own 'lower selves' to break through into behaviour unacceptable to them.

Mason's last point about the limitation of the sexual taboo to a relation between white woman and black man, while casual encounters between white man and black woman are often occasions for boasting, for example, in the Southern parts of the United States, once again highlights the deep irrationality of the white supremacy idea. The racial purity is affected, one way or the other. But the myth which has developed about the Negro's extraordinary sexual prowess, perhaps a projection of the white man's fear of his own sexual inadequacy, creates anxiety that the white woman might experience greater satisfaction with a Negro man. This final blow to the white man's pride in his masculinity had to be avoided at all costs. It was avoided at the cost of all the Negroes who have ever been lynched under the faintest suspicion of intercourse with a white woman.

Several authors have remarked on the lack of evidence for the widespread belief that the genitals of Negro males are larger than those of white males. Dollard, [1] for example, who came across this belief comments on it as follows: 'One thing seems certain—that the actual differences between Negro and white genitalia cannot be as great as they seem to be to the whites; it is a question of the psychological size being greater than any actual difference could be ... the notion is heavily functional in reference to the supposed dangers of sexual contacts of Negroes with white women.'

In summary, then, prejudice seems to be embodied in a particular type of personality, the authoritarian personality. This type bears the mark of an unresolved conflict, the conflict about one's identity, to an extraordinary extent. While this conflict is probably universal, prejudiced persons use it in a peculiar way. Sexual identity is a major component in the conflict; hence the preoccupation with sexual matters in race relations among prejudiced persons.

Psychoanalytic theory maintains that the first sexual desire of the child is directed toward his parent. Fulfilment of this desire is forbidden and consequently becomes strongly repressed. But the repression is incomplete, and the attraction of the for-

---

1. Quoted in M. F. Ashley Montague, *Man's most dangerous myth: the fallacy of race* [22].

bidden fruit stems from this fact. At the same time, the secret belief that out-group members have a clearer identity leads to the assumption that they are sexually superior to oneself, an assumption which creates profound jealousies and intensifies one's feeling of insecurity. The by now familiar mechanism of hating in others what is wrong in oneself leads to the intense emotion of horror, disgust and fascination about inter-racial sex relations.

PREJUDICE AND MENTAL HEALTH

It should be clear from what has been said so far, that recognition of the irrational component in prejudice and of the fact that it often has its roots in a psychological conflict which remained unresolved in childhood is not yet equivalent to saying that prejudice is a type of mental illness. The idea that healthy persons are altogether rational belongs to pre-psychoanalytic thought and can no longer be maintained.

Yet there is sufficient indication of severe disturbance in the picture we have drawn of the prejudiced personality to warrant further empirical inquiry. The most direct way of searching for evidence of the relation between prejudice and mental illness consists in exploring its presence or absence in mental patients. One such investigation by Maria Hertz Levinson[1] was conducted in a state institution for the diagnosis and treatment of psychiatric disorders, an institution to which, however, violent cases and cases for permanent commitment were not admitted. She found that the average degree of prejudice in these patients was, if anything, slightly lower than in the population outside. Furthermore, differences in the severity of the psychiatric disorder were not related to the intensity of the prejudice ;... 'one is likely to find people with more or less severe psychological disturbances in the high, low, and middle quartiles [i.e., measures of prejudice] although we cannot say in what proportion'. Again, with regard to the ordinary psychiatric classifications, no relationship was discovered between any one of them and the absence or presence of prejudice. There is some evidence that these negative results are not due to any peculiarity in the institution in which the study was conducted.[2] However, general

---

1. This study by Maria Hertz Levinson is reported in *The authoritarian personality* [2].
2. See, for example, A. R. Jensen [14].

psychiatric classifications leave much to be desired. A study of the personality dynamics revealed certain differences between the highly prejudiced and the unprejudiced patients. The former, Maria Levinson concludes, 'usually displayed very little awareness of their own feelings and psychological problems. What is more, they tended to resist psychological explanations and to suppress emotions.... The most common symptoms in both men and women were vague anxiety or physical signs of anxiety and rage. The more disturbed patients suffered from feelings of depersonalization, lack of interest, and depressed affect of a more schizoid type. Very many [highly prejudiced] men and women came to the Clinic with somatic complaints...'.[1]

In contrast, this is what the study has to say about the unprejudiced patients. 'They were much more familiar with themselves, more aware and accepting of emotional experiences and problems... [their complaints] very rarely consisted of vague anxiety or physical symptoms alone... the most common single symptom... was neurotic depression with feelings of inadequacy. Most of these patients had inhibitions in some area—sexual, work, social—and felt uneasy in group situations.'

These statements about the functioning of the prejudiced personality in mental illness are much in line with the function of prejudice in general. The tendency to look away from one's own psychological problems and to project feelings of discomfort on hard and fast objects—as, for example, on somatic symptoms—is what one would expect from a prejudiced person. The study of anti-Semitic patients in psychoanalytic treatment mentioned before [1] confirms Levinson's findings. There, the authors say: 'An examination of the clinical diagnoses of these psychoanalytic patients reveals that anti-Semitism is *not* the concomitant of any one clinical category of personality disturbance. The diagnoses cover a wide range of disturbances. Anti-Semitic reactions are found in psychoneurotics of various types; in character disorders..., in psychopathic and psychotic personalities as well as in others with less precisely defined disturbances.' And later on: 'In this broad range of diagnoses and vague symptoms, however, one type of disturbance becomes conspicuous through its absence. None of the cases manifested a genuine, deep *depression*.' This last statement is indirectly corroborated by the finding, quoted before, that it was the unprejudiced patients who manifested depressive tendencies.

The relation between prejudice and mental health has been

---

1. Maria Hertz Levinson, op. cit.

studied also in a less direct manner. On the assumption that psychological disturbances are even more frequent than the large population in mental hospitals would lead one to suspect, a whole set of tests and measures has been devised to diagnose the degree and kind of psychological disturbance in the so-called 'normal' population. Outstanding among these devices is the Minnesota Multiphasic Personality Inventory, generally referred to as MMPI, which has been used by several investigators in conjunction with measures of prejudice to establish the relationship, if any, between them [12].

The MMPI elicits information about several fairly distinct psychological patterns, each of which corresponds to the symptoms and problems of a clinical category of mental disease. For example, there is one group of inventory items which measures the degree of abnormal concern with bodily functions; this corresponds to hypochondriasis. Another group is composed of items related to the clinical category of depression; a high score on these items 'indicates poor morale (of the emotional type) with a feeling of uselessness and inability to assume the normal degree of optimism regarding the future'. Another group provides indications of suspiciousness, oversensitivity and delusions of persecution, corresponding to paranoia. And so on. A summary of various independent studies using these measures to establish the relationship between psychological disturbance and prejudice among American high school and college students emerges with clear-cut results: prejudice was found to be positively correlated with personality features corresponding to hypochondriasis, depression, psychopathic deviations, schizophrenia and hypomania; it was found to correlate negatively with defensiveness and hysteria.

Thus, from two different types of evidence—studies of mental patients on the one hand, and studies of psychological disturbances among 'normal' persons on the other—we arrive at apparently totally opposite conclusions. Not only do psychological disturbances hang together with prejudice in one case but not in the other; what confounds confusion is that one particular clinical entity which was singled out before for comment, depression, is according to one type of evidence present in unprejudiced patients, according to the other, present in prejudiced people.

What is one to conclude from this? Is there or is there not a relationship between prejudice and mental health? Or do we have to admit defeat by stating that at the present level of knowledge and methodology the question is unanswerable?

I believe an answer, and not a defeatist one, can be gleaned from the material so far presented. It requires, however, a digression from the matter of prejudice. For the crux of the confusion is unquestionably the concept of mental health [13].

What do we mean by mental health? Most frequently and most unfortunately the term mental health is used, in euphemistic fashion, as a synonym for mental disease. And somewhat less frequently, but still unfortunately, it is equated with the absence of mental disease. Ultimately, of course, one can define mental health however one likes. But a concept becomes scientifically useful only if it helps to solve intellectual or practical problems. From that point of view to regard mental health as the absence of mental disease is not particularly helpful, for two reasons. First, mental disease is itself as yet a vague and unclear notion; not much is gained by trying to link one vague term to another only just slightly less vague. Second, and this is even more important, the absence of mental disease leaves no scope for making more subtle differentiations between the enormous variety of persons for whom the statement that they are free of mental disease can be made with confidence.

Many psychologists and psychiatrists have, therefore, found it useful to think of mental health as a positive attribute of individuals; its presence in varying degrees helps to introduce these more subtle differentiations. A survey of the many ideas in this field yields, broadly speaking, six major categories of human functioning which present promising approaches to the concept of mental health.

First, there is the idea that mental health is expressed in an individual's attitude toward himself. If he is aware of himself, has a correct image of who he is, can accept himself or has developed a stable sense of identity, he is regarded as mentally healthy.

Second, an individual's style and degree of development and actualization of his potential is regarded as indicative of mental health.

Third, various proposals emphasize the unity of personality, that is, the integration of all psychic functions as the essence of mental health.

Fourth, some authors single out the notion of autonomy; that is, a person's relative independence from social pressures and his ability to act independently under inner regulation.

Fifth, various proposals suggest that mental health is indicated in the adequacy of an individual's perception of reality.

Sixth, mental health is regarded as the ability to master one's environment, which comprises matters such as adequacy to love, work, and play; the ability to meet situational requirements, problem-solving, and the like.

None of these concepts is, of course, free from value connotations. Their suitability will undoubtedly vary from one culture to another. Even within any one culture there is as yet not enough knowledge about the usefulness of these various concepts in predicting behaviour to enable one to choose among them. What is more, it seems quite possible that several of these various concepts are quite closely related to each other.

Yet, notwithstanding these limitations, singly and jointly these efforts to give meaning to the vague notion of positive mental health represent a considerable step forward in thinking about the subject. One implication of having formulated these concepts is the fact that the statement, 'a person is not mentally sick but neither is he mentally healthy', now makes sense. In other words, the opposite of mental disease is absence of mental disease; the opposite of mental health absence of mental health. The extent to which the absence of mental health coincides with, overlaps or is independent of mental disease, and vice versa, is as yet a moot question. But no longer is this question one of speculation only. It can be empirically approached by studying the extent to which one or more of these criteria of mental health are present in persons who are definitely mentally sick. Indeed, some of the clinical observations quoted before clearly suggest that self-awareness, for example, can be present in some mental patients and absent in others.

I have discussed elsewhere further implications of these ways of thinking about mental health, and the problem of converting these ideas into some form of quantification [13]. Here it remains to be demonstrated that this approach to mental health helps to clarify the confusing data presented before about the relation of prejudice to mental health.

If mental health has positive meaning, that is if it is regarded not just as the absence of mental disease, the major apparent contradictions in the data disappear.

The evidence from studies with persons who are sufficiently sick to be under psychiatric care suggests that there is no reason to assume that prejudice and mental illness are related to each other. Mental patients, like the normal population, do or do not entertain prejudiced attitudes; being more or less severely mentally ill is not related to being more or less prejudiced.

The evidence from studies with high school and college students I take to mean that prejudice is related to the absence of positive mental health. There are several reasons for this interpretation. First, the population with which these studies were conducted consisted of young people sufficiently free from mental illness to be able to attend schools or colleges. Furthermore, even though the MMPI was constructed without distinguishing low mental health in the positive sense from mental disease, it does not claim that a person who scores high on any set of items is actually ill. In its authors' careful wording, the various items are designed to measure *similarities* of such persons with psychiatric patients; they do not imply that this similarity amounts to identity. However, this is not the place to enter into a detailed discussion of the problems and promises of personality inventories.

Further support for the idea that prejudice is a sign of low positive mental health rather than of illness comes from a rough and ready confrontation of the personality and behaviour of the prejudiced person with the six concepts of positive mental health.

From the preceding discussion it is clear that the prejudiced individual gives little evidence of the first criterion, a healthy attitude toward himself. The absence of a stable sense of identity is, indeed, the crux of his human condition. He does not know himself, and he does not want to. Projecting his problems on to others has precisely the function of allowing him to avoid looking at himself.

The case is somewhat less clear on the second criterion—that of self-actualization. But it is, perhaps, not an over-interpretation to say that the existence of a deep though unconscious inner conflict is not a condition conducive to the development of one's potentials.

On the other hand, it is fairly obvious that the prejudiced person cannot achieve a unity or integration of all his functions. The defence mechanism or denial of what is wrong in himself interferes with such integration.

Autonomy, too, is outside his reach. For the selection of the target group for his projection is dictated to the prejudiced person by social pressures around him. Unless society has stamped a group as inferior in social position, the prejudiced person will not select it as a target for his hostilities.

In the prejudiced person mental health is equally low according to the criterion of adequate reality-perception. He cannot see individuals, he perceives his own stereotypes. But where reality is overwhelmingly clear-cut, he resorts, as we have seen, to regarding his own positive experiences as exceptions to a fantasied sinister dream world.

The criterion of environmental mastery is, perhaps, the one according to which the prejudiced individual might be judged to have positive mental health. For, as we have seen, his prejudice serves the function of dealing with an inner conflict. He derives from regarding others as inferior a semblance of support for his self-respect. This secondary gain is, to be sure, often not reliable, for any contact with the group he hates—and he often seeks such contact compulsively in an effort to convince himself of the others' inferiority—nevertheless revives his secret doubts about his own adequacy. But it is conceivable that for prejudiced persons without direct contact with the victims of their conflicts, environmental mastery is facilitated by a strengthening of their sense of their own worth.

Much in line with the assumption that mental disease and mental health are two distinct concepts, and that the prejudiced person suffers from a shortcoming in the latter, are a number of empirical studies. Barron [3], for example, ascertained the degree of prejudice of persons in psychotherapy. He discovered that absence of prejudice was the best single predictor of improvement through therapy. This finding can be interpreted in the following manner: while all the persons he studied were sick, some of them had a greater health potential than others. Those free from prejudice had, notwithstanding their illness, more often the resources for positive mental health. The prejudiced persons gave evidence, by the very fact of their prejudice, of impaired positive mental health. It is as if the inflexibility which is the essence of stereotyped thinking and which makes an individual impervious to direct experience were the reason for his shutting himself off from the direct experience of psychotherapy.

Studies of prejudice among criminals support this line of argument. The controversy of long standing as to whether criminals should be regarded as mentally sick may, perhaps, be brought nearer to resolution by introducing here, too, the distinction between mental illness and low mental health. Be this as it may, in the present context one such study is of particular interest, W. R. Morrow's 'Criminality and anti-democratic trends: a study of prison inmates', published in *The authoritarian personality* [2]. Morrow found that prison inmates have a higher average of prejudice than any other group to which similar measures have been applied. The expression of their colour prejudice and their anti-Semitism reveals what the author calls intense status anxiety: to keep the Negroes in their place and to resent the Jews because of their power.

In the light of this evidence it appears justified to conclude that prejudice is a symptom of poor mental health. Whether or not the most violent forms of prejudice are indications of mental illness, as some authors suggest, is as yet a moot question.

IS PREJUDICE INEVITABLE?

Racial antagonism, according to this psychoanalytically oriented interpretation is, then, a deeply meaningful support to the individual of low mental health who strives, however spuriously, for a solution to the basic conflict of personal identity. Do we therefore have to accept it as an inevitable aspect of modern life?

I believe that the psychological need which leads to racial antagonism is indeed universal, and will be with us for the foreseeable future. There is even some reason to believe that the modern trend toward the destruction of caste systems and toward greater democratization of public life intensifies the conflict over the individual's personal identity. Some one hundred and thirty years ago De Tocqueville had already noticed in his observation of the young American democracy the increased difficulty which persons in this political system experienced in finding security through their status in life. Not that the discrimination incorporated in the structure of a caste society is necessarily preferable to that based on prejudice in a democratic society; but where the entire social web justifies the existence of second- or third-class citizens, the exploitation of this pattern as a projection screen for man's troubles with himself will probably be more successful. In such circumstances the defence mechanisms may well achieve their ends, and the sense of identity in each individual may be stronger, whatever caste he belongs to, by virtue of this clear definition of who he is. This is why Kris [15] says that 'only in a society ... whose values include the belief in the equality of all men and in the dignity of the individual, can the fight against prejudice be meaningfully carried on'. Kris, carefully, speaks of a 'meaningful', not a successful fight. Whether, and under what conditions it can be successful is the question confronting us here.

The very universality of the basic conflict underlying prejudice suggests, of course, that this fight can be successful. For not all who experience it are prejudiced. There are people, after all, who can accept the existence of difference without envy or fear. And among them there are many whose positive mental health is also low. In the studies of *The authoritarian personality* it was found that many unprejudiced persons find it very difficult to accept themselves. They are full of self-blame and often ridden by guilt feelings; they tend to be depressed and withdraw from difficulties easily. Often they are worriers, much pre-occupied with themselves. Thus the statement that prejudice is an indication of poor mental health cannot be taken to mean that lack of prejudice is a sign of good mental health. There are many ways of suffering, and many types of unsuccessful effort to deal with inner conflict. The suggestion, often made with tongue in cheek, that the solution of the problem lies in having every prejudiced person psychoanalysed is, to say the least, not very helpful, notwithstanding the fact that psychoanalysts report that prejudice disappears after a successful analysis. Even if psychotherapeutic efforts could be multiplied many times, this would hardly make a dent in the social problem which prejudice presents.

Although the experience of inner conflict may be a necessary condition for prejudice to become a social problem, it certainly is not by itself a sufficient cause. Unless there are groups who, within the social structure, are assigned inferior status irrespective of the personal qualities of an individual member of the group, not even the most pitifully insecure and tortured souls would create prejudice. They have not got the nerve to attack the strong; they need the judgement of the world around them that members of another group are inferior as the kernel of reality to support their imagination before they dare to attack.

Yet, at first blush, there is small comfort to be derived from this second ingredient that is required to produce racial antagonism. For it seems that the organization of societies into in-groups whose power or prestige stems in part from the denial of power or prestige to out-groups will be slow to change. Thus there will be available for a long time to come a convenient projection screen on to which we can throw, as our weakness requires, ambivalence, envy, fear and hate. The existence of these under-privileged groups in many societies can be the result of initial prejudices in powerful groups, as is probably the case in parts of Africa. But this is certainly not the only, or even the most frequent, reason for their existence. The distribution of power and various concomitant political motives such as the need for cheap labour can induce a dominant yet unprejudiced group to bring about or maintain others in a social position so weak that the prejudiced bystander feels free to use them as a target for his hostilities. At this point, another unpractical solution is occasionally advocated: a revolutionary change to eliminate the organization of society into groups which confer different degrees of power and prestige on its members. This proposal is, to say the least, equivalent to postponing the fight against prejudice to the remote future.

There is, however, a third element that is necessary before prejudice can become a major social problem. It is less visible than the other two. Nonetheless it presents the best target for the fight against racial antagonism. There are no ready means either of eliminating the fundamental psychological problem or of changing society radically. But it is possible to attack the *link* between these two conditions. If this link, which is the third factor in the situation, can be destroyed or at least undermined, then there is a possibility of reducing prejudice—on earth and not in heaven; that is, within an imperfect society in which troubled people suffer from their own imperfections and make others suffer the consequences.

All realistic efforts to change prejudice have indeed been aimed at breaking this link. Where they have succeeded they have, deliberately or intuitively, built on the psychodynamics of prejudice. Where they have failed they have neglected this important factor. In what follows some failures and some achievements in the effort to change prejudice will be discussed from the point of view of their relevance to the psychodynamic picture presented here.[1]

A simple and, judging from results, all too simple effort to improve racial attitudes consists of a direct appeal on a rational and ethical level. Sermons, lectures, articles, posters and slogans of all kinds have been directed to the American public, for example. In those cases where their impact was systematically studied, the results were disappointing. Communication research has again and again demonstrated that it is difficult to reach people through public appeal who are not already in favour of the views expressed. This is true not only for matters of prejudice but also for election campaigns, adult education and many other areas. Unless the audience is captive its members turn away from ideas at the slightest indication that they might

---

1. For a discussion of various other efforts to change prejudice see Harding, Proshansky and Chein, 'Prejudice and ethic relations', in: G. Lindzey (ed.), *Handbook of social psychology* [16].

not like what they are about to hear or read. Such 'selective inattention' to disagreeable matters is the most widespread form of propaganda evasion, but not the only one. In a series of experimental studies prejudiced and unprejudiced persons were included in a captive audience of such communications. Here it was found that when the prejudiced person cannot escape noticing that a communication is directed to him, his need to evade the message is so strong that he employs ingenious devices to escape its impact. Dominant among them is his ability to misconstruct and misunderstand what is being said [8]. For example, in public transportation a poster was used showing a group of gay white children playing together with a sad-looking little Negro boy standing unhappily alone. The inscription read: 'Prejudice hurts innocent children'. One prejudiced person, invited to comment on this poster, thought it meant that Negro children prefer to play with other Negro children, and the little boy was sad because somebody wanted him to play with white children. Such astonishing misconstructions occur apparently in persons with reasonably good intelligence. The slightest ambiguity in the material is seized upon in the unconscious effort to evade the message. This is one of the reasons why caricature and satire—by definition ambiguous—are particularly ineffective in reaching the prejudiced. In the United States a satirical cartoon series was once employed poking fun at a Mr. Biggott depicted as a rather ridiculous prudish figure with exaggerated feelings of racial antagonism. What the producers of the cartoon intended was the following perceptual sequence: the prejudiced person would see the similarity between his own racial attitude and that of Mr. Biggott; would notice that Mr. Biggott was an absurd character; would conclude that it was absurd to hold prejudiced ideas; and would, in the final stage of the process, presumably reject his own prejudice so as not to be like Mr. Biggott.

The study demonstrated convincingly that this reasonable and logical process did not take place. Somewhere after the first or second stage the danger to the prejudiced person's self-esteem if he continued along this logical line became obvious to him. And from then on all sorts of devices other than logic came into play in the effort to evade the damage. Misunderstanding, change of topic, invention of bad intentions, accusing the victim of having provoked Mr. Biggott and the like led to a successful avoidance of having to come to terms with the message.

For any attitude less deeply imbedded in the psychodynamics

of an individual, the cartoonist's intention might have brought the desired result. It is quite likely that those who are simply misinformed and not prejudiced for psychological reasons would have reacted as anticipated, though no such case is mentioned in the study. One concludes that the rational or satirical effort to change prejudice has little chance of success.

Starting out with a better understanding of the irrational component in prejudice others have tried to combat it by establishing occasions for direct personal contact between members of different races. The assumption underlying these efforts is that inadequate reality-testing is made all too easy where segregation is dominant in public life. If people are in a situation in which they can see with their own eyes what members of the other group are really like, they will no longer be able to misconstruct reality to suit their own needs. The assumption is reasonable to some extent. We have seen, after all, that the prejudiced person is not altogether autistic in his view of another race. He needs some support from the actual state of affairs, and he receives it most frequently from the inferior social position in which members of the other race are often put. This implies that direct contact will lead to more adequate reality-testing only where members of both groups meet on a basis of equal status. Having Negroes as native servants, it has been shown, may result in pleasant relationships without, however, leading to a reconstruction of attitudes. There exist in many countries many organizations and clubs which are run on an inter-racial basis. Undoubtedly such organizations are an important positive feature in the general climate of opinion and beyond it carry deeper meaning for the participants of both groups in such meetings. From the point of view of changing prejudice, however, all voluntary efforts of this kind are handicapped by the evasion mechanism discussed before. As a rule the prejudiced person goes nowhere near such an organization, so that much of this good-will work only serves to persuade the persuaded.

But, of course, direct contacts on an equal status basis need not occur voluntarily. In industry and commerce, in the army, in schools and in neighbourhoods, such contact is often a requirement of the situation. And it is from studies in these situations that the idea of breaking the link between psychological conflict and the existence of out-groups which accounts for prejudice as a social problem receives support.

Of the many existing studies in involuntary inter-racial contact situations, those in public housing in the United States are, perhaps, most instructive [9, 21, 25]. In the United States low-cost subsidized housing is provided for families whose income is below a certain level and whose accommodation is inadequate. The policy applies without regard to race. However, the implementation of this policy is left to local housing authorities and housing managers. As a result, different principles guide the allocation of flats to Negro and white families in different localities. In some cases, Negroes and white live as next-door neighbours; in others they are assigned to separate buildings; and sometimes they are placed so that a considerable distance—a major street, for example—separates the two groups from each other. This situation provides conditions approaching those required for a controlled experiment, and it has been used for this purpose by several investigators. It should be noted that such housing policies not only imply equal status for both groups; they also create a situation in which the families concerned receive considerable material advantages, however much a white family may be opposed to sharing these advantages with a Negro family next door. Under the circumstances only members of the lunatic fringe refuse to avail themselves of the accommodation if the assignment of flats challenges their prejudices. Most prejudiced people enter this situation and stay in it because the advantages offered outweigh the disadvantage of having neighbours whom they regard as undesirable. This initial compromise is facilitated by the social norms established in favour of integrated living arrangements which are clearly supported by the local authority and the housing manager. The comparison of race relations under these conditions, alike in many ways but different in the degree to which they require direct and personal contact between the races, is revealing: where families live as next-door neighbours relations between the groups become friendly and personal. The consciousness of race recedes into the background and people are accepted and judged for what they are as individuals. On the other hand, where segregation is maintained within public housing, hostilities and prejudice continue to prevail. In the latter circumstances, the way prejudice affects the perception of people could be clearly demonstrated. In one of the housing units in which there were 350 families of each group, with about equal status as measured by income and years of formal education, prejudiced white persons believed that there were many more Negro than white families in this large unit, and that the Negroes were considerably less educated. What is more, they maintained staunchly that the Negroes, too, would prefer to live in even greater segregation. An inquiry among the Negro tenants had, however, shown that virtually all of them were in favour of integration.

It is the positive result, however, which interests us here. How does one understand the change which takes place? There is no indication as to whether a wholesale reorganization of personality has taken place. Indeed, there are good reasons to doubt that that could have happened. Rather, the situation was one in which the prejudiced person's general submissiveness to social norms and to the powers that be was exploited. This, together with the enforced improvement of reality-testing, are the psychological mechanisms which account for the change.

There is much evidence from other sources of the prejudiced person's tendency to conform. The inner conflict which makes prejudice a convenient pseudo-solution also makes the individual yearn to be accepted by the powerful people within the social setting in which he lives. If they condemn prejudice he will comply, just as he will comply if they condone it. The social climate controls the manifestation of prejudice. Psychologically speaking, however, there is less difference than one would like to assume between the politely prejudiced and those given to violent aggressiveness against another race. In the study of psychoanalytic case histories of anti-Semitic patients already quoted [1] one person had been included who had come from Germany to the United States. In Germany he had shared in the rabid anti-Semitism of the Nazis; in the United States he shared the polite anti-Semitism prevalent in the set in which he moved. Nevertheless, however small the psychological difference, socially there is all the difference in the world between societies which favour violence and those which merely tolerate a polite hesitation about contact with another race. It is hence perfectly in line with a psychoanalytic interpretation of prejudice to regard laws against and social controls over the manifestations of prejudice as the most realistic safeguards of a civilized society.

The housing studies include data on the manner of change which occurs under the compulsion of established social norms. It is the behaviour that undergoes improvement long before the corresponding attitudes towards members of the other race start to yield [21]. Thus originally prejudiced white people start being on a first-name basis with their Negro neighbours, visit in each other's flats and undertake mutual baby sitting or common shopping expeditions; but, when asked whether they prefer segregated or integrated housing conditions, they continue for a considerable time to give preference to the former. That behaviour should change before attitude is, again, understandable in the light of the underlying psychological processes. Behaviour is more frequently under ego-control. The function of the attitude is significant for the less conscious part of the personality. Adaptation and change on that level is a much more complex process. It seems reasonable, however, to assume that the change in behaviour also acts as a stimulus to set in motion a change in attitude if for no other reason than because a flagrant inconsistency between what one does and what one thinks is an uncomfortable experience for many people.

However, there are limits even to the change in behaviour, as the following example illustrates. A white tenant in one of the inter-racial housing units had come to accept her coloured neighbours on an equal basis. She reported with some pride that many Negro tenants greeted her familiarly in the precincts of the project by her first name; yet she added: 'I would faint, of course, if they did so in the main street in front of my friends outside.' Apparently, this 'compartmentalizing' of good relations with another group within specific limits is quite frequent. Another study conducted in a mining village of West Virginia reported much the same tendency; underground the work teams were inter-racial and white miners were quite willing to accept Negro leadership. Above ground the miners strictly adhered to the pattern of segregation in their community. [1]

Apparently it takes a fair amount of time before changes in behaviour affect attitudes, and the mechanism of compartmentalization interferes with the ready transfer of norms acquired in one situation to another. That the transfer does occur is occasionally demonstrated. For example, nation-wide polls in the United States indicate that about four-fifths of the adult population prefer residential segregation. Among people who have either worked with Negroes, or who have had some experience with them as neighbours, only two-thirds prefer segregation. And among those who have had both experiences the proportion is reduced to about half [21].

In the light of all this evidence, some cautious optimism about the possibility of breaking the link between psychological conflict and the existence of underprivileged groups in a society is, perhaps, not out of place. Yet the evidence indicating how

1. See Stuart W. Cook's article, 'Desegregation : a psychological analysis' in : *American psychologist*, vol. 12, January 1957.

difficult it is to bring about change is also strong. Perhaps the best known example of the problems confronting the effort to change race relations within one society arises out of the United States' legal action to end school segregation. There can be little doubt that the legal and constitutional battle in the states will be won by the Federal Government. Notwithstanding the various outbreaks of violence and the temporary suspension of some local school systems, close on half a million Negro children who were in segregated schools before the Supreme Court's decision have already had the experience of going to school with white children.

Where the integration of schools has been successfully accomplished, the chances are that children will ultimately grow up with somewhat less prejudice than their parents. Yet, in the transitional period the personal conflicts of many are undoubtedly heightened rather than assuaged. Adults who are inclined to obey authority, find this standard of conduct of little help in a situation where the state authority is in conflict with the federal authority. Children may experience the authority of their parents as conflicting with that of their teachers. The problems thus created in this transitional period are fully discussed in a report by the Group for the Advancement of Psychiatry[7]. Here, only one of these problems need be discussed because it is so often overlooked: the fact that the psychological problems of persons who become champions of racial equality often interfere with their thoughts and actions and thus diminish their effectiveness in working towards the goal to which they are apparently devoted. To some of these persons the first school results achieved by Negro children in desegregated schools came as a major shock: with considerable consistency the average achievements of the Negro children were below those of their white class-mates. Such results could, of course, have been easily predicted from the inferior schooling many Negro children had had before desegregation and from the generally much lower economic standards prevailing in their homes. The surprise of some people at these results indicates that for psychological reasons of their own they found it difficult to accept the existence of any difference between white and Negro. Just as the prejudiced person feels threatened by the recognition of a visible difference between himself and others, so low mental health in unprejudiced persons can also focus on the fact of existing differences. In the latter case, however, psychological purposes are served better by an attempt to deny that differences exist. An obvious demonstration, such as that provided by the school results, shatters the basis on which their identification with the underdog was built. One easy but unfortunate way out of their peculiar dilemma is the expression of suspicion against the good will of anyone who discovers or assumes differences of any kind between races. The denial of differences is as little helpful as the assertion that their existence presents an unbridgeable gulf between the races. Mental health in the positive sense of the term is needed in the proponents of harmonious race relations if confusion and exaggeration are to be avoided.

One final question needs to be considered. If efforts to change prejudice take away from the prejudiced person a convenient pseudo-solution for his problems without, however, helping him to solve these problems and without providing an alternative outlet for his hostilities, is it not possible that the already low mental health of such persons will further suffer? Or that they will seek and find other innocent victims for their aggressive needs? It is very likely that both these questions must be answered in the affirmative, even though in some persons a genuine change of outlook will occur.

The dilemma inherent in these considerations cannot be resolved by psychological thought alone. Indeed, to raise them means to raise the vast problem of the relation of psychology to ethics, a problem which transcends the scope of this essay. All that can be done here is to recognize its existence and to indicate roughly its pertinence.

Psychoanalysis has frequently been accused of undermining ethical principles by understanding and explaining all too well the psychological problems which lead to violence, crime, exploitation and prejudice. This accusation once again hits the wrong target: Freud answered it on one occasion in epigrammatic style: 'Auf dem Divan ist es eine Neurose, im Leben eine Schweinerei.'[1] If social action to protect the victim of aggression does not cure the aggressor, this is hardly an excuse for abandoning the protection. If the aggressor feels compelled to attack other victims, new protections must be created. All societies find it necessary to restrain some impulses and to curb socially dangerous actions.

Yet for the psychologist the dilemma persists notwithstanding his recognition that ethical principles must be maintained even at the expense of doing psychological damage to some. As in medicine the psychologist's professional concern with

---

1. On the analyst's couch—a neurosis; in real life swinish behaviour.

individuals is independent of whether they are good or bad by social standards. A good doctor will set the broken leg of a criminal as carefully as he sets that of a saint. A good psychologist will want to deal with prejudice without doing harm to either its victims or to those who are guilty of it.

The task confronting psychology is therefore to discover or create the conditions under which the basic conflict of identity can be made bearable without the crutch of prejudice. There is no easy and certainly no quick method available to achieve this; some crutch can probably not be avoided. The search for such conditions will probably lead to specific modifications of the environment. For man's greatest achievement throughout the centuries of known history is the creation of protective environments which support many of his needs, however irrational they may be. Perhaps it is not utopian to think that this extraordinary gift for creating a supporting environment could be used in a deliberate and controlled fashion in the service of the psychologically weak among us. To derive one's sense of identity from work, or from stamp collecting, or from mountain climbing may be psychologically as precarious as to derive it from prejudice against underprivileged groups; but it may help one to live without hating either oneself or one's neighbour.

BIBLIOGRAPHY

The titles starred are of general interest and do not require specialized knowledge in psychological theory or method. The most complete treatment of the situation of the American Negro is Gunnar Myrdal's *An American dilemma* (New York, Harper Brothers, 1944). This approach considers historical, sociological, psychological, political and philosophical aspects of the Negro's position in the United States.

1. ACKERMAN, N. W. and JAHODA, Marie. *Antisemitism and emotional disorder.* New York, Harper & Brothers, 1950.
2. ADORNO, T. W., FRENKEL-BRUNSWICK, E., LEVINSON, D. J. and SANFORD, R. N. (eds.). *The authoritarian personality.* New York, Harper & Brothers, 1950.
3. BARRON, F. 'Some test correlates of response to psychotherapy', *J. Consult. Psych.*, Vol. 17, 1953.
4. BETTELHEIM, B. and JANOWITZ, M. *Dynamics of prejudice.* New York, Harper & Brothers, 1950.
5. BRONOWSKI, J. *The face of violence.* London, Turnstile Press, 1954.

6. CARTER, Gwendolen. *The politics of inequality, South Africa since 1948.** London, Thames & Hudson, 1958.
7. COMMITTEE ON SOCIAL ISSUES. Group for the Advancement of Psychiatry. *Psychiatric aspects of school desegregation*, U.S.A., 1957. (Report No. 37.)
8. COOPER, Eunice and JAHODA, Marie. 'The evasion of propaganda: how prejudiced people respond to anti-prejudice propaganda', *J. Psychol.*, 23, 1947.
9. DEUTSCH, M. and COLLINS, M. *Interracial housing: a psychological evaluation of a social experiment*. Minneapolis, University of Minnesota Press, 1951.
10. DUNN, L. C. *Race and biology*. Paris, Unesco, 1951. *(The race question in modern science series.)*
11. HARTLEY, E. L. *Problems in prejudice*. New York, King's Crown Press, 1946.
12. HATHAWAY, S. R. and McKINLEY, J. C. 'A multiphasic personality schedule (Minnesota). I. Construction of the schedule', *J. Psychol.*, 10, 1940.
13. JAHODA, Marie. *Current concepts of positive mental health*, New York, 1958. *(Basic books.)*
14. JENSEN, A. R. 'Authoritarian attitudes and personality maladjustment', *J. abnorm. soc. Psychol.*, Vol. 54, No. 3, May 1957.
15. KRIS, Ernst. 'Notes on the psychology of prejudice', *The English Journal* (Chicago), Vol. XXXV, June 1956.
16. LINDZEY G. (ed.) *Handbook of social psychology*. Vol. 2, Cambridge, Addison-Wesley Publishing Company, 1954.
17. LOEWENSTEIN, R. *Christians and Jews*. New York, International Universities Press, 1951.
18. MACAULAY, T. B. *Critical, historical and miscellaneous essays and poems*, Vol. III. New York, Wm. L. Allison, 1886.
19. MASON, P. *The birth of the dilemma.** London, Oxford University Press, 1958.
20. MERTON, Robert K. *Social theory and social structure*. Glencoe, Illinois, The Free Press, 1957.
21. —— WEST, P. S. and JAHODA, M. *Social fictions and social facts*, 1949. Unpublished.
22. MONTAGUE, M. F. Ashley. *Man's most dangerous myth: the fallacy of race.** New York, Columbia University Press, 1945.
23. SARTRE, Jean-Paul. 'Portrait of the anti-Semite',* *Partisan Review*, 13, 1946. See also, *Réflexions sur la question juive*, Paris, Gallimard, 1946.
24. SOFER, Cyril. 'Working groups in a plural society', *Industrial and Labour Relations Review*, Vol. 8, No. 1, October 1954.
25. WILNER, D.M., WALKLEY, R. P. and COOK, S.W. *Human relations in interracial housing: a study of the contact hypothesis*. Minneapolis, University of Minnesota Press, 1955.

491

ACTION BY UNESCO

Racial doctrine is the outcome of a fundamentally anti-rational system of thought and is in glaring conflict with the whole humanist tradition of our civilization. It sets at nought everything that Unesco stands for and endeavours to defend. By virtue of its very Constitution, Unesco must face the racial problem: the preamble to that document declares that 'the great and terrible war which has now ended was a war made possible by the denial of the democratic principles of the dignity, equality and mutual respect of men, and by the propagation, in their place, through ignorance and prejudice, of the doctrine of the inequality of men and races'.

Because of its structure and the tasks assigned to it, Unesco is the international institution best equipped to lead the campaign against race prejudice and to extirpate this most dangerous of doctrines. Race hatred and conflict thrive on scientifically false ideas and are nourished by ignorance. In order to show up these errors of fact and reasoning, to make widely known the conclusions reached in various branches of science, to combat racial propaganda, we must turn to the means and methods of education, science and culture, which are precisely the three domains in which Unesco's activities are exerted; it is on this threefold front that the battle against all forms of racism must be engaged.

The plan laid down by the Organization proceeds from a resolution [116 (VI) B (iii)] adopted by the United Nations Economic and Social Council at its sixth session, asking Unesco 'to consider the desirability of initiating and recommending the general adoption of a programme of disseminating scientific facts designed to remove what is generally known as racial prejudice'.

Responding to this request, Unesco's General Conference, at its fourth session, adopted the following three resolutions for the 1950 programme:

'The Director-General is instructed

'To study and collect scientific materials concerning questions of race;

'To give wide diffusion to the scientific information collected;

'To prepare an educational campaign based on this information.'

Such a programme could not be carried out unless Unesco had at its disposal the 'scientific facts' mentioned in the resolution of the Economic and Social Council. For the purpose of securing these facts with as little delay as possible, the Department of Social Sciences, at that time under Mr. Arthur Ramos, convened a committee of anthropologists, psychologists and sociologists, whose task was to define the concept of race and to give an account in 'clear and easily understandable terms' of our present knowledge regarding the highly controversial problem of race differences.

By inviting a group of experts to come together to discuss the racial problem, Unesco was taking up again, after 15 years, a project that the International Institute of Intellectual Co-operation had intended, but had been unable, to carry out.

The scientists who met at Unesco House from 12 to 14 December 1949 were of different countries (Brazil, France, India, Mexico, New Zealand, United Kingdom, United States of America). They represented different disciplines; their tendencies were divergent. As the study of man is pursued both in the natural and the social sciences, specialists in both fields were required for a thorough discussion of the racial problem. The scanty representation of the biological sciences on the committee must be attributed to the sudden death of Mr. Ramos and to last-minute withdrawals. The sociologists, who formed the majority of the members, agreed, however, that race had to be defined biologically. The declaration drawn up by this group was published by Unesco on 18 July 1950 and was extremely well received by the general public. It was printed in a considerable number of newspapers in a score of countries and has frequently been quoted in works dealing with the race problem; the Assembly of the French Union, at its meeting on 20 November 1951, adopted a proposal for the publicizing of the statement and its inclusion in school syllabuses in the French Union.

It would have been much too optimistic to hope that, in a sphere in which there are so many conflicting trends and methods, the statement could be considered perfect as it stood. Some of its contentions, and some of the terms used, were much criticized, especially by physical anthropologists and geneticists.

The scientific journal *Man,* published by the Royal Anthropological Institute, and those who criticized this first statement, did not reject its general spirit nor its main conclusions; they felt it would have been better, however, had certain propositions been put forward with greater circumspection. They considered that the document tended to confuse race as a biological fact and the concept of race as a social phenomenon; they also declined to acknowledge as a proved fact that there are no mental differences between racial groups, stressed that there was insufficient evidence to support that view, and urged the need for keeping an open mind on the subject. The statement that 'biological studies lend support to the ethic of universal brotherhood, for man is born with drives towards co-operation' came in for the most frequent criticism.

Some people, not understanding the real significance of the criticisms and comments made on the statement, tended to regard them as representing a victory for racism and the defeat of a naïve humanitarianism. In order to clear up any possible misunderstanding, it was therefore necessary for a second group of scientists, consisting solely, on this occasion, of physical anthropologists and geneticists, chosen, for preference, from among those who had expressed disagreement with the statement, to draw up a text reflecting more accurately the views of scientific circles. Unesco therefore called on 12 scientists, representing physical anthropology and human genetics, who, in the course of discussions lasting from 4 to 9 June 1951, prepared the document contained in this pamphlet. Generally speaking, the main conclusions of the first statement were upheld, but some assertions have been toned down and substantial omissions have been made.

It was important to avoid presenting the new statement as an authoritative manifesto published by Unesco as the last word on the race question. Although the writers of this docu-

495

ment sought to make available the results of the most recent research on the question, it was obvious that they could not make full allowance for the doubts still felt by many of their colleagues. Unesco wished to set forth a document expressing not only the opinions of one group of specialists, but also those of other scientists whom it had been impossible to invite to the meeting held in June 1951. For this reason, it was agreed that the statement should be submitted to as many anthropologists and geneticists as possible, with a request for them to let us have their comments and criticisms before the definitive text was established. This was done.

The reader wishing to become acquainted with these comments will find them published in the brochure appearing in the Unesco series *The Race Question in Modern Science*, under the title *The Race Concept*.

The texts of the two declarations are reproduced below.

STATEMENT OF 1950

1. Scientists have reached general agreement in recognizing that mankind is one: that all men belong to the same species, *Homo sapiens*. It is further generally agreed among scientists that all men are probably derived from the same common stock; and that such differences as exist between different groups of mankind are due to the operation of evolutionary factors or differentiation such as isolation, the drift and random fixation of the material particles which control heredity (the genes), changes in the structure of these particles, hybridization, and natural selection. In these ways groups have arisen of varying stability and degree of differentiation which have been classified in different ways for different purposes.

2. From the biological standpoint, the species *Homo sapiens* is made up of a number of populations, each one of which differs from the others in the frequency of one or more genes. Such genes, responsible for the hereditary differences between men, are always few when compared to the whole genetic constitution of man and to the vast number of genes common to all human beings regardless of the population to which they belong. This means that the likenesses among men are far greater than their differences.

3. A race, from the biological standpoint, may therefore be defined as one of the group of populations constituting the species *Homo sapiens*. These populations are capable of interbreeding with one another but, by virtue of the isolating barriers which in the past kept them more or less separated, exhibit certain physical differences as a result of their somewhat different biological histories. These represent variations, as it were, on a common theme.

4. In short, the term 'race' designates a group or population characterized by some concentrations, relative as to frequency and distribution, of hereditary particles (genes) or physical characters, which appear, fluctuate, and often disappear in the course of time by reason of geographic and/or cultural isolation. The varying manifestations of these traits in different populations are perceived in different ways by each group. What is perceived is largely preconceived, so that each group arbitrarily tends to misinterpret the variability which occurs as a fundamental difference which separates that group from all others.

5. These are the scientific facts. Unfortunately, however, when most people use the term 'race' they do not do so in the sense above defined. To most people, a race is any group of people whom they choose to describe as a race. Thus, many national, religious, geographic, linguistic or cultural groups have, in such loose usage, been called 'race', when obviously Americans are not a race, nor are Englishmen, nor Frenchmen, nor any other national group. Catholics, Protestants, Moslems and Jews are not races, nor are groups who speak English or any other language thereby definable as a race; people who live in Iceland or England or India are not races; nor are people who are culturally Turkish or Chinese or the like thereby describable as races.

6. National, religious, geographic, linguistic and cultural groups do not necessarily coincide with racial groups; and the cultural traits of such groups have no demonstrated genetic connexion with racial traits. Because serious errors of this kind are habitually committed when the term 'race' is used in popular parlance, it would be better when speaking of human races to drop the term 'race' altogether and speak of *ethnic groups*.

7.   Now what has the scientist to say about the groups of mankind which may be recognized at the present time? Human races can be and have been differently classified by different anthropologists, but at the present time most anthropologists agree on classifying the greater part of present-day mankind into three major divisions, as follows: the Mongoloid Division, the Negroid Division, the Caucasoid Division. The biological processes which the classifier has here embalmed, as it were, are dynamic, not static. These divisions were not the same in the past as they are at present, and there is every reason to believe that they will change in the future.

8.   Many sub-groups or ethnic groups within these divisions have been described. There is no general agreement upon their number, and in any event most ethnic groups have not yet been either studied or described by the physical anthropologists.

9.   Whatever classification the anthropologist makes of man, he never includes mental characteristics as part of those classifications. It is now generally recognized that intelligence tests do not in themselves enable us to differentiate safely between what is due to innate capacity and what is the result of environmental influences, training and education. Wherever is has been possible to make allowances for differences in environmental opportunities, the tests have shown essential similarity in mental characters among all human groups. In short, given similar degrees of cultural opportunity to realize their potentialities, the average achievement of the members of each ethnic group is about the same. The scientific investigations of recent years fully support the dictum of Confucius (551-478 B.C.): 'Men's natures are alike; it is their habits that carry them far apart.'

10.   The scientific material available to us at present does not justify the conclusion that inherited genetic differences are a major factor in producing the differences between the cultures and cultural achievements of different peoples or groups. It does indicate, however, that the history of the cultural experience which each group has undergone is the major factor in explaining such differences. The one trait which above all others has been at a premium in the evolution of men's mental characters has been educability, plasticity.

This is a trait which all human beings possess. It is indeed, a species character of *Homo sapiens*.

11.   So far as temperament is concerned, there is no definite evidence that there exist inborn differences between human groups. There is evidence that whatever group differences of the kind there might be are greatly over-ridden by the individual differences, and by the differences springing from environmental factors.

12.   As for personality and character, these may be considered raceless. In every human group a rich variety of personality and character types will be found, and there is no reason for believing that any human group is richer than any other in these respects.

13.   With respect to race-mixture, the evidence points unequivocally to the fact that this has been going on from the earliest times. Indeed, one of the chief processes of race-formation and race-extinction or absorption is by means of hybridization between races or ethnic groups. Furthermore, no convincing evidence has been adduced that race-mixture of itself produces biologically bad effects. Statements that human hybrids frequently show undesirable traits, both physically and mentally, physical disharmonies and mental degeneracies, are not supported by the facts. There is, therefore, no 'biological' justification for prohibiting intermarriage between persons of different ethnic groups.

14.   The biological fact of race and the myth of 'race' should be distinguished. For all practical social purposes 'race' is not so much a biological phenomenon as a social myth. The myth 'race' has created an enormous amount of human and social damage. In recent years it has taken a heavy toll in human lives and caused untold suffering. It still prevents the normal development of millions of human beings and deprives civilization of the effective co-operation of productive minds. The biological differences between ethnic groups should be disregarded from the standpoint of social acceptance and social action. The unity of mankind from both the biological and social viewpoints is the main thing. To recognize this and to act accordingly is the first requirement of modern man. It is but to recognize what a great biologist wrote in 1875: 'As man advances in civilization, and small tribes are united into

larger communities, the simplest reason would tell each individual that he ought to extend his social instincts and sympathies to all the members of the same nation, though personally unknown to him. This point being once reached, there is only an artificial barrier to prevent his sympathies extending to the men of all nations and races.' These are the words of Charles Darwin in *The Descent of Man* (2nd ed., 1875, pp. 187-88). And, indeed, the whole of human history shows that a co-operative spirit is not only natural to men, but more deeply rooted than any self-seeking tendencies. If this were not so we should not see the growth of integration and organization of his communities which the centuries and the millenia plainly exhibit.

15. We now have to consider the bearing of these statements on the problem of human equality. It must be asserted with the utmost emphasis that equality as an ethical principle in no way depends upon the assertion that human beings are in fact equal in endowment. Obviously individuals in all ethnic groups vary greatly among themselves in endowment. Nevertheless, the characteristics in which human groups differ from one another are often exaggerated and used as a basis for questioning the validity of equality in the ethical sense. For this purpose we have thought it worth while to set out in a formal manner what is at present scientifically established concerning individual and group differences.

(a) In matters of race, the only characteristics which anthropologists can effectively use as a basis for classifications are physical and physiological.

(b) According to present knowledge there is no proof that the groups of mankind differ in their innate mental characteristics, whether in respect of intelligence or temperament. The scientific evidence indicates that the range of mental capacities in all ethnic groups is much the same.

(c) Historical and sociological studies support the view that genetic differences are not of importance in determining the social and cultural differences between different groups of *Homo sapiens,* and that the social and cultural *changes* in different groups have, in the main, been independent of *changes* in inborn constitution. Vast social changes have occurred which were not in any way connected with changes in racial type.

(d) There is no evidence that race-mixture as such produces bad results from the biological point of view. The social results of race-mixture whether for good or ill are to be traced to social factors.

(e) All normal human beings are capable of learning to share in a common life, to understand the nature of mutual service and reciprocity, and to respect social obligations and contracts. Such biological differences as exist between members of different ethnic groups have no relevance to problems of social and political organization, moral life and communication between human beings.

Lastly, biological studies lend support to the ethic of universal brotherhood; for man is born with drives toward co-operation, and unless these drives are satisfied, men and nations alike fall ill. Man is born a social being who can reach his fullest development only through interaction with his fellows. The denial at any point of this social bond between man and man brings with it disintegration. In this sense, every man is his brother's keeper. For every man is a piece of the continent, a part of the main, because he is involved in mankind.

The original statement was drafted at Unesco House, Paris by the following experts:

Professor Ernest Beaglehole, New Zealand;
Professor Juan Comas, Mexico;
Professor L. A. Costa Pinto, Brazil;
Professor E. Franklin Frazier, United States of America;
Professor Morris Ginsberg, United Kingdom;
Dr. Humayun Kabir, India;
Professor Claude Levi-Strauss, France;
Professor M. F. Ashley-Montagu, United States of America (Rapporteur).

The text was revised by Professor Ashley-Montagu, after criticisms submitted by Professors Hadley Cantril, E. G. Conklin, Gunnar Dahlberg, Theodosius Dobzhansky, L. C. Dunn, Donald Hager, Julian S. Huxley, Otto Klineberg, Wilbert Moore, H. J. Muller, Gunnar Myrdal, Joseph Needham, Curt Stern.

STATEMENT OF 1951

*drafted by a group of physical anthropologists
and geneticists*

1.   Scientists are generally agreed that all men living today belong to a single species, *Homo sapiens,* and are derived from a common stock, even though there is some dispute as to when and how different human groups diverged from this common stock.

The concept of race is unanimously regarded by anthropologists as a classificatory device providing a zoological frame within which the various groups of mankind may be arranged and by means of which studies of evolutionary processes can be facilitated. In its anthropological sense, the word 'race' should be reserved for groups of mankind possessing well-developed and primarily heritable physical differences from other groups. Many populations can be so classified but, because of the complexity of human history, there are also many populations which cannot easily be fitted into a racial classification.

2.   Some of the physical differences between human groups are due to differences in hereditary constitution and some to differences in the environments in which they have been brought up. In most cases, both influences have been at work. The science of genetics suggests that the hereditary differences among populations of a single species are the results of the action of two sets of processes. On the one hand, the genetic composition of isolated populations is constantly but gradually being altered by natural selection and by occasional changes (mutations) in the material particles (genes) which control heredity. Populations are also affected by fortuitous changes in gene frequency and by marriage customs. On the other hand, crossing is constantly breaking down the differentiations so set up. The new mixed populations, in so far as they, in turn, become isolated, are subject to the same processes, and these may lead to further changes. Existing races are merely the result, considered at a particular moment in time, of the total effect of such processes on the human species. The hereditary characters to be used in the classification of human groups, the limits of their variation within these groups, and thus the extent of the classificatory subdivisions adopted may legitimately differ according to the scientific purpose in view.

3. National, religious, geographical, linguistic and cultural groups do not necessarily coincide with racial groups; and the cultural traits of such groups have no demonstrated connexion with racial traits. Americans are not a race, nor are Frenchmen, nor Germans; nor *ipso facto* is any other national group. Moslems and Jews are no more races than are Roman Catholics and Protestants; nor are people who live in Iceland or Britain or India, or who speak English or any other language, or who are culturally Turkish or Chinese and the like, thereby describable as races. The use of the term 'race' in speaking of such groups may be a serious error, but it is one which is habitually committed.

4. Human races can be, and have been, classified in different ways by different anthropologists. Most of them agree in classifying the greater part of existing mankind into at least three large units, which may be called major groups (in French *grand-races,* in German *Hauptrassen*). Such a classification does not depend on any single physical character, nor does, for example, skin colour by itself necessarily distinguish one major group from another. Furthermore, so far as it has been possible to analyse them, the differences in physical structure which distinguish one major group from another give no support to popular notions of any general 'superiority' or 'inferiority' which are sometimes implied in referring to these groups.

Broadly speaking, individuals belonging to different major groups of mankind are distinguishable by virtue of their physical characters, but individual members, or small groups, belonging to different races within the same major group are usually not so distinguishable. Even the major groups grade into each other, and the physical traits by which they and the races within them are characterized overlap considerably. With respect to most, if not all, measurable characters, the differences among individuals belonging to the same race are greater than the differences that occur between the observed averages for two or more races within the same major group.

5. Most anthropologists do not include mental characteristics in their classification of human races. Studies within a single race have shown that both innate capacity and environmental opportunity determine the results of tests of intelligence and temperament, though their relative importance is disputed.

When intelligence tests, even non-verbal, are made on a group of non-literate people, their scores are usually lower than those of more civilized people. It has been recorded that different groups of the same race occupying similarly high levels of civilization may yield considerable differences in intelligence tests. When, however, the two groups have been brought up from childhood in similar environments, the differences are usually very slight. Moreover, there is good evidence that, given similar opportunities, the average performance (that is to say, the performance of the individual who is representative because he is surpassed by as many as he surpasses), and the variation round it, do not differ appreciably from one race to another.

Even those psychologists who claim to have found the greatest differences in intelligence between groups of different racial origin, and have contended that they are hereditary, always report that some members of the group of inferior performance surpass not merely the lowest ranking member of the superior group, but also the average of its members. In any case, it has never been possible to separate members of two groups on the basis of mental capacity, as they can often be separated on a basis of religion, skin colour, hair form or language. It is possible, though not proved, that some types of innate capacity for intellectual and emotional responses are commoner in one human group than in another, but it is certain that, within a single group, innate capacities vary as much as, if not more than, they do between different groups.

The study of the heredity of psychological characteristics is beset with difficulties. We know that certain mental diseases and defects are transmitted from one generation to the next, but we are less familiar with the part played by heredity in the mental life of normal individuals. The normal individual, irrespective of race, is essentially educable. It follows that his intellectual and moral life is largely conditioned by his training and by his physical and social environment.

It often happens that a national group may appear to be characterized by particular psychological attributes. The superficial view would be that this is due to race. Scientifically, however, we realize that any common psychological attribute is more likely to be due to a common historical and social background, and that such attributes may obscure the fact that, within different populations consisting of many human types, one will find approximately the same range of temperament and intelligence.

6. The scientific material available to us at present does not justify the conclusion that inherited genetic differences are a major factor in producing the differences between the cultures and cultural achievements of different peoples or groups. It does indicate, on the contrary, that a major factor in explaining such differences is the cultural experience which each group has undergone.

7. There is no evidence for the existence of so-called 'pure' races. Skeletal remains provide the basis of our limited knowledge about earlier races. In regard to race mixture, the evidence points to the fact that human hybridization has been going on for an indefinite but considerable time. Indeed, one of the processes of race formation and race extinction or absorption is by means of hybridization between races. As there is no reliable evidence that disadvantageous effects are produced thereby, no biological justification exists for prohibiting intermarriage between persons of different races.

8. We now have to consider the bearing of these statements on the problem of human equality. We wish to emphasize that equality of opportunity and equality in law in no way depend, as ethical principles, upon the assertion that human beings are in fact equal in endowment.

9. We have thought it worth while to set out in a formal manner what is at present scientifically established concerning individual and group differences.

   (a) In matters of race, the only characteristics which anthropologists have so far been able to use effectively as a basis for classification are physical (anatomical and physiological).

   (b) Available scientific knowledge provides no basis for believing that the groups of mankind differ in their innate capacity for intellectual and emotional development.

   (c) Some biological differences between human beings within a single race may be as great as, or greater than, the same biological differences between races.

   (d) Vast social changes have occurred that have not been connected in any way with changes in racial type. Historical and sociological studies thus support the view that genetic differences are of little significance in determining the social and cultural differences between different groups of men.

(e) There is no evidence that race mixture produces disadvantageous results from a biological point of view. The social results of race mixture, whether for good or ill, can generally be traced to social factors.

(Text drafted, at Unesco House, Paris, on 8 June 1951, by: Professor R. A. M. Bergman, Royal Tropical Institute, Amsterdam; Professor Gunnar Dahlberg, Director, State Institute for Human Genetics and Race Biology, University of Uppsala; Professor L. C. Dunn, Department of Zoology, Columbia University, New York; Professor J. B. S. Haldane, Head, Department of Biometry, University College, London; Professor M. F. Ashley Montagu, Chairman, Department of Anthropology, Rutgers University, New Brunswick, N.J.; Dr. A. E. Mourant, Director, Blood Group Reference Laboratory, Lister Institute, London; Professor Hans Nachtscheim, Director, Institut für Genetik, Freie Universität, Berlin; Dr. Eugène Schreider, Directeur adjoint du Laboratoire d'Anthropologie Physique de l'Ecole des Hautes Etudes, Paris; Professor Harry L. Shapiro, Chairman, Department of Anthropology, American Museum of Natural History, New York; Dr. J. C. Trevor, Faculty of Archaeology and Anthropology, University of Cambridge; Dr. Henri V. Vallois, Professeur au Museum d'Histoire Naturelle, Directeur du Musée de l'Homme, Paris; Professor S. Zuckerman, Head, Department of Anatomy, Medical School, University of Birmingham; Professor Th. Dobzhansky, Department of Zoology, Columbia University, New York, and Dr. Julian Huxley contributed to the final wording.)